ReCalling Early Canada

Reading the Political in Literary and Cultural Production

ReCalling Early Canada

Reading the Political in Literary and Cultural Production

JENNIFER BLAIR

DANIEL COLEMAN

KATE HIGGINSON

LORRAINE YORK

Editors

The University of Alberta Press

Published by
The University of Alberta Press
Ring House 2
Edmonton, Alberta, Canada
T6G 2E1

LIBRARY AND ARCHIVES CANADA
CATALOGUING IN PUBLICATION

ReCalling early Canada : reading the
    political in literary and cultural
    production / Jennifer Blair ... [et al.],
    editors.

Papers presented at a conference held
    June 23, 2003 in Hamilton, Ont.
Includes bibliographical references
    and index.
ISBN 0-88864-443-4

    1. Canadian literature—To 1867—
History and criticism. 2. Canadian
literature—19th century—History and
criticism. 3. Politics in literature.
I. Blair, Jennifer, 1975–

PS8077.1.R42 2005   C810.9'358
C2005-902319-8

A volume in *(cuRRents)* , a Canadian literature series. Jonathan Hart, series editor.

Indexed by Judy Dunlop.

The University of Alberta Press is
committed to protecting our natural environment. As part of our efforts, this book is
printed on New Leaf Paper: it contains
100% post-consumer recycled fibres and is
acid- and chlorine-free.

The University of Alberta Press gratefully
acknowledges the support received for its
publishing program from The Canada
Council for the Arts. The University of
Alberta Press also gratefully acknowledges
the financial support of the Government of
Canada through the Book Publishing
Industry Development Program (BPIDP) and
from the Alberta Foundation for the Arts for
its publishing activities.

Canada Council   Conseil des Arts
for the Arts   du Canada

Contents

Foreword

CAROLE GERSON

EACH GENERATION CREATES its own construction and subsequent
reading of its past. In Canada, this undertaking is complicated and
enriched by dramatic shifts in our national narrative. The once dominant "colony to nation" paradigm that informed perceptions of Canada
through the middle decades of the twentieth century, an era that sought
an optimistic and unifying story of two founding nations drawing their
identity from their European parent cultures, has yielded to the multicultural, postcolonial and pluralistic analysis that prevails at the opening
of the third millennium. We do not have many wide-ranging volumes
of critical studies dedicated to early Canadian literary culture; nearly
three decades have passed since the appearance of Lorraine McMullen's
edited collection, *Twentieth Century Essays on Confederation Literature* (1976).
The profound difference between that handy book and the one now in
your hands demonstrates the extent to which new paradigms of cultural
history are reshaping Canada's scholarly climate.

ReCalling Early Canada unites literary studies with cultural studies in a
refreshing and innovative collection that discusses canonical poems
and novels alongside non-canonical writings such as private letters and
journalism, situates writing in relation to other cultural media, including
painting, carving, and photography, and jostles the whole enterprise
of higher culture by inserting a study of the designation of Canada's
National Horse. Whereas the mission of McMullen's volume was to
disseminate a selection of previously published studies illuminating
nineteenth-century Canada's quest to define and advance a national

literature, the mission of this volume is to problematize that enterprise in original and cutting-edge essays that interrogate institutionalization of the national and valorization of the literary. Many of these studies directly relate the past to the present, assessing the selective representation of historic texts, people and icons in preservative formats ranging from editions to museums, and examining current incarnations of historic conventions such as the captivity narrative. Attending to the participation of women, Aboriginals, francophones, expatriates (and horses) in Canada's historical imaginary, authors address the overt and covert politics which underlie the preservation, reception and interpretation of experience that can be accessed only through its surviving material and cultural traces. This dialogue with earlier canons of thought and text breathes fresh life into topics that might have remained moribund, and adds vital new dimensions to our never-ending discussion of Canadian nationhood. The publication of this book, whose very title reminds us that the past is accessible only through the ever-changing lens of the present, represents a milestone and quite possibly a turning point in scholarly discussion of Canada's cultural history.

Acknowledgements

THE RECALLING EARLY CANADA PROJECT, from conference to book, has been enriched, enlivened, and made possible by several wonderful people and institutions.

The editors would like to thank the Department of English and Cultural Studies at McMaster University, and especially its past chair Donald Goellnicht and its Administrative Officer Antoinette Somo, for their support of this project. We also wish to thank Nick Buffo, our capable managerial assistant, as well as John Corr, Benjamin Lefevbre, and Sabine Milz, who made sure that the conference ran smoothly in June 2003.

The Canada Research Chairs Program provided essential support for both the conference and for the publication of this volume. It was Daniel Coleman who first came up with the concept of a project devoted to the study of early Canada and we would like to thank him for his generous administration of these funds, his quiet leadership in this process, and his flexibility as it took shape. Also, *ReCalling Early Canada* benefited from the support of the Social Sciences and Humanities Research Council of Canada in the form of doctoral fellowships and faculty research grants.

Our thanks, as well, goes out to all the participants who took us up on our idea of an intensive workshop style conference—one that required, most notably, a significant amount of work on their part in order for it to function as successfully as it did. In addition, we would like to thank the contributors to this volume, whose ideas challenged us and who accepted our comments and suggestions with such good grace. Finally, we would like to thank people who have become great friends to us at the University of Alberta Press: Peter Midgely, who copy-edited the manuscipt and proofs carefully, Alan Brownoff, whose wonderful design ideas have made this book beautiful, and most especially Alethea Adair, who guided us through the manuscript-to-book process with good humour, efficient correspondence, and a keen eye to the details that matter.

Introduction

ReCalling Early Canada:
Reading the Political in Literary
and Cultural Production

JENNIFER BLAIR, DANIEL COLEMAN,
KATE HIGGINSON, & LORRAINE YORK

◆ ReCalling Early

WHAT IS "EARLY CANADIAN" literature or culture, and how do we look for, uncover, speak, or teach it? How do we address its important and heterogeneous bodies of historical material when "Early Canada" is not, in many ways, an adequate term for the places and times of which we speak? When we call and recall "Early Canada," what is "it" that we call upon, and how does the very name we give to "it" shape in advance what it is that we set out to recall? What habits of mind, conventions of procedure, or institutional protocols shape our inquiry? What challenges are posed by the organization—let alone contents—of archives, by the alterity of past texts, or by recent developments in theory and criticism to our assumptions about how we go about recalling the Canadian past?

Questions such as these occupied the attention of a group of literary and cultural studies scholars who gathered in Hamilton, Ontario for three days' discussion between June 23 and 25, 2003 under the conference title, "ReCalling Early Canada: Reading the Political in Literary and Cultural Production." We conference organizers, all members of the Department of English and Cultural Studies at McMaster University, had been struck by the mismatch between the high interest in early Canadian research topics among relatively new scholars and the paucity of venues for these scholars to meet and share their research. As Michael Peterman has previously noted, there are no scholarly journals or professional associations dedicated to these historical areas of research, so those who work in them tend to rely on the annual meetings of general associations such as the Association of Canadian College and University Teachers of English (ACCUTE), the Association for Canadian and Québec Literatures (ACQL), the Canadian Association for Commonwealth Languages and Literatures Studies (CACLALS), the Association of Canadian Studies (ACS), or the Canadian Association of Cultural Studies (CACS) to bring them together, and they turn to general Canadian literary or interdisciplinary journals such as *Canadian Literature, Canadian Poetry, Essays on Canadian Writing, Studies in Canadian Literature, Topia, Papers of the Bibliographical Society of Canada*, or *The Journal of Canadian Studies* to keep abreast of new developments in the field. We determined, therefore, not only to provide an opportunity for scholars of early Canadian literature and culture to meet one another, but also to organize a conference that would ensure all delegates got a chance to benefit as fully as possible from this singular gathering. As a result, we arranged for a first day of paper-panels, common to most scholarly conferences, so that members of the university community as well as the public could attend and learn about the work being carried out by scholars from across the country, but the second two days consisted of workshops in which the conference delegates were divided into small groups of four or five wherein each delegate received comments and suggestions from fellow delegates who had read each others' full-length papers before arriving at the conference. The chapters in this volume, therefore, emerge from these days of energetic discussion, wonderful conviviality, engaged critique, and stimulating intellectual companionship.

The contents of these chapters demonstrate that the opportunities to recall early Canadian materials are greater than they have ever been, and that, correspondingly, the politics of research in the domains of early Canadian writing and culture are more complex and compelling than ever. In the forty-odd years since the publication of foundational works such as the first volume of *The Literary History of Canada* and the establishment of funding bodies such as the Canada Council and its scholarly division, the Social Sciences and Humanities Research Council of Canada, vast archives of primary material as well as critical commentary have been made widely available, not just in physical collections housed in Ottawa or in various museums or university libraries across the country, but more recently through web-based archives such as those maintained by the Canadian Institute for Historical Microreproductions (www.nlc-bnc.ca/cihm) and Early Canadiana Online (www.cana-diana.org/e/_index.html). In addition, hard-to-access texts have been published in inexpensive editions by institutions such as the Centre for the Editing of Early Canadian Texts, Tecumseh Press, the Canadian Poetry Press, and McClelland and Stewart's New Canadian Library series. Reference works such as the multi-volumed *Canadian Writers and their Works* series published by ECW press, the *History of the Book in Canada* project, with its print and online resources, the *Oxford Companion to Canadian Literature* and the *Encyclopedia of Literature in Canada* as well as the *Dictionary of Canadian Biography* and the Canadian volumes of the *Dictionary of Literary Biography* all have come into publication in this short span of time. It stands to reason that with this increased access to materials from and scholarly commentary upon Canada's past have come intensified debates about the political implications of the methods by which these materials are made available as well as the interpretations that have been made of them. One recent version of these debates can be tracked in the sepa-rate claims made by the prolific, Toronto-based historians Michael Bliss and Jack Granatstein, that "social" history's attention to specific and local phenomena and, in particular, to stratification and differences within Canada has come at the expense of a unified sense of the nation's "public" history as well as in the many rebuttals of Bliss and Granatstein in both scholarly venues (e.g. A.B. McKillop or Bryan D. Palmer in the *Canadian Historical Review*) and popular ones (e.g. Paul Webster's article, "Who Stole Canadian History?" in *This Magazine*). While many of the chapters in this volume clearly disagree with Granatstein's and Bliss's centralist views, ironically, their research benefits from and depends upon the resources provided by the very national institutions— archives, museums, and historical scholarly institutions—in whose establishment and maintenance nationalists such as Granatstein and Bliss have played key roles.

Our purpose in gesturing to these ongoing "history wars" is not to analyze them in detail nor to advocate for one side or another (see Paul Hjartarson's and Anne Milne's chapters in this volume for further discussions of these debates), but to illustrate how multi-dimensional and political the question of historical "recall" truly is. When historians such as Bliss and, more emphatically, Granatstein blame "social" historians for producing and teaching the wrong kind of history, they are not (in their better moments) denying the veracity of the events social historians have studied; rather, they assert that the lenses of social history (such as feminism, race studies, multiculturalism, Native studies, or regional studies) have focused on particular events and not upon others and that this selectivity has produced an unhelpful, even harmful history, one that emphasizes the part over the whole, dissent over agreement, failures over successes, division over unity. Their assessment of what constitutes helpful or harmful history operates on the premise that historical work should be nation-building work, where "nation" can only stand for the coherent and successful. The politics of recollection, then, as demonstrated in this debate, involves questions about the "uses" of particular kinds of historical inquiry, about the ways in which the facts and events of historical research are pre-selected or pre-determined by the approach of the historian, and about how the material objects of the past (texts, images, records, archaeological objects, etc.) themselves are seen to be valuable (or not) and are therefore selected, maintained, and made available to present research in accordance with contemporary non-neutral methods of historical inquiry. Julia Emberley's chapter in this volume provides a dramatic illustration of the ways in which the meanings of photographs from the past can be radically changed when they are "reframed"—that is, when what were understood to be family portraits of First Nations families, for example, are interpreted in relation to the history of residential schools in Canada. The "framing" of the past influences what we understand it to mean, as well as the uses to which it can be put. Based on this "usable pasts" idea of history, what we might call an "easy postmodernism" would conclude that the parts of the past we know about will always and only be the ones that are useful to the present. But what goes missing in this version of the politics of recollection is an awareness—a humbling intuition—of the past as *different* from the present, and if different, then as a challenge to the present; in the words of Tilottama Rajan, what goes missing is a conception of "history as our own unassimilable alterity, our difference from the directions in which 'history' is pushing us; history as the condition for an internal distanciation and for self-reflection on what we do" (428). The signs of this widespread intuition of the alterity of the past persistently trouble the blandishments of "presentist" historiography.

This is how we understand Michael Peterman's lament in his 1997 introduction to *The Journal of Canadian Studies'* special issue on *Writing and Culture in Nineteenth-Century Canada*:

> *in many Canadian graduate departments of English the preoccupation with theory-driven criticism and with value systems in which the contemporary is privileged over the flawed and politically incorrect views that characterized our past has led to the favouring of trend-governed approaches, approaches that often engage in either calculated misreadings of new-world experience or an uninformed and historically irresponsible rendering of that past. Indeed, it ought to be a matter of grave concern today that a young literary scholar interested in what I will call pure historical research into Canada's early writing and culture stands little chance of significant encouragement or support within the academy. (3)*

An unsympathetic reader might dismiss Peterman's gesture towards "pure historical research" with its mirage of sanctity somehow beyond or anterior to the contagions of "political correctness" and "theory-driven criticism" as naïve. Not even traditional historians such as Bliss and Granatstein understand history to be retrievable beyond the influences of the present in this simplistic way. But a sympathetic reader of Peterman's lament would recognize in his call for "pure historical research" and a more responsible rendering of the past an echo of what we have called an intuition or recognition of the alterity of the past, an alterity that constitutes a stubborn challenge to rather than a simple mirroring of the demands of the present. For us, then, the politics of recollection inhabits a tension between what we might call the "directions" of history—between an intuition of our responsibility to imagine accurately, as far as possible, the otherness or difference of the past and the knowledge that our very desire to explore the past, and our capacity for imagination itself, is shaped by present needs and concerns.

This tension is not new—that is, it is not a sign of our being at some kind of vanguard of modernity, or postmodernity, for that matter. One can trace this tension even in the work of scholars who understood historical inquiry to be an objective, unself-reflexive rendering of the "facts" of the past. In his memoir, *Giving Canada a Literary History* (1991), for example, Carl Klinck—the managing editor of the monumental *Literary History of Canada*, co-editor of the *Canadian Anthology* (1955), and publisher of twenty-two books on early Canadian literature—remembers that what made him choose literary history over theology for his MA studies was his dissatisfaction with the impressionistic teaching and research he encountered in his theology classes and his attraction to the scholarly apparatus of footnotes, documentation, and "certified proof" (5) that he encountered in literary history. This commitment to "authoritative facts and logic" he understood to belong to "a world of moral responsibility" (7, 5). Throughout the book, Klinck thinks back upon his quest for a national literary history in these same terms: as he and Reginald Watters composed their biographical sketches for the *Canadian Anthology*, for instance, they "expressed the facts without interpretation or judgment. The whole principle of selection was to give people facts and let them form their own judgments and opinions." By this method, he says, "We helped establish a canon" (88). Klinck's wording here betrays a central problem of historiographical recollection: the "principle of *selection* was to give people facts and let them form their own judgments" (our emphasis). The facts themselves are selected, necessarily to the exclusion of some other facts, and readers are given the illusion of forming their own judgments based on pre-selected facts. But on what basis are these pre-selections made? Klinck is not silent about the overarching motives that drove his quest for literary history. Although he sticks consistently to the methods of what Peterman would call "pure historical research," to the moral responsibility of certified proofs and objective facts, he admits that what provoked him to persevere in his research (despite discouragement and incomprehension from his doctoral supervisors at Columbia University for a dissertation on what was then an unknown literature) was a desire to refute claims made by Ray Palmer Baker in *A History of English-Canadian Literature to Confederation* (1920) about the "intellectual sterility of Ontario." Klinck writes, "the aspersion cast upon Ontario bothered me for many years and caused me to collect evidence to the contrary. In fact, it gave me a program: finding, sorting, and presenting the real bulk of the early literature, not only of Ontario, but of the English in Québec" (34). Thus, although Klinck presents himself as a biographer and historian who preoccupied himself with the objective facts while critics and philosophers such as Northrop Frye went on to make the critical assessments and theoretical formulations (48), nonetheless, the facts he compiled were selected to buttress his, as opposed to Baker's, version of the past. The question of "responsibility" in this instance, then, is worked out in a tension between Klinck's passion to prove Baker wrong and his instinct or belief that his selection of facts would be more "accurate" to the multitudinous reality of the past than were Baker's—a tension between the alterity of the past and Klinck's needs in the present.

Another way to imagine this tension is to conceive of it being produced between what we might call the "directions" of history. Rajan follows Matthew Wickman, one of the contributors to her collection of essays, in identifying several "cognitive figures...that subtend the imagining of history: progress and enlightenment, or mourning and return" (431). The idea of history as linear progress, as the inevitable march of time from the past into the present, is fundamental to the consequent belief that historical inquiry is a genealogical endeavour in which we discover our determining antecedents in the past. This vision of history lies at the base of the oft-repeated statement that if "we" wish to "understand ourselves" (as Canadians, as moderns, as white settler-invaders, as queers on the margins of the nation-state—whatever the collective "we" stands for) we must trace a narrative for how we came to be in the present. This figuration of history tends to trace its "direction" as coming out of the past and projecting into the future. There is an opposite "direction" of history, however, conveyed in the figures of mourning and return, a sense of the present reaching back into what has been lost in the past. The notion of the past as a series of losses that haunts "us" in the present becomes a central topic of Adam Carter's chapter in this volume, where he meditates on the centrality of mourning to figurations of the nation. Peterman's lament over the loss of "pure historical research" and Klinck's desire to establish the "facts" of the past manifest this sense of the past as something we can lose if we are not careful—indeed, as something likely to elude our reach. The idea of the past as something to which we are "responsible" suggests not only the alterity of the past, but also the notion that we in the present can be (must be?) "read by" the past. This "direction" of history questions the hubris of the progressive idea of history, the self-satisfaction that would read the present as more enlightened, more developed and therefore more "correct" than the past. This direction of historical inquiry informs the arguments of Andrea Cabajsky, Robert David Stacey, and Kathleen Venema in this volume, whose chapters warn against the dismissal of earlier forms such as romance, pastoral, or domestic letter writing as naïve or simple as compared to the sophistication we assume for our own writing in the present. It also informs Janice Fiamengo's chapter, which warns against the retrospective claims that recuperate the writings of Sara Jeannette Duncan as feminist subversions of patriarchy when the writer's oeuvre gives evidence of much more ambivalent and unsettled attitudes. The politics of recollection, then, inhabit a space of tension, a tension between the needs of the present and the alterity of the past, a tension between the shaping of the past out of the needs of the present and the reconsideration of the present out of a responsibility to the past, a tension between optimistic figurations of history as progress and elegiac figurations of history as loss, a tension between the multitudinousness of the past and the necessity in all historiography to organize that complex and contradictory heterogeneity under some kind of sense-making rubric.

◆ EmBracing Canada?

THERE IS ALSO SOMETHING of an internal contradiction at play within this volume's project: on the one hand, it gathers together a group of essays under the sense-making rubric of "Early Canada" (with the assumption that there is some productive dialogue to be gained thereby), and on the other, it is acutely aware of the limitations of national classifications in general and of the problematic history of Anglo-Canadian cultural nationalism in particular. In our initial call for papers we asked: "In the face of increasing financial and cultural globalization, what, for instance, is at stake in classifying "Early Canadian Literature" in national terms, in persistently engaging in a specifically political act that marshals the many possible meanings and impulses of a given work of art in the service of building the imagined community of the nation?" To classify cultural products as "Canadian" is to privilege the category of the nation over other possible axes of analysis, to implicitly endorse the idea of the nation-state as a coherent and legitimate social and political entity, to potentially stabilize or shore up the concept of the nation-state in the face of expanding claims of globalization, and, additionally in this particular early Canadian case, to risk falsely projecting a fixed concept of the Canadian nation-state back in time, which lends it an additional antiquity or authenticity not to be found in its actual history of sporadic and contested conquest. Furthermore, to mobilize a Canadian literary-cultural rubric is to raise the possibility of perpetuating a tradition of cultural patriotism among English Canadian critics, a tradition that has tended to create a violently homogenous, Eurocentric, and "monologic story of Canadian culture and criticism" (Pennee, "Après" 208). Nationalist criticism in Canada, so often exclusively focused upon the culture of the country's two so-called founding nations, the English and the French, provides ample evidence for Arun Mukherjee's claim that "Canadian nationalism, for us non-whites, is a racist ideology that has branded us un-Canadian by acts of omission and commission" (89). Concerns such as these motivated us to put the "Canada" in our call, and in this volume's title, under interrogative scrutiny.

Recent arguments against "Canadacentric" modes of study have tended to take one of two (often interconnected) routes: (i) a critique of nationally-based modes of analysis in general or of the character of Canadian cultural nationalism in particular, or (ii) a more temporally grounded assertion that nationally-based thought is outmoded in the global or transnational circumstances that increasingly characterize the early twenty-first century. While these are recent critiques, in a country where querying national identity is a perennial activity, questions of what nationally-based criticism "here" should entail and whether it is to be endorsed are long-standing and recurring (Besner 41; Lecker 7, 10); one earlier example, analyzed in this volume by Andrea Cabajsky, is Napoléon Bourassa's 1865 critique of the ethnic exclusivity of Canadian nationalist narratives. That Canadian literary nationalism operates from a long tradition of exclusion is well-established, but to use that history to dismiss nationally based modes in general is too hasty, for nationalisms are always subject to *context*, to shifts in time and place and constituency, they make different demands on different subjects and ultimately they warrant specifically grounded contextualized evaluation. Notwithstanding the injustices of a certain Anglo-Canadian literary critical nationalism, there are multiple instances of enabling nationalisms, of strategically deployed nationalisms, of decolonizing or popular nationalisms, of nationalisms more and less defined by kinship and territory. The very (essentialized) qualities—of blood, soil, and language—that have often rendered applications of modern western nationalism xenophobic, can, arguably, be used to laudable, decolonizing ends by disempowered groups or nations; although, as Helen Hoy notes, such groups still have to negotiate difficult questions of how to balance competing identificatory allegiances and avoid reductive and exclusionary ones (Hoy 127). They are faced with the dilemma, as George Elliott Clarke has written in his spirited defense of strategic African Canadian cultural nationalism, of establishing their nation's "*difference* from others, while still accommodating *difference* within itself" (*Odysseys* 21).

The concept of confederation, as a negotiated alliance among widely disparate peoples, regions, and cultures, and as a referent to antecedent sovereign indigenous confederacies on Turtle Island, serves as a constant reminder of the diversity that has always undermined the coherence of the Canadian nation-state, which suggests the importance of radically and literally reading early Canada as a site of conflicting confederacies. Within (and frequently poised against) the geopolitical entity of Canada and its enfranchised state nationalism are numerous other contestatory nationalisms, ranging from queer nationalisms to those of the First Nations—a term which itself stands as "a brilliant rhetorical intervention" on the part of Aboriginal peoples "to counteract the racist nationalist discourse of two founding nations" (Mukherjee 82) and to further the "struggle for Aboriginal self-government by fracturing the symbolic unity of any Canadian nation" (Goddard 233). The need for such First Nations' resistance to Canadian nationalism's active re-scripting of Anglo-European discourses of nation—including its naturalization of national belonging—is abundantly clear.

Take, as one example among many, the articulation of a homogenizing Canadian nationalist rhetoric (and mobilization of manpower, in the form of the RCMP) in response to a recent conflict over policing and leadership at Kanesatake, the Mohawk Territory made famous to many Canadians through its assertion of territorial sovereignty during the "Oka Crisis" of 1990. A sampling of federal(ist) rhetoric is suggestive: "Canada's National Newspaper," The Globe and Mail, describes Kanesatake in infantilizing terms as a "tiny, quarrelsome Mohawk territory" (Ha); Canadian Public Safety Minister Anne McLellan, after authorizing the RCMP to police the territory, "call[s] upon everyone in the Kanesatake community to respect the rule of law" ("RCMP"); and journalist Rex Murphy—on (the aptly named) The National—argues that members of the Mohawk Territory should be forced to obey Canadian law in a fashion "identical" to that of every other "Canadian," be they "white people, people of colour, immigrant, or native" (Murphy). The falsity of such an enforced "equality" (of all under the Canadian law) is evident from Himani Bannerji's vantage on "the dark side of the nation" where "'Pan-Canadianism' loses its transcendent inclusivity and emerges instead as a device and a legitimation for a highly particularized form of domination" (105). In the bid to establish a singular ethos of the

Canadian nation, Murphy and, to a lesser extent, McLellan are eager to efface the differences at work between these varied constituents and *the law*: they must work actively *not* to recall that Kanesatake has been the centre of a 300 year-old legal dispute that dates back to Louis XV's deed of land in 1717 that failed to clarify whether it was to be owned by the Seminary of St. Sulpice or by the largely Iroquoian people it was meant to benefit. To insist that the Mohawks of Oka submit equally to a legal system that has perennially denied their equality with other Canadians to assert their rights to this contested land until an agreement-in-principal was finally signed in December 2000 (see Dickason 326–30), is not only to deny this history of legal inequality but also to deny the validity of a different set of Mohawk or Haudenosaunee laws in this case. At issue here is the function of the Canadian law, which Patricia Monture-Angus (one of the first indigenous professors of law in Canada) has identified as an "instrument through which colonialism continues to flow" to the detriment of "First Nations collectively" (*Journeying* 9, 10). She elaborates:

> What needs to be understood is who has done the defining [of Canada]. It has not been First Nations. Many of us do not accept this great lie any longer. We understand the solution lies in our unalienable right to define ourselves, our nations, our governments, and in protecting the laws the Creator gave us. Nor has the restructuring of law and government on Turtle Island to conform to European norms been achieved with the express or implied consent and/or assistance of First Nations. (qtd in Mukherjee 82)

Combining the three above-cited responses to Kanesatake (from the Canadian national newspaper, Cabinet Minister, and news broadcast), and bearing their suppression of the specific history of Kanesetake as reflected in Monture-Angus's words in mind, we see one nation's aggressive attempt to efface the difference and delimit the sovereignty of another by utilizing racialist, paternalistic rhetoric and by applying a singular, violently homogenizing conception of the Canadian law and nation.

This dissemination of nationalist rhetoric (backed by police power) is suggestive of the ways in which the Canadian nation-state—replete with ideological and repressive apparatuses—continues to operate in these avowedly global, or more accurately *trans*national, times. Despite the fact that globalization is often characterized (with some accuracy) as succeeding nationalism, the relation between the two in Canada is not necessarily one of antithesis or inverse correlation. Len Findlay explains that

> The death of the nation-state has been greatly exaggerated. In fact, the nation-state needs to continue for two broadly contradictory reasons, one triumphalist and one dissenting: transnational corporations and the United States both need nation-states as satellites or proxies to talk (down) to, and to help develop the deregulating political and fiscal instruments necessary for further "globalization" of the market economy; at the same time, citizens need nation-states as sites of resistance to such political and economic hegemony exercised by unelected elites and insiders. (298)

The Canadian nation, far from being rendered obsolete by globalization, has instead taken on a complex, sometimes even symbiotic, relation to it; at times seen as abetting transnational corporatism and at others seen, as Findlay suggests, as a means to resist it. Recent Canadian nationalism catalyzed by anti-American sentiments has been viewed both positively, as a site of a local particularism that stands as an empowering antidote to American (neo)imperialism, and negatively, as a "retreat to discourses of nationalism which become short-sighted in terms of the transnational political identifications that might be crucially necessary in our times" (Walcott 33).

This issue of how to configure a desired relation between local specificity and international relevance has long preoccupied Canadian literary critics; see, for instance, Thomas D'Arcy McGee's calls in the 1860s and A.J.M. Smith's in the 1940s for a Canadian "cosmopolitanism"—to use Smith's term—which sought connections to international literary cultures without losing sight of local specificities. Though the effort to locate

African Canadian cultures between Canadian and diasporic Black nation-alisms in the 1990s makes for a very different context from McGee's and Smith's, Rinaldo Walcott's *Black Like Who?: Writing Black Canada* strikes an exemplary balance of the trans/national insofar as it cogently argues for attending to (and at times prioritizing) the transnational dimen-sions of culture produced in Canada as well as retaining a focus on the particularities of local and national contexts. For instance, his analysis of rapper Devon's commentary on police brutality—from the "LAPD" to the "RCMP," "52," and "Peel Region"—illustrates the need to read in terms of "locality and historicity" (say, the particular context of 52 Division's known abuse of Jamaican Torontonians) and transnationally in order to account for the local/national, as well as for that which exceeds its bound-aries (41). For Walcott, "making outer-national identifications with other black peoples is important to the kinds of struggles that might be waged within national boundaries" (45): the transnational functions here, in part, as a means to reconfigure the national.

The Canadian police brutality at issue for Walcott, and for Kanesatake, speaks to the apparatuses that make the nation a lived, imposed, mate-rial reality: all of us within Canada's geopolitical borders must operate within a pervasive and quotidian collection of state-regulated practices and institutions. Arguably these structures affect cultural production as much as other more celebrated influences of climate or canon. The merit of the idea that work produced in Canada will carry a "Canadian dimension" (Clarke, *Odysseys* 10), however fleeting or diverse, arises from a recognition of the common impact of state laws, practices, and cultural institutions. (Think, for example, of those "para-statal" bodies like the CBC or the Canada Council which were critiqued as racially-suspect by Dionne Brand and others in the 1990s [qtd in Mukherjee 88].) As Barbara Godard observes: "'Post-national' though Frank Davey may call the rhetoric of contemporary Canadian fiction, the nation remains the field of its material production, where publishing is organized under the state apparatus of the Canada Council and Heritage Canada" (222). Which is not at all to discount the impact of global capital and the emer-gence of a new transnational world order, but instead to remember the nation's continuing role within that economic realignment in general and upon the field of culture in particular. Thus, despite proclamations that we have arrived at "the end of what has been the epoch of the nation-state" (Readings 193) and despite the clear need for modes of cultural analysis beyond the national, the continuing existence of the nation within globalization, the existence of enabling or decolonizing nation-alisms, and the material effects of Canadian nationalism and its state apparatuses stand as compelling reasons to continue using the nation as "a unit of analysis" (Pennee, "Looking" 81)—that is, to consider the nation as an object of discourse, to examine nationalisms with critical suspicion, to critique, denaturalize, and reconfigure their contents and functions, to endorse what Walcott describes as a "notion of nation... that is constituted through the practices of justice, ethical politics and progressive race relations" (129).

If the nation is still a relevant unit of analysis for current texts (though not one to be privileged or thought of in isolation from other modes of community, migrancy, and power), it is even more apropos when exam-ining late nineteenth-century culture produced during what is known (perhaps somewhat misleadingly) as Canada's "nation-building era": generated during the period when "Canada" was under construction, early Canadian artifacts offer particularly revealing sites in which it is possible to trace the gains and losses of the imposition of the nation—with its demands of cohesion and homogeneity—upon the many and various preoccupations of artists, writers, and cultural commentators. Many, perhaps half or so, of the chapters in *ReCalling Early Canada* (and the volume itself, featuring "Canada" in its title) might be said to em*brace* the nation, in that they both turn to the nation as a privileged unit of analysis (among others) and critique what we might term the nation's *braces*: those structures and mechanisms which gird, support, invig-orate and animate the nation.

Informed by a postmodern suspicion of nationalist master narratives and a postcolonial aim to "circumvent imperial and colonial habits of mind" (Brydon, "Introduction" 11), as well as a historical materialist attention to the power of cultural discourse to shape and determine human perceptions of lived reality, the chapters in this volume tend to view the Canadian nation not as an essence nor a natural phenomenon but as a motivated construction, as what historian Ian McKay has labeled "a historically-specific project of rule" (620). And like McKay, the scholars here mount a "reconnaissance" of Canada (627): they seek to *know it again*, to reCall it, to denaturalize it through a close scrutiny of its mechanics, to question how it has come, and continues, to be in a "terrain that was already thick with alternative, indigenous logics" (Henderson 5). Key questions running through *ReCalling Early Canada* concern the policing of "Canadian" contents: How are the inclusions and exclusions of what is understood as national culture enforced, reinforced, and adapted? How is this culture constructed by relation to and difference from its internal and external others? How are "organic" or "naturalistic" figures such as the family, heterosexual romance, femininity or masculinity, friendship, loyalty, or purity used to regulate and organize the constituent parts of this culture's "integrity"?

In her 1997 assessment of the current state of Canadian literary criticism, Donna Palmateer Pennee notes the centrality of issues of *representation* and the denotative shift this term has undergone in the discipline in the last three or four decades: "Increasingly, the term 'representation' in literary studies has less to do with mimesis...and more to do with the question of representing the different constituencies or voices that populate the country and its literature" ("Après" 203). It is in keeping with this disciplinary trend that many of the chapters which here em*brace* the nation opt to map the gains and losses of its imposition via a multi-pronged focus on representation (attending, to put it simply, to the who and what as well as to the how and why). Which symbols, bodies, tropes, texts, modes, and artifacts are positioned so as to represent the early Canadian nation at particular moments and places in time—and with what consequences? Anne Milne, for example, utilizes a biodiversity paradigm grounded in local knowledges to critique the manner in which the Canadian Parliament recently designated *le cheval Canadien* as Canada's national horse, as a propagandist symbol of a homogeneous, Euro-derived early Canada that forecloses recognition of numerous other regional breeds, histories, and approaches. Kate Higginson looks to another pair of bodies, those of two invader-settler women widowed during the North-West Rebellion of 1885, to show how they were con-

structed as emblematic of the Canadian nation and how this representation both limited the women's ability to represent themselves (if they
were to be readmitted to the national polity) and provided a (dubious)
justification for Canada's harsh retaliation against western Cree and
Métis nations. The expulsion of the Métis from the Canadian nation is
also at work in two contemporary patriotic odes written by G.D. Roberts
and analyzed here by Adam Carter who addresses the linguistic and
historical violence enacted in Roberts' anthropomorphic troping of the
nation as a singular white subject. Nick Mount's examination of the
transnational or continental cultural network significantly responsible
for the formation of the late nineteenth-century English Canadian canon
contends that over-zealous, soil-bound nationalism has unjustly excluded
significant works from that canon that were written by Canadians in
the United States. Robert Stacey's chapter addresses representative literary
modes, noting the ascendancy of romance within Canadian criticism
that has occluded the recognition of alternative rhetorical and imaginative structures, such as the pastoral mode, in which the history of the
nation and/or national culture is presented in terms other than those of
quest, victory and origin.

Postcolonial critics have noted that second world, or settler-invader,
countries have tended to represent themselves, via cultural nationalism, in ways that elide their origins in the usually brutal conquest of
Aboriginal cultures. The chapters here insistently reject what Gary Boire
has dubbed the "Boer syndrome," the exclusive definition of Canada as
a colonized and not a colonizing entity (5), and many focus upon early
Canada's colonization or attempted genocide of First Nations peoples.
Drawing on the work of Anna Johnston and Alan Lawson, Diana Brydon
has observed that "the very notion of 'Canada' is posited on the basis of
this substitution":

> In the founding and growth of cultural nationalism…we can see one vector of
> difference (the difference between colonizing subject and colonized subject:
> settler-indigene) being replaced by another (the difference between colonizing
> subject and imperial centre: settler-imperium). We can see this, with the benefit
> of postcolonial hindsight/analysis, as a strategic disavowal of the colonizing act.

In this process, "the nation" is what replaces "the indigenous" and in so doing conceals its participation in colonization by nominating a new "colonized" subject—the colonizer or settler-invader. (qtd in Brydon, "Canada" 56–57)

While Brydon references "Canada" as a signified, the troubling substitution she pinpoints can be plainly seen in early discussions of "Canada" as a signifier as well. In his well-known Confederation-era lecture, "The Men of the North and their Place in History," Robert Grant Haliburton writes disparagingly of the indigenous derivation of "Canada" from the Iroquois or Haudenosaunee *kanata* which denotes a village or cluster of dwellings:

We have called the Dominion by the name of Canada.... I like Indian names for towns and for provinces...but should we ever become a nation, we need a name that will have some historical traditions, or at least some meaning and significance. What does Canada mean? Is it Indian?...Why should we puzzle history by giving ourselves a name of which it can make nothing? Ex nihilo nihil fit [nothing becomes out of nothing].... Let us revive the grand old name of Norland" (15–16).

Haliburton annihilates indigenous knowledges and histories, turning away from invader-settler relations with Aboriginals in Canada to instead advocate for a relation between colony and metropole, between his new "Norland" (Canada) and the original Viking nation of that name. Resisting such attempted erasures of indigenous epistemology, Lee Maracle's recent poem "*Ka-Nata*" uses the term to denote an indigenous form of community and imbues this referent with a powerful past legacy—"the truth of infinite grandmothers"—and an optimistic future trajectory— "infinite progeny... who cannot forsake *Ka-Nata*":

Ka-Nata
the sleeping giant
will awaken without a howl.
The clatter and clang of machines
will be less deafening
the concrete less barren

Ka-Nata less impossible
and the earth will sing
a song of maternal hope. (111–12)

If Canada is founded upon this unpalatable substitution, this attempted erasure of Maracle's *Ka-Nata*, and if its cultural products reproduce such colonialist annihilations, a pressing issue becomes how to address and redress this situation, how to practice a criticism responsible to the complexity of past texts, and the violences of representation within which they were produced, that remains aware of our own investments and limitations as scholars who often work within formations and institutions that continue to reproduce the inclusions and exclusions of "Canadian" culture. The challenge here is imperative and daunting. As Bannerji states, "the very discourse of nationhood in the context of 'Canada,' given its evolution as a capitalist state derived from a white settler colony with aspirations to liberal democracy, needs an ideology that can mediate fissures and ruptures more deep and profound than those of the usual capitalist nation state" (96). Some, like Arun Mukherjee, place hope in the ability of an ideology of diversity to redemptively reconfigure Canadian nationalism: "Canada needs a new nationalism, one whose grounding premise will be heterogeneity" (92); and this volume's recuperative analysis of numerous little-studied cultural products (non-canonized voices, neglected modes, long-unpublished autobiography) is one small contribution toward such a heterogeneous Canadian culture. Other thinkers, while not denying that "the postcolonial nation remains a potential agent of ethicopolitical transformation in neocolonial globalization" (Cheah 198), point to Canada's distinctly colonial status with regard to First Nations' rights and see little prospect for a new, decolonized Canadian nationalism. They therefore argue instead for (an acknowledgement of) other, extra- and anti-national, ways of imagining and identifying cultural products, and ourselves. Their proposals include moving beyond a nationalist critical methodology into a "consideration of the complex traffic between and within cultures and regions" (Heble, "Sounds" 27), focusing upon concepts like migrancy and diaspora as axes for theorizing belonging (Brydon, "It's"), or, more radically, conceptualizing communities without identity or unmediated by any condition of belonging (Readings 185; Agamben 85). These ideas, too, are very much at play in *ReCalling Early Canada*, in, for instance, Cabajsky's study of Acadian diaspora or Jennifer Blair's examination of the transnational circulation of nun's tales in early North American Protestant collectives. Blair's careful attention to various non-national borders— not only in employing a bicontinental frame for her historical and intertextual reading, but in examining attempts to demarcate the diffusive notion of "sex" and to police boundaries between an inner imagination and an outward behaviour as well as between the cloister and the outside world, and in probing the multiple function of texts themselves as "boundary-keepers"—underscores the rich panoply of boundaries or borders (and their attendant rubrics) which demand analysis. More often than not, however, at least in the case of the early Canada in the texts addressed in the following chapters, nation tends to call upon and yoke other analytical categories together. It makes them readable, or it enlists others to identify as readers as they negotiate the aggressions of invader-settler citizenship, the pressures of migrancy, and the ongoing, historically rooted vitality of aboriginal, "First-" nationalisms as political and spiritual rights of belonging.

◆ **Reading Politics**

"WHO READS A CANADIAN BOOK?" Carole Gerson opens her landmark text on "the writing and reading" of early Canadian literature with this question that Thomas D'Arcy McGee put to the Montreal Literary Club just a few months after Confederation. McGee's immediate answer—"very few, for Canadian books are exceedingly scarce"— was followed by a hopeful prediction for the future of Canadian literature, one that concentrated specifically on *readers*, or what he called "a recognized literary class" that would "by and by be felt a state and social necessity" (qtd in Gerson 3). Gerson offers McGee's attention to readers as an introduction to her discussion of literacy rates in Canada and the overall paucity of Canadian books compared to British and American books in circulation at the time. McGee's remarkable choice of words, however, alerts us to another matter that figures significantly in recent work undertaken in the field of early Canadian criticism, as well as in most of the chapters in this volume. This is the assertion that people in early Canada saw themselves specifically as readers and asked to be "recognized" as such. According to McGee, "readers" became a "class" of people, an identity to which people aspired, through their particular treatment of texts. Often, as Heather Murray has investigated at length in *Come, Bright Improvement! The Literary Societies of Nineteenth-Century Ontario* (2002), a book she calls the "study of a manifestation of readership" (171), these individuals came to be "readers" through the negotiation- and consensus-generating processes of collectives such as the literary club McGee addressed in Montreal. As critics in the academy, we too operate in relation to a collective identity and, accordingly, there are several ways in which the concept of a "recognized reader," that is, one who is not just a producer but also a subject of inquiry, helps us twenty-first century readers to negotiate some of the pressing concerns facing historically oriented criticism of Canadian culture. To address these reader relations is fundamental to the important and necessarily political work that underlies what we have called "reading early Canada."

McGee's confederation-era question, then, gives way to another that Murray poses at the end of her study of early Canadian readers, a question more pertinent to our era of reading and critique. "What," she asks, "of the desire to capture and to understand reading in its 'original' or immediate moment" (161)? The key, she says, to this instructive question is that it identifies two reading subjects. First, there is the critic, who, in taking on such a task, works with and against the credentials of a critical/academic class, if not precisely a "literary class." Second, what the critic reads are texts written by, for, and as often against, *another* set of credentials, a set of credentials our early Canadian reader-counterparts aspired to, and through which they sought to be "recognized," according to McGee, as a "class" of readers. When we do the work of recalling early Canada, then, we are, in part, reading a set of texts that were written with a particular set of readers in mind—a set of people for whom identifying as "readers" meant something in particular, something *different* from what it means to identify as readers now. Early Canadian criticism thus far has consistently probed the relationship between readers past and present, suggesting that we as readers in the present inherit our discursive practices from readers of the past (along with more general cultural knowledge and identifications). This argument that criticism of early Canadian literature could usefully identify a literary and/or discursive lineage was the focus of Lorraine McMullen's 1988 anthology *Re(dis)covering Our Foremothers* and Germaine Warkentin and Heather Murray's 1991 special issue of *Canadian Literature* entitled *Discourse in Early Canada*, the latter of which considered "whether a realignment of agendas might bring into focus the discourse of those who gave birth to the communities we now inhabit," so that students of contemporary Canadian literature might be "more aware of the direct effect of non-canonical genres and institutional frameworks on the way we write today, on what we permit to be said, and what we require not to be said" (9). Working now at a critical distance of more than a decade from these texts, *ReCalling Early Canada* expresses a wariness of a "recalling" activity that is somehow neutral and simply "discovers" our antecedents in the details of the past. We take our cue, then, from these earlier anthologies by advocating a continued focus on readings and readers, yet we do so in order to increase our understanding of the differences inherent in this uneven reciprocity between past readers and ourselves. These differences are evidence of the not-so-simple fact that, as Alberto Manguel has recently reminded us, reading itself has a history, and that this history betrays our "desire to capture it," to revisit it at its "original moment."

Such differences—which might come to stand as signs of Rajan's "unassimilable alterity"—are not going to be easy to identify. We are likely to see ourselves as quite different from McGee's anticipated readers who would mobilize a national citizenry specifically through their acts of reading. After all, to identify a "literary class" as a "state and social necessity" makes at least some of this early Canadian readership seem foreign to those of us who read precisely to *de*stabilize the nation—an endeavour through which, paradoxically, Canada has experienced a "coming into its own" (Carter, "Namelessness" 10). Which is to say,

Canada can now, with the advent of postmodernism, recognize itself and be recognized as a nation even though it has experienced ethno-cultural pluralism since its inception. This is another way in which, despite our supposedly sophisticated critique of "the nation," we have certainly not yet divested ourselves of a sense of "necessity" that is inextricably linked to "state" and social identity. In fact, we might not be as different, whether in process, style, effect or even politics, from early Canadian readers as we think we are or as we aspire to be. Therefore, perhaps our difference from these early readers needs to be thought through another set of parameters. Perhaps we need to think about the relationship between reading on the one hand, and what it means to seek or establish recognition on the other—and, in the process, we might reconsider the extent to which we can throw off our current desire to "come into our own" as part of a "class" of early Canadian critics.

Canadian philosopher Charles Taylor, through an analysis of English/French relations in Canada, famously assessed what he considered to be the uncertain possibilities of a "politics of recognition," and, in so doing, encouraged further critique of political movements aimed at seeking recognition of otherwise excluded cultural groups. In some fundamental ways, this project to "recall early Canada" is a manifestation of what Taylor calls the "demand" for recognition—in this case, however, the recognition of a culturally and temporally distant literary past. First and foremost, the chapters in this volume insist that any and all literary and cultural production produced in or about Canada be recognized as integral to Canadian studies, colonial studies, Victorian studies—all in all, to an expanded national, or transnational, canon. In addressing a variety of textual and visual documents, these chapters also demand that literary criticism recognize the value of texts outside of what has only recently become considered "literary." As Warkentin and Murray have argued, in order to include early Canadian textual production in our classrooms and our scholarship, we must also argue for the inclusion of all discursive material: "a wide linguistic and symbolic world" to "take us outward from our position as scholars of the purely or independently 'literary,' to a consideration of the way in which literature, and the larger category we will call 'discourse,' are constructed by society"

(7). Finally, the fact that Canadian literature is a recognized field for literary criticism, (as it was not, for example, in Klinck's sojourn at Columbia) is itself a triumph of recognition, although this triumph is undoubtedly still encumbered by the fact that it has barely managed to escape its marginalized status in the international literary canon.

To engage in the politics of recalling early Canada, then, is also to voice a concern with the limited structures of protest, identification, and recognition in which we operate—and, perhaps, to venture something new. As several chapters in this volume suggest, "reading the political" in early Canada should be as much about re-conceiving the mechanics of, as well as the relationship between, identity and recognition as it is about which texts and which people have been included and excluded. In general, the contributors assume Taylor's "politics of recognition," insofar as they respond to what Taylor then saw as "new," i.e., that "the demand for recognition is now explicit," made so "by the spread of the idea that we are formed by recognition" and that "misrecognition has now graduated to the rank of a harm" (121). Janice Fiamengo's chapter, in particular, shows that while it is almost impossible to fix Duncan's position on any political issue, when amassed her varied journalistic offerings seem part of a project to detach feminism from an accompanying prescribed identity performance. Duncan, it seems, launched a kind of opposition within feminism by mocking the way in which the demand for political recognition by the "damp females" she satirized was bound to a supposedly authentic female identity—one that, for Duncan, was often unpalatable. In a somewhat different vein, Nick Mount's paper in this volume argues for a recognition of Canadian expatriate writers as a sizeable but often forgotten ensemble in the history of Canadian literary production. But this is also to argue for a detachment of the national label "Canadian" from a writer's place of residence, work, and publication and, therefore, to trouble the process of recognizing an individual and his or her cultural production according to national belonging—a category that so often guarantees easy identifications.

If Taylor's foundational essay calls for a critique of the "demand" for recognition and its apparently unwavering faith in the notion of an authentic identity—as in the current popular epithet "I am Canadian," for example—Alexander García Düttmann's *Between Cultures: Tensions in the Struggle for Recognition* charts in further detail the disparity between identity and recognition. Düttmann's attention to the space "between cultures" can serve as an important reminder that we must acknowledge not only the differences between present and past readers, but also the fact that recognizing both sets of readers' desires redoubles the critical fields of the two sets of reading subjects. For Düttmann, "That which demands recognition differs from itself. It comes out, as it were, it goes beyond itself in a self-referential turn. The fact that it demands recognition means that it is not yet what it is, that it must first show itself to be this or that and thereby assert itself" (6). Here, the reader—even one of McGee's readers—is the product of a relation between the individual-as-reader and the individual-as-other to that reader-identity. In other words, this reader experiences potentially conflicting allegiances to, on the one hand, a collective identity of readers, and, on the other hand, the identifications that he or she has made with other groups and activities, produced under other cultural regimes. Certainly, we can expect that the identificatory processes and pursuits that come with the latter leak into those of the former, and therefore threaten to disrupt the coherence of the collective identity of readers. The "reading," we can imagine, as both activity and product, travels circuitously through the resulting set of recognitions and refusals that ensue from this reader/ Reader.

Murray's *Come, Bright Improvement!* positions such readerly concerns within the context of early Canada. Like Düttmann, Murray insists that we recognize this "manifestation of readership" as a collection of shape-shifting individual and collective processes. Most important, she argues that, as critics, we must recognize how "we make a transition from readers as individuals (or series of singularities) to an aggregate" in order to make "a shift to treating" readers, and also possibly texts of the past, "within the context of intellectual, cultural, and social formations" (166). From McGee through to Murray, we can begin to see that as we enter the picture as similarly and disparately pluralized reading individuals, it is important to acknowledge the distance we encounter when we approach texts and also that the texts we read come as the result of a similar distancing. Even as we wish to be "close," we are, as readers, already two degrees of separation away from a text just by virtue of assuming the position of reader. This redoubled distancing is in place even before we take into account the fact that a given text was produced in the "past." If "doing history" is a project riddled, in ever new ways, with the "unassimilable alterity" of a *past* with which we can only ever partially engage, then to identify as a "reader" means to assume *another* alterity, one that is related to, but also separate from, that which comes of the difference between present and past. This second alterity perhaps holds the best promise for early Canadian literary studies, because it ensures that we will not, in any brash move of critical irresponsibility, decide that we have achieved the collapse of all partitions between ourselves and what we read.

The collapse of difference, as Paul Hjartarson and Cecily Devereux examine in their contributions to this volume, has been a much sought after and renewed feature within Canadian criticism, literature and culture. Hjartarson's chapter and its title, "Wedding 'Native' Culture to the 'Modern' State," offers up various fantasies of contact—marriage, collegial handshakes, twin-ship—for energetic critique. Similarly, Northrop Frye's famous comment that Isabella Valancy Crawford's *Malcolm's Katie* integrates "the literary tradition of the country by deliberately re-establishing the broken cultural link with Indian civilization" provides Devereux with a classic example of this rhetoric of connectedness. Devereux argues that Frye's comment is a faithful interpretation of the cultural work accomplished in this poem, but that we need to recognize this cultural work as the maintenance of the distance between cultures necessary to the colonial project. In effect, both of these chapters show how the collapse of difference can be superficial rhetoric for more complicated alignments and differentiations produced by both early Canadian texts and more recent criticism. In other words, this rubric of sameness and difference, link and rupture, characterizes early Canadian literature *and* its criticism, and this rubric is usually at the service of a dominant class of readers and writers.

Accordingly, distance, separation, and rupture are welcomed by the chapters in this volume, not just in their suspicion of collegial handshakes and healing links but also in their attendance to the political possibilities of disconnection. So Fiamengo notes, for example, Duncan's "[r]hetorical and ideological distance" (6) in her newspaper columns, while Adam Carter identifies the haunting but inevitable possibility that the call to the nation imagined in the national ode might be answered in a muffled, distanced, and/or partial voice. Of course it should not come as a surprise that distance is a prominent subject of discussion in these chapters when, after all, distance is the cardinal theme of a colonial literature. Murray recalls Thomas Campbell's *The Pleasures of Hope* (Edinburgh, 1799) as a once popular example of a text for which distance is not only the subject but also a condition of its production. For Campbell, the distance that "lends enchantment to the view" was the distance between Europe and North America, the continent about which he wrote without ever having been there. By calling attention to this phrase from Campbell's poem, Murray reminds us of our own more or less oceanic reaches of imagination as we write about the past (qtd in Murray x).

Distance, then, is the inevitable condition of our reading as much as it is the condition of colonial Canada, and it is useful to acknowledge what distance has done for the literature and culture of early Canada insofar as it has made an opening for alterity to become prominent in our critical endeavours. After all, so many early Canadian texts are, like Campbell's, both fascinated and encumbered with the geographical distance between Europe and the North American colonies, and often between these "Western" regions and the Indian and African colonies as well. Furthermore, distance is often what produces and maintains the secrets of early Canadian texts, both popular and "literary," until it delivers the matter of their revelations. In Julia Catherine Beckwith Hart's *St. Ursula's Convent, or The Nun of Canada*, two young women must travel back and forth between Canada and Europe in order to solve the secret of their identity and reorganize their incestuous engagements. This was a plot to be revisited by several colonial writers. Isak Dinesen's story "The Caryatides" features a man who, having returned from

Québec to France, discovers hidden documents in the attic of his family home and realizes that he is married to his own sister. Of course, this revelation of the consequential effects of distance via the found document is another classic feature of colonial narratives. In such a story the reader-as-character figures prominently: he or she who reads the found document becomes the producer of the text and often as a result the producer of his or her own identity. Most important, the finding of a revealing document becomes associated with the illicitness of the story it is to reveal, which operates, as in the case of Dinesen's story, upon the *frisson* of cardinal sexual deviance. This was the case in several Canadian novels. George Bourne's *Lorette*, for example, is prefaced with an "Introductory Letter" written by a nameless traveller who claims to have been given the manuscript of the novel that follows when he was visiting Québec, and the manuscript turns out to be, of course, another convent narrative haunted by sexual abuse and the threat of incest.

In early Canada, reading was often predicated upon the dangers of secrets and discovery, both of which are so intimately connected with the colonial condition of being distant, and the resulting precariousness of family history. Perhaps it was for this reason that some of Canada's most adamant readers advocated an abstention from reading. Egerton Ryerson, for example, saw reading as an activity that could be left out of the demanding schedule of Methodist ministers. In his *Doctrines and Discipline of the Methodist Episcopal Church in Canada* (1829), Ryerson advised: "If you can do but one, let your studies alone. We ought to throw by all the libraries in the world, rather than be guilty of the loss of one soul" (49). Ryerson's complicated position—that reading could help convert and sustain lost souls, but that it could also, and perhaps at the same time, lose others—gives voice to the kind of inevitable differencing that comes with identifying as a collective. Reading could be as dangerous to his evangelical project as it was beneficial, as long as there were those who did not identify with the aggregate of Christian readers. If all Canadians were baptized, they would collectively read the Bible and be the better for it; however, if there were "others" to the good Christian readers, then ministers and other converts could not spend time reading: they were to go out and convert these others. Even though a minister could better himself by reading, and better convert others by reading to them, the prudent minister might realize that it was a more efficient use of his time—resulting in a higher yield of new believers—to quickly explain about Methodism, perhaps demonstrate his own faith, and then move on to new audiences. Reading, then as now, was in the way of mass-consumption, but then again it was also necessary to amass the population and then sustain their collective fervour in the absence of ministration.

If reading could sometimes be expendable, then some books, and, by association, their readers, were considered expendable also. In *A Plea for Emigration* (1852), for example, Mary Ann Shadd critiques the quality of books sent to fugitive slaves: "I have often thought if it is really a benevolent act to send old almanacs, old novels, and all manner of obsolete books to them, what good purpose was accomplished, or even what sort of vanity was gratified, by emptying useless contents of old libraries on destitute fugitives?" (67). If, for Ryerson, reading should occur only when it directly contributed to the collective moral good, then Shadd calls attention to the displacement of apparent "goodness" when charity, in the name of fostering good reading and good people through reading, worked more in the service of gratifying the donors than it did in offering any potential "good" to the readers. Generally speaking, and to very different ends, Ryerson and Shadd address the connection between books—and reading books—and the production of "classes of readers" as well as their "others." The others are not just non-readers, as we all too often imagine when we get caught up in discussions of literacy rates, for example. Reading, it seems, was bound to produce others, even when this was the opposite of its presumed "good intentions."

◆ **ReCalling Early Canada...In Literary and Cultural Production**

WHEN WE BEGAN PREPARATIONS for the conference that gave rise to this volume, we carefully thought out the implications and the parameters of our title. The final portion of the title that we decided upon, "in literary and cultural production," was meant to signal to potential contributors that, although all of us were associated with a department that has, until recently, gone under the title "English," we were eagerly receptive to scholarly work on a whole range of cultural texts and practices beyond the specifically literary. In this we were referring, of course, to the marked influence that cultural studies has had in the Canadian academy over the last few years, at the same time that we were wondering about the extent to which this burgeoning field is currently informing the study of early Canada. The response to our call, and the chapters collected here, speak affirmatively to this query: this is very much a meditation on early Canadian cultural texts and practices. From Anne Milne's research on the "national" horse, *le petit cheval du fer*, and the legislation that brought it into its symbolic being, to Jennifer Blair's examination of convent novels for the ways in which salacious confession functioned to sanction the dissemination of important sexual information, and from Kathleen Venema's analysis of kinship and discourse in Hudson's Bay society, to Kate Higginson's consideration of the relation between the writing of two "captive" women and contemporary legal and media-based depictions of feminine vulnerability, cultural practice is a frequent touchstone in these chapters.

As we have argued, for scholars of early Canada, the concept of culture is closely tied to the interactions between variously positioned readers and forms of distance. An intriguing site for observing this interaction is the archive. As we mentioned at the beginning of this introduction, the organizing and ordering of archives is but one of the challenges involved in the project that is "recalling early Canada." The archive eloquently poses the question of cultural value and validation: what parts of history are valued in the keeping, in the reaffirming of cultural value? Of course, such inquiry finds a powerful predecessor in Michel Foucault's probing analysis of the archive in *The Archaeology of Knowledge* and *The Order of Things*. According to Foucault, the archive stores not only its ostensible contents but also the narrative of its own organization, and of its historical period's understanding of knowledge as well as the ordering of that knowledge. As we have noted, generations of early Canada scholars have had varying understandings of what the "archive" that is early Canadian culture consists of, how it takes shape(s), and what its purpose is. Clearly, this volume adds layers to this growing archive, and one of these layers is a fascination with the relations between different kinds of cultural documents and moments. In this respect, *ReCalling Early Canada* draws on the various senses of the Greek roots of the very term "archive": "arkhe," or "beginning, commencement," and "arkheion," meaning "ruler's house or public office." That is, from its inception, the term archive drew upon both the idea of some kind of originary and comprehensive compilation and the notion of institutional orderings of knowledge. Here, in effect, is Foucault's two-fold description of the archive restated: both the contents of knowledge and the institutionalization of that knowledge. And if previous generations of early Canada scholars tended to emphasize the former, we see critics in these pages moving toward a thoroughgoing awareness of the institutionalization of the objects of study and its ideological negotiations. Paul Hjartarson asks why it is that the Tsimshian carver and painter Frederick Alexcee does not figure prominently in the archive that is Canadian art history. In his quest to frame a response to his question, Hjartarson takes us on a journey through the "arkheion" of early Canada, the institutionalization of the narratives of Canadian nation-building that have effaced a great deal of indigenous authority. Among our contributors perhaps none is as explicitly aware of the functioning of the archive as is Julia Emberley; in her chapter on colonial photographic archives and their representations of the "family," the archive becomes an immense photograph album, a collection narrativized and ordered in the Foucauldian sense. Like Hjartarson, she is explicitly critical of the colonizing archive and its power to disrupt and reframe histories and, in Emberley's case, aboriginal kinship systems.

As these examples suggest, there is much at stake, culturally speaking, in recalling early Canada as the negotiated institutionalization of knowledge. In the words of sociologist Pierre Bourdieu, "The struggle in the field of cultural production over the imposition of the legitimate mode of cultural production is inseparable from the struggle within the dominant class...to impose the dominant principle of domination (that is to say—ultimately—the definition of human accomplishment)" (41).

The archive is one such site of what Bourdieu would call "position-takings" on "the definition of human accomplishment." He argued passionately for the importance of studying the interactions among agents or institutions in the fields of cultural production, the better to understand how cultural power circulates and rearranges itself. Clearly, this insight is relevant to the project that is *ReCalling Early Canada*; many of the chapters archived here show scholars of this period taking very seriously the importance of studying the relations among various agents of cultural production (and consumption). And, more than ever, they are departing from the tendency to see archival work on relatively recent historical cultural artifacts as "secondary sources," merely there to bolster their interpretations of a "primary text." As JoAnn McCaig pertinently observes in her book on the cultural production of Alice Munro, "It is my conviction that literary archives are an under-utilized source of useful information about culture, authorship, and literary process" (13). Most urgently, for her, she argues that Munro's archives in Calgary reveal the formation of Munro as an author in a social sense; that is, as a sanctioned cultural player. To quote Bourdieu again, on this consecration of the writer, "the fundamental stake in literary struggles is the monopoly of literary legitimacy, i.e., *inter alia*, the monopoly of the power to say with authority who are authorized to call themselves writers; or to put it another way, it is the monopoly of the power to consecrate producers or products" (42). Of course, as Bourdieu would have hastened to point out himself, his comments apply to far more than literary authors. It is in this spirit that Pamela Banting, in "The Archive as a Literary Genre," paints a picture of the archive as participating both in institutional power and its unseating; it has "creative, subversive powers" and yet it betrays its "support of, and participation in, the existing structures of power and authority" (119) very much in the way that Bourdieu suggests.

This is a markedly different understanding of the archive than those that have held sway in the humanities. There has tended to be a methodological and theoretical divide between scholars who identify themselves as archival scholars, often working in earlier periods of study, and those who take up more recent subjects of analysis, and who make less intensive use of archives. But as many of the chapters in this volume attest, such a distinction is, now more than ever, misleading. Archival research and cultural studies approaches need not be, as they are often thought, distinct pursuits, with scholars of more traditionally historical approaches using the archive and cultural studies scholars turning away from it as a traditional, even antiquarian pursuit. In these papers, the archive, cultural studies assumptions, and continentally inspired critical and literary theory find a shared space for discussion and mutual enrichment.

As we have suggested, this volume, *ReCalling Early Canada*, is itself an archive, functioning in all of the intricate ways that the concept of archive suggests. On a basic denotative level, it archives a number of discussions held in a particular time and place, at a specific meeting of early Canada scholars. This is an important function to be sure, the lack of such occasions for meeting and discussion in the field being what they are. But the volume functions as an archive in many more ways than that and reaches beyond any specific occasion to a much larger audience. It archives a whole new discussion about what the study of early Canada can be, posing new questions and engaging a range of methodologies that reach outside of scholars' primary fields of specialization. In many ways, the archive that is *ReCalling Early Canada* does what Foucault suggested thinking differently about authors and authorship could do. It allows new questions to be asked. As Foucault wrote in "What is an Author?," the older questions, like the traditional concepts of the archive as the sum of its contents, were about matters of supposedly verifiable data: "Who is the real author? Have we proof of his [sic] authenticity and originality? What has he revealed of his most profound self in his language?" Instead, we find scholars in this volume consistently paying attention to the questions that Foucault foresaw emerging from a renewed understanding of authorship:

> "What are the modes of existence of this discourse?"
> "Where does it come from; how is it circulated; who controls it?"
> "What placements are determined for possible subjects?"
> "Who can fulfill these diverse functions of the subject?" (138)

However much these questions resonate with the questions about early Canadian literary and cultural production that our contributors pursue in these pages, many might have difficulty agreeing with the final, ringing question that Foucault posed in "What is an Author": "What matter who's speaking?" As many of these chapters energetically maintain, it *does* matter "who's speaking" in the archive that is early Canada. It matters in richly complex and sometimes disturbing ways. We return, then, to one of our own questions, posed at the beginning of this introduction and posed, earlier, to prospective contributors to this volume: "When we call and recall 'Early Canada,' what is 'it' that we call upon and how does the very name we give to 'it' shape in advance what it is that we set out to recall?" Our contributors "call upon" many vital questions and issues in the chapters that follow: the alterity of the past, the nation as rubric, contestatory understandings of history, the making of readers, and much else besides. These issues surface in this volume, not just as matters of critical urgency for the project of recalling early Canada, but also as the conditions of its making, a making that must be, it seems, projected as a retrieval, as if from a certain territory, constituency, subject, or moment in time, and into another. This is an exciting and necessary time to be ReCalling Early Canada.

1

Wedding "Native" Culture to the "Modern" State

National Culture, Selective Tradition and the Politics
of Recalling Early Canada

PAUL HJARTARSON

*The purpose of the National Gallery in arranging this exhibition...is to mingle
for the first time the art work of the Canadian West Coast tribes with that of our
more sophisticated artists in an endeavour to analyse their relationships to one
another, if such exist, and particularly to enable this primitive and interesting
art to take a definite place as one of the most valuable of Canada's artistic
productions. (National Gallery of Canada [2])*

*That there has been a meeting and that some sort of marriage has resulted is
what pours out of our literature and our painting. (Saul, Reflections 191)*

◆ Frederick Alexcee's Baptismal Font and the Politics of Recall

IF YOU HAVE NEVER HEARD OF the Tsimshian carver and painter
Frederick Alexcee[1] (1853?–1944), you are not alone. Although many people
have seen his artwork, and although some have been deeply moved by
it, few will recall the artist's name: he simply does not rank among the
people whose life story the Canadian nation has felt is "worth recording."
His name seldom appears in art histories and there has been no system-
atic attempt to identify or catalogue his work. A few of Alexcee's creations,
however, have escaped this general neglect. In a recent article on the
Museum of Anthropology (MOA), Michael McCullough listed a baptismal
font carved by the artist (*Figure 1.1*) as one of the museum's six treasures.

1

"It commands," he declares, "a special place in the hearts of frequent museum goers." For McCullough himself, "The font comes off as a haunting statement about the merging of European and Native American cultures. In that," he asserts, "it captures what the MOA is all about"(14). Others share McCullough's fascination with the font. "The image of Freddie Alexie's Baptismal Font has haunted me," Gitsan artist, curator and writer Doreen Jensen remarks, "since I first noticed it in the Museum of Anthropology quite a few years ago."

> The piece has a powerful beauty and a mysterious quality. I first noticed how two images were brought together: the very classic Tsimshian style of the head, and the European religious robe starting with the crisp line of the neck then draping over the body, with wings attached. The forms seem to fit, but at the same time don't fit. Alexie combined these two very different aesthetics into one carving, and the result is a dynamic tension. The figure's head seems to be turning ever so slightly, with the eyes actively looking. (9)

Jansen's comments about the baptismal font are contained in *Objects and Expressions*, a book published in 1999 to celebrate the golden anniversary of the museum's opening; fifty people associated with the museum were asked to choose their favourite objects and comment on them. Jensen chose Alexcee's font. When she first saw the font, she knew nothing about the artist. McCullough's and Jensen's comments might suggest that Alexcee's font has been given a place of prominence in the museum. Nothing could be further from the truth; it is just one of thousands of artifacts on display. Unless you search for the baptismal font, you might well leave the museum without noticing it. And why *would* you search for it? Unlike Emily Carr or Lawren Harris, Alexcee's name is not widely known; his artworks are not national icons; indeed, in most articulations of the national tradition his work is ignored.

"As a form of public space," art historian Carol Duncan writes,

> [art museums] constitute an arena in which a community may test, examine, and imaginatively live both older truths and possibilities for new ones. It is often said that without a sense of the past, we cannot envisage a future. The reverse is

FIGURE 1.1: *Frederick Alexcee, Baptismal Font, Tsimshian, 1886. Wood and paint, 82.5 cm height x 62.5 cm depth x 60.6 cm width. Courtesy UBC Museum of Anthropology, Vancouver, Canada.*

also true: without a vision of the future, we cannot construct and access a usable
past. (133)

Although Duncan argues that "art museums are at the center of this process in which past and future intersect," the dynamics of that interaction are far from clear (133). Alexcee's artwork is arguably part of the history of Tsimshian culture and of Canada's past as a settler-invader colony. The question has always been whether Tsimshian culture in general, and Alexcee's work in particular, would find a place in the nation's future. Alexcee's baptismal font has never, it must be noted, achieved the status of art: unlike the work of Carr and Harris, it is held as an artifact in a museum of anthropology. When Marius Barbeau, an anthropologist and ethnologist working for the museum branch of the Geological Survey of Canada, first saw Alexcee's art in Port Simpson in the winter of 1915, he "overlooked" it:

> *This artist, I was told, was a fisherman of humble extraction. He was neither a full-blooded Indian nor a true white man. As he did not count among the Tsimsyan chiefs, whose pedigree and history were worth recording, I overlooked him, and I left Port Simpson in the spring, knowing no more about him than I had learned during the winter evening at the mission; he sat there with the others in the audience, silent—he could not speak English very well—while the missionary commented on [the lantern slides of] his cartoons and drawings. (Marius Barbeau, "Frederick Alexie" 21)*

Alexcee himself, "neither a full-blooded Indian nor a true white man," seemed beneath consideration (21). In the subsequent decade, however, Barbeau kept encountering Alexcee's art. "More and more," he writes, "their strange quality beckoned and puzzled me; they remained outside the regular categories of Indian and Canadian art" (21). Would they—could they—become part of what Duncan terms "a usable past"? The issue here is the nature of tradition. To "recall" any person, event or object from the past, Raymond Williams argues, is inherently a political act. To recall is in fact to construct and what is being constructed is either the tradition itself or an alternative or oppositional response.

Narrative is mobilized in that act of recall: tradition is a form of story-telling; and a national tradition forms part of what Homi K. Bhabha terms "nation as narration." To "recall" someone or something from the past is to shape that past in the interest of what Williams aptly terms a "pre-shaped present." "For tradition," he argues,

> is in practice the most evident expression of the dominant and hegemonic pressures and limits. It is always more than an inert historicised segment; indeed it is the most powerful practical means of incorporation. What we have to see is not just "'a tradition' tradition" but a selective tradition: an intentionally selective version of a shaping past and a pre-shaped present, which is then powerfully operative in the process of social and cultural definition and identification. (115)

Tradition is, in short, "a version of the past which is intended to connect with and ratify the present" (116). The present is "pre-shaped" because, in the view of those who espouse a national tradition, it is the past that shapes the present and not the present that shapes the past. To recall early Canada is necessarily to enter the space of the nation and to engage in dialogue with nation as narration.

If Frederick Alexcee's artwork has not found a place in the national tradition, is it possible that it does not fit the story Canada seeks to tell about itself? In whose interest is that "usable past" being shaped? In this essay I analyze what is at stake in "recalling early Canada" at present and focus that analysis on two articulations of a selective tradition for the settler-invader colony, one recent and one more removed in time. Both projects developed out of perceived crises in which the hegemonic order felt compelled to reaffirm the "pre-shaped present" by articulating its relation to a "shaping past." The more recent crisis is centred on the near success of the Parti Québécois's 1995 referendum on sovereignty while the earlier crisis occurred in the decade following World War I and was precipitated by the settler-invader colony's participation in the Great War. In both cases, the hegemonic order in Canada interpreted the perceived crisis as a problem in citizenship and education; in both cases, too, the "necessary education" (Williams, *Marxism* 117) in citizenship was carried out by nationalist movements; and, in both, that work centred on the articulation of national culture. In the following pages I juxtapose the hegemonic response to these two crises. While I consider several different responses to the Québec referendum, I centre my analysis on the book John Ralston Saul wrote in its aftermath, *Reflections of a Siamese Twin: Canada at the End of the Twentieth Century*. Within that text, I focus on Saul's representation of the place of First Nations in his vision of Canada. I have chosen to examine *Reflections of a Siamese Twin* not only because it is perhaps the most influential recent attempt to "recall" Canada's past but also because Saul himself has been instrumental in numerous national initiatives taken since 1995 to reaffirm the "pre-shaped present" by re-articulating its relation to the "shaping past." I centre my analysis of the post-World War I crisis on an event Saul himself "recalls" in *Reflections of a Siamese Twin*: the first joint exhibition held by the National Gallery of Canada and the newly created national museum, the Victoria Memorial. (On January 5, 1927 that museum was created out of the Museum Branch of the Geological Survey of Canada by Order-in-Council.) Titled *Exhibition of Canadian West Coast Art—Native and Modern*, the show opened in Ottawa in December 1927 and travelled to Toronto and Montreal the following year. Although primarily recalled as the exhibition that created Emily Carr as a national icon—that is certainly how Saul represents the show—*Exhibition of Canadian West Coast Art—Native and Modern* is also the moment in Canadian history when Frederick Alexcee's work was consigned to obscurity. There is certainly no mention of Frederick Alexcee in Saul's text. In this essay I focus my analysis on the representation of First Nations in these moments of recall because, as Terry Goldie, Alan Lawson and others have argued, the cultural traditions of settler-invader colonies such as Canada are largely shaped by the invaders' response to the aboriginal people on whose land they settled.

In juxtaposing these events and issues, and the historical crises of which they are a part, my purpose is neither to equate the historical events or crises nor to deny the many differences that inform them; rather, I seek a better understanding of culture's relation to the state and what it might mean to "recall early Canada" at this time.[2] My analysis is grounded in the work of Raymond Williams, particularly in

FIGURE 1.2: *Catalogue Cover*, Exhibition of Canadian West Coast Art—
Native and Modern. *Designed by Emily Carr. National Gallery of Canada.*

his concepts of tradition, institution and formation. In "The Future of Cultural Studies" Williams argues that "a central theoretical point...at the heart of Cultural Studies" is:

> that you cannot understand an intellectual or artistic project without also under-standing its formation; that the relation between a project and a formation is always decisive; and that the emphasis of Cultural Studies is precisely that it engages with both, rather than specializing itself to one or the other.... (151)

"The importance of this [point]," Williams observes, "is that if we are serious, we have to apply it to *our own* project, including the project of Cultural Studies"(152). Williams's point, it seems to me, is equally appli-cable to the project of "Recalling Early Canada": we cannot understand that project without also understanding its formation and in that analysis the relation between project and formation is decisive.

◆ **The Québec Referendum, the Crisis in Historical Memory, and the "Necessary Education"**

There is a crisis in the transmission of our society's memory. In fact, I think there is no real memory. (Mark Starowicz, director of Canada: A People's History*)*[3]

THAT THE NEAR SUCCESS of the 1995 Québec referendum on sover-eignty precipitated a crisis for the hegemonic order is apparent both from the flurry of educational and cultural initiatives launched in its aftermath and from the debates occasioned by the narrow federal victory. What is at stake, proponents of these initiatives argue, is the survival of the nation. The problem, they contend, is that Canadians share neither a common history nor the values that history should instill; the issue, in short, is citizenship. The solution, they argue, lies in education, in a common "recall" of early Canada. Many of these educational and cultural initiatives originate in the work of two organizations. One is The Dominion Institute, an organization founded in 1997 "by a group of young people concerned about the erosion of a common memory in Canada" (http://www.dominion.ca/English/home.html). (According to its 2002–2003 report, titled *The Dominion Institute: Championing the Cause of Canadian History* and available on its website, the institute has "a full-time staff of six, a yearly operating budget of $250,000 and yearly programming expenditures of $1,000,000.") This is the organization behind the annual Canadian history surveys, the annual "Lafontaine-Baldwin" lecture, the Memory Project, the Great Canadian Questions, Passages to Canada, "ourheroes.ca" and a multitude of other web-based resources designed for use by school teachers and students. The other organization is Historica, a charitable foundation established in 1999 with an initial $25 million donation from philanthropist Charles Bronfman, chairman of New York City-based Seagram Co. Ltd.; its mandate is "to provide Canadians with a deeper understanding of their history and its importance in shaping their future" (http://www.histori.ca/foundation/strategy.jsp). This is the organization behind the Heritage Fairs, Heritage YouthLinks, Heritage Teacher Institutes and, of course, the Heritage Minutes. In 2000 *Historica* acquired the online version of *The Canadian Encyclopedia* from McClelland and Stewart; it also helps bankroll the Dominion Institute. According to Red Wilson, one of the founders of Historica, his own children

...never gained more than a superficial understanding of Canadian history. "Most of what they were learning was related to specific episodes or themes—the role of women in society, for example, or aboriginal issues.... Those are important but what was missing was an understanding of how this country came to be, why we are organized as a federation, and what role the British and French and other European ancestors played in all this." (Maclean's Dec. 13, 1999)

Jack Granatstein, Dominion Institute board member and author of *Who Stole Canadian History?*, puts the issue more bluntly. Why teach the divisive stuff, he asks, and why foster multicultural examinations of our past? "The aim of every Canadian and of all levels of government should be to welcome immigrants and turn them into Canadian citizens as quickly as possible…. Not one cent of federal, provincial, or municipal government money should be devoted to fostering retention of their cultures" (Webster 5).

As Granatsein's comment suggests, analysts who conceive the crisis as a problem in citizenship tend to trace that problem to the teaching of Canadian history. "Who killed Canadian history?," he demands in the book that takes his question as its title. (The provocative title both fosters and feeds the sense of crisis.) Briefly put, Granatstein argues that Canada has failed to teach its own history and that "we" have consequently deprived ourselves of a common past and a national culture. With little knowledge of that common past, Granatstein argues, Canadians have no reason to seek a common destiny; as a result, he warns, Canada's future as a nation is at risk. While the majority of historians might agree that Canadians need to know more about their history, many disagree both with Granatstein's analysis of the problem and his prescription for change. A.B. McKillop, for example, writes:

> Who killed Canadian history? No one. Nor is it dying. The historical profession is as active and engaged in studying the many Canadian pasts as it has ever been…. Canadian history did not die, only the Granatstein version of Canadian history. The old foundational myth of a British North American colony triumphing over physical circumstance on its way to autonomy and maturity as a nation served Canadians for decades as a means of establishing a consensus about past achievement, and at its best this old national history had the power to persuade and to inspire. But many historians subsequently concluded that it masked as much as it revealed. (295)

As McKillop rightly suggests, in Who Killed Canadian History? Granatstein is ultimately less concerned with the profession of history than with the collapse of "foundational" myths, and with them, of a certain representation of the nation.

While Granatstein resists the demise of these myths, others welcome the change. In National Dreams: Myth, Memory and Canadian History, Daniel Francis acknowledges that these foundational myths "were willingly embraced by generations of Canadians as our national dreams, the truth of our history. They provided an explanation of our past and satisfied a deep need to feel that we were engaged in an important national enterprise." But, he adds:

> The master narrative excluded many people...who did not see themselves reflected in the stories; or worse, felt belittled by them. These people—Aboriginals, minorities, working peoples, women—have had to force their way into the story of Canada by inventing narratives of their own. For someone like myself, raised on the conventional narratives, it is tremendously invigorating to witness the process.... At the same time, the old master narrative does not give up without a fight. People with a vested interest, emotional or otherwise, in the old myths resist their subversion by new voices. As a result, there is a high level of anxiety evident in the culture these days, a feeling on the part of many people that the familiar Canada they have always known is under siege. They are right, of course. Canada is being reimagined. But this should be a cause for celebration, not concern. (172–73)

Although attention has focussed on the threat posed by the possible separation of Québec, other factors have contributed to what Granatstein describes as Canadians' "growing concern that the nation is in danger of fragmentation"(xvii): as Francis's comments suggest, these include the increasing strength of First Nations' challenges to the national *status quo*, the continuing interrogation of the nation by feminist and labour historians, and the *de facto* transformation of the nation through immigration. The founding myths of Canada have been destabilized and history has once again openly become a site of struggle. "If Canada is to survive," Granatstein declares in *Who Killed Canadian History?* with a certain quiet desperation, "we must know what the nation was, is, and will be" (xvii).

The destabilization of the old national myths is forcing the hegemonic order to re-articulate the relation between Canada's "shaping past" and its "pre-shaped present." Perhaps the most influential attempt to rethink that relationship is John Ralston Saul's *Reflections of a Siamese Twin*. Saul wrote *Reflections* in the immediate aftermath of the 1995 Québec referendum and it centres on his analysis of that event. He is a founding member of the Dominion Institute; the influential LaFontaine-Baldwin annual lecture was named in honour of the historical moment he argues is central to Canada's nation-narration; and Saul himself delivered the inaugural lecture in Toronto in 2000. Although he offers the 500-plus pages of the text as his reflections on "Canada at the end of the twentieth century," Saul broaches the topic of the 1995 referendum campaign in the opening pages (11) and returns to it repeatedly throughout the book. (Chapter 18, "An Existential Moment," for example, analyses the "unity rally" held in the closing days of the 1995 referendum campaign.) Although Saul's primary concern in *Reflections of a Siamese Twin* is the relation between anglophone and francophone Canadians and the relation of Québec to the federal government and to the other provinces, he does offer a vision of Canada as a whole and seeks to reshape the story the nation tells about itself. It is in this context that he affirms aboriginal experience and argues that First Nations are one of three "deeply rooted pillars" (81) upon which the nation was built. Although I support his acknowledgement that First Nations played a foundational role in the development of the nation, I believe that Saul is caught in a contradiction: on the one hand, he affirms aboriginal experience and argues that Canada is built on a "tripartite foundation"; on the other, he grounds his arguments in histories and concepts that celebrate settler-invader culture and appropriate First Nations authority. At various points in *Reflections* Saul seems aware of the contradictions in which he is caught and struggles to resolve them. I propose to examine one of those moments of struggle: his recall of *Exhibition of Canadian West Coast Art—Native and Modern* exhibition. Both *Reflections of a Siamese Twin* and the 1927 exhibition articulate the relation between "Native" culture and Canada as a modern nation-state. While Saul, like many others, remembers the 1927 exhibition as the event that first brought Emily Carr's painting to the attention of the nation, others have rightly argued that it appropriated "Native" culture to build a national tradition.

◆ John Ralston Saul Recalling the "Marriage" of Native and Modern

SAUL TAKES THE TITLE for his book from Jacques Godbout's novel, *Les Têtes à Papineau*. In the opening pages of *Reflections of a Siamese Twin* Saul offers the following summary of Godbout's novel:

> The heroes are Siamese twins. They have one body, two heads and two separate but interrelated personalities. Together they are very interesting. Most people want them to be separated—to be normalized. Banalized. To become like other people. To give up their real non-conformity for perhaps a more self-indulgent, less demanding sort. Gradually they lose track of their sense that to be different is a positive. In the end they agree to be separated, and so conform to the norm. (14)

In Saul's analogy Québec and the rest of Canada (ROC) are these "interesting" Siamese twins; the norm in question is what he characterizes as a "monolithic European model" of the nation-state. Against this model, Saul sets Canada. The European model, he asserts, "...could not work here" (102) and something different emerged:

> Elements were put in place very early on through European-Native treaties. The change of colonial regimes in 1763 was followed by seventy-nine years of groping in the direction of the final element to this triangular pact. It was formalized in 1842. Louis-Hippolyte Fontaine, standing in the legislature in Kingston, described this agreement as a binding handshake. His with Robert Baldwin. They were the original Siamese twins. (11–12)

In this version of a "shaping past" and a "pre-shaped present," the Canadian nation is grounded in "a complex accommodation with place and circumstance" (104) whose continuing strength lies in a certain genius for moderation and compromise epitomized by Baldwin and Lafontaine.

As an example of a New World nation constructed on the European model, Saul offers the United States: "it is," he argues, "the European state personified" (102). Canada, in contrast, is "profoundly un-European" (102). The argument here, and throughout *Reflections of a Siamese Twin*, is structured on a series of binaries: European/ un-European, the United States/ Canada, monolithic/ pluralistic, exclusive/ inclusive, simplistic/ complex, and so on. Saul's point is not, of course, that the United States is ethnically homogenous but that it conceives of itself monolithically and acts exclusively. Or, as Saul would have it, the USA has historically dominated within and without: within, it waged war against its aboriginal peoples (103); without, it seized Texas and California, asserted its power over Central America, and so on. If the key concept of the nation-state is domination, the crucial binary is "domination" versus "accommodation." Because Canadian settlers could not "conquer" the harsh northern land or its aboriginal peoples, Saul argues, "a more complex accommodation to place and circumstance" developed (104). According to Saul, "The single most important element of this progress was the impossibility of domination over nature or society. The marginality imposed by climate was a specific constant reminder that progress would in general be built on alliances and interdependence" (107). Thus, according to Saul, while the United States is monolithic and exclusive, Canada is pluralistic and inclusive.

What, then, of the "tripartite foundation"? If the Canadian nation has been constructed on "a tripartite foundation," on "three deeply rooted pillars, three experiences—the aboriginal, the francophone and the anglophone" (81), how does the aboriginal experience enter into the "complexity" that is Canada? Into the handshake between Baldwin and LaFontaine? Into Saul's analogy of the "Siamese twins"? *Reflections of a Siamese Twin* seems, finally, to rest on a contradiction: on the one hand, Saul's use of the Siamese twin analogy, his repeated reference to Baldwin and LaFontaine, and his reliance on binaries suggest that Canada consists, in fact, of two "founding peoples," of two—not three—realities; on the other hand, Saul maintains that Canada is built on a "triangular foundation" (88) and he speaks of a "triangular pact" (12). There are times, however, when Saul himself seems aware of that contradiction. For example, lauding Canada's success as a constitutional democracy, he writes:

> *The specific point here is the longevity of the experiment. And the complexity of it. The original triangle*—because despite our prolonged denials, the Natives have always been part of the bargain—*is like a multi-jointed box which can fold and unfold in many ways.* (12; emphasis added)

It is tempting to suggest that *Reflections of a Siamese Twin*, like the "original triangle" of which it speaks, is itself "a multi-jointed box which can fold and unfold in many ways." For, if it is true that Canada's First Nations peoples "have always been part of the bargain," it is also true that they have seldom been granted a voice at the bargaining table. They were not present when Baldwin and LaFontaine joined forces in 1842 nor did they have a seat at the bargaining table in 1987 when the Meech Lake Accord was being formulated. They were nonetheless "part of the bargain."

Although Saul's formulation of the nation's "triangular foundation" explicitly acknowledges the experiences of First Nations, the account he offers of Canada's history in *Reflections* effectively denies them a significant role: they are not one of the "Siamese twins"; they play no role in the Baldwin-Lafontaine story; what is more, they have no part in the seven other "strategic acts" (171) by which, according to Saul, Canada was built. What, then, is their role in the nation? Anna Johnston and Alan Lawson's conception of the settler-invader colonies is helpful here. As they point out, "In general, historical definitions of 'settler [-invader] colonies' have relied on the presence of long-term, majority white racial communities, where indigenous peoples have been out-numbered and removed by colonial policies and practices" (361). Canada falls into this category, as do Argentina, Australia, Brazil, New Zealand and many other "New World" nations. In the 1980s, Johnston and Lawson note, "analysts of colonialism and postcolonialism began to re-examine the implications of 'settler colonies,' often starting by reinstating the more historically accurate term "settler-invader" to emphasize the violence that the single, ostensibly benign, term 'settler' concealed" (362). According to Johnston and Lawson, settler-invaders should be conceived as "uneasily occupying"

a place caught between two First Worlds, two origins of authority and authen-
ticity. One of these is the originating world of Europe, the Imperium—the source
of the Second World's principal cultural authority. Its "other" First World is that
of the First Nations, whose authority they not only replaced and effaced but also
desired. (370)

As Lawson pointed out in an earlier article, "The address of the settler is
toward both the absent(ee) cultural authority of the imperium and the
effaced, recessive cultural authority of the Indigene" (29). If "there are
always two kinds of authority and always two kinds of authenticity
that the settler subject is *con/signed* to desire and disavow" (26), his or
her relationship to them is very different: on the one hand, the settler
represents and very often mimics imperial authority and authenticity;
on the other, he effaces Indigenous authority and appropriates Indigenous
authenticity. "The national," Lawson argues, "is what replaces the indigenous and in doing so conceals its participation in colonization by
nominating a new colonized subject—the colonizer or settler-invader"
(30).

Although Saul affirms that First Nations are one of three founding
peoples, the narrative he advances in *Reflections* re-enacts the settler-
invader culture's appropriation of indigenous authenticity. Saul defines
Canada as an "animist country" (107) and he links that animism both to
place—"the North"—and to First Nations' culture. Against animism
Saul sets materialism (186). (That opposition needs to be understood in
relation to the other binaries he establishes in *Reflections*.) For Saul,
animism, like pluralism, is a function of geography. "Being in the
north," Saul argues, "is a central factor in our animism.... It is a condition in and of itself, one which makes it impossible to turn away for
more than brief periods from an animist approach to our existence." He
hastens to add, however:

This is not to minimize the role that Native animism has played in the approach
of our society. Europe has the clear memory of its animist roots in the Greek
myths. But the memory is so distant and intellectualized that those roots are no
longer perceived as having been animist. In Canada, only a little over a century

ago, those same myths were alive and well in the indigenous cultures. When Duncan Campbell Scott was writing his Native-filled poetry and taking part as a civil servant in the undermining of that civilization early in the twentieth century, he was dealing with people whose "material and spiritual lives were not severed." Today that culture is still very much alive. (190–91)

This is another of the troubling passages in *Reflections*. I am troubled both by the implicit equation of First Nations peoples with the land and by the foundational narrative Saul advances. Once upon a time, he intones, Europeans *were* animist; increasing rationalism and materialism, however, have seriously attenuated that animism. For Saul, that attenuation is readily apparent in European art. "After all," he argues, "the arts, once separated from an animist sense of place, became profoundly static. That is the European inheritance" (198). By contrast, First Nations people, the indigenous inhabitants of the north can, it seems, be nothing other than animistic. In Saul's narrative, European settler-invaders rediscover their animist roots in the Canadian north and in the art of aboriginal peoples. If European art is "profoundly static," First Nations art is full of the "animist sense of place." In this view, European settler-invader culture is revitalized through its contact with aboriginal art.

In the passage cited above, First Nations myths stand in relation to settler-invader culture as Greek myths to European culture. In other words, despite Saul's subsequent affirmation that "Today [First Nations'] culture is still very much alive," the implied narrative is that, like the culture represented by the Greek myths, indigenous culture belongs to the past. In the next paragraph Saul describes the meeting of First Nations' and settler-invader culture as a marriage:

...[O]ur situation has produced a peculiar and difficult meeting between an extremely sophisticated animism more or less unbroken in history and an almost unconscious animism re-adopted and re-adapted by those of us who have arrived from places where it has been reduced to the vague reminder of a distant past. That there has been a meeting and that some sort of marriage has resulted is what pours out of our literature and our painting. "The disturbing thrilling

awareness is that there really is a world outside of language which, creatures of language ourselves, we translate with difficulty." Our creativity has been a constant reworking of that difficulty. (191)[4]

The problematic term here is the pronoun "our": while at the outset of the passage that pronoun may refer both to First Nations and to settler-invader peoples, in later sentences it stands in for the nation. This passage is taken from a chapter titled "Animism." There, and in the following chapter, titled "The Animistic Image," Saul celebrates the literature and painting of settler-invader culture, and particularly the work of the Group of Seven and their contemporaries, including Emily Carr. There is only passing reference to First Nations culture. In these chapters, as in the book as a whole, indigenous authority is effaced and indigenous authenticity appropriated: the national replaces the indige-nous.

If, for Saul, *Exhibition of Canadian West Coast Art—Native and Modern* exemplifies the "complexity" that is Canada, the paintings of Emily Carr represents the "marriage" of First Nations and European culture. Saul refers to the exhibition in demonstrating that regionalism "turns its back on the complexity which makes each region uncover its best" (39). Characterizing Carr as "the quintessential B.C. painter," and noting that "for a long time she was more or less ignored at home," Saul asks how she gained national recognition. Here is the answer he offers:

Marius Barbeau, the great French-Canadian ethnologue, used his base at the National Museum in Ottawa to save much of what we know of Québec folklore and Native folklore. He also had a particular interest in the Tsimshian people in B.C. Through this, he came to know about Emily Carr. Her painting, centred on the essential West Coast traditions—that is, of the Natives—struck few chords in the local white population.... In 1927 Barbeau convinced Eric Brown, at the National Gallery, to mount a show which hung works of the West Coast artists such as Carr along with Native art.... Interestingly enough, the very idea of hanging art and artefacts together, suggesting an inclusive, animist approach towards art, may be a Canadian invention. In a sense this is a demonstration of our long-standing acceptance that place and humans are part of a continuing whole; as opposed to the rational view that humans must humble nature in order to reconstruct it in their own image.... The 1927 Ottawa show was the turning point in Carr's career. On that trip, she met the Group of Seven.... Of the seven, Lawren Harris in particular became her friend and supporter.... Over the years he kept encouraging her and buying her pictures. It wasn't until 1938 that Vancouver accepted her. (39–40; emphasis added)

Note the place of Tsimshian people in this narrative. The "essential West Coast traditions" may be Native but in Saul's "recall" Emily Carr becomes "the quintessential B.C. painter." After the initial reference, Tsimshian culture is not mentioned again; certainly Tsimshian artists never become central to the story. "It was in good part Barbeau and Carr, and indirectly Harris," Saul declares, "who brought the West Coast Native images into the Canadian imagination until they became central to the way Canadians saw themselves" (40). First Nations peoples remain the silent partner in Saul's "triangular pact"(12).

◆ **The Great War, the Crisis in Citizenship and "the Great Wave of Education"**

Growing support for labour radicalism, agrarian populism, and the enfranchisement of women illustrated the generative impact of the war on popular social thought affecting citizenship rights. Grass roots support for radical visions of a post-war Canadian citizenship and nationhood disclosed the depth of the crisis of the old order. (Mitchell 10)

As the title of the 1927 exhibition suggests, its organizers were themselves intent on relating Native art to modern settler-invader painting. Jointly organized by the National Gallery and the newly established Victoria Memorial Museum, *Exhibition of Canadian West Coast Art—Native and Modern* displayed together for the first time in Canada First Nations "artifacts" alongside work by white, settler-invader artists, most of them Group of Seven members and their contemporaries, who had recorded their impressions of the Pacific northwest and its aboriginal peoples. In December 1927 the exhibition opened in Ottawa; in January 1928 it moved to the Art Gallery of Toronto; and, in February, it moved again to the galleries of the Art Association of Montreal. The First Nations artifacts, all of them from the Pacific northwest, ranged from small carvings and masks to dugout canoes and carved house poles while the modern art consisted primarily of sketches and paintings but included several sculptures and some crafts that incorporated designs derived from First Nations culture. The review in the *Ottawa Citizen* made the organizers' argument for them: "What a tremendous influence the vanishing civilization of the West Coast Indian is having on the minds of Canadian artists," the *Citizen* declared ("Canadian Art History," Dec. 2, 1927). The reviewer's comment affirmed not only that Native people were "vanishing" but that their art lived on in the culture of the nation. Today *Exhibition of Canadian West Coast Art—Native and Modern* is primarily remembered as Saul represents it in *Reflections of a Siamese Twin*, that is, as the exhibition that introduced Emily Carr's art to the Canadian public.[5] The significance of the exhibition, however, far exceeds the putative "discovery" of Emily Carr's painting. The exhibition was a defining moment in the cultural construction of Canadian national identity following World War I—the moment in which settler-invader culture, working through the National Gallery and the new national museum, appropriated First Nations art for the nation. In *Exhibition of Canadian West Coast Art—Native and Modern* the National Gallery and the national museum sought to invent a "native" tradition for the national art that by the mid to late 1920s was increasingly identified with the painting of the Group of Seven.

This joint project emerged out of an earlier sense of crisis: the threat to the Anglo-Canadian order posed by Canada's participation in World War I. The perceived menace was at least fourfold. One threat was posed by "enemy aliens," that is, by the non-English immigrants who settled the country, particularly the west, in the two decades prior to the outbreak of war and who came from countries with which, after August 1914, Canada was at war. Another danger centred on organized and organizing workers whose "unrest" led to the Winnipeg General Strike in the summer of 1919 and to the creation of the modern surveillance state in

FIGURE 1.3: *Installation Photograph.* Exhibition of Canadian West Coast Art—Native and Modern, *Ottawa. National Gallery of Canada.*

Canada. With the success of the Russian Revolution, "socialist revolutionaries" threatened to displace unionizing workers as the most potent force acting against the state. That "socialist revolutionaries" could be, at once, both "enemy aliens" and "workers" only served to magnify the perceived menace. These dangers were in addition to the long-standing threat posed by the existence in Canada of a large francophone population centred in Québec, a division exacerbated by the conscription issue.

Once war had ended, the top priority of the state, business, and their allies among middle-class intellectuals was "to contain the threat to authority posed by the surging working-class militancy" and to protect and entrench the British character of the nation (Mitchell 6). In "'The Manufacture of Souls of Good Quality': Winnipeg's 1919 National Conference on Canadian Citizenship, English Canadian Nationalism, and the New Order After the Great War," historian Tom Mitchell writes:

Canada's business elite and its allies among Canada's middle-class progressives
interpreted the post-war malaise as a crisis of citizenship which threatened the
stability of the social order and the destiny of the emergent Canadian nation.
They sought to address this condition by casting the post-war order in a particular
idiom of citizenship informed by a common Canadianism rooted in Anglo-
conformity and a citizenship framed in notions of service, obedience, obligation
and fidelity to the state. (21)

If the problem was "citizenship," the answer, many argued, was education. In *A Study in Canadian Immigration*, published by Ryerson Press in 1920,
W.G. Smith, for example, writes,

What is needed is a new crusade of young Canadians in whom the fires of patriotism burn, who will man the outposts of Canadian nationality. In times of war a
half-million of our best were enlisted in a gigantic struggle of destruction. In
times of peace can there not be a brigade or two of equally ardent spirits who will
engage in the work of construction? The final completion of the immigration task
is a great wave of education carried on by patriots who will prepare the highway
of the future. (397)

What Smith proposes is, in effect, a cultural war on "aliens." Although
this campaign was directed at non-English-speaking subjects, particularly those involved in the settlement of the west, its broader concern
was Canadians as a whole. As Mitchell argues, in the 1920s middle-
class English Canadian nationalism dislodged social reform as the content
of Canadian progressivism (19).

The National Gallery's support and advancement of the Group of
Seven was one manifestation of that nationalism. The National Gallery
had been incorporated by an Act of Parliament in 1913; Eric Brown's
appointment as Director of the National Gallery dates from three years
prior to that time. That the new gallery actively promoted the nationalism that developed out of the post-war crisis is apparent from its
Annual Reports. As Joyce Zemans notes, in its *Annual Report* for 1921–22, the
National Gallery lists as its "key responsibilities" "nation-building and
the establishment of a common heritage for Canadians" (11). The connec-

FIGURE 1.4: *Great War Veterans Association demonstration at City Hall. Winnipeg, June 4, 1919. Archives of Manitoba N12296.*

tion between the painters who would subsequently form the Group of Seven and the National Gallery dates from at least 1914. The bonds were strengthened by the inclusion of A.Y. Jackson, Fred Varley, Arthur Lismer, Frank Johnston, and Lawren Harris among the artists commissioned as part of the Canadian War Memorials Project to record Canada's war effort. When, following World War I, Canada was invited to participate in the British Empire Exhibition at Wembley, the bonds between the newly formed, nationalist Group of Seven and the newly established gallery were strong. The success of the Group paintings at that exhibition strengthened both Brown's position as Director and the Gallery's connection to the Group and its definition of modern art. In "Art Museums and the Ritual of Citizenship," Carol Duncan argues that "museums can be powerful identity-defining machines. To control a museum," she argues, "means precisely to control the representation of a community and some of its highest, most authoritative truths" (101–2). By 1927, the Diamond Jubilee of Confederation, Brown had effective control of the National Gallery and he used its resources to promote the nationalist painting of the Group of Seven and educate the nation.

◆ Frederick Alexcee and the "Mingling" of "Native" and "Modern"

Museums not only collect and store fragments of culture; they themselves are part of culture: a special zone where living culture dies and dead culture springs to life. (Durrans 125)

WHILE THE GROUP'S yearly exhibitions at the Art Gallery of Toronto consolidated its position at the forefront of art in Canada, the Gallery focussed its resources on building a national tradition around the Group. *Exhibition of Canadian West Coast Art—Native and Modern* was part of that effort. As Saul recognizes, it was the first exhibition in the dominion that sought to bring together two fields of study: Canadian art, which was the concern of the National Gallery; and anthropology, which was the purview of the Victoria Memorial Museum. While the landscape paintings of the Group of Seven represented the nation as an unpeopled northern wilderness, the anthropologists at the national museum were busy transforming First Nations peoples into ethnographic objects. These discursive formations—one defining and producing objects of "art"; the other, ethnographic artifacts—were brought together in the exhibition organized by Brown and Barbeau. This leads us to yet another first: *Exhibition of Canadian West Coast Art—Native and Modern* was the first exhibition to represent "Native art in an institutional setting for aesthetic as opposed to ethnographic reasons" (Hawker 241). As Scott Watson argues, the exhibition sought to appropriate Native art to modern white painting so that Canadian art could have what he aptly terms "a rooted relationship to place" (62). To do so, Watson argues, "It was necessary to wrest native art from anthropological discourse and its emphasis on the specifics of culture and to make the art speak again in a language of humanist aesthetics" (62).

The exhibition catalogue can be divided into three parts: an introduction (itself in two parts); an annotated listing of the West Coast Indian artifacts titled "West Coast Indian Art"; and an unannotated list of non-Native art titled "Works of Canadian Artists." In his introduction to the catalogue, Eric Brown writes:

The purpose of the National Gallery in arranging this exhibition of West Coast Indian Art combined with the work of a number of Canadian artists who, from the days of Paul Kane to the present day, have recorded their impressions of that region, is to mingle for the first time the art work of the Canadian West Coast tribes with that of our more sophisticated artists in an endeavour to analyse their relationships to one another, if such exist, and particularly to enable this primitive and interesting art to take a definite place as one of the most valuable of Canada's artistic productions. (2)

Other than Carr, the only painter Brown names is Paul Kane. Through the use of Kane's name, Brown creates the impression that the exhibition surveys Canadian art from the mid nineteenth century to the present; in fact, of the twelve non-Native artists represented in the show, fully ten are either Group of Seven members or their contemporaries.[6] Although Brown declares that the National Gallery's purpose in "mingling" the artwork of Canadian West Coast tribes with that of modern painters is to "analyse their relationships to one another, if such exists," his comment clearly constructs and regulates that relationship: the artwork of the West Coast peoples is "primitive"; the landscape painting of the settler-invaders, "sophisticated." Further, the work of the West Coast peoples belongs to the past and is in need of classification and labelling; that of the modernist artists represents the future and needs no such interpretation.

Because the exhibition was jointly sponsored by the National Gallery and the Victoria Memorial Museum, the catalogue contains not one introduction but two. The second is by Barbeau who, as the national museum's ethnologist, comments on the artifacts.[7] As Douglas Cole points out in *Captured Heritage: The Scramble for Northwest Coast Artifacts*, Barbeau was one of the many collectors in the 1920s who bought northwest coast artifacts, both for museums and personal gain. In his opening paragraph, Barbeau makes it clear that northwest coast artifacts were a hot property, rich in cultural capital, in the 1920s:

The decorative arts of the West Coast tribes of British Columbia have achieved world-wide fame. They are extensively represented in the state museums of

Europe and America. And they favourably compare with the well-known aborig-
inal arts of Mexico, Africa, and the South Seas. Thiebault-Sisson, the French art
critic, wrote last year: "Between the specimens of Canadian West Coast art and
those of the Bantus of Africa or of the ancient Aztecs of Mexico, there is an obvious
analogy. They seem related to each other. Yet, the art of the Canadian tribes has
advanced further than the others and discloses a much finer culture." (3)

While the comparison of the artifacts to those of the Bantus and Aztecs
is meant to suggest their relative cultural value, it also groups them
with "specimens" not just of vanishing peoples but of "prehistoric" civi-
lizations. In the anthropological discourse of the day, First Nations
artifacts were collected and First Nations cultures were studied as though
they *were* prehistoric. In the second last paragraph of his introduction,
Barbeau clearly indicates the value of First Nations' culture to the
national project. "A commendable feature of this aboriginal art for us,"
he writes, "is that it is truly Canadian in its inspiration. It has sprung
up wholly from the soil and the sea within our national boundaries"
(4). Throughout the 1920s and 30s Barbeau advocated that contemporary Canadian artists use what he regarded as the legacy of Native art to
produce a modern national culture. That certainly seems to have been
the message conveyed by the exhibition. "For the exhibition organizers," Scott Watson argues, First Nations art "was seen as a decorative
art that identified Canadian nationality and which could be easily
assimilated into the already arts and crafts based, Art Nouveau inflected,
national landscape school epitomized by the Group of Seven" (63). The
death of Native culture was both a precondition of the exhibition itself
and the reason for the sudden popularity of Native artifacts: "Having
first of all destroyed many aspects of Native culture," Daniel Francis
writes in *The Imaginary Indian*, "White society now turned around and
admired its recreation of what it had destroyed.... By a curious leap of
logic, non-Natives became the saviours of the vanishing Indian" (36).

The effacement of First Nations' authority is readily apparent in
Canada's deplorable record on aboriginal land claims. Scott Watson points
out that *Exhibition of Canadian West Coast Art—Native and Modern* "took place

in the very year, 1927, when an amendment to the Indian Act made it a criminal offense to raise money to represent land claims" (63; cf. Tennant 111–12).[8] Susan Crean acknowledges that opening the exhibition only months after passage of the amendment may have been "happenstance" but she terms it "symbolic nonetheless": "It meant the issue of ownership was settled politically and legally, and it was now safe to admit that the land in British Columbia was not empty but full of history and ancient artifacts that could be represented as primitive art and exhibited with deference" (240). The exhibition sought to indigenize settler-invader culture, that is, to replace First Nations peoples with forms of white indigeneity. And it succeeded: it negotiated a place between the authority and authenticity of the imperium and that of First Nations. Nowhere is the cultural construction of national identity more apparent than in the differential treatment of Emily Carr and Tsimshian artist Frederick Alexcee. *Exhibition of Canadian West Coast Art— Native and Modern*, I have argued, transformed Carr's paintings into national icons. Two paintings by Frederick Alexcee were also hung in the exhibition. Alexcee's painting were not listed with Emily Carr, Lawren Harris, and others among the "Works by Canadian Artists" but among the artifacts of "West Coast Indian Art"; that is, in the terms set out in colonial discourse, Alexcee's paintings belong to anthropology rather than art. Here is the catalogue entry:

No. 118 The Alexee Paintings

The two paintings by Frederick Alexee...might be placed among the primitives of Canadian art here exhibited. They are worth special notice. In European countries primitive paintings have been prized for their naïveté, their charm, and the historical perspective which they confer upon the development of art. In Canada this category has so far eluded search, if we except Indian art pure and simple. Alexee's work possesses something of the quality which we should expect from such primitive painting, and he himself is an old Tsimsyan half-breed of Port Simpson, B.C. What he depicts in his many pictures is Port Simpson, his tribesmen, their legends and their former battles. His sense of colour is limited; his composi-

FIGURE 1.5: *Frederick Alexcee, Beaver at Port Simpson. Oil on cloth, 43 x 137 cm. Wellcome Institute Library, London, England.*

> *tion is as a rule excellent; and the movement is spontaneous and spirited. Artists have already expressed their admiration for his efforts, which are carried out in both oil and water colour.* (13)

About this catalogue entry, at least two things are worth noting. First, the paintings themselves are never named.[9] The entry is preoccupied, as colonial discourse habitually is, with how to classify this "artifact." Second, as Ronald Hawker points out, "While Alexcee's work is accepted as charming, the word primitive is transferred from a description of his art to a kind of racial slur on his ethnic background. The phrase 'Old Tsimshyan half-breed' hangs in the air without dignity" (242).

The 1927 joint exhibition was perhaps the only time Frederick Alexcee's work was included in a curated show and Barbeau himself appears to have been the primary, and perhaps only, champion of the artist's work. That work, however, was widely collected and interest in it has grown in recent years. In one of two articles on Alexcee published in the early 1990s—the other article is by Hawker—Deidre Simmons writes:

> *To date, I have found four paintings, fifteen carvings, thirty-eight glass slides and have evidence of two paintings, one drawing and two carvings that remain elusive. His work is found in public collections across Canada, notably the Vancouver Museum, the University of British Columbia, the Art Gallery of Ontario, the*

Manitoba Museum of Man and Nature, and the Canadian Museum of Civilization.
One painting is in the collection of the Wellcome Institute for the History of
Medicine in England and the Thomas Burke Memorial Washington State
Museum has examples of his carved miniatures. (84)

The number of works held in both private and public collections is probably much larger: in his article Hawker mentions several works not
known to Simmons and I can report, in addition, that the Glenbow Museum
holds a painting, two drawings and several carvings.[10] Knowledge of
Alexcee's life is almost as sketchy as the provenance of his work. Hawker
summarizes the little that is known:

> *According to Barbeau, Frederick Alexie (also sometimes spelled Alexcee, Alexei,*
> *or Alexee) was born in Port Simpson in 1853. His father was part of a small group*
> *of Iroquois brought to the Pacific coast in the 1820s by the Hudson's Bay*
> *Company. His mother was a Coast Tsimshian, and thus Frederick belonged to the*
> *gispawadawada clan of the Giludzar Tsimshian. His Coast Tsimshian name was*
> *Wiksamnen (meaning Great Deer Woman) and he was apparently trained as a*
> *halait carver responsible for the production of naxnos or secret society parapher-*
> *nalia. His surviving art shows strong influences from the Western tradition. This*
> *is particularly true of some canvas paintings...and a group of lantern slides now in*
> *the collection of the Vancouver Museum.... He did curio pieces for the tourist*
> *trade. As well, carvings of two priests in the Museum of Northern British*
> *Columbia and a baptistry...originally housed in a Port Simpson church and now*
> *at the University of British Columbia's Museum of Anthropology, are attributed*
> *to him. He passed away sometime in the early 1940s. (231–33)*

Alexcee's best best-known work is undoubtedly the baptismal font.
According to Simmons, it was "collected by the Reverend George Raley
circa 1886":

> *Raley's notes state that it was the "first representation of an angel by an Indian*
> *carver" and that it was used in the church at Port Simpson. The head of this*
> *winged angel has the features of a European man but reflects Indian masking*
> *traditions. The body mass is blocked out in totem pole fashion and is dispropor-*

tionate to the head size. The drapery of the robe is exquisite, following the grain of the wood although the wings were made with less care from a separate piece of wood. (85)

The font is characterized by its hybridity, that is, "the creation of new transcultural forms within the contact zone produced by colonization" (Ashcroft et al 118). As Hawker's brief biography indicates, Alexcee was not a "half-breed" as the colonizers themselves would understand that term; what his art embodied, however—and what so disturbed colonial authority—was the "mingling" of First Nations and European traditions in the art he created. While Emily Carr's "marriage" of "Native" and "modern" culture in her paintings was—and is—celebrated, Alexcee's creation of mixed forms both disturbed and haunted colonial discourse. It disturbed that discourse because it threatened to deprive "the imposed imperialist culture, not only of the authority that it ha[d] for so long imposed politically, often through violence, but even of its own claims to authenticity" (Bhabha, qtd in Young 23). It haunted and fascinated settler-invader culture because it remained outside categories colonial discourse both imposed and understood.[11]

♦

IN THIS CHAPTER I have argued that recalling any event, person or object is inherently a political act. To develop that argument I have focussed on two acts of recall: John Ralston Saul's recall of *Exhibition of Canadian West Coast Art—Native and Modern* in *Reflections of a Siamese Twin*; and Marius Barbeau and Eric Brown's recall of First Nations culture in their catalogue to the 1927 exhibition. In Saul's account, the exhibition illustrates the involvement of Canadians from all parts of the country in the creation of national culture and the success of what he terms the Canadian "experiment." Although he acknowledges that the meeting of European and First Nations cultures was "difficult and peculiar" (191), and although he is more concerned with French-English relations than with First Nations, he nonetheless regards the meeting of European and First Nations cultures as foundational to the nation. "That there has been a meeting," he declares, "and that some sort of marriage has resulted is what pours out of our literature and our painting" (191). In Saul's view, the 1927 exhibition—particularly the work of Emily Carr— epitomizes the originality of the experiment that is Canada. Against that view, I have argued that *Exhibition of Canadian West Coast Art—Native and Modern* is the moment when settler-invader culture appropriated First Nations culture for the nation. I have developed that argument by examining the 1927 exhibition and the contexts surrounding its organization and development. Against Saul's celebration of Carr's painting, I have placed the work of Frederick Alexcee; his baptismal font, I have argued, just as fittingly epitomizes the originality of the Canadian experiment. If Canada were pluralist and inclusive, as Saul affirms, it would celebrate Alexcee's work alongside the painting of Emily Carr; if Canada were pluralist and inclusive, the National Gallery would routinely display First Nations art alongside artwork produced by settler invaders. In "mingling"— to use Eric Brown's term—West Coast Indian artifacts with modern settler-invader art, *Exhibition of Canadian West Coast Art—Native and Modern* sought to articulate both a tradition of Canadian art and a vision for the nation. But, as John Barrell demonstrates in another context, "the demand for a holistic, representative vision of society could only be represented in a discourse that was *at the same time* obsessively fixed upon, and uncertain of, the boundaries of society, and the margins of the text" (qtd in Bhabha 296). The attempt to join "Native" and "modern," ethnographical artifacts and modernist works of art, thus becomes less an affirmation of unity than the policing of boundaries. The catalogue of the 1927 exhibition is just one instance of Williams's selective tradition at work, "an intentionally selective version of a shaping past and a preshaped present, which is then powerfully operative in the process of social and cultural definition and identification" (*Marxism* 115). As Williams points out, "This struggle for and against selective traditions is understandably a major part of all contemporary cultural activity" (117). So much is at stake in the interpretation of the past. The need is not just to "recall early Canada" but to articulate the relation of past to present.

Given the current conflict over Canada's foundational narratives, and the educational campaign being waged by the hegemonic order, that struggle has never been more fraught or more meaningful.

ACKNOWLEDGEMENT

This essay is part of a larger project on Canadian cultural nationalism in the 1920s. I gratefully acknowledge funding provided by the Social Sciences and Humanities Research Council of Canada and by The University of Alberta.

NOTES

1. Born Wiksamnen, Great Deer Woman, in Port Simpson, B.C. c. 1857, he was baptized into Christianity as a youth and took the name Frederick Alexcee. His surname has been rendered variously as Alexie, Alexee, etc. (See Simmons 91, endnote 1.) I have followed Simmons in adopting the spelling Alexcee; I have not, however, changed the various spellings used in the documents I cite. See Simmons and Bear.

2. There is another issue here I shall not pursue: the role of crises—real and manufactured—in fostering nationalist movements.

3. Starowicz, head of documentary production for CBC Television, made this statement at the McGill Institute for the Study of Canada conference titled "Giving the Past a Future." He was a keynote speaker at the conference. He is quoted in the *McGill Reporter*; see "Cultural apartheid in the digital age." In *Making History*, Starowicz discusses his participation in this conference.

4. The quotation within this passage is from Don McKay's "Local Wilderness," *The Fiddlehead* 169 (1991): 5–6. Saul's source for the quotation is Stan Dragland's *Floating Voice: Duncan Campbell Scott and the Literature of Treaty 9*; Dragland quotes McKay on 45–46.

5. Because the *Exhibition of Canadian West Coast Art—Native and Modern* has been remembered largely for the "discovery" of Emily Carr, most studies of the exhibition have been undertaken by Carr scholars and it has figured prominently in biographies of the painter. See, for example, the biographies by Tippett (139–66) and Shadbolt (107–09). For revisionist interpretations, see

Francis's *The Imaginary Indian* (34–38), Scott Watson's "The Modernist Past," 62–63, and Crean 196–202. See also the articles by Hawker and Simmons.

6. In addition to Carr, the non-Native artists included Lawren Harris, Edwin H. Holgate, A.Y. Jackson, Paul Kane, J.E.H. MacDonald, Peggy Nichol, Walter J. Phillips, Annie D. Savage, Charles H. Scott, Frederick M. Bell Smith, F.H. Varley, and Florence Wyle.

7. In *Reflections of a Siamese Twin* Saul cites this introduction [197].

8. Section 141 of the Indian Act, drafted by D.C. Scott and passed by Parliament in 1927, states: "Every person who, without the consent of the Superintendent General expressed in writing, receives, obtains, solicits, or requests from any Indian any payment or contribution or promise of any payment or contribution for the purpose of raising a fund or providing money for the prosecution of any claim which the tribe or band of Indians to which such Indian belongs, or of which he is a member, has or is represented to have for the recovery of any claim or money for the benefit of the said tribe or band, shall be guilty of an offence and liable upon summary conviction for each such offence to a penalty not exceeding two hundred and fifty dollars and not less than fifty dollars or to imprisonment for any term not exceeding two months" (Tennant 111–12). This section immediately followed the anti-potlatch provision (section 140).

9. Perry Bear identifies the two paintings as follows: "One of the paintings depicts a battle between Haidas and Tsimshian at Fort Simpson, with the bay and fort in the foreground and mountains beyond especially well-executed, while a second shows Fort Simpson in its earliest days, with totem poles still prominent" (11). Bear does not identify the source of his information. Since these paintings, *A Fight Between the Haida and the Tsimshian at Fort Simpson* (oil on oilcloth, Canadian Museum of Civilization, cat. No, VII–C–1805) and *Indian Village of Port Simpson* (watercolour on paper, Art Gallery of Ontario) were owned by Barbeau and A.Y. Jackson respectively, and acquired in the year preceding the exhibition, Bear may be assuming that Barbeau chose to include them. For a brief account of the purchase of the paintings see Barbeau, "Frederick Alexie," 21. Note, however, that Barbeau does not identify these paintings as the two included in the 1927 exhibition. Simmons reproduces both works in her article.

10. The painting, oil on treated sailcloth, is titled *Fishing Scene* (A.65.60) and measures 67 x 71.5 cm. One of the drawings, a black ink wash drawing on cardboard, is titled *Three Sailboats on a Stormy Sea* (A.64.32.2) and measures 10 x 18.5 cm; the other, in pencil, is titled *Fort Simpson* (A.64.32.4) and measures 7.35 x 17 cm.

11. I cannot adequately discuss the hybridity of Alexcee's work within the space of this chapter. On hybridity see Young.

2

Feminine Vulnerability, (neo)Colonial Captivities, and Rape Scares

Theresa Gowanlock, Theresa Delaney and Jessica Lynch

KATE HIGGINSON

RAPE HAS LONG BEEN USED ALLEGORICALLY to figure threats to the national body; during the late nineteenth century the condition of the new Canadian Dominion was frequently represented in visual and print media by a young, besieged woman.[1] See, for example, the 1891 electoral poster in which Sir John A. MacDonald poses as the hero who staves off the capture, and implicit gang rape, of Miss Canada by Uncle Sam's henchmen (*Figure 2.1*). While this poster overtly targets the danger of proposed Liberal free trade with the United States, it also—in casting McDonald as a citizen enfranchised with speech and power and Miss Canada as an emblem of possessable national land rather than of citizenry—reiterates a set of conventions explicating feminine vulnerability, paternal protection, and heterosexual desire. This is more than either a politically motivated repetition of the archetypal damsel-in-distress or a citation of the Western tradition of feminizing desired territory: in depicting the figure of the white single woman in need of nationalized paternal protection, the poster references not only contemporary North American worries concerning white slavery and the emergence of "redundant," public, and unsupervised women, it also references the colonial discourses of captivity tales and rape scares more generally. This field of public discourse includes the Canadian colonial rape scare of 1885, in which the (apparent) rape of two "captive" invader-settler women by their Cree "captors" during the North-West Rebellion (NWR)[2] was portrayed in central Canada as an "issue of national security," as a threat to the colonial body as a whole. The assumed fate, "worse than death," of

FIGURE 2.1: *"Uncle Sam: 'Seize her, fellows! Now's your chance! Ah ha! Miss Canada, you shall not escape!' Sir John: 'I think you had better call some other day gentlemen.'"* Conservative Party Campaign Poster, c. 1891. C.J. Patterson, Sabiston Litho. & Publishing, Montréal. National Archives of Canada (C–111243).

Feminine Vulnerability, (neo)Colonial Captivities, and Rape Scares

these two women, Theresa Gowanlock and Theresa Delaney, was sensationalized and widely circulated in the Canadian press to rouse antipathy
toward Louis Riel's call for Métis and First Nations rights to responsible
government. I will begin by examining how these women, after having
been billed as Miss Canada-esque figures in need of rescue, chose to
narrate their experiences as feminized icons of national vulnerability,
and will conclude by considering a more recent, (neo)colonial captivity
and rape scare—that of American Private Jessica Lynch during the
invasion of Iraq in 2003—which bears striking similarities to the sensationalized colonial "captivity" of the two Theresas.

In the autumn of 1885, just months after the end of the NWR,
Gowanlock and Delaney penned autobiographical accounts which were
published together as *Two Months in the Camp of Big Bear: The Life and Adventures
of Theresa Gowanlock and Theresa Delaney* by Gowanlock's brothers-in-law in
Toronto, with an eye to profits for the familial publisher, to securing
federal pensions for the authors, and to reintegrating the supposedly
violated women into respectable Canadian circles. One fascinating feature
of this dual captivity narrative is how differently the two women position themselves in their respective textual bids for national approbation.
Gowanlock's text overtly stages its acceptance of the feminine vulnerability proffered by captivity narrative conventions and by late nineteenth-
century Canadian domestic and legal prescriptions of normative femininity. Gowanlock accounts *for* herself: her text is a tampered ledger
arguing her worth by deftly balancing the qualities requisite for a violated
woman to be repatriated into the fatherland or national family. Yet if
Gowanlock adopts, performs and manipulates a scripted feminine
vulnerability for her own ends, what Fredric Jameson would term the
"political unconscious" of her text also bears witness to the costs or
trauma of the material vulnerability forced on women in this time and
place. Her narration of sexual violation is displaced into a figurative
realm where substitutable objects "speak" the rape she is prohibited
from enouncing, and her chronologically-organized text is often interrupted—ruptured—by depictions of abuse; combined, these substitutions
and ruptures mount a broad, if subtle, critique of the options available
for women—both white and First Nations—in colonial Canada. While

Gowanlock's fashioning as a frail flower captive is haunted by the risks vulnerability carries, Delaney rejects such vulnerability by consistently scripting herself as a capable maternal and colonial agent instrumental not only in her own rescue from captivity (thereby deflating the claims of her male rescuers) but also in the rescue of young Cree women from "ignorance" by instructing them in "civilized" domestic practices. Her text becomes a political platform from which she asserts her value to the Dominion as a public maternal agent of colonization, a claim that anticipates (in both its scope and racial prejudice) the demands of Canadian maternal feminists at the turn of the century. If Gowanlock performs a vulnerability not unlike that of Miss Canada in Figure 2.1, Delaney's stance is better captured by the maternal feminists as depicted on the cover of *Grip* in March 1889 (see *Figure 2.2*). The role of the Canadian woman, again shown in relation to the nation's *prima* citizen, Sir John A. (here drawn as an infant, see detail), is cast in terms of maternal capability instead of paternal protection.

Two Months illustrates the divergent strategies adopted by relatively privileged settler women to navigate and manipulate the norms— gendered and racialized, social, legal and economic—of citizenship in late nineteenth-century Canada. Despite living in a "global" era, we must not assume that now, more than a century later, we are beyond the nationally motivated rape scare, as the recent case of American POW Jessica Lynch illustrates. In this (neo)colonial rape scare of 2003— as in that of the Theresas in 1885—*race* remains pivotal to national belonging, feminine vulnerability remains widely coveted, and rape remains paradoxically both highly saleable (as sensationalized threat) and essentially unspoken (as personal female testimony).

This chapter engages in a comparison of two nationalistic rape scare scenarios featuring iconographic, feminized captives, and as such it functions as a limited cross-historical genealogy of a specific (neo)colonial form of captivity. This comparison, this decision to recall or consider Jessica Lynch via the antecedent of Gowanlock and Delaney, raises one of the major themes of this volume: the politics of historical and cultural *recall*. What is at stake in such a cross-historical pairing? Perhaps it risks reinforcing presentist assumptions of recall as a unidirectional

Vol. XXXII.—No. 11.   TORONTO, MARCH 16th, 1889.   No. 823.

WOMAN'S SPHERE.

THE ATTORNEY-GENERAL, ONTARIO.—"Er—personally, I may say, I regret it, but you see the Legislature is still of opinion that woman's proper sphere is to look after the babies, and not to vote."

SUFFRAGIST.—"So it is; and yonder are a couple of political babies that require looking after in the worst way, but we must be enfranchised before we can take charge of them!"

FIGURE 2.2: *Cover from* Grip *(16 March 1889) and detail of same. Reproduction courtesy of the William Ready Division of Archives, McMaster University Library.*

WOMAN'S SPHERE. *The Attorney General, Ontario:* "Er—personally, I may say, I regret it, and you see the Legislature is still of the opinion that women's proper sphere is to look after the babies, and not to vote." *Suffragist:* "So it is, and yonder are a couple of political babies that require looking after in the worst way, but we must be enfranchised before we can take charge of them!"

process in which the past operates only as a source of origins or explanations for a present time assumed to have "progressed" beyond the past; yet the comparison offered here speaks not to our transcendence of the racist motivations underlying colonial captivity but rather to their continuity into the twenty-first century. This emphasis on continuity itself may unintentionally endanger the necessary recognition of what the introduction to this volume terms the "unassimilable alterity" of the past to the present, the constant tension between the presentist needs of scholars and the inaccessibility, the elusive multiplicity of the past. I flag this alterity here to minimize this risk and to caution against a too reductive or falsely extensive mapping of aspects of one instance from 1885 onto another from 2003. Yet given the potency of current (North) American (neo)colonialism both globally and domestically, if reading Lynch's rape scare by way of Gowanlock and Delaney's emphasizes otherwise minimized aspects of it—of race and gender oppression, of the continuing injustices of colonization and state racism—the risks attendant in this form of cross-historical recollection may well be ones worth taking.

◆ **The Case of Gowanlock and Delaney as Colonial Rape Scare**

THERESA GOWANLOCK AND THERESA DELANEY were recent arrivals from Ontario in what is now Saskatchewan in April 1885 when, during the NWR, their husbands and seven other white men at Frog Lake were killed by Cree warriors from Big Bear's band. The Theresas were then held "captive" by Big Bear. Captivity, however, is a problematic term both for the situation of Gowanlock and Delaney (who believed themselves to be imprisoned captives, although recent historians indicate that Big Bear and the Woods Cree were trying to protect the women by taking them into their camp) and for the captivity narrative genre in general, which, in setting white captivities as the norm, effaces the more prevalent and various practices of whites confining First Nations peoples (Carter, "Captured" xxiv; Stonechild and Waiser 118). The contemporary media[3] paid little heed to the ambiguously captive state of the two women, tending to call instead, as in this *Toronto Morning News* editorial, on Canadian men to avenge the women's wrongs: the Canadian Dominion was to "impress upon the Indians that the honour of a white woman is sacred, and that outrage and murder will be promptly avenged, no matter at what cost" (qtd in Carter, "Captured" xxvi). This editorial was one of many which falsely sensationalised the "outrages" (including slavery, sexual assault, dismemberment, and murder) Gowanlock and Delaney reportedly suffered at the hands of the Cree, and which served to mobilise support for the efforts of the Canadian Field Force to rescue the two women and capture Big Bear; eventually the forces pursuing the Frog Lake Cree swelled to include more than two thousand men (Mulvaney 421–23; Dempsey 179).

Jenny Sharpe, in her assessment of the Indian Mutiny of 1857, has noted that "rape is not a consistent and stable signifier" but one that "surfaces at strategic moments" of imperial anxiety and is often implicated in the management of rebellions and in the consolidation of colonial control: "When articulated through images of violence against women, a resistance to [imperial] rule does not look like the struggle for emancipation but rather an uncivilized eruption that must be contained" (*Allegories* 2, 7). Sharpe's theorization of the tactical value of the colonial rape scare may be aptly applied to the case of Gowanlock and Delaney, whose captivity was repeatedly cited to justify the Dominion's territorial expansion and repression of the rights of First Nations peoples.[4] In 1885, images of First Nations men as threats to the honour of white settler women in the North-West permitted the enforcement of increasingly stringent segregationist (reservation) policies following the NWR, which in turn freed up prairie land for Euro-Canadian settlement. The Canadian government rewarded each of the 5,000 "rescuers" in the Field Force with 320 acres of western land ("Reward"). The eventual surrender of Big Bear and other Cree leaders to Canadian authorities served as a coerced assent to Canada's insistence that they confine themselves to their assigned reservations. The supposed "outrages" suffered by Gowanlock and Delaney were cited in Canadian Parliament in 1885 as a means to prevent the extension of the franchise to First Nations men in Western Canada (Carter, *Capturing* 79). Thus, one sanctioned, sensatiolized captivity was, in essence, used to justify another: the internment of First Nations people on Western Canadian reservations. Gowanlock and Delaney's rape scare—like many a traditional North American captivity story before it—proved valuable to the settler-invasion project.

While the mechanics of such colonially useful rape scares have been examined by a number of critics,[5] there has been less analysis of the responses offered by the women subjected to these alleged outrages. Once studied primarily by Canadian historians, if at all, *Two Months* has recently begun to attract the attention of feminist and literary scholars: Eve Zaremba reprinted Gowanlock's portion as an example of writing under privation in *Privilege of Sex: A Century of Canadian Women* (1974), Lalage Grauer classified its literary traits (1992), Sarah Carter penned a ground-breaking historical contextualization of the text (1997), Cecily Devereux (for one) now teaches it in a course on Victorian imperial narratives, and Jennifer Henderson devotes a lengthy and theoretically compelling chapter to it in *Settler Feminism and Race Making in Canada* (2003). This emergence of literary interest in *Two Months* occurs in conjunction with a correlated factor: the recently increased availability and status of this text (as well as many other early Canadian writings), including its valuation, preservation and circulation by a number of institutional apparatuses. Long available only in its original form, in microfiche (through the Peel Bibliography Series [1977] and the Canadian Institute for Historical Microreproductions [1982], and in the multi-volume *Garland Library of Narratives of North American Indian Captivities* [1976]), *Two Months* is now much more readily accessible both in Sarah Carter's new print edition (1999) and online in e-text versions (through *Early Canadiana Online* [1998] and *Project Gutenberg* [2002]).

In addition to this material dimension of the text's reproduction and revaluation, we also need to consider the production or situation of ourselves as agents of *recall*. For instance, although Henderson and I adopt divergent frames of contextualization in our contemporary readings of *Two Months* (Henderson's emphasizing the disciplinary function of the settler woman and late nineteenth-century white slavery and purity campaigns, and mine privileging colonial captivities and rape scares) there are a number of congruencies in our analytical foci. We both examine the dynamic of the Theresas as simultaneous agents and subjects of colonial governance, the interrelation between *Two Months* and contemporary legal discourses of sexual violation, and Gowanlock's subtle critique of the Canadian government's designation of Native and non-Native women as dependents. This set of congruencies speaks, speculatively, to the operation of *recall* central to the theme of this volume, to the process by which earlier texts are (re)located by current scholarship. To what extent, we might ask, are these two analyses directed by time and place, by our instruction and membership in similar (ideological) institutional settings at the same disciplinary moment, and to what extent by our writing in response not only to *à la mode* theories but also to recently "rediscovered," reprinted, newly available primary material?

◆ Gowanlock's Bid for Respectability and Repatriation

WHAT SPURRED Gowanlock and Delaney to write *Two Months*? Historian Sarah Carter has classified *Two Months* as fitting "squarely within the 'frail flower' mould" (*Capturing* 104), a captivity typology which, according to June Namias, arose in conjunction with the popularity of sentimental fiction and Victorian True Womanhood during the mid nineteenth century and which features a miserable, vulnerable, non-adaptive, helpless female captive: "This heroine turns frailty, motherhood, cleanliness, and disgusting Indians into highly saleable works" (Namias 24, 36). While Gowanlock's narrative conforms to many of the conventions of the frail flower tale, and while her brothers-in-law who published the text may have had the saleability of this genre in mind, the pro-nationalist content of *Two Months*—as Stuart Hughes notes and Carter traces in detail in *Capturing Women*—suggests that Gowanlock and Delaney were less interested in selling books *per se* than in selling their story: specifically, in demonstrating their respectability in order to convince the Dominion to grant them pensions to compensate for their hardships during the Rebellion. In the late nineteenth-century economics of colonial *peuplement*,[6] where the spinster was superfluous and the "mother of the race" prized, Gowanlock and Delaney—as newly widowed, childless women, emerging from (and perhaps "contaminated" by) an "uncivilized" Native uprising—were at risk of falling short of the criteria requisite for national heroines, particularly ones seeking recompense for the tribulations of trying to "carry civilization into the remote places of the west" (Gowanlock 43). Here Gowanlock and Delaney can be seen attempting to strike a balance typical of most white heroine authoresses of North American "Indian" captivity tales: to attest to the colonially useful threat of their violation without unduly critiquing the failure of the colony to protect them from such a threat in the first place, to shy away from analyzing the condition for the possibility of their violation and to foreclose criticism of colonial authorities through adamant praise of the colony (often in the form of policy endorsements or dramatically scripted rescue scenes). After emerging from "captivity," the two Theresas were *suspect* in a number of registers: not only colonially as failed "mothers of the race" or as daughters failed by colonial paternal protection, but also, within a socio-legal nineteenth-century Canadian context, as potentially violated women. For while vulnerability was frequently conceived as a desirable Canadian norm, violability was not: only "respectable" women were seen to be rapeable, because they, unlike other classes of women, were assumed to possess a defensible purity. A raped woman had to meet a stringent set of (racialized and classed) conditions in order to be deemed innocent and worth re-*patria*-ting into a *pater*nally-defined Canadian society.[7] The repeated support for Canadian federal policy voiced in *Two Months* needs to be read in conjunction both with Gowanlock and Delaney's pursuit of national worth and respectability, and with their concomitant anxiety concerning the economic and sexual vulnerability of "redundant," single or non-normative women within a masculinized colonial economy.

Both constituent halves of *Two Months* espouse Canadian nationalism. Gowanlock's narrative is quick to tap into the racist anti-Métis and anti-Cree sentiment then raging in Ontario: the first page of her text thanks the "brave" Canadian military men who endured hardships to "vindicate the law" (3), the body of her text perpetuates offensive characterizations of the Cree as "barbarians" (34), while the next-to-last section reproduces a lengthy poem by Cleomati valorizing "Canada's noblest and best" who routed "Riel who's [sic] name we detest" (41–42). Gowanlock is equally supportive of the Canadian platform to settle the North-West; her text's praise of the North-West's beautiful landscape and hospitable climate (11) echoes the expansionist rhetoric of the "Utopian West" then prevalent in immigration propaganda (Francis 107, 111, 120). Gowanlock also refrains, in *Two Months*, from any obvious critique of the government's implication in the causes of the rebellion. In con-cluding her story, she demurely refuses to speculate upon the "real cause for this dreadful act" (43), notwithstanding that her text often inadvertently points to one of the readily identified causes of the violence at Frog Lake: the Indian Agency's starvation of Big Bear's people.

In addition to Gowanlock's stated support for various government policies is her obvious attempt to textually style herself a respectable Canadian "lady"—an amalgam of raced, classed, and gendered traits—in order to render herself a suitable candidate for governmental rescue and recompense. To this end, Gowanlock's text adopts a blend of femi-nized genres (frail flower captivity, travelogue, domestic guide), explicitly addresses a female audience, and includes a typically feminine self-deprecating preface. Gowanlock, unlike Delaney, accepts her popular billing as a helpless widow and attempts to capitalize upon the chivalric obligations owed (by the government) to a ladylike captive. The upper-class and Ontario-based demographic of *Two Months*' target audience is suggested by its publication in Toronto, its dedication to "Our Sisters the Ladies of Canada,"[8] and the disposable income assumed by the adver-tisements (for winter vacations to the southern United States and for high-end stoves) for Toronto businesses included in the original edition. The dedication is worth underlining as it encapsulates a major drive of Gowanlock's text: the desire to qualify as a valued member of the figura-tive national family and, more specifically, to belong to this sorority of racially and socio-economically privileged English Canadian women. Gowanlock uses a similar familial analogy when she bills herself as a "fair daughter of Ontario" (44). In her introduction, Gowanlock again "especially" thanks "the Ladies" of Canada for their sympathy and kind-ness (3) and, at the end of her tale, she encloses a letter from a Winnipeg matron which espouses a *sisterly* sympathy which she "shall never forget" (36–37). Gowanlock's further claim that she "entered upon the duties of the household with a lightness of heart equal to that of any matron" (38)—where a *matron* denotes a married woman of "rank or status" (OED)—reiterates the ascendant classed nature of her self-portrait.

Gowanlock's specifically *classed* self-portrait responds to the contemporary valuation of white women in the North-West. Mariana Valverde explains that in late nineteenth-century Canada, "[w]omen did not merely have babies: they reproduced 'the race'...through their childbearing they either helped or hindered the forward march of (Anglo-Saxon) civilization" (4). Nor were all adult women, even those with children, eligible to mother the race: "The heavy emphasis on women's role as moral teachers of children...privileged those women whose cultural and racial background marked them as more adult, more evolved, more moral, and better 'mothers of the race'" (20). The demand for "mothers of the race" in the North-West in the late nineteenth century was, as a Manitoban immigration pamphlet put it in 1889, "practically unlimited" (qtd in Jackel 66). Anglo-Canadian racism towards indigenous populations of the North-West barred First Nations women from such a valued national maternal role (a rejection of the long-standing local practice of mixed-marriage which Kathleen Venema addresses in her chapter in this volume), but the desired class status of the white mother of the North-West was hotly contested in Canadian and British circles. Jessie Saxby commented to British readers in 1888 that "It seems terrible to us that our own girls should have to cook the food, knead the loaves, mend and make garments, be, in short, their own domestic servants and tradespeople!" (70). Yet, according to settler women polled in the North-West in 1885, it was precisely this ability to carry out extensive manual labour that suited a woman to North-West settler life ("What Women").

If, as hegemonic British Victorian ideology had it, "the widest definition of the middle class...was that of keeping servants," and, consequently, if respectable, Victorian middle-class women "could not bear on their bodies the visible evidence of manual labour" (McClintock 85, 153), how were settler women to be "respectable" or "middle-class" in a territory where "Every woman is a servant [because] labour is so scarce" (qtd in Jackel xviii)? Here we see the difficulties inherent in any simple attempt to transpose a metropolitan ideology onto a colonial context (an enterprise certain Canadian pioneer women attempted, while others adopted what D.M.R. Bentley has dubbed the "the gender-blurring *topos* of the female Crusoe" [96]). Even in the metropole, as Anne McClintock perceptively notes, for those who sought bourgeois respectability yet could not afford its prescribed idleness, manual domestic work had to be done covertly which created the "historically unprecedented labour of rendering invisible every sign of [domestic] work" (161–62). So it is with Gowanlock's *elision* of the "sordid actuality of daily life in the backwoods" (Inness 198).[9] For the reader of *Two Months*, Gowanlock's pre-NWR domestic life at Frog Lake consists of enjoyable Sunday drives, pleasant walks, and the making of lace (9, 10, 23). Her careful omission of other domestic chores—which stands in stark contrast to her minute accounting of such activities within Big Bear's camp—allows her the requisite matronly claim to a home "where all was in beautiful order" (9) without having to disclose her own participation in manual domestic labour which could damage her bid for feminine respectability.

Central to Gowanlock's bid for national approbation is her self-fashioning as an "Angel in the House" possessing the classed sensibility necessary to successfully mother the race. To this end, Gowanlock not only erases manual labour from the "domestic bliss" (44) of her Frog Lake home, but writes of her husband as the sole source of warmth in her "heart and fireside" (3) and diligently applies the "hallmark" equation of Victorian domesticity—cleanliness equals respectability (Davidoff 80)—to differentiate herself from the "unclean" Cree and Métis whose tastes, she claimed, "lay in a direction the opposite to domestic" (12). For Gowanlock, cleanliness becomes a useful, polyvalent measure: "In every other part of their life, so in the domestic [the Cree] were unclean" (23). As Mary Douglas has famously observed: "There is no such thing as absolute dirt: it exists in the eye of the beholder" as an "omnibus compendium which includes all the rejected elements of ordered systems" (2, 35). The eugenically inflected "mother of the race" is a component in such an ordered system—the politics of *peuplement*—and in her pursuit of this matronly respectability, Gowanlock's ascent is facilitated by scripting a complementary descent of her First Nations captors into domestic chaos. Gowanlock paints vivid scenes of disorder, violence, and improvidence within Big Bear's camp (here using a chaotic run-on sentence structure for increased effect): "dogs howling, and babies crying, and Indians beating their wives, and carts tumbling over the banks of the trail, and children falling, and horses and oxen getting mired down in the mud, and squaws cutting sacks of flour open to get a piece of cotton for string, leaving the flour and throwing away the provisions..." (24). Gowanlock's location of the Cree within a classed paradigm of difference is clear when she writes: "I would rather be a maid-of-all-work in any position than slush in an Indian tepee, reeking as it is with filth and poisonous odours" (23). Her use of the term "slush"— which the OED defines as "A slovenly or dirty person: a slut. A drudge"— highlights the overdetermined nexus of the evaluative schemas of hygiene, manual labour, and sexual purity: the common vocabulary of racism, sexism, and classism. The conjunction of class vulnerability and sexual availability is suggested often in this text. Gowanlock's evaluation of a Cree woman's lifestyle relative to that of a maid-of-all-work was not a novel one, for in *Winter Studies and Summer Rambles in Canada* (1838) Anna Brownell Jameson utilizes a similar juxtaposition: "Compare [the life of a Chippewa woman] with the refined leisure of an elegant woman in the higher classes of our society, and it is wretched and abject; but compare her life with that of a servant maid-of-all-work, or a factory girl—I do say that the position of the squaw is gracious in comparison, dignified by domestic feelings, and by equality with all around her" (516). It does not suit Gowanlock's purposes, as it did Jameson's, to lodge an argument for gender equity in this example. Instead, she claims the vantage of Jameson's "elegant woman in the higher classes" to render Cree domesticity abject. While identifying herself with "elegant" Toronto "ladies," like those shown aiding the war effort in the *Illustrated War News* (Figure 2.3), Gowanlock includes the image of the Native drudge as a foil (see Figure 2.4). Winona Stevenson has noted that projecting the European ideal of womanhood onto Aboriginal women was a crucial

FIGURE 2.3: *"Toronto Ladies Receiving and Packing Contributions for Volunteers at the Front."* Illustrated War News, *Toronto, May 9, 1885. Grip Publishing Co. Reproduction courtesy of the Baldwin Room Special Collection, Toronto Metropolitan Library.*

FIGURE 2.4: *"Beasts of Burden."* Illustration from Two Months in the Camp of Big Bear, *13. Reproduction courtesy of the Canadian Institute for Historical Microreproductions.*

"criterion for contrasting savagism with civility" (56). Gowanlock not only uses Victorian precepts of domestic femininity to *class* herself a worthy candidate for rescue, but she also (much like other frail flower captives) turns such precepts against the Cree in order to further underscore the worth of the rescue effort in removing her from such abjection.

Gowanlock not only utilizes definitions of hygiene grounded in Victorian domestic ideology, but also implements one of its techniques—that of household accounting—to further argue her worth. At one level, Gowanlock's half of *Two Months* functions precisely as a domestic ledger, (creatively) tracing the debts and payments accrued during her captivity. As such, it can be read as a product of a rationalised Victorian domestic discourse which instructed matronly women to embrace accountability, to measure accurately, to supervise, and to "invariably...punctually and precisely" keep an account-book (Beeton 6; Davidoff 86). Or, as Catharine Parr Traill reminded Canadian settlers in 1855, "It is best to keep a true account in black and white, and let the borrowed things be weighed or measured, and returned by the same weight and measure" (23). A rhetoric of debt and payment runs through Gowanlock's text and is brought to bear in order to add credence to her judgments of moral standing. Thus, the Plains Cree are depicted as the recipients of "everything" (15) who owed a debt to Mr. Gowanlock and Mr. Delaney by whom they were "constantly fed" (12), and they are targeted as "ungrateful characters" (13) and "vicious...freebooters" (13) who do not honourably discharge their debts. Gowanlock is eager to keep the "Reds" in the red as it were, and generous or chivalric acts done her by indigenous peoples prove difficult for Gowanlock to account for without disrupting her claimed entitlements. Her narrative makes note of chivalric acts—like the Cree boys' tendency to give her flowers (32) and Andre Nault's kindly exchange of his dry blanket for her wet one (33)—but in each case Gowanlock quickly deflates the value of the act by sharply condemning the character of the Cree or Métis in question. The tension implicit in Gowanlock's unjustified reprimands marks the limits of her colonial logic of accountability to integrate such acts into a system based upon assumptions of racial superiority (in which white males are most eligible for chivalric roles).

If Gowanlock's carefully recorded measurement of debt and payment facilitates her self-exoneration from indebtedness to either her Cree captors or her Métis "protectors," she also makes use of the logic of debt and repayment to argue that her narrative itself functions to discharge her debt to those who rescued her. In the opening pages of her text, Gowanlock highlights her indebtedness to the nation and reiterates her "bounden duty to give the public a truthful and accurate description of my capture" in order to repay the "debt of gratitude I owe to the people of this broad dominion" (3). She also, crucially, argues that her fulfillment of the public's "desire" for such an account discharges her, in that it "repay[s]" her "debt of gratitude," and leaves her free to honourably "bid the public a grateful farewell and seek my wished for seclusion from which I would never have emerged but to perform a public duty" (4).[10] In this, the effectual closing line of Gowanlock's text is a blended culmination of the arguments we have traced in her narrative to this point: a desire for the secluded private sphere befitting the matron Gowanlock aspires to be, an assertion that *Two Months* in fact performs a useful national "duty" which justifies Gowanlock's rescue, and an antici- pation of federal reward couched in the diction of a retiree's final speech before heading home to enjoy a federal pension.

In using this rhetoric of debt and gratitude Gowanlock participates in a larger late Victorian deployment of economic logic to mask the oppression of colonialism. Jenny Sharpe notes that, following a number of Native insurgencies in British colonies in the second half of the nine- teenth century, "the crisis produced by anticolonial rebellion [was] managed through a recoding of European self-interest as self-sacrifice and native insurgency as ingratitude" (*Allegories* 8). This is precisely what Gowanlock attempts. She depicts settlers as the fearless agents of civilization who had left "comfortable homes in the east" in order to "elevate the Indian and make him a better man" (43). Despite noting that her husband took "every kind of work he thought would pay" (44), Gowanlock persistently identifies the motives of settlement as prima- rily moral (self-sacrificing) rather than commercial (self-interested). In fact, she conveniently blends the two to argue that the commercial was in fact moral, that settler enterprises like her husband's mill operated as a "blessing to those Indians" (45). That Big Bear's warriors did not recognize this "blessing" is recorded as "unaccountable" ingratitude (43). Here, and in Gowanlock's rather ridiculous refusal of the possibility that settlers could be "extortioners or land-grabbers" (43), we see her brutal erasure of prior First Nations' economies and claims to the North-West.

◆ Traumatized Text: Tracing Gowanlock's Economic and Sexual Vulnerability

GOWANLOCK'S USE of economic rhetoric speaks to both an overt aim of her text—to garner economic recompense from the Dominion—and to the less acknowledged, more subtly written, anxieties that motivate the overt aim—her persistently marked fear of economic vulnerability. I want now to examine the latter. Fredric Jameson has labelled such hidden narratives the "political unconscious" of a text and argues that this "repressed and buried reality" will speak to a Marxian vision of an uninterrupted history of class struggle (20). Jameson's formulation is useful in explicating the role of the vulnerable First Nations women who preoccupy Gowanlock's text, and who appear to signify Gowanlock's anxiety concerning her own class position and social use-value. Carole Gerson has observed a similar strategy in the writing of Susanna Moodie and Catharine Parr Traill, who "negotiated past the silences imposed by Victorian decorum, especially upon middle-class women, by expressing some of their own publicly unspeakable desires and concerns [such as disempowerment, fear, and maternal anxiety] through their literary representations of Indian women" (11, 16). Gowanlock's writing is everywhere stamped with signs of sexual and economic trauma: realms fascinatingly bound to each other in her text, and in late Victorian Canada in general. Her autobiography shows the (quasi)inscription of rape: it illustrates that the explicit telling of rape can remain a prohibited speech act—unsaid—yet be revealingly inscribed into the structure of the text through the exchange of objects symbolically representative of subjects.[11] This preoccupation with traumatic vulnerability not only speaks of Gowanlock's anxiety about her class position and her fear of redundancy, but also signals her recognition of vulnerabilities common to Native and non-Native women that exist *beyond* the bounds of Big Bear's camp within the Canadian settlement economy in general. In so doing, this preoccupation maps the psychic costs of feminine frailty, and repeatedly fissures the surface of her explicitly pro-settlement, pro-nationalist narrative. To analyze the political unconscious of Gowanlock's text is to provide a necessary extension to her overt claims for national worth and to see an underlying, albeit muted, criticism of the norms of feminine vulnerability lodged in the narrative's discordant ruptures and images of abuse.

Gowanlock's anxieties about the role of women within the Anglo-Canadian economy of settlement, particularly single or spinster women, were grounded in contemporary transatlantic debates concerning the increasing numbers of "redundant" women "who have to earn their own living, instead of spending and husbanding the earnings of men" (Greg qtd in Poovey 1). Within the late nineteenth-century Canadian imaginary, this type of single female figure took on "enormous cultural relevance" with the emergence of the "public woman," the unmarried working woman, in Canadian cities (Strange 3–5, 11). The trepidation evident in Gowanlock's approach to issues of female dependence and economic stability signals a larger contemporary (inter)national dialogue on appropriate roles for women.

The political unconscious of Gowanlock's portion of *Two Months* can be traced in its preoccupation—in numerous moments proclaimed to be "incidental"—with images of sexually and physically vulnerable First Nations women. An incident is "something that occurs casually in the course of...something else, of which it constitutes no essential part; an event of accessory or subordinate character" (*OED*). Two of Gowanlock's chapter titles contain the word "Incidents" and appropriately enough it is in these chapters that she describes "subordinate character[s]": indigenous women at risk. While these women may be of subordinate character within the North-West's invader-settlement economy, they are far from "accessory" to mapping the political unconscious of Gowanlock's story; indeed they speak her fear that she too may be "no essential part" of the national body—hence the spirited counter-argument as to her national worth, outlined above.

In her opening chapter, Gowanlock describes her departure from her "father's house" and her travel to Battleford as "full of incident and adventure"—the "incident" in this case being her encounter with a "number of half-famished squaws" (5). This motif is reiterated in the second chapter, "Incidents at Battleford," in which Gowanlock details the hardships endured by Battleford's impoverished Native women (7). This enumeration is preceded by one such woman asking Mr. Gowanlock "why he did not live with [Mrs. Gowanlock], and if she were well" (6): a question which foreshadows Gowanlock's fear of losing two means of (financial) security: her husband and her health. What, the text implicitly asks, is to separate her from the "drudgery" of the Native women she observes? In chapter eleven, entitled "Incidents by the Way," Gowanlock presents a compendium of First Nations women at risk: an orphaned daughter (25), a dying wife (26), a violently murdered "insane squaw" (26), and a "most *strange* procedure" in which four "crying and singing and clapping" First Nations women in the camp were "tied up until morning" by "some of the Indians" (26; emphasis added). Just as the narrative placements of her earlier "incidents" follow her potentially stressful emergence from the "sacred precincts of the paternal hearth" (3), so the "incidents by the way" occur in the chapter immediately following the traumatic degradation of her trousseau and, hence, the symbolic desecration of her marriage (23). Thus, it is as a (figuratively) freshly widowed woman that Gowanlock lashes out at the Cree as wife-beaters and explicitly and repeatedly names her fear of "be[ing] put in with Indians" and "work[ed] to death" (24), "of being taken away by [the Cree] and made to work for them like their squaws" (25).

I want to return to Gowanlock's use of the term "strange." It is how she describes the procedure of binding the four Cree women (an incident which remains unglossed in the text), but it is also the discordant descriptor she attaches to Métis customs, in an earlier chapter, after spending the night at a "nice and tidy" Métis home replete with fresh baked bread, fish and potatoes eaten over a clean white tablecloth, a clean bed, and a warm breakfast (8). Why should a household scene so resonant with Victorian ideals of domesticity be so "very strange"? Perhaps the answer lies in Gowanlock's use of the term in a *Globe* interview in which she comments that after the killings, "strange to say, [the Cree women in the teepee I was taken to] did not ill-treat me, but took my shoes off and dried them for me, and offered me something to eat" ("Big Bear's"). For Gowanlock, then, it is not the Cree women's difference that is strange; instead, "strange" (or strangeness) describes how odd Gowanlock finds the ability of the other to be the same, to embody those domestic ideals to which she subscribes. Hence, one might speculate that the familiar strangeness of the bound Cree women for Gowanlock was in her identification of their plight with that of other women, like herself, caught within what she terms (albeit in a different sense) the "confines of civilization" (3).[12]

Both Gowanlock's overt anti-Cree writing and her less conscious probing of First Nations women at risk express a deep aversion to the vulnerability that accompanies the servitude and manual labour of "drudges," working-class women, and fallen women (the latter frequently assigned domestic labour as penance [Strange 17]). Indeed, her description of her rescue from the Cree camp foregrounds her escape as one from domestic servitude. When she heard the police arrive,

> *Mrs. Delaney was making bannock for the next morning's meal, while I with cotton and crochet needle was making trimming for the dresses of Mrs. Pritchard's nine half-breed babies.... I threw the trimming to the other end of the tent, and Mrs. Delaney called upon Mrs. Pritchard to finish making the bannocks herself... Rescued! at last, and from a life worse than death. (34–35)*

While Gowanlock in this passage overlays the threat of rape—the "fate worse than death"—with the threat of economic vulnerability or cross-racial servitude—a "life worse than death"—it is worth remembering that the two were closely intertwined (at times mutually constitutive) in nineteenth-century Canada.

Dominion newspapers during the NWR described Gowanlock as being "owned by a buck" and the "victim of foul outrages on the part of the Indians" ("More Indian"). To respond in a public narrative to these dominant images of her violation must have posed a dilemma for Gowanlock: regardless of whether or not she had in fact been raped, she had to negotiate a course between the values of Victorian femininity, which suggested that prudent and respectable women (their virtue often figured as protective armour) were all but immune from such defilement, and the potential expectations of her Ontario readership for whom her violation was a significant motivating factor in the "terrible excitement" surrounding the pursuit of Big Bear and in her subsequent stature as a heroine (Plummer 65; Pederson 200). Negotiating this course results in what Lalage Grauer has characterized as a dualistic narrative which swerves between avowals of suffering and assertions that she was not harmed (131).

In Gowanlock's story, rape is a frequently suggested possibility which is never explicitly resolved: she often draws attention to the threat of her rape by Cree or Métis men, and she hints that "Big Bear's braves" did not keep their promise not to harm her (19), yet she neither overtly denies nor overtly writes of her rape. In so doing, Gowanlock takes up a structure historically utilized by women writing of rape: an obsessive inscription (the repeated raising of the spectre or threat of rape) and an obsessive erasure of sexual violence (her refusal to explicitly deny or stage it). Having observed this pattern of "striking repetition of inscription and erasure" in numerous writings of rape, Lynn Higgins and Brenda Silver contend that the "trace or sign of imperfect erasure can have many meanings.... In the tension between attempt and failure to reveal violation, the story that often gets told is that of an inability to tell the story" (2, 5). Other examples of this pattern can be found in Richardson's *Clarissa* (1748), in which the climactic act of rape is never itself described, in Flora Annie Steele's *On the Face of the Waters* (1896), in which the catalyzing act of the rape of British women during the Indian Mutiny, is left unwritten, and in W.T. Stead's "The Maiden Tribute of Modern Babylon" published in the *Pall Mall Gazette* just weeks after the rescue of Gowanlock and Delaney in July 1885. Stead's scandalous series on white slavery used a line of asterisks to connote the rape of the virginal young "Lily": "'There's a man in the room! Take me home; oh, take me home!' / ******** / And then all once more was still" (Stead qtd in

Devereux 13). A similar absence of descriptive representations of rape characterizes contemporary Canadian discourse in general; in her study of sexual assault in Ontario during this era, Karen Dubinsky notes a "near total silence on the topic in the writings of nineteenth-century women" (14). Dubinsky explains that in Canada at this time women's fear of rape "seemed to revolve around public disgrace and community disapproval" (15). Gowanlock and Delaney were no doubt subject to such shame, and in an interview in the *Globe* Gowanlock is eager to "correct some infamous and outrageous stories that have been circulated throughout the press without regard for their authenticity" and to assert that she was "not hurt nor ill-treated in any way" ("Big Bear's").

Notwithstanding Gowanlock's denial of rape in the press (and Dubinsky's historical work is suggestive of why Gowanlock, aspiring to respectability, could not say otherwise), her text is marked by traumatic references to (potential) sexual violation. Stuart Hughes has called *Two Months* a "rather hysterical" account (243), and I wonder if his choice of *hysteria*—with its historically misogynist denotation of emotional illness generated by the *womb*—is more resonant for this text than he may have intended. Gowanlock's highly emotional and often disjunctive writing is, I think, the result of anxieties specific to the bearer of a womb: the pressure to reproduce the race and to guard against "improper" violation. In *Two Months*, disruptive shifts in chronology and content often follow on the heels of Gowanlock's observation of her sexual vulnerability. For instance, when she first arrives in Big Bear's camp and is surrounded by the men who have just killed her husband, she interrupts her description of their threatening behaviour toward her to tell, in lengthy ethnographic detail, of a Cree baby, "done up in a moss bag" (17). Mary Louise Pratt, amongst others, has demonstrated that this type of "manners-and-customs" ethnographic discourse is a "widespread and stable form of 'othering'...whose work is to codify difference" (Pratt 139; Grauer 132). Perhaps Gowanlock resorts to this type of codifying language to invest herself with authority, as well as to stabilize the threat she felt at that precise moment in the narrative. Nor is it insignificant that the ethnographic object she chooses—a bound baby who looks nearly "dead"—mirrors her own sense of bondage. We encounter a similar disruption when she interrupts the telling of her near rescue by the North-West Field Force, during the Cree Thirst Dance, to pronounce upon missionary work among Native peoples (28–29). Gowanlock's anxiety concerning the Thirst Dance prompts this chronologically disruptive recourse to established subjects of cultural intervention in the North-West.

What in the Thirst Dance arouses Gowanlock's anxiety? It is one of many instances in the text where First Nations people utilize items which once belonged to white invader-settlers, and such "misuse" of these domestic objects repeatedly elicits a noticeable response from Gowanlock. As the Thirst Dance begins, Gowanlock prays that the police—her "dispensers of law and order" (38)—will arrive and prevent it (28), but her description maps instead their symbolic defeat. Her table linen strewn from the poles of the lodge and her thimbles worn as bodily decoration suggest the degeneration of Victorian domestic order and the triumph of a First Nations economy or epistemology; the Cree wearing both police uniforms and lace veils would seem to represent the mixing of masculinity with femininity, the defilement of that paternal system of power which Gowanlock had hoped to summon to her rescue. For Gowanlock it is not only that these objects represent a collapse of the values of settlement governance, nor solely that these clothes are traumatic triggers for her because the new object-use recalls the desired old (pre-captivity) usage,[13] but that, in addition, these resituated domestic objects seem scripted to suggest a narrative of sexual violation which she is not permitted or does not desire to express otherwise. When Urania White, a Caucasian captive in 1862, first saw the Sioux children of her camp playing in silks she began to laugh, until the "laugh died on [her] lips" and she grew faint as she thought, "Where did these things come from? What tales could they tell if power were given them to speak?" (qtd in Derounian-Stodola 155). In Gowanlock's text, I am interested in a slightly different formulation of this schema wherein such resituated clothing does have the power to "speak" (albeit subtly) of sexual persecution and violation.

The arch-villain in Gowanlock's story is a Métis, Peter Blondin, who "purchased" her (at a cost of $30 and a horse) from "Big Bear's braves" shortly after the killings. After buying her, Gowanlock records that

Blondin "asked me to go with him, but I refused; and he became angry and did everything he could to injure me. That man treated me most shamefully" (18). Here Blondin enters the popular contemporary register of the racially demonized white slaver. It is not until her closing chapter, when she is safely back in Ontario, that Gowanlock returns to tell in detail of Blondin's "evil intent" to make her live with him (39). She concludes that "By the help of God I was saved from him; and a life worse than death. If the worst had come I would have drowned or killed myself; but it did not" (39). Was Gowanlock saved from a *fate* or a *life* worse than death? Might this slippage between terms suggest her escape from co-habitation if not from rape? For in textual moments like the strangely unconcluded scene in which Blondin torments Gowanlock by parading before her wearing her husband's underclothing, there is a potential coded enactment of his (sadistic) sexual dominance, of his possession of a husband's intimacy (see also Henderson 129). At the least, in Gowanlock's description of Blondin's use of "her" domestic possessions is a mirroring of his attempted use of her: when Blondin offers Gowanlock her husband's overcoat as "*his*," he mimics his offensive attempt to seduce or purchase her with goods taken from her own house (20). At most, we might *speculate* that the violation of Gowanlock's trousseau—the contents of that ultra-symbolic womb-like chest "misused" by her captors and scattered and muddied on the camp's ground— and Blondin's odd strutting about in Mr. Gowanlock's undergarments speak of intimate physical contact and of Gowanlock's rape.

By framing Gowanlock's writing of rape within a legal context (and her text as governmental plea does essentially lay her *case* before a group of jurors), we can elucidate contemporary definitions of rape and the reasons Gowanlock may have felt compelled to shape her narrative as she did. Both Karen Dubinsky and Constance Backhouse have written legal histories of rape in Canada in this period, and their list of requisite criteria for the successful prosecution of a late-Victorian Canadian rape case are remarkably similar to the characteristics Gowanlock attributes to herself and her situation in *Two Months*. The most important factor in the outcome of a sexual assault case was the woman's perceived character, her "respectability" and "reputation"; women deemed irresponsible or engaged in a sexual praxis outside nineteenth-century mores were held culpable for their own "misfortune" and received no legal protection from rape (Dubinsky 24–26, 18; Backhouse 111). Respectability not only belonged predominantly to the upper classes, but was also usually confined to Caucasians (Backhouse 98). Given Gowanlock's desire for the Dominion to assume (fiscal) responsibility for her "misfortune," one can see the necessity of establishing her respectable, white, middle-class character—a project she takes on with vigour in her text. Respectable women were more likely to succeed in court if they could demonstrate their physical resistance to the rape (Dubinsky 23; Backhouse 103); Gowanlock's threat to commit suicide (à la Clarissa) should Blondin attempt to rape her demonstrates this requisite physical resistance (while, in keeping with captivity tale conventions, retaining a star role for the male who would rescue her from needing to resort to such an end). Finally, Backhouse notes that the most successful cases (apart from those in which women died defending themselves) were those of attempted rather than successful rape (111). This too fits with Gowanlock's writing of a text that underscores the threat of rape without ever detailing or confirming its fulfillment. Given the period's stringent delineation of which women (usually white, married or otherwise-supervised, upper- or middle-class) were considered "rapeable" and worthy of protection and compensation and which were not, and, given the closely linked aspects of sexual and socio-economic vulnerability in these cases, it is perhaps not surprising that Gowanlock approached her defence with calculated care, aiming to fulfil all of the requisite definitions for respectability deserving of recompense.

◆ Delaney as Domestic Instructress: Anticipating Maternal Feminism

REDUCTIVELY, we might argue that while Gowanlock was driven to demonstrate *respectability*—"to be regarded by society as being proper, correct and good"—Delaney desired a different object relation, to be *respected*—"to be admired because of [her] qualities or achievements"

(*OED*). While Delaney, like Gowanlock, craved national approbation and recompense, she was less keen to be passively judged upon her proper domestic feminine attitudes than to be admired for her competency and skill. If Gowanlock's text suggests the strategic wisdom and costs of playing upon long-standing assumptions of feminine vulnerability to justify rescue, Delaney's, in contrast, attempts to justify her rescue by demonstrating her quasi-professional national value as a civilizing agent useful to the Dominion's settlement-invasion enterprise.

Both Theresas organize their narratives chronologically and each story moves from a childhood home in Ontario or Québec to a marital home in the North-West and back again (on the newly completed CPR line), but only Gowanlock notes her happiness at returning to the "wished for seclusion" of her parental home (4). Delaney, while introducing her narrative with a standard feminine disclaimer concerning her lack of literary skill and an additional caveat that she writes from "a duty imposed...by gratitude" to those Canadians who have helped her (51), appears to relish the opportunity that the writing of the text gives her to voice her political thoughts in a public forum. Aware of the social prohibitions facing female politicians, Delaney nevertheless writes knowledgeably about settlement policy, farming practices, and Indian Affairs. She notes: "It would not become me, perhaps, to comment upon the manner in which the country is governed, and the Indians instructed, for I am no politician.... But I cannot permit this occasion, the last I may ever have, to go past without saying plainly what I think and what I know about the north-west and its troubles" (61).

Like Gowanlock, in *Two Months* Delaney is careful to concur with Dominion policy on settlement and Indian Affairs (her disapproval falling instead on the Hudson's Bay Company and its anti-assimilation policies). Her account is no doubt intended both to establish her husband's proper conduct—as a Farm Instructor employed by the Dominion government to convert the Woods Cree to agricultural practice—and to secure herself a pension in the wake of his death in the line of duty. Yet I think Delaney's account, in underlining her political knowledge of her husband's affairs and her own analogous work as an instructor of Woods Cree women, also suggests that she too was a useful (if unofficial) Dominion employee. Delaney was what we might call a "Domestic Instructress": inviting the young Woods Cree women to her house to teach them "cleaning, scrubbing, washing, cooking, sewing, fancy work" and observing that "they would feel as proud when they could perform some simple little work, as a child feels when he has learned his A.B.Cs" (64). Here Delaney (intent on depicting herself as a capable maternal teacher) exhibits a racist tendency, then prominent in Anglo-evangelical women's missionary work, to infantilize indigenous women rather than see them as peers (Valverde 10). She writes more than once of the Cree as "her children" or "children of the forest" (61, 64). Of her "Indian protegees" Delaney writes that "With time and care good housekeepers could be made of many of them and it is too bad to see so many clever, naturally gifted, bright creatures left in ignorance and misery.... How many a flower is left to blush unseen, and waste its fragrance in the desert air" (64). How different this suggestion that Delaney's domestication efforts are *rescuing* these women from supposed misery is to the popular paternalistic rhetoric of rescue surrounding the Theresas' captivity.

Indeed, Delaney often refuses the position of vulnerable *rescuee*. Her text opens with the assertion that she had an "important role" in the NWR as a "heroine" (52), and culminates with a "rescue" scene in which she, again, plays an important—active and assertive—role. Whether it even qualifies as a rescue in her version is debateable given her crucial role in its success. After almost two months in Big Bear's amalgamated camp, a small group of Métis—including the Pritchard family who had been harbouring Gowanlock and Delaney—had managed to break off and take a separate course. In this smaller camp one evening, Delaney was making bannock when Pritchard "ran in and told me that the police were outside." It was, writes Delaney, at that "moment we ran the greatest of all our risks. The police had taken us for a band of Indians, and were on the point of shooting at us when I came out and arrested the act" (74). Unlike Gowanlock, who writes a rather passive, domestic rendition of this scene, Delaney scripts herself as an agent interacting with, even "arresting," the "police." In so doing she not only deflates the paternalistic rescue typical of captivity tales, she arrests an act of misrecognition and performs a significant, resistant act of self-classification. Thus, although Delaney's story is, like Gowanlock's, marked by a fear of sexual assault, a sense of her vulnerability is countered and transformed by descriptions of her abilities, knowledge, and capacity to act and to self-identify.

Delaney's self-fashioning as a Domestic Instructress—with her emphasis on the value of women carrying their domestic skills into a semi-public sphere of colonial governance—resonates with the precepts of turn-of-the-century Canadian maternal feminism, which held that a woman's essential motherly traits gave "her the duty and the right to participate in the public sphere...[to be] social housekeepers responsible for tidying up and humanizing the industrial capitalist system" (Kealey 12). First wave maternal feminist Nellie McClung was twelve years old and living on her family's Manitoban farm when she first heard of the two Theresas in 1885. In her autobiography she recalls:

> The fate of the women was a shivery subject for conversation. Up to that time the "trouble" was a vague and abstract state, far away and impersonal, but now the menace had come out into the open, and the evil had assumed a shape and image; painted savages, brandishing tomahawks and uttering blood-curdling cries had swarmed around the lonely and defenceless farm houses, and overpowered those two women... (Clearing 182)

McClung's recollection provides an apt description of how media stories "assume a shape," how they are sold to us, and how, in this case, the Theresas were ascribed the forms of vulnerable white women. The young McClung imbibes the media's racial caricatures of the Cree and dreams at night of "shrieking savages" attacking her. Significantly, it is not soldiers or police who come to her nocturnal rescue but her mother, who "would feed [the Natives] currant buns and get them persuaded to go back [to their reserve], and make their baskets and behave" (185). When a group of neighbouring Natives do arrive at her farm a few weeks later to sell their baskets, it is as Nellie dreamed: everyone sits in the kitchen while her mother dispenses cups of tea and soothes ailments with her medicinal remedies. Just as Delaney emphasizes that those

Cree who had been instructed by her were not rebellious, McClung's story finds a practical solution to Indigenous insurgence in the feminine domestic sphere. Three decades later McClung argued for a "new chivalry": "Let us give women every weapon whereby they can defend themselves; let us remove the stigma of political non-entity under which women have been placed" (In Times 42). McClung's call resonates both with Delaney's frequent refusal of typical feminine vulnerabilities (her self-scripted role as rescuer suggesting that she can "defend" herself) and with Delaney's valuation of the colonial woman's utility within extra-domestic, at least marginally public, capacities.

Indeed, Two Months is particularly interesting for its complex and at times internally-conflicted vision of female citizenship in late nineteenth-century Canada. While Gowanlock's performance of feminine vulnerability is apparently and strategically in accordance with expectations of the Victorian frail flower captivity genre and with nationalistic representations of Miss Canada like that found in Figure 2.1, a glance back at this Miss Canada, so dependent upon a protective masculinized citizen, should remind us that Gowanlock's narrative also attests to the costs, the material and psychic tolls, of such prescriptions of sexual and economic vulnerability. In her narrative, Delaney, while embracing the white-supremacist logic of the colonial settlement project, does "arrest" certain expectations of conventional feminine vulnerability. Her call for a public maternal role, which was taken up by a subsequent generation of feminists challenges the allegorical rape and paternal protection of the nation with a maternal morality of care. Two Months, with its divergent constituent halves, is a record of relatively privileged colonial women utilizing—while simultaneously revealing the costs and limitations of—Victorian ideals of domestic femininity in relation to Métis and First Nations cultures in an attempt to negotiate more secure or fulfilling roles for themselves within the paternalistic economy of settlement in the North-West during the late nineteenth century.

◆ Jessica Lynch's Captivity as (neo)Colonial Rape Scare

IN KEEPING WITH this volume's theme of *recalling*, and the bi-directional temporal process it invokes, let us examine the currency of the (neo)colonial rape scare. If one considers *Two Months* as a plea for governmental recompense, it was a successful one: Gowanlock and Delaney each received federal pensions of $400 annually. These unconditional pensions, as Sarah Carter reminds us, should be compared to that of Jane Quinn or Owl Sitting, the Cree widow (with child) of Thomas Quinn, the Indian Agent killed at Frog Lake; given that Delaney's pension was based on her husband's rate of pay and given that Quinn's government salary was larger than Delaney's, it is scandalous that Jane Quinn was granted the paltry sum of $12 per month on the condition that local authorities certify her as morally worthy (Carter, *Capturing* 124–25).

Lest the racism (not to mention the state-supervised "morality") of this recompense seem passé, we might turn to a recent (neo)colonial rape scare: the rescue of Private Jessica Lynch (a nineteen-year-old, white, injured, American POW) from an Iraqi hospital in Nasiriya in April 2003. The American military mobilized approximately a thousand personnel in order to seize Lynch from the hospital where she was reportedly being "tortured" (implicitly raped) by her "barbaric" Iraqi captors. This dramatic rescue garnered extensive front-page coverage in the Western media at a point when the war was coming under increasing criticism at home (see, for instance, *Newsweek's* cover featuring Lynch: *Figure 2.5*). As one American soldier explained: "We are finally war heroes. We pulled out the POW last night. Makes me feel as if it was all worth it" ("Saved" 56). "For the US military, the story of Private Lynch arrived just in time" and became "the most oft-told story of the Persian Gulf War II" (Eviatar; Potter). More than one commentator has noted that this story—its fortuitous timing, its filmed footage, its "all-American" heroine (a blonde, baseball-playing, beauty queen)—seems fit for Hollywood, and indeed the event has generated numerous media spinoffs. And Hollywood it was: Jessica, far from being tortured in the

FIGURE 2.5: *Cover, Newsweek, April 14, 2003.* © 2003 *Newsweek, Inc. All rights reserved. Reprinted by permission.*

Nasiriyan hospital, received the best available care; the Iraqi doctors, far from being "barbarous" captors, had tried to return Jessica to the American forces (who shot at their ambulance before ascertaining its purpose); and so on. For many months after her "rescue," the U.S. Pentagon appears to have restricted media access to Lynch and prohibited her from addressing the public, which is one way, among other ways, in which Lynch's captivity experience has been constructed as unspeakable. The BBC's *Correspondent* hailed the Pentagon's handling of Lynch's situation as "one of the most stunning pieces of news management ever conceived" (qtd in Eviatar).

To borrow Nellie McClung's phrasing, through Jessica—and Pentagon media-spinning—the war had "assumed a shape and image." It is worth noting which shapes were selected and which bypassed in this process. Just as the Theresas garnered more media coverage than other more pro-Cree whites, Métis or First Nations people in Big Bear's camp in 1885, Jessica's image has been more widely circulated than those of other women (and men) in similar circumstances: a quick scan of *New York Times* coverage in the three months following the event indicates that Shoshana Johnson, a black Army cook taken prisoner at the same time as Lynch and later released, received less than half the coverage Lynch did, while Lori Piestewa, a Hopi-Mexican-American from Jessica's unit whose body was found in Nasiriya and who is the first Native American servicewoman to die in combat, received only a tenth of the coverage allotted to Jessica. Who is deemed a suitable poster-girl for the American troops? What is the normative centre of the imagined national family? In 2003, as in 1885, whiteness remains key. As does feminine vulnerability. For Gowanlock, this vulnerability was written as a genteel Victorian femininity befitting a "sister" or "daughter" of the Dominion; for Lynch, it is apparent in the media's focus on her small stature, youth, and love of children.

In not entirely dissimilar moments of (neo)colonial crisis, both the Theresas and Jessica found themselves circulating in popular media accounts as the victim-heroines of nationally useful rape scares. Not only were their sensationalized plights used to mollify the citizens at home as to the justness of the invasion at hand, they were also used to rouse the vindictive fury of the nation's armed forces against the "barbarous violators" of these emblematic women. Journalist Rick Bragg provides a clear snapshot of this dynamic at work in his authorized biography of Lynch—*I Am a Soldier, Too: The Jessica Lynch Story* (2003)—when he introduces us to Seth Bunke, a U.S. Marine posted to Nasiriyah who "is the opposite of Jessi, except for the color of his hair. His arms are

long and thick with muscle and his legs look like pulpwood logs..."
(122). Bragg explains that

> *in the streets of Nasiriyah, the story of the young woman [Lynch] in the hands of*
> *the brutal Fedayeen took hold in the minds of the young marines, and it mush-*
> *roomed: She was being tortured, in the most cruel ways, every day, every hour.*
>
> *"I took it personally," said Bunke. "I took it right to heart. I have a sister. She's*
> *nineteen. I thought of Jessi, and I thought of her. I thought of the people who*
> *would do that. I wanted to kill them.*
>
> *"I killed thirty-four of them." (124)*

Not only do we see how Lynch is perceived as a "sister"—a beloved member
of an imagined American national family—and how her exaggerated
fate served to motivate American retaliation, but we also see a typical
example of how Lynch is figured in specifically feminine terms "opposite" to the prototypically masculine strength and stature of the marine.
Not only are their relative sizes contrasted; Seth's ability to fight is also,
implicitly, staged as opposite to Lynch's role as victim. Which leads us
to one of the significant *costs* attached to this role Jessica and the
Theresas were forced to occupy (Gowanlock's narrative enumerates
others): the lack of capacity or ability ascribed to the feminine captive.
While Bragg, and others, frequently assert Lynch's difference from her
male "rescuers," she—in her well-known first post-rescue speech act—
asserts her equality: "I'm an American soldier, too" (131). Though Bragg
dismisses this as a careless comment, it proved a prescient one given
that her situation sparked renewed debate on the viability of female
soldiers. In her column in the *Globe & Mail*, Margaret Wente wrote: "Call
me sexist. But I confess I'm troubled by the thought of girls like Jessica
and single mothers like Shoshana being rounded up at gunpoint by
fedayeen and other men who've never heard of the Geneva Conventions."
Putting aside the problematic assumption that it is primarily foreign
fedayeen who violate the Geneva Conventions, it is striking that even a
proclaimed feminist like Wente believes young women—notwithstanding
their military training—to be vulnerable and unsuited to military
service. One might imagine Private Lynch as fulfiling Delaney's implicit

demand of public leadership roles for women, yet the popular coverage of Lynch as a vulnerable feminine captive is also reminiscent of Sir John A., the masculinized citizen, protecting Miss Canada, a feminized icon of the nation. North American women may now be soldiers, but their national publics still yearn to protect them from the dangers of the "frontier."

If the rhetoric of paternal protection applied to Jessica Lynch draws on a long discursive history (of which the rescue of the Theresas constitutes an earlier articulation) so too does the form taken by this narration of rape: the sensationalism, the demonization of a racialized rapist, and the unspeakable nature of the rape act itself all harken back to the conventions of the colonial rape scare and captivity tale. Colonial ideology reverberates in the diction Bragg employs to infer Lynch's rape: "savagery," "torment," "horror" (170, 79, 164). News headlines announcing the publication of Bragg's I Am a Soldier, Too fixate on the fact that the book "reveals" Lynch's rape, and this, in combination with the million-dollar deal Knopf signed for the biography, underline the fact that rape, at least when configured nationalistically, sells ("Jessica"). Rape operates in Bragg's text as the climactic event—the darkest of the "tortures" Lynch endured—yet, it remains in the realm of the sensational, connoted again and again by insinuation or in euphemistic terms. Bragg's repeated reference to Lynch's "lost three hours" and their "horrors" and "torments" is, to be fair, partially necessitated by the fact that Lynch cannot remember the three hours in which medical records suggest "she was a victim of anal sexual assault" (96). This last sentence is the only—fleeting—description of the act of rape in non-emotive, medical terms in I Am a Soldier, Too and it is followed by a Stead-like asterisk, after which Bragg describes where Lynch's bloody uniform was found. Stead's "much mocked" asterisks, as Cecily Devereux has observed, mark both the rape of the victim and her "disappearance from representation" (13); Bragg's all too serious asterisk functions similarly in that it hushes any actual description of the act, forecloses upon a victim's recollection of the violation, and contains the rape within an imagined, unwritten domain which allows it to be claimed not only by the victim but by others as well (in this case, the American military). Other injuries are not treated in Bragg's text as the rape is, but are catalogued in concrete denotative terms. Lynch's rape, then, functions as the primary motivation for a text in which it is essentially unspoken: cloaked in shadowy inference, the act remains in the realm of the politically useful sensation, a national act rather than a personal one voiced by its victim. The pattern of inscription and erasure found in Gowanlock's text, and which has characterized Western representations of rape for centuries, persists.

As does the captivity narrative convention of returning the captive happily home to "civilization" at the close of the tale. Like Gowanlock and Delaney's, Lynch's narrative traces a journey from home to away to home again—from a protected paternal space, to a captivity induced by a failure of that protection, to a rescue which (partially) reinstates it. Bragg's concluding description of Lynch has her returning to a yearned for "normal life"—that of the American wife and mother (201). Not only does Lynch return to "the sacred precincts of the paternal hearth" (Gowanlock 3), but she is scripted to replicate this domestic realm by becoming what would, in Victorian parlance, have been termed "a mother of the race." Cecily Devereux has observed that the figure of the white slave (a vulnerable feminine captive) has operated as the exploited obverse of the mother of the race—"she is the 'mother of the race' torn from the nation before she could undertake to produce its next generation" (15). It was such an obverse status—a flipped face, a change of fortune, a redress of "misfortune" or violation—which Gowanlock strove for in her bid for renewed membership in the Dominion's national family. Bragg, having established that Lynch admirably discharged her debt to the nation, mobilizes these worn feminine categorizations to argue for Lynch's deserved retirement to the private contentment of motherhood. It is a story both familial and familiar.

Thanks to Donna Palmateer Pennee for working with me on a much earlier draft of this chapter, to Sarah Carter for her useful historical study of *Two Months in the Camp of Big Bear*, and to all of my fellow *ReCalling Early Canada* workshoppers and editors.

NOTES

1. For further analysis of the anthropomorphization of Canada in 1885, see Adam Carter's paper in this volume.

2. The North-West Rebellion is the conventional name for the Métis and First Nations uprising over land rights led by Louis Riel in 1885, but following the compelling anti-colonial logic of those who have renamed the Indian Mutiny a "War of Independence" (Sharpe "Unspeakable" 25), we might usefully query the implications of this terminology.

3. While there was obviously variation in the coverage granted the two Theresas, racist anti-Métis propaganda spurred English Canadians to set aside their usual differences and unite against Riel, and this relative cohesion is evidenced in the articles about Gowanlock and Delaney; hence we can talk fairly confidently of their general treatment by a nationalist Canadian press.

4. Jennifer Henderson cites Gowanlock and Delaney's agency and authorization to speak publicly as reasons to dismiss the applicability of Sharpe's model of rape discourse to their case (104); but to do so ignores the fact that during their two months in Big Bear's camp Gowanlock and Delaney had no such recourse to speak publicly to Canada, no public agency in this sense, and were vociferously spoken *for* and circulated as objects within the Canadian media.

5. See the work of Jenny Sharpe, Nancy Paxton, Norman Etherington, and Sarah Carter.

6. The French term *peuplement*—literally to people, to populate, or to stock—is more effective than "settlement" in evoking the numerous discursive mechanisms that imperialism employed to regulate and monitor female sexuality and, hence, colonial reproduction (Higginson 174). Michel Foucault uses the term to denote a late nineteenth-century European imperial "politics of settlement" or state racism which mobilized a mythic concern with

protecting the blood of the "race" in order to revitalize political powers exercised through "devices of sexuality" (149).

7. For a detailed discussion of rape and seduction laws in nineteenth century Canada and Britain, see Henderson (114–18).

8. This dedication was printed in the original 1885 edition of *Two Months*, but is omitted from Sarah Carter's 1999 edition, which is the edition to which my citations refer.

9. Whereas Misao Dean has aptly demonstrated how Catharine Parr Traill, in transplanting British domestic ideology to Canada, modified it to accommodate manual labour *as* feasibly feminine, Gowanlock—perhaps influenced by the fairly urban nature of her target audience in Ontario—chooses instead to *efface* descriptions of manual labour from her domestic life in Saskatchewan.

10. Henderson also comments upon the strong rhetoric of indebtedness at work in Gowanlock's preface and argues that it serves as a means of protest against the subtle coercions or moral performances extracted by an indebted subject position (122–23, 138).

11. For more on the discursive constraints facing nineteenth-century raped women in Canada and the "language of inference" they established to (not) speak of sex, see Jennifer Blair's paper in this volume.

12. Henderson arrives at a fairly similar conclusion (although by a different analytical route), noting that Gowanlock's narrative offers a "subtle critique" of the constraints faced by the "freed 'proper lady'" by drawing parallels between the space of captivity and the "doubtful freedom that will be on offer within the father's house" (134).

13. For more about how clothing has functioned as a traumatic trigger in Victorian female captivity narratives, see Derounian-Stodola (154–56).

Historiographical Revision and Colonial Agency

Napoléon Bourassa's Jacques et Marie

ANDREA CABAJSKY

THIS CHAPTER EXAMINES the connections between historiographical fiction and colonial agency in Napoléon Bourassa's *Jacques et Marie: souvenir d'un peuple dispersé* (1865), the first Canadian work of historical fiction to render the expulsion of the Acadians in 1755 the subject of serious novelistic treatment.[1] *Jacques et Marie* is a romantic allegory of the Acadians' tragic encounter with British imperialists. Its allegorical plot is organized by tropes of motherhood and kinship that, however conventional to historical fiction, are deployed here in the service of imagining the viability of Acadian culture in diaspora. *Jacques et Marie*'s revisionary historicism deserves more serious consideration than it has received to date for its literary nationalism which locates the Acadian diaspora at the symbolic roots of Canada's historical identity.

Although it is out of print, when first published, *Jacques et Marie* represented a formative contribution to the movement of French Canadian cultural nationalism that spanned the decades between the 1860s and the 1880s and which helped to shape binationalist discourse in the Confederation era. In choosing to examine a novel that has never been translated into English, this chapter foregrounds the fact that the long overdue project of reconsidering, or "recalling," early Canadian historical fiction is impeded by the number of early texts that, although pivotal to the literary histories of English and French Canada, remain untranslated and are thus too often studied independently of one another.

E.D. Blodgett (2003) has rightly described the author of *Jacques et Marie* as the "now neglected Napoléon Bourassa" (31). *Jacques et Marie* was originally published serially from July 1865 to August 1866 in *la Revue canadienne*, a journal that Bourassa co-founded. A second edition appeared in 1866, which was followed, twenty years later, by an abridged, unauthorized edition by Cadieu et Derome.[2] *Jacques et Marie* survived some of the twentieth century as a heavily abridged children's book, edited by Eugène Achard (1944).[3] As Robert Viau suggests, Bourassa (1827–1916) is remembered less as a novelist and more as a painter of murals (62), or as the son-in-law of revolutionary leader Louis-Joseph Papineau and father of former Québec Premier Henri Bourassa.

Jacques et Marie stands out among early Canadian novels for its portrayal of Acadians as members of a culture intent upon, and capable of, sustaining their cultural integrity in diaspora. Yet it is also representative of early historical fiction in its preoccupation with the connections between narrative modes and communal identity—that is, between the stories that nations tell about themselves and the approaches to history that structure and authorize them. Writing during the socially and politically transformative decades that led up to and immediately followed Confederation, French Canadian authors, Bourassa among them, engaged with questions of colonialism and nationalism by exploring the interconnectedness of history, culture, and politics. Like their English Canadian counterparts, from John Richardson in the mid nineteenth century to William Kirby almost a half-century later, French Canadian historical novelists (Aubert de Gaspé, père, Bourassa, Boucherville, Marmette) struggled variously to fuse or disentangle nationalist and imperialist mandates in order to imagine a bicultural Canada within the British Empire. Their novels' combined treatment of intercultural contest and rapprochement has shaped the thematic richness and ideological capaciousness of Canada's early historical fiction, written in both official languages. Yet recent scholarship on the genre of historical fiction remains largely divided into English and French Canadian disciplines, owing in part to the surprising lack of available translations.

In his foreword to the second edition of the *Bibliography of Canadian Books in Translation* (1977), Philip Stratford famously cautions that it seems "strange that a country like ours which has accepted the idea of fostering two languages and two cultures for over 200 years should have made such a small contribution in the way of translation" (ii). Stratford's cautionary tone is understandable. In central Canada in the nineteenth century, translations often quickly followed the success of original texts, but many works that were translated prior to 1900 are currently out of print. Novels by Mrs. Leprohon, Kirby, John Talon Lesperance, Philippe Aubert de Gaspé, père, Joseph Marmette, and Laure Conan were rapidly translated, sometimes within a year of their first publication, and were frequently reissued.[4] In French Canada, translations of Mrs. Leprohon's *Antoinette de Mirecourt* (1864) and Lesperance's *The Bastonnais* (1877) were so popular that they were taken for French-language originals (Hayne 40). In English Canada, Aubert de Gaspé's *Les Anciens Canadiens* (1863) remains the most celebrated example of a French-language historical novel, translated three times, by three different translators, and reissued under three different titles.[5] Overall, however, early historical fiction is noticeably under-represented in the field of literary translation, so that untranslated originals remain largely accessible to bilingual scholars alone.[6]

It may not be surprising, then, that there exist so few comprehensive comparative studies of early historical fiction. In English Canada, the most recent book to consider the genre at some length remains Dennis Duffy's *Sounding the Iceberg: An Essay on Canadian Historical Novels* (1986) which, as its title implies, presents a short treatment of some of the major themes that have preoccupied writers of English- and French-Canadian historical fiction from 1832 (the publication date of *Wacousta*) to 1983. Duffy rightly points out the need to study English- and French-Canadian historical novels together because, "[r]emote as the cultures may appear to one another, they share preoccupations common to national literatures...[that is,] the imaginative representation of nationalist ideologies" (v). Duffy's study is limited, however, by its reluctance to extend its comparison beyond the existence of these national "preoccupations," a limitation to which Duffy himself draws attention when he admits that he "do[es] not discuss the unexpected parallels between literatures seemingly so diverse" (v). Such a disciplinary treatment of historical fiction unfortunately upholds a "two solitudes" view of

Canadian literary production that overlooks the genre's complicated internal dynamic of intercultural dialogue, historical revision, and ideological critique.

We can learn an important lesson from Maurice Lemire (1970), who argues that it is important to study novels by Mrs. Leprohon, Kirby, and Lesperance within the context of early French Canadian literary nationalism if one is to understand English Canadian novelists' attempts to inscribe themselves into "le mouvement national" of nineteenth-century French Canada (xi). Although Lemire's bicultural corpus is limited largely to three English Canadian novelists, his discussion of Leprohon, Kirby, and Lesperance is valuable for underlining the important lesson that "their works are not foreign to French Canada" ("leurs oeuvres ne nous sont pas étrangères"; xi).[7] By extension, in choosing to examine a French Canadian historical novel in an anthology largely intended for English Canadian readers, I am proposing that it is necessary to treat comparatively the development of Canada's two officially recognized national literatures, especially when studying the historical novel, a genre that is inextricably linked to the rise of literary nationalism in early Canada.

◆ **Diagnostic History, Dismantled Domesticity**

PUBLISHED TWO YEARS before Confederation, *Jacques et Marie* looks back at a nation that is itself looking both backward and forward. The novel's temporal layers (1865 and 1749–60) intersect with its three narrative voices: those of the historian, the editor, and the novelist. *Jacques et Marie* occasionally reads like a history book, for it aims to correct the aporias in metropolitan histories of the expulsion which are incomplete, the narrator insists, due to the fact that many of the documents referencing the event went missing from archives in Halifax and London. In an editorial voice that appears in the main narrative as well as in the historical endnotes, Bourassa repeatedly harkens back to these aporias and informs his readers that he has been compelled to correct them by transcribing the oral tales told to him in his childhood by deportees residing in L'Acadie, Québec, where he was born. Bourassa reminds his readers that *Jacques et Marie* is unique, both formally and thematically, for it represents the first time that deportees' testimonies have been recorded and disseminated in literature. By reminding his readers of the novelty of his historical narrative, Bourassa also calls into question the authority and veracity of metropolitan historiography which, in its failure to record details of the expulsion, commits a discursive "acte bien mauvais" (28) that recalls the event itself.

From dedicating *Jacques et Marie* to the French historian Edme Rameau de Saint-Père,[8] to translating prolonged excerpts from metropolitan documents dealing with Acadia, Bourassa repeatedly attempts to legitimate *Jacques et Marie*'s historicism by resorting to the authority of precedent, most notably the precedent set by Nova Scotia's first historian. Quoting from Thomas Chandler Haliburton's *Historical and Statistical Account of Nova Scotia* (1829), Bourassa expresses his mistrust of official accounts of the expulsion:

C'est une chose remarquable, dit Haliburton dans une note de son livre, qu'on ne rencontre aucune trace de cet événement important parmi les papiers du secrétariat provincial à Halifax.... Dans le registre des lettres du gouverneur Lawrence, qui existe encore, aucune communication du bureau du commerce (Board of Trade) depuis le 24 décembre 1754 jusqu'au août 1756.... On a paru s'étudier à cacher les détails de cette affaire. (364)

(It is remarkable, Haliburton tells us in a note to his book, that one does not encounter any record of this important event in the papers at the provincial secretariat in Halifax.... In the register that contains letters by Governor Lawrence, no correspondence exists from the Board of Trade between December 24, 1754 to August 1756.... It seems as though some attempt was made to hide the details of the affair.)

Situated within the interstices of metropolitan historiography, *Jacques et Marie* aims to expose the gaps in official historical records of the expulsion. And, as the figurative supplement to those historical records, the trope of femininity that shapes the novel's counter-historical narrative undergoes some alarming transformations when charged with representing the material "débris" of history (29).

Two women in *Jacques et Marie*, Jacques's mother, "la mère" Hébert, and Jacques's fiancée, Marie Landry, represent the allegorical and cultural significance of a feminized body for Acadian values. The following passage underscores their importance. A few months before the expulsion, Jacques has already been separated from his family for a number of years, for he has been participating in uprisings against the British. He has fought in Acadia as one of the French Commander Vergor's troops and will eventually participate in the Battle of the Plains of Abraham under the command of Lieutenant Charles Deschamps de Boishébert. On his way to Grand-Pré to rejoin Marie after almost six years in exile, Jacques encounters a group of displaced Acadians whose makeshift settlement has been discovered by the British and burned to the ground. In conversation with the fleeing Acadians, Jacques discovers that his family had, until a few days before, been travelling on foot with them. To his dismay, he learns that two of his older brothers have just died and that his mother died two days before of physical exhaustion and emotional fatigue. Jacques also learns that she was buried by her husband beneath a tree not far from where he is standing. That night, he hears, in the distance, the howling of wolves, so he detaches himself from his regiment to investigate. To his horror, he finds himself fast approaching the tree beneath which his mother has been buried, for he recognizes it by the sign of the cross he has been told his father etched into it to mark the spot. When Jacques reaches the tree, he finds that wolves have unearthed his mother's corpse and are feasting on it—indeed, they have practically cleaned it to the bone. All that remains is her dismembered skeleton. Jacques gathers her remains and deposits them at the bottom of a riverbed nearby so that her spirit may rest in peace (172–73).

The image of mother Hébert's dismembered corpse registers on a number of levels the challenges that inhere in *Jacques et Marie*'s attempts to narrate a violent history of intercultural conflict whose excesses literally and figuratively erupt in the trope of the female body. First, the imagery recalls the narrative's repeated descriptions of Acadian families as "dismembered" ("des familles démembrées"). Traditionally in historical fiction, the family has stood allegorically for the longevity of a nation and the fruitfulness of its culture. In *Jacques et Marie*, the historical novel's key conventions, such as the trope of kinship, change in emphasis whereby the prevalence of broken Acadian families, and their haphazard reconstitution in diaspora, render territorial dislocation, alienation, and heartbreak the features of Acadianness. Because of the cyclicality of recent Acadian history, defined as a series of hostile invasions by the British, the traditional Acadian family comprised, as in the example of the Landry family, of two parents and eighteen children, is now little more than a patchwork of surviving members and neighbours.[9]

Mother Hébert's death in exile and burial at the roots of a tree, itself a transgenerational symbol of longevity, underscore the tension between diasporic routes and cultural roots that has become a conventional feature of Acadian literature,[10] and which, in *Jacques et Marie*, threatens to pull the Acadian community apart. As a symbol of the violence of imperial encounter, mother Hébert's dismembered body signals an important ideological shift in metropolitan-colonial relations that the narrative enacts and that it registers in the ways it deploys its tropes. For example, the positive symbolization that potentially inheres in the trope of mother Hébert, such as that of cultural longevity, captured in both the organic metaphor of a tree and its roots and in the image of a kind and generous mother-figure, is foreclosed by the brutal imagery of a dead and dismembered body. The question of what readers should do with the symbol of mother Hébert remains an important one. We could conclude with Roger Le Moine that mother Hébert is merely an incidental character (19) and thus ignore her. To do so may lead us to draw similar conclusions to those of Rainier Grutman (1997) who complains of the overdetermined literary conventions that disrupt *Jacques et Marie*'s plot (160). To do so may also lead us to overlook the important work that Bourassa's novel performs in authorizing colonial historiography and in making Acadian history meaningful. Nevertheless, in underscoring the novel's overdetermined conventions, Grutman does inadvertently land on an important point. To appreciate the ways in which *Jacques et Marie* revises Acadian history, it is necessary to consider mother Hébert, not in terms of her importance as a character (which is, admittedly, minimal, for she never once speaks), but rather, in terms of her significance as a trope.

In his important study of colonial discourse and literary agency, Srinivas Aravamudan (1999) proposes an understanding of tropes grounded etymologically in Ephraim Chambers's eighteenth-century definition: a trope is "a word or expression used in a different sense from what it properly signifies. Or, a word changed from its proper and natural signification to another, with some advantage" (1). Tropes are thus, as Aravamudan suggests, "transitive," for they "swerve" from a "proper and natural" meaning to another (1). The trope thus implies a process of metaphorizing that turns in on itself—new meanings are produced in new contexts, while residual, or surplus, meanings are left behind as tropes are reincorporated into new contexts. Aravamudan concludes the following: "the negative position suggested by an unincorporated and unincorporable remainder also allows tropes to be reappropriated by resistant positions and redeployed by the agency that comes from those positions" (5). In colonial literature, tropes can thus function as discursive "agents of resistance" (4). Taking as our starting point the understanding that tropes connote a process of displacement as well as refiguring, the symbol of mother Hébert's dismembered body becomes a radical symbol of the materiality of lived experience, that is, of the sustained emotional and physical strains that define the Acadians' day-to-day conditions in flight from their pursuers. The dismemberment of mother Hébert's corpse thus registers in terms of a linguistic surplus the excessive violence that haunts the narrative's attempts to represent meaningfully the lived conditions of the past.

◆ Appetizing Figures, Distasteful Characters

IN HIS ONLY NOVEL, Bourassa, writing as a romantic nationalist and revisionary historian, represents the history of imperial competition in Canada as the encounter between unique and historically incompatible national characters, each the result of specific origins and developments. As a means of imagining Acadian resistance to the encroaching imperialists, the narrative connects the women in *Jacques et Marie* with an idealized notion of a domestic and pastoral idyll. This idyll contains two components: the first defines Acadian community by the pure motives and innate generosity of its members. In *Jacques et Marie*, the Acadians naturally understand their place in society, crave neither material improvement nor social mobility, and are aware that their individual values are synonymous with those of the larger community to which they belong (see Lemire 100; Viau 64–65). The second involves what Mikhail Bakhtin has described as an idyllic chronotope, "a blend of natural time...and the everyday time of the more or less pastoral (at times even agricultural) life."[11] This idyllic temporality, Bakhtin suggests, "possesses its own definite semicyclical rhythm, but it has fused bodily with a specific insular idyllic landscape, one worked out in meticulous detail. This is a dense and fragrant time, like honey, a time of intimate lovers' scenes and lyric outpourings, a time saturated with its own strictly limited, sealed-off segment of nature's space" (103). Before the arrival of the British, the village of Grand-Pré is a bounteous place where trees produce fruit in excess, where the fruit hangs off branches with such ripe, delicious weight that the branches themselves stretch languorously to the ground. The courtship between Jacques and Marie begins when, one warm spring day, Jacques feeds Marie juicy red strawberries. When Marie allows Jacques to wipe "le fruit inoffensif" from her face, she also inadvertently provides him with the opportunity to explore her face, especially "the round of her chin" ("la partie la plus arrondie du menton"; 50). The villagers of Grand-Pré exist as though in their own temporal sphere, in a kind of perpetual present where time seems to stand still. Indeed, the Acadians exist in such harmony with nature that, even after the expulsion, their abandoned sheep herd themselves home of their own accord, although to a deserted and burning village (268). An obvious Biblical intertext, the sheep's return to a deserted village represents, on one level, the Acadians' displacement and longing to return home. On another level, it also signals the notion that, even after the Acadians have been chased from their homes, nature itself acts as a kind of mnemonic that recalls the way of life that is organic to the region. Acadia's idyllic temporality remains inherently antithetical to the post-Enlightenment linear and aggressive conception of historical progress that the imperialists import to Acadia and use to justify their expansionist enterprise.

The disinterment and dismemberment of mother Hébert's corpse by wolves recalls the various images the narrative employs to define the rapacious character of the British imperialists. While some of the real historical figures that the novel impugns for their role in the expulsion include New Englanders (Colonel John Winslow and his troops) as well as Englishmen (Governor Charles Lawrence and Admiral Edward Boscawen), Bourassa chooses not to dwell on their different origins and instead groups them together under an overarching rubric of British imperialism. *Jacques et Marie* channels much of its critique of the British into a fictional character, Captain Butler, whom it defines as a kind of hybrid animal, a cross between a hyena and a fox, as "cruelty united with deceit" ("la cruauté unie à la fourberie"; 62). While the Acadians are described as an "ephemeral" people, the British are defined by their corporeality, specifically, by their bloated bodies and excessive appetites. The uniformly cruel and gluttonous Butler wears an outdated moustache that, we are told, makes him look like a carnivore (62). The imperialists also display a liking for English cuisine, in their noticeable preference for the bland vegetable celery and the distasteful Stilton cheese (277). The narrative's portrayal of such culinary tastes as no less than disgusting represents a barely veiled criticism of metropolitan assumptions about Englishness as a standard against which the civilization and tastes of other cultures are to be measured.[12]

The distasteful English cuisine is also a metonymy for the imperialists' moral character, which the narrative defines as barbarous and devilish and links to its subplot of justifying Acadian resistance as divinely sanctioned. The following scene makes this clear. In one of the novel's most powerful and disturbing accounts of psychological and imaginary revenge, Jacques, who has survived an attempt by the British to have him executed, secretly returns from hiding. With the help of his friends, Jacques sets fire to the presbytery in which the British are engaged in a debauched banquet celebrating the expulsion. The soldiers are groggy with drink and Butler himself, their superior and the King's representative in the village of Grand-Pré, has passed out from drunkenness. The front of his jacket is covered in spilled drink so that when the young Acadian men set fire to the presbytery, Butler is enveloped in flames:

> *La liqueur essentielle, au contact du feu, s'allume subitement, et de petites flammes bleuâtres, agiles et caressantes comme des vipères, se mettent à courir autour des bras et des jambes, le long de la poitrine du capitaine; elles s'enfoncent dans son cou, se jouent dans ses moustaches et ses cheveux crépus; elles s'agitent et frissonnent en serpentant sur cette figure apétissante, comme dans un accès de joie. (289)*

> *(When it made contact with the fire, the alcohol suddenly ignited and small blue flames, as agile as the caress of vipers, began to run along the captain's arms and legs and the length of his chest; they plunged into his neck, played in his moustache and woollen hair; they shivered and tossed and wound their serpentine way along his appetizing face in a fit of joy.)*

The narrative is almost pornographic in its enjoyment and detailed description of the flames caressing Butler's burning body. The consuming appetite of the English is, in an ironic twist, consumed by the fire of Acadian revenge as Butler's body, encircled by "serpentine" flames, quickly transforms into an "effigy" (289). Given *Jacques et Marie*'s repeated descriptions of the events surrounding the expulsion as a "holocaust," which the *Oxford English Dictionary* defines as "a sacrifice wholly consumed by fire," then Jacques's fiery revenge figures as the revenge of colonial microhistory on a seemingly inexorable British imperialism, of imperialism's victims on their imperialist persecutors.

As defenders of the Acadians' proprietary claims to their ancestral lands, Acadian men, such as Jacques, are characterized by their militant patriotism. By contrast, as retainers and reproducers of the displaced culture, Acadian women are charged with maintaining an idyllic temporality which each group of displaced Acadians attempts to restore in its

efforts to re-establish communal harmony in exile. *Jacques et Marie* conceives of these partially restored communities, however temporary they
may be and however haphazardly reconstituted, as pre-modern, pre-
political places where local identity is defined by shared customs and
history, and where the clear transmission of cultural values relies on
mothers themselves to sustain them. For example, by the end of the
novel, Jacques is eventually reunited with Marie, having finally discovered her in a makeshift community hidden deep in the woods of Lower
Canada, only to find that she has taken the place of his own mother as
a provider of care for Jacques's dying father. *Jacques et Marie* can thus be
seen as enacting a typical gendering of patriotic duty that conflates
womanly virtue with cultural integrity, natural with national values.
Such connections between gendered behaviour and cultural nationalism, as well as femininity and cultural longevity, characterize much
historical fiction from Sir Walter Scott to Bourassa, and beyond. Why,
then, re-examine them in the context of *Jacques et Marie*?

In *Imagined Communities*, Benedict Anderson considers the discursive
longevity of nations in his famous discussion about "how and why"
nations come to imagine themselves as "antique" (xiv). The fact that
nationalist discourses mask the relative newness of nations with narratives of antiquity foregrounds what Anne McClintock has rightly identified
as a "temporal anomaly within nationalism...that is typically resolved
by figuring the contradiction in the representation of time as a natural
division of gender" (358). Thus, women come to represent the authentic
body of national tradition. Such a gendering of the nationalist sense of
time has its analogue in imperialist discourse, which casts colonial
societies as feminized and backward in order to justify imperial expansion as a beneficent project of cultural improvement or modernization.
Colonial societies are thus typically understood in terms of their anachronism. *Jacques et Marie*, however, attempts to resist such a conflation of
femininity with backwardness, coloniality with anachronism. While it
is difficult to ignore the essentialist gender politics at work in *Jacques et
Marie*'s static representation of Acadian women, at the same time, it is also
necessary to recognize the important work that the novel is performing
in carving out an alternative, anti-imperial temporality to accommo-

date the Acadian diaspora, work that bolsters Salman Rushdie's claim that the empire does not merely write back, but does so "with a vengeance" (8). Nationalism in *Jacques et Marie* is thus grounded in a nationalist sense of time that is both anti-imperial and purposefully anti-modern.

Continuously relocating the Acadians in geographically isolated and culturally homogeneous communities within the ever-changing and shrinking boundaries of New France, *Jacques et Marie* portrays the Acadians as resolutely segregational. Bourassa transforms the cyclicality of the Acadians' diasporic history into a site of potentiality whereby the Acadians can exist independent of a linear and aggressive imperialism. In the Prologue, Bourassa defines history as a Gordian knot (28), a definition that recalls the intricate knot tied by Gordius, King of Gordium, who resided in Phrygia, now central Turkey. The exiled Phrygians became known to the Greeks as a source of slave labour, so that *Jacques et Marie*'s comparisons of the Acadians to Phrygians recalls to readers that, after the expulsion, the Acadians were used by the British as slave labour, primarily in the American colonies.[13] In tracing the roots of recent history to a mythic past, however, Bourassa also normalizes his conception of history as a process structured by cycles of invasion and displacement and shaped by the inexorability of imperial conquest and diaspora. Such a conception of history works to legitimate the Acadians' segregationalism along similar lines to those expressed by Robin Cohen: "[t]he more ancient and venerable the [diasporic] myth, the more useful it is as a form of social distancing from other ethnic groups...even in the teeth of dispossession and discrimination" (184). By retrojecting recent history into a mythic past, *Jacques et Marie* suggests that the conquest by the British was anticipated by history as is, then, the Acadians' survival in diaspora.

The word "diaspora" derives from the Greek, *dia*, meaning "through," and *speirein*, meaning "to scatter." For the Greeks, "diaspora" denoted a population's dispersal due to the forces of colonization. For Jews and Africans, as well as for Acadians, the meaning of the word changed. It took on a more tragic meaning and came to signify an anticipated return home. Today, the term has acquired yet another set of meanings, which includes a positive relationship between migrants, their adopted homes, and their "imaginary homelands," to borrow Rushdie's phrase. Emphasizing "diaspora" as a "heuristic device," Avtar Brah (1996), for example, has argued that "the concept of diaspora offers a critique of discourses of fixed origins," and reminds readers that, "[p]aradoxically, diasporic journeys are essentially about settling down, about putting roots 'elsewhere'" (181–82). Such an understanding of the term, one that is theoretically empowering, can also make it quite challenging to revisit earlier texts that uphold notions of diaspora that are grounded in ideologies of return, and to resist seeing such ideologies as regressive. It is necessary, however, to try to understand these earlier texts in the historical context in which they were written. That the Acadians will not put down roots until they achieve their projected return from diaspora is foregrounded in *Jacques et Marie*'s abundant images of processions (comprising painful departures, arrivals in exile, expulsions, and funeral processions) as well as images of the various roadways, waterways, and hidden pathways that they use to avoid discovery by the British. While these images are characteristically Biblical in their suggestion of an uprooted, meandering people, they also represent an Acadian mapping of a fallen landscape that facilitates the furtive communiqués, secret departures, and secret returns that challenge British attempts to superimpose their own maps and place names onto the landscape and which reflect Bourassa's larger revisionary historicism that tropes Acadian history into a narrative of anti-imperial resistance.

◆

IN *JACQUES ET MARIE*, Bourassa adjusts the model of historical fiction standardized by Sir Walter Scott, whose Waverley novels celebrate the distinctiveness of local culture while simultaneously justifying the absorption of that culture into a larger colonizing entity. Instead, for Bourassa, the historical novel becomes a medium for resisting the absorptive pressures of territorial expansion. Le Moine has suggested that a stock plot of French Canadian historical fiction is its happy ending, whereby a hero and heroine marry and look forward to a happy life together (17).[14] This plot, he rightly suggests, was meant partly to satisfy the ultramontanist censors of the period, the religious elite in Lower Canada who cautioned against the negative moral influences of novel-reading and only grudgingly approved those novels that imagined the reconciliation of "l'honneur" and "l'amour" through the marriage metaphor. While such a metaphor may have satisfied the censors—and Bourassa, too, for he was a pronounced ultramontanist—in *Jacques et Marie*, the harmony implied in the symbolism of marriage is challenged by the inescapability of historical fact. Instead of signalling the possibility of marital bliss, the reunion in exile of Jacques and Marie, after their separation of almost twelve years, foregrounds the tragedy of recent history. For, at twenty-five years of age, Marie may not be able to have a typical family—that is, she may not be able to have the eighteen children she had originally planned to have when she became engaged to Jacques at thirteen, at a time when she aspired to emulate her own mother, who had eighteen children of her own. Moreover, although the narrative does suggest that Jacques and Marie will marry, it stops just short of envisioning that ceremony. Instead, the novel concludes with another ceremony, the funeral of Jacques's father. The ceremonial weight of the funeral, together with the fact that five years of constant fighting have, the reader is told, virtually wiped out a generation of young men, will alter the traditional form of the Acadian family for generations to come.

Jacques et Marie was published during a period of nationalist resurgence in French Canada that was inspired by the publication of François-Xavier Garneau's *L'Histoire du Canada* (1845–48). Following in Garneau's footsteps, romantic nationalists insisted that, in politics as in letters, historiographical revision was a necessary step towards repairing the French Canadians' wounded pride after the fall of New France, as well as towards strengthening their self-knowledge and collective political voice in the context of Confederation-era debates about biculturalism. While literary critics have tended to view *Jacques et Marie* independently of Bourassa's other writings, it is important to recall that Bourassa published his only novel concurrently with monthly essays that he wrote for the *Revue canadienne*. In a short essay published in 1864 about a meeting of the Art Association of Montreal that he attended, Bourassa insists that French Canadians must realize that an accommodation of national characters, one to the other, is required in order for political consensus to be realized between two historically antagonistic cultures ("Quelques Réflexions" 171). Given *Jacques et Marie*'s publication at the height of Confederation-era debates about French Canada's historical and cultural character, its message about Britain's sustained violence towards the Acadians suggests Bourassa's more complicated attitude towards intercultural reconciliation and the kind of historical self-understanding required for biculturalism to be viable in the first place. *Jacques et Marie*'s revisionary historicism should thus be understood as a reminder to French Canadians that a broader understanding of the fall of New France, grounded not only in a knowledge of the fall of Québec in 1759, but also in the expulsion of 1755, should inform their historical self-understanding. In his lifetime, Bourassa tried three times to find a translator for *Jacques et Marie*. Although his attempts failed, his desire to see *Jacques et Marie* translated may have sig-nalled his belief that a revisionary narrative of Acadian history might not have been unsuited to English Canadian readers.

NOTES

1. The publication of five works about the expulsion, two American, one English Canadian, and two French Canadian, preceded that of *Jacques et Marie*: Catherine R. Williams's *The Neutral French: or the Exiles of Nova Scotia* (1841), a novel that Roger Le Moine describes as little more than a costume drama whose plot is a mere "aventure abracadabrante" (108); Longfellow's well known elegiac long poem, *Evangeline* (1846); Clotilda Jennings's *The White Rose in Acadia* (1855), which Carole Gerson suggests is a "sentimental" exploration "of the event's historical complexity" (122); Charles DeGuise's adventure tale, *Le Cap au diable* (1863); and *L'Acadien Baptiste Gaudet* (1863), published serially in the *Courrier de Saint-Hyacinthe*, whose author is identified as P. de S*** (see Viau 56–58).

2. For more on *Jacques et Marie*'s publication history, see Le Moine 124–33.

3. Achard founded the Librairie générale canadienne in 1940 during a period of intense social and literary activity which saw novelists reject the traditional messianism that had shaped earlier accounts of Acadian history. Achard both authored and edited texts, including *Jacques et Marie*, which appeared in the "Collection pour la jeunesse canadienne, Romans et légendes sur l'histoire du Canada." For more on Achard's prolific editorial career, see Viau 150–55.

4. Three novels by Mrs. Leprohon were translated within a year after first being published. *The Manor House of De Villerai* (1860) was translated in 1861 by her nephew through marriage, Joseph-Édouard Lefebvre de Bellefeuille, as *Le Manoir de Villerai*; *Antoinette de Mirecourt; or, Secret Marrying and Secret Sorrowing* (1860) was translated by Joseph-Auguste Genand (Bellefeuille's colleague at the ultramontanist newspaper, *L'Ordre*) as *Antoinette de Mirecourt; ou Mariage secret and chagrins cachés* (1864); and *Armand Durand, or, A Promise Fulfilled* (1868) was also translated by Genand and published as *Armand Durand, ou La promesse accomplie* (1869). Two novels published in 1877 were also translated prior to 1900: Kirby's *The Golden Dog*, translated by Pamphile Le May as *Le Chien d'or* (1884); and Lesperance's *The Bastonnais. Tale of the American Invasion of Canada in 1775–76* (1877), translated by Aristide Piché as *Les Bastonnais* (1896).

5. *Les Anciens Canadiens* was translated within a year of its original publication by Georgiana M. Pennée as *The Canadians of Old* (1864), then a quarter of a century later by Sir Charles G.D. Roberts, under the same title (1890). It has also been recently translated by Jane Brierley (1996). Roberts's controversial translation has an active publication history. It was reissued several times in the late nineteenth and early twentieth centuries: in New York by Appleton (1890; 1897; 1898), in Boston by Page (1905; 1910), and in Toronto by Hart, or Hart and Riddell (1891; 1898) and Copp Clark (1905). It was reprinted again, later in the century, by McClelland and Stewart in their "New Canadian Library" series (1974). For more on the publication and translation histories of *Les Anciens Canadiens*, see Hayne.

6. There have only been a handful of recent translations of early French-Canadian historical novels, including Claire Rothman's translation of *Le Chercheur de trésors, ou, L'influence d'un livre* (1837) by Philippe Aubert de Gaspé, fils, issued as *The Influence of a Book* (1993). In Québec, *Le Chien d'or* was reissued by Stanké in 1989, while *Les Bastonnais* was reprinted by Éditions des deux mondes in 1984, with a preface by Maurice Lemire.

7. All translations in this essay are my own.

8. Edme Rameau de Saint-Père's *La France aux Colonies* (1859) contains such a sympathetic account of Acadian history that Bourassa is compelled, in a note, to identify "M. Rameau" as a "compatriote" (369). Like Bourassa,

Rameau cites Haliburton's suspicion of missing information at the archives in Halifax when he too finds his research hindered by missing documents.

9. These unconventionally broad notions of kinship quickly became conventional to Acadian fiction. Twentieth-century Acadian novels that revisit the themes of broken families and interrupted courtships include Madame Alexandre Taschereau-Fortier's *Les Orphelins de Grand-Pré* (1931), Antoine-J. Léger's *Elle et lui, idylle tragique du peuple acadien* (1940), Albert Laurent's *Épopée tragique* (1956) and, perhaps most famously, Antonine Maillet's *Pélagie-la-Charette* (1969). For his discussion of Taschereau-Fortier, Léger, and Laurent, see Lemire 99–119; for his discussion of Maillet's oeuvre, see Viau 225–46.

10. See, for example, Maillet's fiction.

11. For her related precedent-setting examination of the connections between the idyllic chronotope and literary nationalism, please see Ferris 130–33. Ferris examines these connections in the context of early nineteenth-century Scottish and Anglo-Irish national romances.

12. In this respect, *Jacques et Marie* recalls its predecessor, *Les Anciens Canadiens*, whose sustained descriptions of characters' culinary tastes form part of the novel's larger aim of cataloguing quickly disappearing French Canadian customs, celebrations, and cuisine. See especially the chapters "La fête du mai" and "La Saint-Jean-Baptiste" in *Jacques et Marie*.

13. The Phrygian mode, we may recall, is one of the ancient Greek modes and is defined by its warlike and religious character, again strengthening the connections between religion and militant patriotism that *Jacques et Marie* advocates through such characters as Jacques and his father.

14. Le Moine's optimistic reading is not uncommon to criticism of *Jacques et Marie* and has been echoed more recently by Duffy (8–9) and Viau (69).

Romance, Pastoral Romance, and the Nation in History

William Kirby's The Golden Dog *and Philippe-Joseph Aubert de Gaspé's* Les Anciens Canadiens

ROBERT DAVID STACEY

TWO OF THE MOST SUCCESSFUL NOVELS produced in Canada in the nineteenth century were William Kirby's *The Golden Dog* (1877) and Philippe-Joseph Aubert de Gaspé's *Les Anciens Canadiens* (1863, trans. Brierly 1996[1]). De Gaspé, writing in French, and Kirby, writing in English, managed to do what few Canadian novelists have done since: write works which, with the help of translation, were as popular with the other linguistic group as with their original readerships. Given this broad bilingual appeal, it is perhaps not surprising that the novels are in many respects quite similar. Indeed, both works are historical novels that revisit the Conquest of New France as a means of understanding bicultural relations in the crucial decades bracketing Confederation. Likewise, both novels are strongly allegorical love stories, the chief markers of national and historical significance being romantic, desiring couples, their families, and the various dwellings to which they are attached.

Despite these similarities, however, the novels express radically divergent views of historical process and the role of the nation within that process. Though both novels have been read as romances and have been cited as exemplary or illustrative of the centrality of the mode of romance in nineteenth-century Canadian literature, de Gaspé's novel is better described as *pastoral* romance. This is a crucial distinction, since in each novel the narrative of changes affecting the various national symbols is not only an allegory of the polity in crisis and, eventually, in transformation, but also an allegory of the *logic* of that transformation. That is to say, the representative couples and homesteads presented in these texts are figures of national and/or ethnic belonging, but their *emplot-ment* within the narrative process of each novel makes them figures of history as well. This essay is concerned with the form of each novel's narrativization of history. *The Golden Dog* embodies a view of history and the Canadian national "family" that, though more pessimistic than most works of romance, is "absolutist" and unequivocal in accordance with a romance modality. The historical argument of *Les Anciens Canadiens*, on the other hand, exhibits a pastoral logic. Opposing the principles of triumph and transcendence upon which romance is based, de Gaspé's novel is rather more equivocal and uncertain. History, for de Gaspé, is an ongoing and perpetually incomplete process of accommodation; the nation is imagined less as a unified or homogeneous whole than as a plurality of *conversations* between distinct parties. Both romance and pastoral have been accused of being escapist (the pastoral especially so). What I hope to show here, above all else, is that pastoral, no less than romance, constitutes an inescapably political negotiation of social responsibilities. The manner and meaning of each text's engagement with the political differ, though, along modal lines. Questions of form surrounding each novel therefore have serious implications, not only for our understanding of the ideological assumptions of each author, but for our understanding of the political and cultural legacy of nine-teenth-century Canadian literature more generally.

In this essay, I speak of romance and pastoral in terms of modality rather than genre. Usually invoking a level of generality not shared by other literary typologies such as genre or kind, mode can be a fairly nebu-lous concept. Here, I have adopted what Fredric Jameson calls a "semantic" theory of mode (*Political Unconscious* 108). In contrast to a "syntactic" approach to literary categories, which is descriptive and taxonomic, a semantic understanding of mode prioritizes an idea of its form as inherently meaningful; that is to say, it insists that modes, in and of themselves, *embody an idea*, make a statement, or propose a concept about human beings' relationships to one another and to the world(s) they share. Northrop Frye's generic theory is perhaps the best-known and most influential of the semantic school. Because Frye attributes to what he calls the major narrative "genres" of romance, comedy, tragedy, and satire a particular concept—so that the form of comedy, for instance, is inherently "about" one generation overcoming the obstacles thrown up by an older generation and the consequent crystalization of a new social formation—Jameson points out that these genres actually function as modes, since each implies a distinct, fundamental relationship to the world. In *Metahistory: The Historical Imagination of Nineteenth-Century Europe*, Hayden White adopts Frye's generic categories, calling them "tropological modes" which, he argues, "underlie and inform" (ix) the work of the major nineteenth-century historians. Mode, White suggests, is a "prefigurative element" that precedes the texts which enact a message in accordance with the mode of their composition. One does not therefore "use" or "employ" a mode so much as contract to work *within* it; it may be useful to think of mode as a kind of register in which certain meanings are enabled while others are disabled. Mode is therefore an inescapably intentional concept insofar as it is, to use a Kantian term, *purposive*. One works within a particular mode because it—and not another—has the power to enable certain "realizations."

According to Paul Alpers in *What is Pastoral*, the kinds of realizations enabled by literary modes vary according to a ratio of human "strength relative to the world" internal to each (44). For Alpers, texts can be classed according to the degree of power they accord their subjects: a differential of control over circumstance. This idea owes a great deal to Frye's apportioning of the modes of fiction according to their heroes' "power of action, which may be greater than ours, less, or roughly the same" (*Anatomy* 33)—a crucial concept that cuts across compartmentalized notions of form, content, theme, and social context. For Frye, the meaning of a particular mode—its semantic content—is the range of possibilities enabled or activated by the hero's "power of action." In romance, he writes, that power is "superior in degree to other men and to [the] environment" (33). Consequently, romance is for Frye an inherently "proletarian" and revolutionary mode that expresses a collective capacity to overcome negativity and opposition. In contrast to this, Alpers defines pastoral as a mode of lost or limited power: pastoral embodies a necessary "acceptance of limitation" (9). He points out that though pastoral shares with romance a basically dialectical, that is to say, binary and agonistic structure, the pastoral invariably stops short of presenting what Frye calls the moment of *anagnorisis*, the "exaltation of the hero" (*Anatomy* 187). While romance is "about" the triumph of good over evil, right over wrong, pastoral rejects such clear-cut distinctions, opposing heroic transcendence with unresolved conflict; it is the mode, not of triumph, but of personal and political *uncertainty*. For this reason the shepherd is the archetypal pastoral character: though charged with certain responsibilities, the shepherd is always at the mercy of forces beyond his control—be it the weather, his lord, or the strength of erotic desire. The shepherd's "power of action," his "strength relative to the world," is, in other words, quite low, being actually or nearly insufficient to the problems with which he is faced. The romantic hero is, in contrast (and by definition), above such vulnerability.

Pastoral deals with situations of personal and political constraint by adopting a principle of compromise that finds its formal embodiment in various tropes of uncertainty. Pastoral singing contests, for instance, typically end in a tie or are interrupted before a final decision has been reached. This tendency to "end without concluding" is especially notable in pastoral romance, whose lack of narrative drive opposes it at the most basic level to romance proper where a quest structure predominates. In this way does pastoral also distance itself from Georg Lukács's reading of the historical romance as the forging of a "middle way" between "opposed extremes" (35). This (rather "comic") dialectical synthesis is no more congenial to a pastoral modality than the dialectical reversal implied in Frye's *anagnorisis*.

The question of cultural synthesis and/or *anagnorisis* is especially crucial with respect to The Golden Dog and Les Anciens Canadiens—not only because they are explicitly concerned with cultural conflict and the military conquest of one people by another, but because they are national allegories whose representation of the nation depends on a particular understanding of historical *process*. Our own understanding of the allegorization of this process largely depends on our sense of each novel's mode. The relevance of a pastoral modality to Les Anciens Canadiens, de Gaspé's story of the loss of New France, is perhaps already obvious. For not only is the pastoral inherently suited to the dramatization of reduced circumstances, of duress, subjugation, and disappointment, its characteristic "acceptance of limitation" entails an ironic approach to power relations potentially attractive to an author who, in Marie Lessard's words, "appartient à la nation des vaincus" (86).

Significantly, however, in her own comparison of these novels, Lessard treats both *Les Anciens Canadiens* and *The Golden Dog* as romances, thereby sacrificing a potentially rewarding sense of their modal difference. Not surprisingly, she sees the novels as occupying similar ideological positions—a notion with which I take issue in the following pages. It must be said that Lessard is not alone is assimilating pastoral to romance, a critical habit that has been encouraged by the work of Frye. Though Frye's "semantic" understanding of genre as mode is indispensable to the way I have set up pastoral here as a meaningful, intentional form based on a particular "power of action," his own take on pastoral is extremely limiting. For Frye, the pastoral is not a distinct mode with its own body of forms and unique "modal message," but the central archetype of romance itself. As a world "associated with happiness, security and peace" where "the emphasis is often thrown on childhood or on an 'innocent' or pre-genital period of youth, and the images are those of spring and summer, flowers and sunshine" (*Secular Scripture* 53), Frye's pastoral designates both an original moment of plenitude and, projected into the future, the *goal* of the romantic hero's quest. Needless to say, this utopian dream world differs strikingly from Alpers' understanding of pastoral. By stressing pastoral's "acceptance of limitation" and its refusal to endorse heroic solutions to social problems—i.e. heroism itself—Alpers explicitly questions whether pastoral could ever serve as the archetypal or generic "core" of romance, described by Frye as "the epic of the creature, man's vision of his own life as quest" (*Secular Scripture* 15).

An "idyllic" version of pastoral such as Frye's has been the dominant view in Canadian criticism, and has invited some readers to see the pastoral as a falsely naïve or politically mystified mode of writing, such as when Walter Pache, in "English-Canadian Fiction and the Pastoral Tradition," defines pastoral as an "escape into a world of illusions" (18). On the contrary, pastoral constitutes a significant literary means of dealing with situations of extreme hardship and radical uncertainty. This is not to say that pastoral is free of idyllic elements. Some kind of utopian impulse is probably essential to the pastoral mode, and through the work of Frye and Jameson we can see the potential value of this impulse. But what differentiates pastoral proper from what might be called "idyllic pastoral" is the latter's explicit intolerance of conflict or contradiction *within itself*, its "monologicality." It is not the absence of the idyllic which characterizes the best kind of pastoral, but rather the presence of *something else* in conflict with the idyllic. This dialectic makes possible the (uncertain) exploration of difference that I hold to be essential to the mode and that makes it such an attractive and useful mode for any writer of historical fiction interested in exploring social difference without necessarily finding ways of transcending it.

Because, as Harry Shaw points out in *The Forms of Historical Fiction*, "historical novelists depict ages significantly different from their own and may aspire to represent the workings of historical process itself, they are faced with the task of creating characters who represent social groups and historical trends" (30). For this reason, there is greater abstraction and a stronger thematic impulse in the historical novel than there is in most realistic fiction. This fact has urged an association between historical fiction and the mode of romance which Angus Fletcher notes is a "natural, popular medium for allegorical expression" (Fletcher n. 221). But we should not let this association overshadow the potential role of the pastoral as well, for as Fletcher also points out, pastoral is "the central tradition of English allegory" (184). In the context of Canadian literary criticism, the connection between historical fiction and romance has been asserted repeatedly, at least since Desmond Pacey's *Creative Writing In Canada* (1952), in which he suggested that the "historical romance" was the dominant mode of Canadian fiction throughout the nineteenth and early twentieth centuries (68).[2] Such a view has further undermined an awareness of the role played by pastoral in that literature. Certainly, a reading of *Les Anciens Canadiens'* distinct handling of issues that are central to the mandate of the nineteenth-century historical novel—namely cultural inheritance, social conflict, and national identity—suggests the need to recognize historical *pastoral* romance as a genre of nineteenth-century fiction. If, as I suggest below, there is something about pastoral form that speaks to a tradition of Canadian political compromise—a tradition firmly established in the nineteenth century, yet which the "dominant" mode of the period, romance, ultimately opposes—such a recognition is all the more called for.

◆

THE GOLDEN DOG opens on the ramparts of Québec in 1748, amid the work of *habitants* who have been summoned to the city in order to improve the city's fortifications against an impending British attack. Though the *habitants* themselves are "ready to risk life and fortune for the honour and dominion of France" (7), their presence in the city represents a disruption of the natural order brought about by the war. Benefiting from this disruption is the Intendant Bigot, head of the Grand Company, or Friponne, whose royal ordinances permit it to exact labour and foodstuffs from the peasants at little or no cost while simultaneously enjoying a monopoly as supplier for the military. Needless to say, this situation is resented by the *habitants*, who at the beginning of the novel are already weary of seeing "their bread taken" by the Frippone (7), but resented also by New France's other great business association, *Les Honnêtes Gens*, led by the *Bourgeois* Philibert, whose store on *la rue* Buade gives the novel its name. Though war serves the interests of Bigot and the Grand Company, it is damaging the business of the Bourgeois, whose sincere hope is for "the comforts of peace [to] take the place of war and destruction" and for the "husbandman...[to] reap for himself the harvest he had sown, and no longer be crushed from the exactions of the Friponne" (563). Not surprisingly, in the conflict between the two companies— additionally fueled by the deep personal animosity, with its roots in the Old World, between Bigot and the *Bourgeois*—the *habitants* are squarely on the side of the *Bourgeois* and the *Honnêtes Gens*. Despite the *Bourgeois'* bourgeois inclinations and city connections, his (somewhat improbable) defense of the interests of the *habitants* asserts an idyllic harmony between their respective sectors of the economy. This "romantic" use of pastoral imagery is dramatically underscored by Bigot, who, when he is nearly overrun by riotous supporters of Les Honnêtes Gens who have gathered to protest their mistreatment at the hands of the Friponne, calls his assailants "vile moutons" (125).

If the habitants are sheep in The Golden Dog, their shepherds occupy the ranks of the seigneurial class. The Bourgeois Philibert, Kirby makes a point of stressing, is also "noble by birth" and lord of the estate of Belmont. In the opening scenes of the novel, "the rich and powerful feudal Lady of the Lordship or Seigneurie of Tilly" (12), and her niece, Amélie de Repentigny, literally act as shepherds by conducting their censitaires from the seigneurie to their work of defense at the city ramparts. Amélie, who is affectionately dubbed "queen of the shepherdesses" (93) by her brother Le Gardeur (whose own name has shepherd-like connotations), embodies many of the graces and values Kirby associates with the ancien régime of New France, especially religious piety, dedication to family, and an unshakeable faith in the aristocratic feudal order.

In keeping with romantic convention, Amélie and her brother—like Archie Cameron of Locheill in de Gaspé's novel—are orphans, and live under the protection of their aunt. Though the Lady de Tilly keeps a house in the city, her primary dwelling is the country estate whose "green woods and still greener meadows" (293) receive the novel's most consistent and intense idyllic treatment. The road that runs through the extensive property traverses

> stretches of cultivated fields—green pastures or corn lands ripening for the sickle of the censitaire. Sometimes it passed through cool, shady woods, full of primeval grandeur—part of the great Forest of Tilly.... Huge oaks that might have stood there from the beginning of the world—wide-branching elms and dark pines overshadowed the highway, opening now and then into vistas of green fields where stood a cottage or two, with a herd of mottled cows grazing down by the brook. (281)

Matching this primordial (and seemingly pre-political) landscape is the manor house, an antediluvian edifice whose hoary exterior gives way to a "profusion of social feeling" (306) within. This "hospitality," the narrator informs the reader, is a "marked characteristic of the people of New France" (306).

But the Seigneurie de Tilly is more than merely typical in this regard: it is *emblematic* of an entire social *mythology* Kirby identifies with New France. Lessard points out that the Tilly estate represents the noble past of New France as a "lieu libre de toute corruption" (92). This follows the logic of romance whose use of the pastoral idyll is inevitably tied, in Frye's words, to "the vision of a social ideal" ("Conclusion" 240). This vision, Frye goes on to say, is usually "associated with childhood, or some earlier social condition—pioneer life, the small town, the *habitant* rooted to his land—that can be identified with childhood" ("Conclusion" 241). Accordingly, the reader is not entirely surprised to learn that the *manoir* de Tilly is a "seat of memories" and "second home" (104) for Pierre Philibert, son of the *Bourgeois*, whose heroic rescue of the drowning Le Gardeur when they were children sparked Amélie's feelings of gratitude and esteem which, in the intervening years, have turned to *amour*.

In an extended pastoral inset comprising three chapters, Amélie and Pierre return to the "rustic seat" of their youth, accompanied by Le Gardeur, the Lady de Tilly, and her *censitaires*. The movement is an explicit (but temporary) reversal of the changes brought about by the war, a return to the "natural" order. As the title of the inset's first chapter, "Cheerful Yesterdays and Confident Tomorrows," indicates, the return home is meant also to (re)connect past and present with the idea of a prosperous future—a providential plot which recent events, including military alarms, Bigot's continuing extortions, and France's refusal to answer the defensive and fiduciary needs of its fledgling colony, have very much put in jeopardy. The engagement of Amélie and Pierre, who pledge their troth on the idyllic grounds of the Tilly estate, symbolizes New France's "confident tomorrow." As foreshadowed by the burst of thunder at the moment of the proposal's acceptance, however, both the relationship and the colony are doomed.

Time reveals Le Gardeur to be an agent of this doom, though an unwitting one. Despite his name, Le Gardeur is a weak character, easily misled by others. Amélie and Pierre have brought him to the country in order to rid him of the excesses and vices to which he has lately become accustomed in the city. In this respect, Le Gardeur is rather more like a lost sheep than a shepherd. Separated from flock and family, he has fallen in with the Grand Company, an association which eventually leads to a drunken rage wherein he kills his sister's father-in-law-to-be, the *Bourgeois* Philibert, exactly according to the plans of the Intendant Bigot for whom the *Bourgeois'* presence in the colony has become intolerable. The assassination takes place in a busy city square. Generally speaking, Le Gardeur's corruption at the hands of the Grand Company reiterates a symbolic contrast between city and country that follows the polarizing tendencies of romance form. Informed that one of Bigot's cronies, the Chevalier de Paen, has made the trip to the seigneurie in order to retrieve Le Gardeur, Amélie proclaims: "Le Gardeur is lost if he return to the city now! Twice lost! lost as a gentleman, lost as the lover of a woman who cares for him only as a pastime and as a foil to her ambitious designs upon the Intendant!" (433). The woman in question is the ironically-named Angélique des Meloises, who throughout the novel is consistently aligned with the demonic aspects of the city from which, unlike every other significant character in the novel, she does not once venture forth. Le Gardeur's fascination for Angélique ultimately causes his downfall, as she is all too willing to trade on his devotion to serve the aims of the Intendant whose connections at the court at Versailles she is intent on exploiting to the utmost of her considerable abilities.

But if the city is a place of corruption, it is only because it has been corrupted. Québec, it should not be forgotten, is also the seat of government, headed at this time by the "brave" and "skillful" Count de la Galissonière (2). Its walls are a symbol of French sovereignty and "Canadian" pride. In *The Golden Dog*, Kirby shows the rot within its walls as imported, having arrived with Bigot following his defeat at Louisbourg. This idea of contamination followed by creeping decay *from the inside* marks a departure from the structure of romantic *agon*—conceived as a pitched battle between the forces of good and evil—in the direction of the gothic's uncanny, whose false appearances and categorical confusions tend to make such clear distinctions problematic.

The gothic turn serves an obvious political purpose, however, in that it enables Kirby to cast the defeat of New France as a *betrayal* of its best by its worst, and not as a heroic or moral victory for the British: "The fall of Quebec, and the capitulation of Montreal were less owing to the power of the English than to the corrupt misgovernment of Bigot and Vaudreuil, and the neglect of the court of France of her ancient and devoted colony" (670). Though the "gothic romance" was already well-established as a genre by this time, the novel's departure from traditional romance form also conforms to the demands of contemporary history which, in the immediately post-Confederation context of the text's composition, required the development of narrative structures through which bilateral hostility between English and French Canada might be minimized or avoided. Had this formal adjustment not occurred, it is unlikely the nationalist critic Maurice Lemire could state that of all English Canadian novelists Kirby "est seul à pénétrer aussi profondément la mentalité canadienne-française" (qtd in Sorfleet 132). I will suggest below, however, that such generosity and good will with respect to Canada's "other" founding nation is perhaps rather more apparent than it is real.

The novel's historical argument is thus inseparable from its gothic effects. These are almost always achieved by an inversion of the idyllic trope. The very countryside itself has been infiltrated by the "Devil" Bigot whose palace, Beaumanoir, is described in terms strikingly different than those of the *manoir* de Tilly. Having made the trip to the remote dwelling to summon Bigot and his men to a council of war at Québec, the young Philibert remarks: "The château seemed a very pandemonium of riot and revelry, that prolonged the night into the day, and defied the very order of nature by its audacious disregard of all decency of time, place, and circumstance" (51).

Beaumanoir may not yet be rotten to the core, however, for hidden in a secret chamber in the depths of the palace is the beautiful and good Caroline de St. Castin—tellingly described as "a stray lamb" (174) by Angélique. Caroline, whose honour has been compromised by Bigot's seductive designs, is nevertheless forgiving, and her "purity of heart" nearly stirs the Intendant to compassion. Being a "lamb," however, she is for the slaughter, and her murder at the hands of the infamous poisoner La Corriveau at Angélique's behest (Angélique considers Caroline a rival for the affections of the Intendant) once again announces an invasion/ inversion of the idyll. La Corriveau, who recites her prayers backwards "to keep on terms with the devil" (472), repeats the performance of her mother, the murderess Marie Exilli, who "fled to New France in the disguise of a paysanne" (364), by dressing as a "simple peasant" in order to gain entrance to Caroline's secret chamber and commit the crime.

The murder of Caroline indicates a final betrayal of the "social ideal" represented in the novel and a last lost opportunity for the colony's redemption. Caroline is

> the only one who, had she been spared, might by her sweet influences have made a better and a nobler man of [Bigot], and, who knows? might have checked his career of extravagance and corruption, and turned his undoubted talents to the benefit instead of to the ruin of New France! Caroline de St. Castin, had she lived, might have averted the conquest of the Colony, which was mainly lost through the misgovernment of Bigot, and his waste of all the public resources that should have contributed to the defence of New France. But it was not to be! (516)

In a fairly overdetermined manner, the death of Caroline—like the breakup of Amélie and Pierre, the corruption of Le Gardeur, and the dismantling of *Les Honnêtes Gens*—both precipitates and symbolizes the fall of New France. But insofar as history—"the ruin of New France"— operates as a pre-existing constraint (the "But it was not to be!") that determines *avant la lettre* the outcome of these allegorical plots, the actions of these characters cannot really be understood (even in the context of the novel's own plot) to have *caused* these historical changes. Consequently, their inherent significance to the novel's presentation of *history as process* is less than certain.

Caroline's death thus marks a transition in *The Golden Dog* from the benign and harmonious world of the idyll to the "fallen" world of actual history, literalized by the fall of New France. As such, though, her death also marks the novel's entrance into a world in which meaning is no longer immanent in life, but outside it—that is to say, the world of allegory itself, a world in which, as Jameson describes it, things have been for whatever reason utterly sundered from meanings, from spirit, from genuine human existence" (*Marxism and Form* 71). In allegory, any natural connection between objects and their meanings is replaced by an understanding of that connection as arbitrary and impermanent, a matter of the allegorist's will and not some power inherent in the objects themselves.

Since in allegory meaning is never resident, never contained in the discrete sign, but somewhere else, somewhere *later*, it is possible to see allegory's treatment of its own significations as a kind of mortification. The allegorical sign must *ruin* itself: sacrifice its own meaning, its own value, in the name of another meaning, its referent, to which it can serve only as an empty pointer. In his discussion of Walter Benjamin's theory of allegory, Richard Wolin writes, "allegory devalues everything tainted by this-worldliness—the material content of its personages, emblems and situations—turning them instead into lifeless signposts of an enigmatic path to the absolute" (66). Like allegorical signs in the general sense, then, the representative characters and couples of *The Golden Dog* are mortified, ruined, insofar as they become most meaningful in their passing away, their negation in the face of history. The characters' hopes, promises, struggles for recognition—everything making up the level of "private" desire and human agency in the novel—count for nothing so much as their own abortive quality. These personal tragedies—bankruptcy, death, unrequited love—are always, in *The Golden Dog*, set against the irony of history itself, the "But it was not to be!" that says, at every attempt to do or say something meaningful, *it won't matter*. Indeed, one of the most striking features of *The Golden Dog* is its tendency to leap forward in time, out of the present of the narrative, to some point in history from which perspective the stated meaning or import of a present situation is cancelled out:

> *Poor girl! she did not foresee a day when the women of New France would undergo trials compared with which the sword stroke that kills the strong man is as the touch of mercy; when the batteries of Wolfe would for sixty-five days,*

shower shot and shell upon Quebec, and the South shore, for a hundred miles together, be blazing with the fires of devastation. Such things were mercifully withheld from their foresight and the light hearted girls went the round of the works as gaily as they would have tripped in a ball room. (191)

This ironic view of history as a perpetual undoing of intention finds its embodiment in the ruin itself, regarded by Walter Benjamin as the allegorical text *par excellence* inasmuch as its "earthbound exposition of history as the story of the world's suffering...is the very essence of allegorical perception; history takes on meaning only in the stations of its agony and decay" (in Jameson, *Marxism and Form* 73). Kirby's description of château Beaumanoir as it could be seen in his own time, a century and a quarter after the (fictional) murder of Caroline, as a "pile of destruction" (516), serves as a reminder that history is a process of ruination in which all human meaning finds its end. The decay of Beaumanoir, which is also the decay of our own "beautiful houses," announces the ultimate negation of all human signification: with it expires "all that was left on earth to perpetuate the memory of the beautiful and unfortunate Caroline de St. Castin" (517). This graveyard sentiment similarly touches the death of the *Bourgeois* Philibert: for, though he "was a man fit to rule an empire, and who did rule the half of New France," the "great leveller had passed his rule over him as he passes it over every one of us" (617).

The irony of history is finally the tragedy of history.[3] But this tragedy points to a final mortification of the allegorical figures of *The Golden Dog* that has serious implications for the novel's *national* representations. In the final analysis, Kirby's historical romance is less an allegorical retelling of the tragic fall of New France than an allegory of the tragedy of history itself. In some sense, the fall of New France becomes merely an allegorical sign for the process of history, a reconfiguration that reduces all the past to a "lifeless signpost" (to use Wolin's expression) on the road to oblivion. Yet to view all history in this way has a peculiarly local effect; it allows Kirby to stand before the ruins of New France in order to declare an end to French history in Canada.[4] The very form of *The Golden Dog* has the effect of sealing off a French national past from a

Canadian national present—of declaring an end to it and whatever powers of self-definition and national differentiation it, in 1877, might still hold for the French Canadian. In a reversal of Frye's claim that "[t]he frequent association of romance with the historical...is based... on the principle that there is a peculiar emotional intensity in contemplating something, including our own earlier lives, that we know to have survived" (*Secular Scripture* 176), *The Golden Dog* suggests the possibility of a particular consolation, for its English reading public at least, in contemplating something that has *not* survived, and need not, therefore, be accommodated.

While consistent with Kirby's well-known Loyalist sympathies, such a view is perhaps less consistent with his expressed belief in "One Canada" as the successful merger of the qualities of both founding nations into a single "mainstream." "The grace and polish of France are needed in the civilization of this great continent by the side of the rough energies of England. Happy the State that can unite them both! Such a one I see quickening in the womb of the future" (417), proclaims Peter Kalm, sage friend and councillor of de la Galissonière. But inasmuch as such a "happy" and "united" state, through synthesis, denies French Canadian proprietorship of an historical and cultural legacy that can only assert the sort of difference abhorrent to a "One Canada" model of national belonging, it manifests itself as a cultural termination that merely reproduces the effect of Kirby's allegorical ruins. Even so, *The Golden Dog* would like to assert otherwise: over against its various "pile[s] of destruction," the novel concludes with the narrator's declaration that the edifice that once housed the eponymous enterprise remains standing on *la rue* Buade, still bearing an inscription commemorating the *Bourgeois*' feud with Bigot. In some way this demonstrates—or is meant to demonstrate—the survival of a French cultural legacy into the present day. But as the text which inspired Kirby to write *The Golden Dog*, J.M. LeMoine's *Maple Leaves*, reveals, at the time that Kirby sat down to write his novel, the building on *la rue* Buade had already become a symbol of the unified and harmonious "happy state"; it was the new Dominion post office.

◆

THE GOLDEN DOG is, in the end, rather *unequivocal* in its presentation of French-English relations. Its idyllic aspects produce or derive from a very un-pastoral feeling of *total* defeat while the novel nevertheless manages to maintain a romantic valorization of the ideas of heroism and military glory despite their passing (in fact, these are to be valued especially because they have vanished). In contrast, de Gaspé's response to the fall of New France in *Les Anciens Canadiens* is rather more balanced, in keeping with its consistent pastoral modality.

To be sure, de Gaspé's novel makes its pastoral affiliations fairly overt, even employing a number of the conventions of classical pastoral, including an invocation to the muses, a debate, a singing contest, an exchange of gifts, and a version of the flower catalogue in which the narrator names all the species of tree growing on the lands of the d'Haberville Seigneurie. The novel's commitment to a pastoral mode of discourse is similarly registered in its manner of narration which employs both direct address and free indirect discourse in accordance with the conventions of pastoral romance. More significant, however, is the tone that de Gaspé adopts: a light, self-deprecating—even, at times, maladroit—manner of speaking (this orality is also key) that demonstrates the purposeful *under-utilization* of the powers of language that distinguishes the pastoral style. "This book," de Gaspé tells the reader,

> will be neither too dull nor too clever. Too dull—well, an author must have some
> self-respect! As for too clever—then he runs the risk of only appealing to people
> with plenty of wit; and so, like a candidate under constitutional government, the
> aspiring author favours quantity over quality in his readers. (21)

This democratic moderation is certainly in contrast with what Leonard Early refers to as the "stylistic excesses" (25) of *The Golden Dog*, and establishes a fitting rhetorical context for de Gaspé's modulated and qualified approach to telling history.

Tonal moderation finds its formal counterpart in the looseness of the novel's plotting, and in de Gaspé's transgressions of accepted novelistic practice—*Les Anciens Canadiens* most definitely lacks what is sometimes called a "well-made" plot. Most commentators on the novel have remarked that though a narrative thread connects the novel's varied incidents, it does so only nominally, with a modicum of logical causality. Especially in the first half of the novel, before the plot (such as it is) has reached the point of the British attack of 1759, the reader is presented with a succession of fairly static tableaux highlighting different Canadian traditions and points of historical interest. The story of La Corriveau, for instance, appears in *Les Anciens Canadiens* as an embedded tale: on the road to the Seigneurie, the servant José amuses the novel's young protagonists, Archie and Jules, by recounting a convoluted story originally told to him by his now "defunct" father about an encounter with the murderess' ghost. What little momentum such plotting affords is further retarded by the not one, but two sets of notes—generally containing personal reminiscences—included by the author. These pull the reader out of the action so that he or she is constantly flipping *between* scenes rather than moving *through* them. Romance, too, exhibits an episodic structure, but in narrative pastoral this feature is exaggerated to the point where the text can appear more like an anthology or album than a story *per se*: "the episodes tend to be set-pieces, of a similar character, often centring on or issuing in a song, a poetic performance, or a recited tale" (Alpers 67). Pastoral form is therefore inseparable from the novel's folkloric preoccupations; it enables de Gaspé to introduce (and therefore preserve) all manner of traditional ballads, folktales, and anecdotes.

Given that the novel's various acts of testimony and preservation are part of a larger "struggle" on the part of the author and his "countrymen" to "keep their national heritage intact" (152) in the face of "the humiliating reproach of being a conquered people" (151), we are invited to consider at least one other way in which pastoral modalities are central to the novel, for in the pastoral, an attempt is made to find strength in weakness, or alternatively, to reveal strength to be disadvantageous in some way. Generally speaking, pastoral promotes a "double attitude" with respect to its characterizations. To quote William Empson, the figures of pastoral are always "in one way better, in another not so good" (14). Maurice Lemire, in his discussion of *Les Anciens Canadiens* in *Formation de l'imagination littéraire au québec*, describes the novel's handling of political difference in terms that are strongly reminiscent of this pastoral double attitude. The novel, he says, endeavours to show how "on peut être à la fois vainqueur et vaincu, agresseur et victime, Anglais et Français. Le roman *Les Anciens Canadiens* transpose dans une diachronie ce qui n'est perçu que dans une synchronie" (Lemire 84).

This acutely ironic experience of psycho-social ambivalence, which stems from a simultaneous identification with essentially opposed points of view, is expressed "diachronically" in the novel in the form of a friendship between two young men, each representing one half of the equation. Jules d'Haberville is the son of a Seigneur and naval officer; being French, he is destined in the course of the novel to be both "vanquished" and "victimized." His counterpart is Archie Cameron of Locheill, the orphan son of a Scottish "highland chieftain" killed during the Battle of Culloden, and brought to Québec by a Jesuit uncle. Archie and Jules meet at school where Jules, out of pity for the "poor exile" (25), invites Archie to spend vacations at the family Seigneurie where, like Pierre Philibert, he meets the woman he is destined to love but never marry in Jules's sister, Blanche. Before long, Archie is effectively adopted by the d'Habervilles who treat him as "one of [their] own" (33) and he and Jules begin to "call themselves brothers" (34). Though not exactly "English"—a point of some consequence, in that his Scots background allows de Gaspé to draw certain parallels between Scottish and French-Canadian history with respect to life under English rule—Archie is English-speaking, and after joining the British army fulfills his role as "victor" and "aggressor."

This divided structure can be understood as a version of the pastoral device of the double plot, best exemplified by those "prince and pauper" narratives in which persons of radically different "walks of life" switch places or enter into some kind of arrangement that allows each to experience life as the other. The two halves of such narratives, Empson tells us, "make a mutual comparison that illuminates both parties" (34). The traditional use of the double plot in pastoral writing is for reconciling class conflicts. In *Les Anciens Canadiens*, the classes are national and *linguistic* rather than economic.[5] To the extent that the double plot represents a schematic simplification in which each "class" is represented by a single person whose relationship to his group is ideal, we are dealing with an allegorical system. In *Les Anciens Canadiens*, character functions as "rhetorical configuation, the presence of idea as statement, a theme" (222), a quality E.D. Blodgett associates with Canadian novels in general, and with Canadian pastoral narratives in particular. Rarely, then, do Jules and Archie act in a manner which does not overtly reflect their group belonging—this is only marginally less true in the case of Archie who serves the additional function of being a cultural neophyte requiring an introduction to the customs, songs, and folktales provided in the novel's set pieces. The implicit suggestion that the cultural otherness that distances Archie from an awareness and understanding of French-Canadian life is analogous to the *historical* otherness of de Gaspé's contemporary readers who are similarly ignorant of "their own" history and folklore is intriguing, and appears to be borne out by the novel's subsequent presentation of historical process.

Yet behind this allegorical abstraction there is a peculiarly psychological model at work, as suggested by the earlier quotation from Lemire which presents *Les Anciens Canadiens* as a displaced manifestation of de Gaspé's own conflicted loyalties.[6] The reconciliation of national-linguistic classes enacted in the double plot depends on the idea of a mental *expansion*, the goal being an enlarged understanding, a frame of mind in which opposites can be counterpoised—held in suspension without threatening to overwhelm the subject. This is also the principle at the heart of *concordia discors*, a quality associated with pastoral writing since Virgil. As the psychological imperative of the double plot, *concordia discors* is compensatory and recuperative rather than destabilizing and symptomatic, which is why the ironies of *Les Anciens Canadiens* do not coalesce in a feeling of tragic loss as they do in *The Golden Dog*, but accommodate each other in a potentially supportive and enriching way. Consequently, the pastoral double plot reveals itself to be the formal embodiment of a politics of recognition in the novel whereby each part, Archie (English) and Jules (French), requires the other for a sense of its own meaning.

The presence of the double plot in *Les Anciens Canadiens* therefore announces the novel's intention as a story of national reconciliation.

But the friendship between Jules and Archie is not simply an allegory of an achieved state; it also serves as the basis for an allegory of the *process* by which that situation is achieved—namely, a war between France and England culminating in the conquest of New France. The double plot is, after all, a double *plot*, unfolding in time—hence Lemire's stress on the "diachronic" aspect of the novel's ironic attitude to those feelings of belonging constitutive of a national identity. As the embodiment of an historical *crisis*, then, the relationship between Jules and Archie suffers an initial estrangement perhaps less typical of the pastoral romance than of the historical novels of Walter Scott in which, as Lukács says, "the split of the nation into warring parties always runs through the centre of the closest human relationships" (41).

Like Kirby, de Gaspé depicts New France before "the fall" as an idyll of childhood innocence, class co-operation, and harmony between humanity and nature. As in Kirby's novel, again, the ruination of this state is presented as the result of a betrayal:

> Wood and meadow were studded with a medley of bright colours, and the bird's cheerful warbling greeted the arrival of spring in the year seventeen thousand [sic] and fifty-nine. Everything in nature smiled. Only man seemed sorrowful and downcast.... A sombre shadow hung over all New France, for, like the wicked step-mother in the fable, the motherland had abandoned her Canadian children. (de Gaspé 150)

Much more than Kirby, however, de Gaspé stresses the role of the *English* in making this betrayal felt. Hence, the loss of the idyll, representing New France's violent subjection to the forces of historical change, is a seen as both a betrayal and an attack. In a perverse reversal of circumstances, New France is orphaned by its "motherland" and attacked by Archie, the "English" orphan, who as a member of General Moncton's forces is required to set fire to the very dwelling "where, for ten years, he had been welcomed like a child of the house, and where a poor, outlawed, and exiled orphan, he had found a second family" (155).

By destroying the home which for him, no less than for the reader, represents the cultural identity of New France, Archie becomes, in the prophetic words of Marie, the "domain witch," "a raging wolf" before whom "the old, the sick, the women and children flee like ewes" (122). Needless to say, this creates a rift between Archie and his adoptive family, and the second half of the novel is largely taken up with his efforts to redeem himself in their eyes. In particular, though, Archie's transformation into an English "wolf" has serious consequences for his relationship with Blanche, who, like Amélie, is tellingly described as a "lovely shepherdess" (123). In de Gaspé's own take on national allegory this rather precipitously introduced love story serves, not unlike that of Pierre and Amélie in *The Golden Dog*, as an instance of "symbolic non-consummation" (Shek 9). As a "shepherdess," Blanche is simply unable to forego her responsibility to the "ewes" whose interests she must continue to protect. As a consequence, even though she loves Archie, Blanche rejects his proposal of marriage, stating: "Am I, a d'Haberville, to set the example to the noble daughters of Canada by being twice conquered?" (241).

But whereas the failure of romantic love and the wreck of idyllic relations represent a definitive and irrevocable loss in *The Golden Dog*, this is not the case in *Les Anciens Canadiens*, whose response to these catastrophes is rather more qualified and measured. Though Captain d'Haberville returns from battle "a ruined man" (191), and his home is reduced to a "pile of ashes," he begins the laborious process of rebuilding almost immediately. In contrast to the images of domestic ruination with which *The Golden Dog* ends, the d'Haberville's home is eventually reconstructed, though on a smaller scale: "After seven long years of grim privation, peace and even happiness began to return to the d'Habervilles. Although they now lived in a building of fairly humble appearance, which had replaced the spacious and richly-appointed manorhouse of the days before the conquest, it was a palace compared to the grist mill they had left behind that very spring" (203). Nothing expresses the modal message of pastoral better than this depiction of *partial* restitution, *relative* happiness, and *comparative* comfort. The very form, then, of *Les Anciens Canadiens* embodies de Gaspé's attitude to the Conquest as a necessary "acceptance of limitation," though not a terminal one. The author's additional claim that the people of New France may actually "have benefitted from the cessation of Canada, for the Revolution of '93 with all its horrors barely touched this fortunate colony, then under the protection of the British Flag" (151) further emphasizes a pastoral interpretation of history which seeks perspectives from which a loss might be reconfigured as a possible gain.

In a like manner, Blanche's rejection of Archie's proposal of marriage becomes the basis of continued relations between them, though necessarily on a redefined basis. (This is in marked contrast with Amélie and Pierre's breakup, which is symbolically equivalent to the death of Caroline in Kirby's novel.) Archie first settles in the area, then, following years of amicable visits, finally moves into the rebuilt d'Haberville home with Blanche and Jules who, notably, has married an English woman (whose allegorical function is emphasized by the fact that she is not given a name). While Jules's situation does serve as a counterpoint to the final arrangement between Archie and Blanche, the latter relationship is the more crucial. Though Archie and Blanche never marry, the pain of this situation diminishes over time as friendship replaces "the more ardent feeling" that had "clouded" their earlier interactions (251). From the perspective of romance, this situation is far from ideal, but this is rather the point. The novel ends with some elegiac musings on the part of its aging author, while the *narrative* concludes with an image of Archie and Blanche gathered with Jules and his family in a "small drawing room" (252); Archie, "now nearing sixty, is playing chess with Blanche" (252). This final image of Archie and Blanche as together, but separate, symbolizes the idea of cultural sovereignty and "intactness" de Gaspé had insisted upon at the outset, and speaks to his vision of English-French relations in the transitional period between the Act of Union in 1840 and Confederation in 1867, which the publication of *Les Anciens Canadiens* preceded by only four years.

Les Anciens Canadiens is without a doubt a reconciliation narrative, but in accordance with the novel's "inner form" the shape that reconciliation takes is decidedly a pastoral one. Blanche and Archie both reconcile themselves to, and are reconciled within, an arrangement in which their differences are not finally overcome, not transcended, but *accommodated*. The final image of Archie and Blanche growing old together, lovingly surrounded by someone else's family, expresses the idea of a political compromise that carries with it certain compensations. The game of chess—fully in keeping with the conventional emphasis in pastoral writing on contests and amusements—reduces national warfare to the benign proportions of a game. Nevertheless, it suggests on-going tensions and negotiations, albeit within a secure framework. Paul Alpers distinguishes pastoral narrative from other kinds of storytelling on the basis of its style of ending which "suggests a poised, even secure contemplation of things disparate or ironically related, and yet at the same time does not imply that disparities or conflicts are fully resolved" (69). To a large extent, then, the ending of *Les Anciens Canadiens* simply reaffirms what is already implicit in its use of the double plot.

It may be that allegory itself must be reread in relation to this final realization, since the theory of allegory, which seemed appropriate to a discussion of *The Golden Dog*, seems much less congenial to the pastoral thematics of *Les Anciens Canadiens*. In contrast to an understanding of allegory as a ruination of meaning, an idea that depends on a sense of the disappearance of meaning into the unbridgeable gulf between the allegorical sign and its referent, a version of allegory based on a less polarized and absolute conception of this relation might be better suited to a literary mode for which a rapprochement between classes is the explicit goal. Such an alternative view is offered by Angus Fletcher who, rather than stressing a radical disjunction between allegorical signs, stresses instead their contact. For Fletcher, allegory "above all is a case where the expression 'extremes meet' is not metaphor" (224). That an idea of meeting might be built into the very structure of one of its central tropes seems most fitting for a text that consistently imagines bicultural exchange as an encounter between discrete parties whose autonomy and difference remain unthreatened, but whose separateness is in some profound sense eased by the contact. This idea turns out to be crucial to *Les Anciens Canadiens,* whose final image of Blanche and Archie expresses a sentiment not at all unlike that of the epigraph of Hugh MacLennan's own allegorical novel of English-French relations, *Two Solitudes*: "Love consists in this, that two solitudes protect, and touch, and greet each other." If, as is often pointed out, the optimism of MacLennan's title is too often overlooked, it may be because its pastoralism is as well.

Finally, an allegory of "meeting" has important implications for the representation of historical process in *Les Anciens Canadiens*. Whereas in *The Golden Dog* allegory gravitates in the direction of tragedy and irony, in *Les Anciens Canadiens* it veers toward metonymy, a figure of contiguity and relation. As an historical trope, then, metonymy expresses a "meeting" between past and present. It opposes *The Golden Dog*'s tragic sense of historical endedness, the past's perpetual disconnection from the present, on which basis Kirby was able to neutralize the cultural legacy of New France by viewing it as something radically "other"—not just "over," but somehow also "away." For de Gaspé, who struggles both *for* and *with* this cultural legacy because it is his own, the past only has meaning to the extent that it is connected to the present.

Admittedly, de Gaspé's stance is far from a revolutionary one. Andrew Ettin reminds us that the "pastoral attitude toward power, though perhaps subversive, is not the substance of constructive rebellion" (165). This is worth keeping in mind, especially given the fact that *Les Anciens Canadiens* has been extraordinarily popular with anglophone readers. But if not quite "rebellious," neither is the pastoralism of *Les Anciens Canadiens* merely reactionary; rather, it represents—or enables the representation of—an approach to cultural difference based on an idea of mutual recognition. Indeed, because *Les Anciens Canadiens* is not unequivocal it stands as a remarkable illustration of the "non-monolithic" commitment to "complexity" and "uncertainty" that John Ralston Saul has recently described as "the genius of the Canadian experiment" ("Think"). While this is perhaps too optimistic a vision of Canadian political culture, it is more-or-less consistent with Charles Taylor's idea of Canada as a "post-unanimist" society that accepts, in principle at least, the "legitimacy of multiple options" (131). Such an arrangement, remarks Jonathan Kertzer, "may produce a fractious Canadian family, but its very multiplicity can have the virtue of guarding against extreme forms of intolerance" (171). In such a society, open-ended debate necessarily takes the place of any final determination, and so Taylor, Saul and Kertzer all look with approbation upon the perpetually incomplete character of the Canadian social experiment. In its expression of a nonmonolithic, debate-driven, inconclusive political philosophy, de Gaspé's pastoral romance can be read as an early, perhaps even constitutive, embodiment of this imperfect ideal.

NOTES

1. For this essay, I have relied on Jane Brierley's excellent 1996 translation of the second edition of 1864. I would like to thank Leonard Early for his helpful comments on an earlier version of this work.

2. See, for example, Ronald Hatch's "Narrative Development in the Canadian Historical Novel," Dennis Duffy's *Sounding the Iceberg: An Essay on Canadian Historical Novels*, and Carole Gerson's *A Purer Taste*.

3. The tragic implications of *The Golden Dog*'s history of New France are noted by J.R. Sorfleet: "For Kirby tragedy is the lesson of history and tragedy is the reality of life" (146). This is in marked contrast to Margot Northey's claim that a "sense of optimism and secure goodness" prevails in the novel (29).

4. While the English, Kirby makes clear, do not accomplish the end of New France, which ruins itself, it is given to them to *pronounce* it. This is accomplished in any number of ways in the novel. But in one striking instance, General Wolfe literally (and literarily) sings the death of New France in an allusion to the most famous ruin poem in English language, "recit[ing] Gray's Elegy with its prophetic line—'The paths of glory lead but to the grave.' As he floated down the St. Lawrence, in that still, autumnal night, to land his forces and scale by stealth the fatal heights of Abraham, whose possession led to the conquest of the city and his own heroic death" (267–68).

5. This, understandably, has been a matter of some concern for contemporary critics of the novel. In "Patriotism and Class Interest in *Les Anciens Canadiens*," Enn Raudsepp quotes Léandre Bergeron as saying the novel is "so anti-revolutionary, so monarchist, so Catholic, one would think it was written by a medieval monk" (107). Her own reading of the novel as a defense of "aristocratic privilege that takes precedence over nationalism" (109) is suggestive, though in my opinion somewhat weakened by its failure to take into account de Gaspé's membership in a professional class (he was a lawyer and civil servant—though not a very good one, given his three-and-a-half year stint in debtor's prison) whose emergence in the second half of the nineteenth century is now generally understood to have been instrumental in the rise of French Canadian nationalism. Also disappointing is the essay's

reliance on an idea of pastoral as *necessarily* a vehicle for the expression of "escapist fantasies from social, political, or economic subservience" (106).

6. Certainly, such a view is encouraged by the author's biography—titularly a seigneur until the system was abolished in 1854, de Gaspé was married to a woman of English descent with whom he shared an extreme fondness for British art and culture, a taste which finds its most obvious expression in *Les Anciens Canadiens*' indebtedness to Walter Scott.

5

Anthropomorphism and Trope in the National Ode

ADAM CARTER

THE DECADES following Confederation in Canada saw the publication of a number of patriotic poems, frequently self-titled "odes," by some of the best-known poets of these years, notably: Sir Charles G.D. Roberts's "Canada" (1885) and "An Ode for the Canadian Confederacy" (1885), William Henry Drummond's "The Habitant's Jubilee Ode" (1887), William Wilfred Campbell's "Ode to Canada" (1896), and Duncan Campbell Scott's "Fragment of an Ode to Canada" (1911). Most of these poems, as D.M.R. Bentley has remarked in his recent study of the poets of the Confederation era, are absent from contemporary anthologies of Canadian literature employed in classrooms and there has been correspondingly little critical attention devoted to them (71, 77). This holds true even for the works by Roberts and Scott who, as two of the central "Confederation Poets," have subsequently become canonical figures for what has conventionally been looked to as the originary phase of a self-consciously Canadian literature. In some respects such a lack of critical interest in these nationalistic poems is not surprising. Such poetry may well strike a contemporary reader as being bombastic in tone as well as formally and thematically predictable. After all, if we want *that* kind of poetry we have the national anthem and who needs much more of it? While criticism has recently been engaged in reading a wide array of cultural production as "national allegory," these poems seem too forthright in their nationalistic and/or imperialistic sentiments to require any subtle exegesis of their allegorical meanings. Furthermore, the excessively nationalistic sentiments of some of the earlier Canadian literature have been the cause for self-conscious uneasiness, if not embarrassment, at least since F.R. Scott parodied what he regarded as a parochial, nationalistic zeal amongst his Canadian poetic predecessors in "The Canadian Authors Meet" (1927), a poem which critiques the literary atmosphere of the day for being too "heavy with Canadian topics" (9) and concludes: "O Canada, O Canada, Oh can / A day go by without new authors springing / To paint the native maple, and to plan / More ways to set the selfsame welkin ringing?" (21–24). If he was familiar with the patriotic poems I have listed above, the young F.R. Scott might well have characterized them as being amongst the worst offenders within such a tradition. Certainly the apostrophe to the nation parodied through triple repetition in this concluding stanza recalls, in addition to the patriotic song that has since become the national anthem, a central convention of these national odes. The current concern with the multicultural, diasporic and even "post-national" in Canadian literature would seem to reinforce Scott's critique of such nationalistic sentiments, if not for all the same reasons.

While it is not my intention to launch a defense of the national ode, I do want to suggest that such works are well worth examining today. The national ode is pre-eminently a *national imagining*, an address to, and a figuring forth of, the nation and as such these poems might be brought into productive dialogue with contemporary criticism's concerns with the nation as, in Anderson's ubiquitous phrase, an "imagined community"—with the interrelations of the discourses of literature and nation, aesthetics and ideology. Furthermore, the ode as a poetic form may prove to be a suggestive one to contemplate in relation to national imaginings, the function of which might form a complement to attempts to understand the relationship between nationalism and mourning. From such landmark texts as Ernst Renan's "What is a Nation?," to Benedict Anderson's *Imagined Communities*, to Marc Redfield's recent *The Politics of Aesthetics: Nationalism, Gender, Romanticism*, historians and literary scholars have attempted to trace and comprehend the central role of mourning within national imaginings. Just what is this peculiar affinity that nationalism has for the mourning of the dead and for dwelling upon death, loss and defeat more generally? The ode, as a lyric which is generally encomiastic in nature, can be viewed as the opposite of the lyric form most centrally devoted to mourning—the elegy. But as Paul de Man once suggested, this may make ode and elegy "generic mirror images" (*Rhetoric* 261) of each other, forms which are engaged in seemingly opposite but perhaps after all complementary operations, just as in nationalist rituals the mourning solicited at the tomb of the unknown soldier or upon Remembrance Day, and the more festive celebrations invited upon Canada Day or the Fourth of July, serve much the same ends in instilling a patriotic oneness amongst the citizenry. Finally, the national odes are productive texts with which to study the operation of the tropes of nation that have recently occupied critics and are of concern to several of the contributors to this volume: the nation as nature, as spirit, as family, but most pre-eminently perhaps, as a human subject. It is the function of this last trope, which I will describe as anthropomorphism (although personification and/or prosopopoeia are equally appropriate in some contexts and will arise in the course of the analysis) that I wish to focus upon in this essay and to consider in relation to some suggestive comments on the role of such a trope in both nationalist discourses generally and lyric poetry specifically. For the purposes of brevity and focus, but also because these particular poems strike me as a particularly suggestive pair for this line of inquiry, I focus on Roberts's "Canada" and "An Ode for the Canadian Confederacy." What I want to suggest, broadly, is that anthropomorphism functions in each poem to trope the nation as a specific kind of singular subject and thereby enacts a violence that is both linguistic and historical. In the final section of the essay, however, I consider how the poems are haunted by the failure of the desired nation-subject coming into being.

◆

ROBERTS WAS A LIFELONG BELIEVER that, as Fred Walker has written, "good poetry could be written on a patriotic theme and [he] attempted to put this belief into practice" (48). In 1942, toward the end of his long career, he edited *Flying Colours*, a collection of patriotic verse from Canada, Great Britain—"Sister Dominions" (*Flying* xii)—and the United States. By this point Roberts was aware that such poetry was out of step with the internationalist intellectual currents of modernism which did not seem to regard patriotism as, in Roberts's words, "a subject quite worthy of their verse" but in his foreword to the collection he defends patriotic poems as being "in the great tradition of English verse from Chaucer down, a tradition demanding simplicity and clarity as the first prerequisites in any poetry which seeks to reach the human heart" (Flying vii) and likewise suggests that effective patriotic poetry is traditional in form, a necessary factor toward achieving the desired emotional effect.

"Canada," and "An Ode for the Canadian Confederacy" appeared in 1886 in Roberts's second collection of poems, In Divers Tones. Both poems, however, were written in the eventful year of 1885 (Adams 56), the year of the North-West Rebellion. Neither poem makes direct reference to these events (and the first poem which dates from January 1885 predates the armed conflicts) although, as I will discuss, the Rebellion appears to be a motivation for the latter poem, which strongly alludes to it in its closing lines. The poems, Roberts's biographers have suggested, are in part a reflection of the enthusiasm Roberts maintained briefly in his twenties during the mid-1880s for complete Canadian independence, a position partly inspired by Macdonald's election slogan of 1878, "Canada for the Canadians" (Adams 56), and partly held in reaction to the political views of his recent employer, Goldwin Smith, owner of The Week, where Roberts was employed as editor and an individual described as the "apostle of annexation" to the United States (Pomeroy 67). By the 1890s, however, Roberts's politics shifted to support the Imperialist Federation for which his former teacher and mentor Sir George Parkin was a chief proselytizer. Indeed as Barrie Davies has asserted: "All of the so-called Confederation poets, and I include Isabella Valancy Crawford and Pauline Johnson, supported the concept [of the empire and of Canada's place within it]" (21). While to readers today, as well as to some anti-imperialists of the time, such a position might seem to contradict or preclude a strongly nationalistic outlook, Carl Berger has noted that most of the imperialists were, in their own minds at least, strongly nationalistic. They regarded the British empire as the necessary vehicle for Canada not only to be a nation at all, but to attain a great national status within the world (Imperialism 4). Supporters of the Imperialist Federation in Canada, employing the central rhetoric of the empire as a family, looked to and actively exhorted Canada as the younger more energetic "son" to assume the mantle of empire from the aging British parent. In his preface to *Flying Colours* the octogenarian Roberts is careful to stipulate, as Fred Walker notes, that "a continued loyalty to the imperial Motherland, although not exactly patriotism, is close enough to count for his purposes" (48). Thus nationalism and imperialist loyalty were not mutually exclusive from Roberts's perspective.

In keeping with Roberts's much later comments on the appropriate form of patriotic poetry both "Canada" and "An Ode for the Canadian Confederacy" are traditional in form. Neither poem, however, follows the complex stanzaic structure of the traditional Pindaric ode, although the latter poem, comprised of three stanzas, may faintly allude to its triadic structure. "Canada" consists of fourteen quatrains with generally iambic tetrameter lines rhyming a b a b throughout. Unlike the other poems I have listed in this group, "Canada" is not a self-titled ode. It does on the one hand, however, strongly evoke the ode which William Sharpe once defined as "any poem finely wrought, and full of high thinking, which is of the nature of an apostrophe, or of sustained intellectual meditation on a single theme of general purport" (qtd in Jump 2). Indeed, "Canada" could be described as an ode insofar as the ode is a lyric which, as Norman Maclean has said, is "massive, public in its proclamations" (qtd in Abrams 137). Yet insofar as praise or celebration characterizes the ode, "Canada" can only with difficulty be described as one. The poem hovers between celebration and chastisement of the nation, a celebration of Canada's sublime potential for greatness coupled with a chastisement for the nation's failure to recognize and act upon this potential. The chastisement is intended as a kind of prod to the nation to begin to achieve its "destiny" (10) and is expressed in a series of challenging interrogatives that characterize the first part of the poem such as: "How long the ignoble sloth, how long / The trust in greatness not thine own?" (5–6). Evidently the poem achieved its desired affect upon certain readers, as W.D. Lighthall, in the preface to his 1889 anthology *Songs of the Great Dominion* which included the poem, declared that it "stirs the heart of every true Canadian like a trumpet" (qtd in Adams 57). The

poem was in fact frequently anthologized, even in a 1891 volume entitled *Younger American Poets* (Pacey 414), and was often known under its
alternate title "O Child of Nations." E.M. Pomeroy's 1943 biography of
the poet reports, somewhat incredulously, that it "was sung throughout
the land as a sort of national anthem" (xix).

Following what Jonathan Culler has identified as conventions of the
ode, "Canada" consists of "a series of apostrophes that name an addressee
in various metaphorical ways" (147). The nation as a whole is the addressee
of the poem and as the offspring of Britain it is figured first as "the
lion's brood" (7), then as a ship swiftly and courageously navigating the
waters of the world under "the flag that bears the Maple Wreath"—the
flag itself a key symbol of the desired nationhood. Somewhat contradic-
torily in this respect, the nation as ship appears to be figured as both a
sailboat, "[t]hy white sails swell with alien gales" (22), and as a steamship,
"the black smoke of thy pipes exhales" (24). As is fundamental in nationalist imaginings, the land also functions in the poem as a central symbol
of nation. One stanza magisterially invokes the entire West, North and
Eastern expanse of the country in its reference to "soft Pacific slopes"
(41), "Strange floods that northward rave and fall" (42) and "Acadia's
chainless tide" (43). As I discuss more fully below, historical battles then
feature as testimony of the nation's heroic character. Further metaphoric
vehicles the poem draws upon in delivering its stirring patriotic call
include a rhetoric of sleep, or dream, and awakening and correspondingly an imagery of darkness and light.[1] Indeed the metaphoric vehicles
and imagery are so various and shifting that one of the only sustained
critical discussions of the poem prior to D.M.R. Bentley's recent *The
Confederation Group of Canadian Poets* (71–78), dismisses the poem in a New
Critical aesthetic judgment for its lack of organic unity. Fred Walker
asserts that the poem's "thought is often unclear, its internal structure
is complicated, and its images show more variety than simplicity or
coherence. Overall, it is more of a logical and rhetorical construction
than a thing of beauty showing real patriotic feeling" (50).

One trope, however, organizes and dominates, we should perhaps
even say *subsumes*, the others in the poem from start to finish, and thus
the poem does seem to be something less of a hodgepodge, and some-

thing more of a coherent tropological movement, than Walker had recognized. This is the trope of anthropomorphism wherein the nation is conceived of, and addressed as, a singular human subject. Anthropomorphism is central in the poem from the first stanza in which Canada is apostrophized as a large ungainly child.

> O Child of nations, giant-limbed,
>> Who stand'st among the nations now
> Unheeded, unadored, unhymned,
>> With unanointed brow, — (1–4)

The trope of the nation as a bumbling, unknown child remains consistent through the first four stanzas until the shift of vehicles toward the ship of state. But the convention of apostrophe itself, so characteristic of the ode, always implies a kind of anthropomorphism, in that it is predicated, at one level of reading at least, as Culler has argued, upon addressing a thing or an abstraction (such as a nation) as a subject capable of comprehending and replying to the speaker (142). Thus, even when the metaphoric vehicles of nation shift in this poem towards other things like sailboats, steamships, and the land, the address to the nation remains constant and anthropomorphism thereby remains implicit.

In the concluding stanza anthropomorphism becomes again explicit. In the first stanza quoted above, the quick succession of four adjectives indicating some form of praise and recognition but beginning with the negating prefix "un" announces the negativity, figured as darkness or night, that must be surmounted if the nation is to mature from being a childlike "Falterer" (25) characterized by an "ignoble sloth" (5) and "indolence" (9) to "Achieve thy destiny, seize thy fame" (10). The success of this movement from childhood to heroic "manhood" (14), from dark to light, obscurity to recognition, is promised in the poem's closing stanza:

> But thou, my country, dream not thou!
> Wake, and behold how night is done, —
> How on thy breast, and o'er thy brow,
>> Bursts the uprising sun! (53–56; emphasis added)

The concluding image of the nation, seen now as a gloriously lighted face, formally encloses the poem within the unity of the dominant anthropomorphic metaphor with which it began.

◆

THE "HISTORY OF NATIONS," writes Etienne Balibar

> ...is always already presented to us in the form of a narrative which attributes to these entities the continuity of a subject. The formation of the nation thus appears as the fulfilment of a "project" stretching over centuries, in which there are different stages and moments of coming to self-awareness...which...all fit into an identical pattern: that of the self-manifestation of the national personality. (86; emphasis added)

In its charted path toward full self-consciousness, national history, it would seem, is indelibly Hegelian. But what accounts for, and what is at stake in, this peculiarly persistent tendency in nationalist discourses—what might be described as nationalism's master trope—to conceive of the nation as, rhetorically transform it into, a singular human subject? Nationalism is arguably modernity's most powerful discourse of citizenry and belonging; in some respects it is all about being a subject, a self amongst other selves. Furthermore, if we join contemporary scholars in dating modern nationalism to the mid to later eighteenth century, then the nation is contemporaneous with modern notions of autonomous subjectivity deriving in complex ways from the Enlightenment and the Romanticism that worked within and against it. In these respects it is unsurprising that the nation should be imagined collectively as a larger-scale version of what its citizenry are interpellated to become individually. Yet to recognize this fact is to invite further questions, such as what kind of subject, specifically, is being interpellated with the invocation of such a trope and what agenda is being served in the imagining of the nation as a particular kind of singular subject?

In his foreword to the second edition of Imagined Communities, Benedict Anderson notes that a key shortcoming of the work's first edition was its failure to recognize and account for "an important structural alignment of post 1820s nationalist 'memory' with the inner premises and conventions of modern biography and autobiography" (xiv), a perceived shortcoming he attempts to address with a couple of thought-provoking pages in a section entitled "The Biography of Nations" which concludes the later edition. National history is, Anderson here contends, conceived of biographically as the narrative of a maturing individual. As a new form of consciousness which, however, does not generally recognize itself as a new form of consciousness, nationalism requires a narrative to construct retrospectively its origins, continuities, and development, to define who "he" or "she" is, just as the adolescent is taught to recognize herself in the yellowing photographs of the happily gurgling infant on the sofa and the toddler on the tricycle. Thus from the anonymous millions living and dead who share, or once shared, the geographical space now defined as a nation, exemplary lives, achievements and sacrifices are selected and emplotted to create a narrative characteristic, even genetically deterministic, of "us" (204–6). The key effect of history as a national *biography* is that these lives, achievements, sacrifices have now become, in the words with which Anderson concludes the book, "our own" (206).

Roberts's "Canada," in figuring the nation as a maturing subject and in actively exhorting the nation to come to a self-awareness of itself, which is to say of its inner greatness, likewise sketches a suitably heroic biography for this subject from carefully selected fragments of history which serve as further synecdoches of the nation's character.[2] Shifting out of the metaphors of the ship of state, the poem invokes the nation's past as that which should convince it of its greatness of character:

> O Falterer, let thy past convince
> Thy future,—all the growth, the gain,
> The fame since Cartier knew thee, since
> Thy shores beheld Champlain! (25–28)

Canada's biography is here instigated through an exchange of gazes between mature, active European subjects and an infantile Canadian subject. The poem proceeds from this supposedly originary moment of the Canadian nation in its discovery by Europeans, to eulogize the heroism and sacrifice of the nation in exemplary battles from "Québec" (30) to "Queenston" (34), "Lundy's Lane" (34), "Chrysler's Farm" (39), and "Chateauguay" (39). According to this biographical sketch the nation needs to attain self-consciousness of its manliness because it has already long been acting as a man. As is characteristic of so much biography, this is not a narrative of fundamental change or discontinuity but of the discovery of an underlying identity and continuity—"the self-mani-festation of the national personality" of which Balibar speaks.

In this brief history the French defeated at Québec are commended along with the English:

> *Montcalm and Wolfe! Wolfe and Montcalm!*
> *Quebec, thy storied citadel*
> *Attest in burning song and psalm*
> *How here thy heroes fell! (29–32)*

In the retrospective biography of the nation the defeated French figure not as combatants against the establishment of English rule in North America, but as "fellow Canadians" whose heroism and sacrifice figure as essential attributes of the nation's personality. The geopolitical strug-gles of globalizing empires become transformed into what Anderson has aptly described as "the reassurance of fratricide" (199)—the peculiar pathos of brother slaying brother which must be ceaselessly remem-bered and forgotten in producing the powerful bonds of nationhood.[3] As David Bentley has remarked in an insightful analysis of the poem, the historical references work to provide "an hallucination of racial reconciliation that deploys an invented tradition to displace the harsh realities of Canada's past and present" (76).

Anderson's reflections on how nations are conceived of in terms of the life of an individual are not, in the main, critically motivated. He is attempting, importantly, to understand the nature and the powerful appeal of what he regards as nationalism's relatively new form of consciousness. Nationalism's success in troping the many as the one and the aleatory and fragmentary as the genetically destined, through history conceived of as a singular biography, must simply be understood as one of its key structural devices. Other scattered reflections upon the function of anthropomorphism in national discourses, however, have tended to invite a more critical attitude toward this rhetorical manouevre. For Balibar, "such a representation clearly constitutes a retrospective illusion, but it also expresses constraining institutional realities" (86). One key aspect of the illusion is that each nation is seen to consist of a particular "invariant substance" (86) which determines its personality and which is passed on from generation to generation. To trope the nation as a human subject and, furthermore, a national personality, is an essentializing and totalizing gesture which falsely covers over historical contradictions and discontinuities as well as the structural inequalities and differences of race, gender and class. Ian Balfour, in an important study-in-progress on the relation of the nation to the aesthetics of the sublime (an aesthetic category which is strongly invoked to figure the nation in both of Roberts's poems), reinforces Balibar's critical view of this process noting that "it is not so fortuitous that this infinitizing of the nation [in the aesthetics of the sublime upon which so many national imaginings draw] coexists with the imperative to represent that nation as a subject. The heterogeneity of any nation resists representation in the modality of a subject, even if it is ceaselessly forced to occupy such a position, a subject position so to speak" (27). In the context of the study of Canadian literature, Jonathan Kertzer likewise points to how social and historical contradictions are reduced to the more comforting realm of psychology in the personified nation:

> ...a common figure of speech (Canada loyally took up arms in the First World War to defend her Mother) permits political strains and social contradictions to be recast in psychological terms, thereby making them susceptible to psychological resolution. History may present a panorama of irreconcilable conflicts, but when they are framed by a psychological model—the nation as person—they can be resolved as if they were merely personal problems. (6)

Anticipating this more recent critical inquiry is Northrop Frye. Invited to give the Whidden Lectures at McMaster University in Canada's centennial year of 1967, later published as *The Modern Century*, Frye clearly felt pressure to speak on a national theme, to give a kind of address to the Canadian nation. He would, however, not meet this expectation, choosing rather to discuss the culture of the preceding "modern century" more broadly. In defending his choice of topic at the outset of these lectures, Frye makes some very suggestive remarks about some of the dangers of a conventional rhetoric of nation which, even in the seemingly benign, subdued context of Canadian cultural nationalism, he maintained that one should remain aware of and maintain a critical distance from. Amongst other things he singles out the anthropomorphizing of the nation in nationalist discourse, a rhetorical manoeuvre which he saw as pervasive and potentially pernicious, in part because such rhetoric is seldom recognized or examined as figural but comes to be taken literally as a being. Frye writes:

> *There is for instance, the assumption that Canada has, in its progress from colony to nation, grown and matured* like an individual: *that to be colonial means to be* immature *and to be national means to be* grown up. *A colony or a province, we are told, produced a naive, imitative, and prudish culture; now we have become a nation, we should start producing sophisticated, original, and spontaneous culture.... Analogies between the actual growth of an individual and the supposed growth of a society may be illuminating, but they must always be, like all analogies, open to fresh examination. The analogy is a particularly tricky form of rhetoric when it becomes the basis of an argument rather than merely a figure of speech.* (15–16; emphasis added)

At worst, Frye suggests, such a forgotten figure is not "open to fresh examination"; it reifies social reality, closes the society off to the kinds of reconceptualizations and renegotiations that would characterize it as multiple, open and democratic. Frye states in his concluding comments to these lectures that the "Canada to which we really do owe loyalty is the Canada that we have failed to create" (122–23). It is the "buried or uncreated ideal" of a less alienated world which "all nations have" (122) as a utopian impulse, however faint and however subject to degradation. Thus Frye cautions us to resist the reification and totalization embodied in the trope of the nation as a biologically developing individual. Although Frye has been broadly critiqued over the last two decades for a universalizing humanism, he here demonstrates himself as conscious as any poststructuralist of the possible ideological entrapments of anthropomorphizing metaphors of the nation.

Frye here sounds curiously, though suggestively, like the Paul de Man of such late essays as "Anthropomorphism and Trope in the Lyric" (whence I borrow my title) and "Autobiography As De-Facement," wherein de Man similarly warns of the dangers inherent in, but also the inevitability of, assertions of an unbroken continuity between the linguistic and tropological, on the one hand, and the phenomenological (the experiencing subject) on the other hand. Through such elisions language becomes anthropomorphized as *voice*, and as a name which assumes a *face*.[4] For de Man the unbroken continuity between the linguistic and the phenomenal can only be asserted through a violence which de Man equates with ideology (*Resistance* 11). Since de Man is specifically concerned with anthropomorphism in the lyric, touching at one point specifically on the ode, his theoretical reflections provide a useful bridge between the more general reflections on anthropomorphism in nationalist discourses by the theorists touched on above, and Roberts's patriotic poems. At the same time, Roberts's poems illustrate perhaps more clearly than any text discussed by de Man in these essays, the potential dangers inherent in such a process. Lyric and autobiography are two "figure[s] of reading" (*Rhetoric* 70)—de Man resisted the designation of either as genres—that most strongly compel the assertion of the continuity of the linguistic and the human. Roberts's "Canada" as a lyric which sketches something of an (auto)biography[5] would appear, then, doubly to compel such an elision, and since the name which assumes voice and face is as vast, complex and political a construct as a nation's, the ideological implications of such a process ought to be particularly suggestive.

"Anthropomorphism," de Man writes,

is not just a trope but an identification on the level of substance. It takes one entity for another and thus implies the constitution of specific entities prior to their confusion, the taking of something for something else that can then be assumed to be given. Anthropomorphism freezes the infinite chain of tropological transformations and propositions into one single assertion or essence which, as such, excludes all others. It is no longer a proposition but a proper name. (Rhetoric 241)

Following the process de Man here traces, Roberts's "Canada," as I have suggested above, likewise gathers the poem's "chain of tropological transformations" (darkness, light, a ship, land, battles) into the "single assertion or essence" of the nation as subject, a subject whose face, as the poem concludes, is just coming into the light as "o'er thy brow / Bursts the uprising sun" (55–56). "Canada" becomes more than a mere sign subject to potentially endless significations and tropological configurations, but a proper name with a singular human face. Furthermore, the name and face will be in possession of a voice. "Thy sons await thy call" (44), the poem declares and the poem's concluding image of the nation-subject gloriously entering the light intimates that this call will not be long in reaching them.

The dominant political implications of this rhetorical manoeuvre in the poem seem unmistakable. Not only is the nation-subject, as will be abundantly clear from the discussion thus far, a specifically male subject, it is a specifically racialized subject:

> The Saxon force, the Celtic fire,
>> These are thy manhood's heritage!
> Why rest with babes and slaves? Seek higher
>> The place of race and age. (13–16)

The essentialism enacted in troping sign as being, is further enacted to trope being as subject to the determinations of superior and inferior essences of "race" (16) or "blood" (20) as the poem articulates the widespread ideology of a Canada which properly belongs to white Northern European races.[6] In a chiasmatic crossing, the racialized subject now stands not as effect of language but as an entity which exists prior to it as its origin, as that which in an ideological enclosure, as de Man says, "can then be assumed to be given."

◆

"An Ode for the Canadian Confederacy" is a shorter poem written later in the same year of 1885. The poem consists of three twelve-line stanzas with a regular but slightly more complex pattern of rhyme and line length in each stanza. In key respects, however, the poem recalls the earlier "Canada." Once again there is a series of apostrophes to the nation and again the nation is anthropomorphized as the "Child of Nations" (36), although this now occurs in the last line of the poem as opposed to the first. The nation's attributes in terms of its sublimely powerful landscape are celebrated as "iron coasts by rages of seas unjarred" (28), and these external attributes become the outer image of the "strong hearts" (25) of its citizens. Thus anthropomorphism and naturalization function, as they often do in nationalist imaginings, to assert a mirroring dialectic between subject and object, the people and the land.

As with the earlier poem, but even more centrally, "An Ode for the Canadian Confederacy" employs the trope of awakening. The first lines of the first and second stanzas exhort the nation to awake from dream: "Awake, my country, the hour is great with change!.... Awake, my country, the hour of dreams is done" (1, 13). As with the earlier poem, the trope of awakening relies upon corresponding vehicles of darkness, "this gloom which yet obscures the land" (2) and light, "the keen confronting sun" (15), the "morn of splendour" (16) and so forth. Once again what the nation is to awake to is a self-consciousness of "the greatness of thy fate" (14), a fate of such sublime proportions that it can indeed inspire "dread" (14) but which must not for that reason be shirked by "faint souls" (15). This awakening is once again specifically figured as the achievement of name and the recognition of Canada, in an imagined realm of nation-subjects, by the other nations of the world: "This name which yet shall grow / Till all the nations know / Us" (21–23).

The trope of the nation attaining its articulate voice concomitantly with this achievement of name is also more central to this later poem.[7] Across the entire nation the poem asserts: "A deep voice stirs, vibrating in men's ears" (5). As Derrida has taught through his early deconstructions of the "phonologocentrism" of western metaphysics, there is no more fetishized sign than voice for the living, breathing presence of a subject and for the stable, irrefutable meaning that such a subject is believed to provide with this voice. Thus it is unsurprising that the poem's anthropomorphism should centre around attending to such a national voice. I will return in the final section of the paper to consider the thematics of voice and voicelessness in greater detail.

History is at once more absent in this latter national ode—there are no specifically historical references such as we examined in the earlier poem—and yet more menacingly present, lurking in the distance, toward the Western horizons invoked in the opening stanza with its militaristic overtones: "giant peaks our western bounds command" (4). Both poems centre around awakening to a destiny which while assuredly sublime remains, perhaps of necessity, vague; there can be no one thing to do, nor even a short list, in achieving such greatness. Yet in this latter poem, the call to awaken seems decidedly more urgent—"the hour is great with change" (1)—and, the intimations of what must be done, decidedly more violent. The difference in tone is suggested at the outset by the titles of the two poems. Whereas the first forthrightly asserts the singular name "Canada," the latter's "Canadian Confederacy" employs the nation's name only as an adjective modifying a noun designating a collection of parts, hence indicating the possibility of the fragmentation of the collection which haunts this ode as historically it has haunted Canadian nationalism. Furthermore, to refer to Canada as a "confederacy," rather than as a dominion, has an unconventional ring and may evoke, with the poem's publication less than two decades after the American Civil War, the name adopted by the secessionist Southern states and perhaps as well such influential First Nations confederations as those of the Iroquois peoples. In the events of 1885 in Canada such a reference to secession and alternate confederations would furthermore, and more immediately and menacingly, invoke Louis Riel's secessionist provisional government of Métis and First Nations peoples declared March 18, 1885, for which Riel invented the name "Exovedate," to mean "taken from the Flock" (Morton 76), a declaration of the very fragmentation Roberts's national ode exhorts against.

As the poem reaches its conclusion, it becomes progressively more explicit that the call to the nation to self-consciousness, maturity and the achievement of voice and name, is simultaneously a call to violence, including blood sacrifice, in the name of the nation to quell the threat of dissolution posed by rebellion. This begins with a seemingly benign reference in the penultimate line of the second stanza which asserts that Canada, in becoming recognized as a nation, must show "heart and *hand* / Loyal to our native earth, our own Canadian land!" (23–24; emphasis added). That loyalty demonstrated by the people's "hand" functions as a metonymy for a willingness to use power against a fragmenting insurrection becomes more clear in the final stanza's opening apostrophe: "O strong hearts, guarding the birthright of our glory, / Worth your best blood this heritage that ye guard!" (25–26). Further references to the sublimity of the landscape follow to reinforce the value of this heritage followed by an even more direct allusion to the conflict for territory and political control: "Shall not our love this rough, sweet land make sure, / Her bounds preserve inviolate, though we die?" (31–32).

The final four lines of the poem parallel the close of the earlier "Canada" insofar as this poem likewise concludes with the image of the nation becoming a proper name and hence achieving its recognition on a world stage. Once again, however, the tone and imagery of the latter poem is decidedly distinct. Whereas the first poem concludes with the image of the nation's face emerging into the light of the "uprising sun" (56), this poem concludes:

> O Strong hearts of the North,
> Let flame your loyalty forth,
> And put the craven and base to an open shame,
> Till earth shall know the Child of Nations by her name! (33–36)

The image of light required to complete the poem's movement from dream to wakeful self-consciousness is no longer that of the natural sun but of flame which (as in the myth of Prometheus) can connote technology and destruction as surely as it can connote the passions of the heart or the rays of consciousness, especially when the word appears as a verb in the imperative: "Let flame your loyalty forth." The connotations of technology and violence are appropriate enough insofar as it was a newly-built CPR railway line as well as the superior weaponry of an industrialized central Canada which greatly enabled the defeat of the Rebellion.

The de Manian perspective through which I have partly framed the analysis of these poems suggests that the violence invoked in the closing lines of the poem as the text asserts the nation's achievement of a recognizable proper name, which likewise implies a recognizable face attached to this name, is not simply coincidental but paradigmatic of all monumentalized, anthropomorphized assertions of meaning. Roberts's national odes likewise attest compellingly to the validity of de Man's remarks in his late essays concerning not only the ideology of the aesthetic, but more specifically that such violence must be understood as belonging to the materiality of history as fully as to linguistic, textual operations and the meanings we impose upon these operations. If Roberts's "craven and base" are indeed the rebellious Métis and First Nations peoples of 1885 and the challenge they seemed to pose, from a certain dominant power perspective, not only to the nation's geographical imaginary ("*A mare usque ad mare*") but also to its racial imaginary ("the Saxon force, the Celtic fire"), then the nation conceived as singular human subject attempts to violently expel this heterogeneity as the condition of the possibility of merging name and voice with the singularity of a human face. In this respect "shame" and "name" are aptly rhymed in Roberts's concluding couplet as the expulsing, exteriorizing gesture of shaming functions as a necessary precondition to achieving the interiority of a unified consciousness.[8]

It will be worthwhile to consider briefly, in conclusion to this section, the implications of the ways the nation is engendered in these two poems. Anne McClintock's comments on conventional gender roles assigned within nationalist discourses are germane to comprehending the gender divisions here. McClintock writes: "Women are represented as the atavistic and authentic body of national tradition (inert, backward-looking and natural), embodying nationalism's conservative principle of continuity" (359). Thus, as territory requiring protection by those who properly possess it against improper violation, the nation in the above passage from "An Ode for the Canadian Confederacy" is engendered female. Such protection will concomitantly ensure the continuity of national tradition and national boundaries, albeit a very short-lived tradition in the Canada of 1885. It is "Her bounds" that the citizenry are to "preserve inviolate" (32) and with this successfully achieved it is "her name" that the "earth shall know" (36).[9] "Men, by contrast," McClintock argues, "represent the progressive agent of national modernity (forward-thrusting, potent and historic), embodying nationalism's progressive, or revolutionary principle of discontinuity" (359). This male gender role for the nation is likewise reproduced in both poems. The citizenry in "An Ode for the Canadian Confederacy" who are called to action, are male; the ears attuned to the nation's forthcoming call are specifically "men's ears" (5). The "allegory of manly maturation" (Coleman 84) rehearsed in "Canada" is all the more resoundingly male as the nation is prodded to awareness of "thy manhood's heritage" (14) contained in the nation's superior racial strength and its heroic actions in battle. In realizing itself to be a man already Canada will continue to act like a man and become a recognized agent on the world stage. These differently engendered aspects of the nation trouble both poems' interpellation of a singular nation-subject by implicitly inscribing gender hierarchies and divisions within the rhetoric of national unity, divisions and hierarchies which further reproduce those of the poems' historic moment. Historically, the disenfranchised and domesticated woman is, officially at least, denied almost all agency, national, heroic, historic or otherwise. Furthermore, as I shall trace in the final section of this paper, a division within the nation, here engendered as the division between a masculinized national agency and an inert, feminized national body, haunts the rhetoric of national unity in various ways, most notably as the division between the living and the dead, suggesting an ineradicable divisiveness and instability at the nation's core.

◆

"Between life and death, nationalism has as its own proper space the experience of haunting. There is no nationalism without some ghost."
—Jacques Derrida "The Onto-Theology of National Humanism" (15)[10]

THE MAIN LINE of my analysis has focused upon how Roberts's nationalistic poems, by interpellating the nation as a particular kind of human subject, gesture toward a singular, monumentalized nation and how this process enacts a linguistic violence which simultaneously bears the traces of the violence of its historical moment. Any reading lessons drawn from de Man, however, would be radically incomplete without some concomitant attention to what was, perhaps, his central concern, namely, to "demonstrate...the impossibility of closure and of totalization (that is, the impossibility of coming into being) of all textual systems made up of tropological substitution" (*Rhetoric* 71). I wish, then, to conclude my analysis with some consideration of the compelling ways in which Roberts's poems demonstrate such an impossibility, a process de Man variously named "disfiguration" or "de-facement" (*Rhetoric* 76, 81). To pay attention to the poems' own "de-facements" is not to exonerate the political vision expressed in the poems by suggesting that the vision is fundamentally double edged or "indeterminate"; I do not think it is. Such attention, rather, may further open a space for the critique of such a vision by drawing out the failures that inhere its very articulation.

A trope which is central to both of Roberts's poems, part and parcel of their anthropomorphic address to the nation as a human subject, is prosopopoeia, which handbooks of literature sometimes define as synonymous with personification (Abrams 69) but which de Man, more tellingly in this context, understands specifically as "the fiction of an apostrophe to an absent, deceased or voiceless entity which posits the possibility of the latter's reply and confers upon it the power of speech" (*Rhetoric* 76).

De Man further suggests that a "latent threat...inhabits prosopopoeia, namely, that by making the death [sic] speak, the symmetrical structure of the trope implies, by the same token, that the living are struck dumb, frozen in their own death" (*Rhetoric* 78). De Man's statement is as elliptical and challenging as it is intriguing.

The threat of prosopopoeia, but also its negative insight, seems partly to inhere in the realization of the impossibility of a tropological, linguistic representation, or construct (a nation in our case) coming into being in a fully living, present, face-to-face manner. Nations have existence but, as I will elaborate, not of this kind. Insofar as we identify with such a voiceless abstraction, as nationalistic poetry solicits us to do, we risk in turn being "struck dumb, frozen in [our] own death." In the following, concluding look at Roberts's national odes I read the "intimations of mortality" (to borrow David Krell's twist on Wordsworth) in these poems, contained in the references to voicelessness, meaninglessness, absence and death, as registering an "ontological instability" (Redfield 58) in the nation as it strives to recognize itself, and unify itself, as a singular, living subject and yet simultaneously recognizes that it is not and cannot be such a subject. Following Marc Redfield's deconstructively inflected reading of Anderson, I understand the ways the poems draw attention to such negativity and death as part of nationalism's work of mourning whereby it attempts, on the one hand, to recoup such loss for the nation's "continuous arc of an unfolding identity" (54) and yet, on the other hand, how it glimpses in such moments the impossibility of recouping such loss, glimpses the limits of national imaginings which both produce and disfigure them.

Despite their clarion patriotic calls to a nation, figured as being in the bloom of youth and vitality, to attain maturity, self-realization, activity, the achievement of voice and the recognition of name, the poems are haunted by the opposite of such imagined virtues of the living. The very occasion for the poems is a pressing concern that the nation, existing under a "gloom which yet obscures the land" ("Ode" 2), is characterized, rather, by inactivity, "ignoble sloth" and "indolence" ("Canada" 5, 9); as well as by anonymity or namelessness as it lies "[u]nheeded, unadored, unhymned...unanointed" ("Canada" 3–4). While the poems urge a movement out of such a spectral half-light into the world of the wakeful living, they seem harried throughout by the fear that this will not be achieved and will result in dissolution, voicelessness and death.

"An Ode For the Canadian Confederacy," as I have suggested, most stridently posits the nation's attainment of voice, "From ice-blue strait and stern Laurentian range / To where giant peaks our western bounds command, / A deep voice stirs, vibrating in men's ears" (3–5). Yet if this sound is indeed the voice of the nation, it must somehow be *our voice* and emanate from us. The poem, however, only allows that it "[vibrates] in men's ears / *As if* their own hearts throbbed that thunder forth" (6–7; emphasis added). Roberts's "as if" marks, much as in Kant's critique of aesthetic judgment, a seductive analogy but not an identity, between this sound and the voice of the nation's people as it might *speak from the heart*. The line marks a further hesitation as to whether such a voice genuinely articulates desire either individually or collectively. The reference to "their own hearts throbb[ing] that thunder forth" is, on the one hand, a good figure for, in Wordsworth's phrase, "the spontaneous overflow of powerful feelings" (304), but such a roar cannot be particularly articulate about desire, especially when it is ambiguous in the first place that the noise emanates from us. Finally, and perhaps most fundamentally, the opening stanza as a whole marks an ambiguity as to whether the noise is voice at all. If it is voice it must be capable at some level of articulate, comprehensible language. In this respect as well, however, the poem both asserts and denies such a predication. In the line following the "as if," "sound" (7) substitutes for "voice." Is this substitution simply an aesthetically pleasing variation of voice? One way of avoiding the sorts of stammering repetitions which could not be said to constitute any meaningful voice? "Sound" is again subsumed within "voice" in the next line which suggests, indeed, that it is only intended to be a synonym for voice: "A sound wherein who hearkens wisely hears / The voice of the desire of this strong North" (7–8). Or does "sound," in keeping with the introduction of the "as if," mark a hesitation as to whether this noise is or is not voice? Those who "hearken wisely" understand the sound as voice, yet what they hear and comprehend is the voice of this "North whose heart of fire / Yet knows not its desire /

Clearly, but dreams, and murmurs in the dream" (9–11). Even as voice, then, this sound hovers between semi-articulate expression and the inarticulate, semi-audible "murmurs" of a nation lost to consciousness.

To sum up the ambiguities of the stanza: the sound may not be our voice, it may not articulate our desires and it may not even be a voice at all. Yet the poem also urges its reader to identify with the sound as our voice, expressive of our desire and, emphatically, to act upon such an identification. Such a series of identifications, or elisions, between language, subject, sense, referent and action, constitutes one of the key meanings, for de Man, of the term "aesthetic ideology." The poem, as de Man theorized of the lyric and, indeed, "of all textual systems made up of tropological substitution" (Rhetoric 71), solicits us to embrace and to act out the very aesthetic ideology it simultaneously critiques in self-reflexively pointing to the tropological nature of such identifications.

By far the most specific and arresting reference to voicelessness, however, occurs in "Canada" where we are informed toward the end of the poem that while "Thy sons await thy call" (44), patiently attend their interpellation as patriots by the nation's voice (a voice which significantly has not arrived): "some Canadian lips are dumb / Beneath Egyptian sands" (46–47). Desmond Pacey's edition of Roberts's poems glosses these lines as "a reference to the Canadian forces involved in the Egyptian wars of the 1880s. Some Canadian soldiers were in the army which attempted to relieve General Gordon at Kartoum...the capital of the Egyptian Sudan [which]...fell to the forces of El Mahdi in 1885" (416, 426). Even in the absence of such helpful historical context, however, the evocation of these mute nationalized "lips" of corpses buried beneath the sands of a far away land, stands as a peculiarly stark image of voice-lessness as death and, thus, a "de-facement" of the longed for nation-subject and its national voice. The "latent threat" of prosopopoeia theorized by de Man—that in addressing the dead, or the non-human, and expecting a reply, the living might be "struck dumb" and enter "the frozen world of the dead" (Rhetoric 78)—strikingly marks the poem in this instance.

Nationalism's peculiar relation to death and mourning, as I suggested at the outset of this essay, has long been noted and is present in both of these poems. "An Ode for the Canadian Confederacy," in confronting the seeming threat of national dissolution posed by rebellion, rousingly asks: "Shall not our love this rough, sweet land make sure / Her bounds preserve inviolate, though we die?" (31–32). Some variously suggestive attempts have been made to comprehend the relationship of nation and death. Anderson points to nationalism's partial affinities with earlier religious systems, how it substitutes as a more secularized structure of meaning for addressing some similarly fundamental first and last questions: To what end are we born? What can be the meaning of our death? The "idea of nation," Anderson writes, provides "a secular trans- formation of fatality into continuity, contingency into meaning" (11). In national imaginings, death frequently becomes troped as heroic sacrifice which permits the nation to live on. The living in turn owe a debt to these dead as well as to the spectral unborn paid in part by their own willingness to sacrifice themselves for the nation. Thus nation- alism exists, as Derrida suggests, "*between* life and death" (15; emphasis added) as a transaction with ghosts and as the scene of a haunting.

Redfield's reading of Anderson suggests a further, less pathos-laden way of understanding nationalism's relationship to death and mourning which pertains to the nation's particular kind of existence, or *half-life*. The "fundamentally and irretrievably faceless" (49) nation is produced, imagined, through technologies of mass communication, technologies which themselves consist of dead matter (from the graphic signs on flags and newspapers, to radio wires, television tubes and computer chips) as well as the spacings and deferrals, the mute and invisible *différance*, through which any structure of representation signifies (50–54). In this sense as well the nation is "between life and death," produced in a flickering play of presence and absence. Furthermore, "technical repro- duction captures its referent thanks to procedures that are inherently and essentially iterable, alien to the identity they construct and docu- ment" (Redfield 53). Much the same technologies produce the nation in Belgium and Brazil as in Canada, and such technologies are equally capable of producing non-national and anti-national identities as well. If such a *technics* is the material base of the nation then "the commu- nity...is irretrievably exposed to an alterity that is never unreservedly 'outside' the community but labours at its heart, constituting its intimacy" (Redfield 54). Thus the nation is predicated on a "misrecognition of its origins." The nation misrecognizes itself in the strident narrative of the maturing, living subject who is uniquely and singularly himself, while it is daily produced in anonymous, iterable, non-living technologies. The mourning in nationalistic aesthetic projects represents both the obscure intimation of this predicament which "corrodes the identities it enables" (53), and the effort to recuperate, collect, such negativity and loss into the affirmation of the living, singular and unique nation-subject. Thus the movement between life and death, unity and dissolution, name and namelessness, that I have been tracing in Roberts's nationalistic poems.

Few deaths could appear so challengingly meaningless, so radically contingent or external to the nation as a life lost in a (now long forgotten) imperial conflict in a distant land. In such a colonial predicament it is difficult even to say that one "died for one's country." Yet drawing on the rhetoric of imperial solidarity that Carl Berger has argued underwrites dominant versions of Canadian nationalism at this historical moment (*Imperialism* 4), Roberts's "Canada" recoups even this loss for Canada's national becoming. The penultimate stanza of the poem, directly following the reference to "Canadian lips...dumb / Beneath Egyptian sands," consists of a strange apostrophe to the Nile river, contingent one presumes to the bodies of these Canadians. "O mystic Nile! Thy secret yields / Before us; thy most ancient dreams / Are mixed with far Canadian fields / And murmur of Canadian streams" (49–52). We are on the move again in this stanza, out from the unmoving, anonymous but nationalized bodies beneath the lifeless sands of the desert to the mythical life-giving river which, thanks to this gift of death, in an image of intermingling (from the dissolution of the corpses?) begins to attain consciousness of Canada and to bestow upon the nation the recognition of name and face it lacks, a recognition affirmed as immanent in the concluding stanza with its triumphant image of the face of the nation coming into the light of the sun

Furthermore, through this sacrifice the "mystic Nile['s]" "secret yields / Before us." The orientalist trope of the "ancient" mysteries of the East may function in part to lend the desired Canadian nation a hoary antiquity and mystique upon which nations, as Anderson has suggested (192–99), although quite modern imaginaries, seem to be structurally dependent. Such a sense of antiquity has always posed a particular challenge to Canadian nationalism and its indelible sense of being a traditionless invention—of being in Earl Birney's phrase, haunted "by our lack of ghosts" (296)—which may explain why Roberts feels the need to infuse the national spirit with some borrowed ancientness. In terms of my analysis, however, what is more remarkable is that the shift from the absolute voicelessness of the lips beneath the sands to the immanent, heightened promise of meaningful voice and language somehow occurs *because* of these deaths, some profound knowledge is to be revealed but is as yet a "murmur" (52). In the final stanzas, then, the poem both balefully recognizes and triumphantly denies the alterity, anonymity, voicelessness and death that exist as a prior condition to troping the nation as a singular, living subject.

In this last respect "Canada" bears comparison with Roberts's "Collect for Dominion Day" a patriotic sonnet also written in 1885 and the poem which contains his most explicit reference to the North-West Rebellion. The "collect" of the title plays on the double sense, most directly a short prayer, but also an imperative to gather together the fragmented, dispersed body of the community, as symbolized in the religious ritual of the Eucharist. The poem consists of a prayer to God, to the "Father of nations" (1) to "make this people one!" (9). The Father is called upon to be like a Blacksmith and "Weld, interfuse them in the patriot's flame,— / Whose forging on thine anvil was begun / In blood late shed to purge the common shame" (10–12). The mourning of the dead is thus similarly limited in this poem, seen as part of the necessary process of creating a healthier—"the fever of faction done" (13)—more unified national body.

"Canada" and "An Ode for the Canadian Confederacy" are both harried by death and characterized by the most strident affirmations of the living vitality of a nation-subject. Instances of mourning are swiftly recouped within the affirmative celebration of the ode as a poetic form. "Aesthetic nationalism," Redfield suggests, "needs to acknowledge and quarantine loss....too much mourning would be crippling.... The task of nationalism, particularly of what Anderson calls 'official nationalism,' is to monumentalize such scenes and fence them off" (71, 73). The national ode, in this respect, would seem to be paradigmatic of nationalist aesthetic education. If one groups under the idea of national mourning not only its most obvious objects such as fallen soldiers, but all intimations of national "de-facement" in voicelessness, namelessness, dissolution, meaninglessness and the non-human, then one more readily glimpses why "too much mourning would be crippling" to the interpellation, the calling into presence, of a nation-subject. But the negative knowledge of the failures that inhere in this aesthetic nationalist project may be another way of understanding the "secret" obscurely intimated to "us" by virtue of those distant, invisible, and mute "Canadian lips."

NOTES

1. Anderson has commented on the "astonishing popularity of this trope" (195) of awakening in nationalist imaginings and the trope is indeed central to both of these poems.
2. In this respect the poem rehearses what Daniel Coleman has aptly named "the Canadian allegory of manly maturation" (84, and passim). Bentley directly comments on the "masculinist assumptions of the opening stanzas" of "Canada" (73).
3. William Henry Drummond's "The Habitant's Jubilee Ode," likewise relies heavily on this rhetoric in constructing Drummond's characteristically rustic and comical habitant as both a proud Canadian and dutiful subject of empire.
4. David L. Clark provides an excellent discussion of the later de Man's theory of language in "Monstrosity, Illegibility, Denegation: De Man, bp Nichol, and the Resistance to Postmodernism." See also Barbara Johnson's "Anthropomorphism in Lyric and Law," for a lucid contemplation and application of de Man's ideas on anthropomorphism.
5. An autobiography in the sense that the poem self-consciously represents its situation to be a Canadian speaking to Canadians of Canada as a maturing subject.
6. See Carl Berger's "The True North Strong and Free" for a seminal exploration of this ideology in Canadian politics and culture.

7.   Rather ironically, given F.R. Scott's early parody of this kind of poetry, Roberts's ode anticipates by some seventy years Scott's "Laurentian Shield" (1954) which likewise invokes as its central trope a nation awaiting its language to articulate its desire: "This waiting is wanting. / It will choose its language / When it has chosen its technic, / A tongue to shape the vowels of its productivity" (8–11).

8.   See Eve Kosofsky Sedgwick's "Shame and Performativity: Henry James's New York Edition Prefaces" for a detailed theoretical exploration of shame and identity.

9.   The gendering of the nation is here in keeping with Kate Higginson's exploration in this volume of female captives and the cartoon figure of "Miss Canada" as national allegories which likewise invoke a rhetoric of chastity and rape to figure social and political conflict.

10.   I am grateful to Robert Brazeau for alerting me to this infrequently cited essay and for stressing its significance.

Letitia Mactavish Hargrave and Hudson's Bay Company Domestic Politics

Negotiating Kinship in Letters from the Canadian North-West

KATHLEEN VENEMA

IN JANUARY 1840, in Campbeltown, Scotland, twenty-six-year-old Letitia Mactavish married James Hargrave, an aspiring, middle-aged, Hudson's Bay Company (HBC) officer. After the requisite wedding tour and a month in London while James dealt with Company business, the Hargraves travelled to James's post at York Factory on the west coast of Hudson Bay in what is now northern Manitoba. Except for one eight-month furlough to England and Scotland in 1846–47, Letitia Mactavish Hargrave would live at York Factory for the next eleven years. Historians describe Hargrave variously as "sensitive, witty and intelligent" (Ramsay qtd in MacLeod lv) and as possessing a "lively and impetuous temperament" (Warkentin 410). However lively and intelligent she may have been, Hargrave could not have known that her acerbic, witty, observant, often self-critical, letters "home" from York Factory would constitute one of the earliest records of colonial activity in the Canadian northwest from the perspective of a British woman.

Hargrave's earliest letters describe her adventures in London before departing for York Factory. "I don't care much about paintings as I always rushed to the portraits and could not be troubled with the small historical affairs," she writes, for instance, after a visit to the Royal Art Gallery just days after she and James arrived in London. "I liked [the portraits]," she continues, "when they were as large as life but was sick of the insignificant ones" (MacLeod 37–38).[1] If this account is accurate, Hargrave's behaviour at the art gallery inverts the focus that her own cultural productions will take. In the many letters she subsequently writes from York Factory, she focuses primarily on subjects that the larger masculine world of the North American fur trade would have considered small historical affairs indeed: her travelling companions' complaints about food; an unfortunately-phrased prayer before supper; how much her female contemporaries typically ate; quarrels with, or between, servants; the most comical of her children's verbal productions; and, regularly, gossip from the colony at Red River.

Although Hargrave's writing manifests characteristics of what has been broadly categorized as women's writing (Buss 3–21; Smith 7–8; Spacks 38–42, 259), her preferred genre reflects geographical isolation much more than it does gender. As I discuss below, the majority of HBC employees lived out their terms at isolated posts scattered across northern North America; because they did, the Company's business could be carried out only if these men exchanged what became hundreds of thousands of letters with one another and with Company headquarters in Montreal and London. Indeed, the HBC's extraordinary dependence on its employees' letter-writing capacity has not yet been either fully appreciated or explored.

Free of the obligation to write business letters, Hargrave writes letters that provide an alternate version of fur-trade reality, and she does so at a time of massive social and economic change. Prolific, and keenly aware of letters' dialogic potential, Hargrave informally and often inadvertently documents the "small" and "insignificant" ways in which members of a complex, idiosyncratic, and tensely hierarchical social system negotiated through a world of shifting kinship ties. She employs an unlikely discursive form to do so, often reconstructing, in her letters, portions of conversations in their original "voices." Like ventriloquism more generally (Davis 151), "epistolary ventriloquism" enables Hargrave to explore her own, legitimate, identity in relation to the often less-secure identities of others and "Others," those explicitly marginalized by shifting fur-trade mores. Hargrave's epistolary ventriloquism, that is, unintentionally records for posterity voices that would otherwise never be heard in official fur-trade history.

Jennifer S.H. Brown and Sylvia Van Kirk, social historians who have dramatically revalued women's importance to the North American fur trade, regularly depend on information they gather from Hargrave's letters. Neither historian, however, considers the writing *as writing*. I propose, therefore, to read Hargrave's letters in specifically generic terms, in terms of the negotiation that all epistolary writing engages in, and as a unique technology for managing family relationships and kinship ties across vast distances in space, time, and ideological orientation. In the chapter that follows, I describe how epistolary's formal constraints, repeated anxiety about the legitimate constitution of "family," and ventriloquized perspectives on the bonds of kinship combine in Hargrave's letters to unsettle the powerful HBC's domestic policies in what became the Canadian northwest. I begin by sketching the historical context.

◆ **The Nineteenth-century fur-trade world**

FUR-TRADE SOCIETY was changing at the time that Hargrave was writing, and it was changing, ironically, because women like her were entering the social scene (Van Kirk 5). Until ten years before Hargrave's arrival, "white" women had been largely unknown in "Rupert's Land," the HBC's massive northern North American territory (Merk xi), primarily because of explicit proscriptions against them (Van Kirk 3, 34, 173–74). That state of affairs began to change when George Simpson and some of his senior officers determined that genteel British wives might well be the social enhancements that their status required (Van Kirk 172). George Simpson, Governor of the HBC and its unofficial alpha male, enjoyed almost unlimited power within the fur-trade empire (Morton 65; Galbraith, *Imperial* 17–21; Galbraith, *Emperor* 208; Van Kirk 181–82). Like most British men in the fur trade, Simpson availed himself of the patterns of domesticity and intimacy that had developed between fur traders and North American First Nations women. Specifically, Simpson "had women" at various fur-trade posts and fathered numerous children by these women (Brown, *Strangers* 122–26; Van Kirk 161–63).

For the first ten years of his fur-trade career, that is, Simpson's behaviour reflected and reinforced certain patterns of intimacy and domesticity that had developed in fur-trade society. It did not, however, reinforce other patterns, notably, the long-term loyalty and fidelity with which many fur traders honoured their First Nations and mixed-blood "country wives." "When George Simpson came into [the fur-trade] environment as an officer of the highest standing," Jennifer S.H. Brown explains,

> he was able to secure as his partners the lower-status daughters of older company men, exploiting their misunderstandings of his attitudes and intentions toward them. He also influenced the domestic conduct of some of his new colleagues... Their behaviour after 1821 showed the effects of his example...reinforc[ing] an instrumental view of country alliances and marriage in general, while fostering an emphasis on home (British and Canadian) kinship and friendship ties. (Strangers 131–32)

Indeed, when George Simpson determined, in the late 1820s, that he needed a wife who would properly reflect his social, political, and economic status, he began and ended his search for her in England (Van Kirk 172, 183; Morton 163). In London, in February 1830, after spending several months searching for a wife, Simpson married his eighteen-year-old cousin, Frances Ramsay Simpson (Galbraith, *Emperor* 103–5; Morton 163–64). Frances was the daughter of his uncle, Geddes Mackenzie Simpson; perhaps more importantly, she was a physically beautiful woman, one who admirably embodied all the qualities of a quintessentially fragile nineteenth-century "lady."

On the surface, George Simpson's marriage to Frances and his decision to bring her with him to Rupert's Land reflected what were purely personal choices. Simpson's personal choices, however, had far-reaching and almost inevitably negative consequences for the First Nations and mixed-blood women of the fur trade, instigating, as those choices did, a radical revision of female power and legitimacy that placed upper-class "white" women securely at the top of a new social hierarchy (Van Kirk 200–203). Though some fur traders deplored Simpson's choice and his insensitive dealings with his "country wife" at the time of his marriage in Britain (Van Kirk 187–89), many others admired and emulated him (Brown, *Strangers* 130). James Hargrave, later Chief Factor at York Factory, was among the latter group. When James Hargrave decided, in the late

1830s, to marry, he returned to Scotland, where he had been born and raised, to do his courting. And it was in Scotland that he met and married Letitia Mactavish, the sister of close fur-trade friends (Brown, "Changing" 36; *Strangers* 41–42).

Letitia Hargrave's presence and her discursive activity in Rupert's Land were thus a direct result of the way George Simpson's legitimate marriage had unsettled the social hierarchy of the fur-trade world. Hargrave's subsequent letters "home" necessarily negotiate the new distance that separates her from her family in Scotland. With resonant historical irony, Hargrave's subsequent letters home sustain and nurture family ties at a point in the Canadian northwest when acknowledged kinship claims marked the limits and the boundaries of legitimate social existence. In the unique social context of the nineteenth-century fur trade, acknowledged familial-affiliative claims enabled women and their children to live valued, legally recognized lives. Powerful HBC officers and men who refused to recognize the claims of their "country wives," however, often condemned them and their mixed-blood children to social derision and disregard, and, in the long-term, the ravages of cultural near-annihilation.

I turn now to a closer examination of the letters themselves.

◆ **Nineteenth-century fur-trade letters**

VERY EARLY in her new life, Letitia Hargrave discovers how profoundly fur-trade society was sustained by gossip. "We have been much diverted with the people at Stromness," she writes to her father on June 18, 1840, from the final port-of-call for HBC ships heading to North America:

> *They are all extremely attentive and the way they entertain us is to tell us all the scandal of our predecessors who have called here. Of course Mrs Clouston [the wife of the HBC agent at Stromness] does not do this, but all the other people we have seen have repeated every word said by ladies or gentlemen and every thing they have done while here. We are now perfectly sick of hearing of Hudson's Bay—* (54)[2]

Hargrave, though she explicitly deprecates the Stromness people's conversational preferences, consistently trades herself in what Patricia Meyer Spacks respectfully describes as gossip: "the stuff of private life made substance for public speculation" (259). And Hargrave gossips with particular style. Though not for the first time since leaving Campbeltown, Mactavish Hargrave's letters from Stromness evidence her predilection for what we might call "epistolary ventriloquism"—the partial reconstruction of conversations, some of which she only knows about secondhand, often in the specific and peculiar "voices" of her various companions.

"She ordered me up on one hand and Mrs Finlayson on the other," Hargrave writes, for instance, about one of her Stromness hostesses and continues: "Hargrave [i.e. James] was then ordered to sit by me and Mr R. Rae to say grace, which he did by looking very devout and saying, 'For what we *have* received, Lord make us thankful'" (52; emphasis in text). In the same letter, she describes the increasingly curious behaviour of one of the other "ladies" of their party. "Miss Allan," she writes of the middle-aged woman who was travelling to Rupert's Land to take over the girls' school in Red River, "has been the death of us all. She has actually broken out altogether and makes such a disturbance, at table especially. Imagine our feelings when, on the cover being taken off a large plum pudding, she shouted, 'Oh! not half boiled!'" (52). This early in the journey, moreover, Hargrave's letters already evidence the innuendo, hearsay, gossip, strategizing, and status-negotiation that characterized the HBC women's complicated, conversational world. In the following excerpt from the same letter, Hargrave refers to: Mrs. Isobel Finlayson, a sister of Frances Simpson's, who was travelling with the Hargraves and whose HBC husband outranked James Hargrave; Mrs. Potter, who was Mrs. Finlayson's maid; and Margaret, who was Hargrave's maid. "I am sorry to say," Hargrave writes,

> that Mrs Finlayson's highly educated & most recherché cook...has been making vainglorious displays of ornaments...to the sailors so as to alarm her neighbor Mrs. Potter who confided to her mistress under promise of secrecy that Marg[are]t & she think it necessary for the sake of their character to cut her as much as possible. Mrs F[inlayson] spoke to me & I have told Marg[are]t to cousen her [i.e.

the cook] & endeavor to entrap her into getting tipsy, w[hi]ch Mrs P[otter] says
she has already done, so that we may get rid of her before leaving this wh[i]ch
w[oul]d be a comfort. (52)

By patiently tracking the way information travels in this complicated, female world, we can identify the various voices at play: the aggrieved Mrs. Potter's, in confidence to her "mistress"; the implied conversation, within that reported confidence, between Mrs. Potter and Margaret Dunnett, the Hargraves' servant, about how dangerous the cook's behaviour might be for their reputations; Mrs. Finlayson's subsequent appeal to Hargrave; and, finally, the latter's instructions to Margaret for trapping the offending servant in the midst of her vices.

Significantly, all these apparently natural and apparently trivial topics—the Stromness people's love of fur-trade gossip; Mr Rae's peculiar emphasis during prayer; Miss Allen's unmannerly outbursts; and the strategies "ladies" employ to dismiss "unsuitable" servants with cause—are being communicated by letter. This is long distance gossip, epistolary gossip that "throws voices" across half a continent and an ocean, gossip that, in the most basic definition of ventriloquism, makes voices appear from somewhere other than their actual source (Connor 13–14; Davis 137). Like the male employees of the HBC, women like Frances Simpson, Isobel Finlayson, and Letitia Hargrave, "incorporated" into the Company by marriage (Callan 1–5) and brought to live "in the country," were profoundly limited in their subsequent communications with family and friends. What we know about Hargrave's geographically and socially isolated life at York Factory and what we know about the lives of the fur-trade participants she chooses to ventriloquize, we know because she spends the next eleven years writing letters "home."

Despite the broadening interest in the social history of the fur trade (Van Kirk; Brown; Burley; Payne; Podruchny; Beattie and Buss), the Hudson's Bay Company's extraordinary dependence on letter writing has not yet been studied seriously. Fur-trade historians note, however, that it was George Simpson who strictly regularized HBC employees' writing and implemented a highly refined system of letter exchange, both amongst the various posts and between himself and the people in charge of those posts (Galbraith, "Introduction" xv; Glazerbrook xxv). "Paradoxically," says Brown of the remarkable archive that now exists of these letters, "the geographical remoteness of the traders from each other is precisely what now facilitates studying them as a group.... Their literacy...became a vehicle for maintaining the community and now aids the study of it" (*Strangers* xii). If HBC traders' relative literacy effectively created the discursive world of the early Canadian northwest, surprisingly little attention has been paid to their letters as texts that, within the constraints and the possibilities of generic form, "do discursive work" by emerging out of, and responding to, lived social exigencies.

Scholars and theorists of epistolary writing exhibit no surprise at the lack of attention. Indeed, they regularly argue that the textual dimensions of epistolary are vastly understudied in proportion to the genre's prevalence and the powerful social forms it takes (Barton and Hall 1–2; Decker 4, 20, 36; Earle 1). They also agree that while the genre is multiform, it possesses certain stable features, including, most importantly, the real or metaphoric distance that its form negotiates; its always tenuous existence between public and private spheres; its dialogic reciprocity; and, relatedly, its construction of the writer's and the reader's personae (Altman 13, 117; Decker 14, 46–47, 80; Ditz 62, 72–73; Hasselberg 99–100; Steedman 117–18). At their most extreme, theorists of epistolary claim that the form is, by its very unstable characteristics, productive of every other writing genre that has developed (Bazerman 15, 27; Derrida, qtd in Kaufmann 17).

For their part, Hargrave's letters provide a vivid and historically significant instance of a female voice simultaneously constrained and enabled by epistolary form (Goldsmith vii). Of the generic features associated with epistolary form, three stand out, both because of their particular significance in Hargrave's unique circumstances and because they combine to demonstrate her letters' rhetorical richness. First, the letters regularly evince the tension between private and public worlds and the two worlds' very different negotiations of power. Second, the letters reflect the confusion that separation in time and space entails, between what is *here* and what is *there*, what is *now* and what was, or will be, *then*. And they reflect how that confusion is intensified when "family" means something very different *here* than it did *there*, *then* than it does *now*. Interwoven into the discursive texture that results is the letters' third notable feature: their frequent ventriloquism of the other voices, often the marginalized voices, that Hargrave employs to meet episto-lary's dialogic demands.

◆ Public private letters: locating "family"

JANET GURKIN ALTMAN's extensive study of epistolary form describes many of the textual and social features that fictional epistolary shares with its "real-life" counterpart. "As a reflection of self, or the self's rela-tionships," Altman explains, "the letter connotes privacy and intimacy; yet as a document addressed to another, the letter reflects the need for an audience, an audience that may suddenly expand when that document is confiscated, shared, or published" (186–87). Hargrave discovers early in her career as an incorporated wife that private letters made public can be dangerous things. Her most egregious miscalculation of epistolary output appropriate to her place in HBC society occurs in a May 14, 1840 letter to her mother, after a visit to George Simpson's family at Gravesend. In this excerpt, "old Mrs. Simpson" is Frances Simpson's mother, George Simpson's aunt and mother-in-law. "I have also had a walk with old Mrs Simpson," the incriminating letter begins and continues:

> I thought all along that the Gov[erno]r's wife had a melancholy look & the old lady fairly let out that the said gov[erno]r is very fashious. It began by her speaking of her love for gardening & how she wished she had a little more money to beau-tify her little shrubbery, that for 34 years she had got all her husband had to give & he never w[oul]d look at a single account of her outlay nor ever been other than satisfied with her endeavors to economize, whilst Frances dared not miss sixpence or there was a rumpus, she must not attempt to advise in any one way nor speak in support of what he does not see fit to do or hear. I observed all this but thought it was simplicity. For one thing she sat with the tea tray on Sunday even[in]g, she asked if she sh[oul]d ring & have it taken away. Altho' he was done, he said nothing & there it remained for long, & two or 3 other matters of the same kind. If

she speaks at all in opposition to him he bids her hold her tongue as she knows
nothing about it—Her mother said she told her that if she w[oul]d exert herself &
have a little mind of her own the Gov[erno]r w[oul]d be a better husband & she a
much more useful wife. But she says she won't as she w[oul]d rather submit than
run the risk of an argument. I don't mean that he is bad or cross to her, but he
treats her & the little girl exactly alike. She says it is the arbitrary habits he
acquired in the North. (25–26)

Mere hours after sealing and sending this detailed account of the Simpsons'
domestic relations, Hargrave writes hurriedly to her sister Florence:

My dear Flora,

The reason for my writing so very soon after I sent away Mama's letter is that I
find I was rash in committing to paper what I said of the family affairs of a person
of whom I spoke yesterday. I have been desired by Mr H[argrave] never to let such
a thing escape me as the hopes of all connected with us would be knocked to the
ground were it ever suspected that such a subject had ever been mooted. I did not
say that I had done so and I am sure that there is no danger of its ever transpiring
from anything I have said or you heard of the matter. (29)

Various voices are ventriloquized here: "old" Mrs. Simpson; Frances
Simpson; Governor George Simpson; James Hargrave; indeed, at one point,
depending on how we read the pronouns, we even hear "old" Mrs. Simpson
ventriloquizing Frances. The two letters together, moreover, suggest
that Hargrave learns very early on that though she may, as she describes
it in an early letter to James Hargrave, be "leaving society" (5), she is also
entering a highly regulated "society," a society quite different from anything
she has known and one in which George Simpson wields more social
power than she has heretofore encountered. Her letters on this particular occasion, in fact, position *her* as an illegitimate speaker, someone
who has to learn, as almost all colonial wives do (Gartrell 166–67), both
her literal and her figurative place. Hargrave learns here that the power
she wields is power to censor herself: epistolary missteps could destroy
her family's future with the HBC.

When Hargrave refers to "all connected with us," that is, she introduces a central feature of the complex fur-trade world: specifically, its
basis in kinship ties. After a lengthy, cutthroat, occasionally deadly, and
economically disastrous competition, the Hudson's Bay Company and
the North West Company (NWC) amalgamated in 1821 under the first
company's name. Much of Jennifer Brown's 1980 study describes how
the amalgamation brought traders with different family, ethnic, economic, and geographical experiences into an often less-than-unified
concern (111). Brown also describes how the former NWC men, including
James Hargrave and Letitia's influential uncle, John George McTavish,
usually belonged to strong kinship, clan, and friendship networks (98).
Hargrave's phrase, "all connected with us," would include, at this point,
her paternal uncle John George McTavish,[3] her husband James, and the
two of her six brothers whom John George McTavish had, by this point,
introduced into the fur trade.

Like George Simpson, and, indeed, enormously influenced by him,
"Uncle John" George McTavish had "put off" his "country wife" only after
marrying a young Scottish woman named Catherine Turner (Van Kirk
184–88). In the spring of 1830, in fact, shortly after their respective
weddings, Catherine Turner McTavish and Frances Simpson, with their
husbands and a massive entourage, made the first ever trip by British
women, by canoe, from Montreal into the heart of the northwest (Van
Kirk 186). Uncle John's various "country marriages" up until this point
(Van Kirk 46) had produced numerous children, a circumstance with
which his family in Scotland was aware and which his new bride
learned about on her "honeymoon."

"I wish you heard Mrs. [George] Simpson's account of Mrs. J[oh]n
[George] McTavish's introduction to her eldest daughter, a girl of 13,"
Hargrave writes to her mother from Gravesend, a week after penning
the reckless letter described above. "As soon as they arrived at Montreal,
Uncle had told her," she continues, referring to her uncle's expectations
that his new wife would act as stepmother to his mixed-blood children.
Hargrave's subsequent description is one of her most resonant recre-
ations of event, character, and conversation:

Mrs S[impson] says [Mrs. McTavish] had evidently suffered, but said nothing,
till one day after dinner at Lachine, with all the gentlemen sitting & Mrs Simpson
and herself the only ladies,...the Gov[erno]r's serv[an]t threw open the door with
a flourish & announced, "Miss McTavish". Uncle rose & took her up to his wife,
who got stupid but shook hands with the Miss who was very pretty & mighty
impudent. Her father then proceeded to caress & make [sic] of her. Mrs M[cTavish]
got white & red & at last rose & left the room, all the party looking very uncom-
fortable except Uncle & the girl. Mrs S[impson] followed & found her in a violent
fit of crying, she said she knew the child was to have been home that night but
thought she w[oul]d have been spared such a public introduction. All the way up
to Moose [Factory] Uncle spoiled & indulged her in a provoking way & she was
often very impertinent to her step mother, who however never took notice of it &
always when writing told Mrs S[impson] that Mary was a very affec[tiona]te girl
& she had become very much attached to her. (34–35)

Hargrave's ventriloquism here takes a form that recurs throughout her
letters: she not only recounts someone else's story in a version of their
own voice, she frequently recounts one person's account of yet another
person's story. Her re-telling here, of Frances Simpson's account of
Catherine McTavish's introduction to the eldest of her "country children," describes a scene of radical social encounter focalized from the
perspective of the acutely anxious but "legitimate" British wife. This is
not, in the telling, a happy meeting. And the telling continues:

When [the Simpsons and the McTavishes] parted at Moose [Factory], Mrs
M[cTavish] had no idea that she was to have at least other 2 [sic], of a different
family, but they arrived soon after herself...Uncle has certainly six daughters. Mrs
S[impson] met a child at Red River and was sure it was one....Their mother was
the York squaw who was brought, during a severe illness Mrs S[impson] had, to
give her eldest baby a drink. She says she was a complete savage, with a coarse
blue sort of woolen gown without shape & a blanket fastened round her neck. It
was she who lost all her family & her husband when the Gov[erno]r's son-in-law
upset the canoe. Mrs Simpson asked Hargrave the particulars of that story while
her husband was present. He looked very melancholy— She evidently has no idea
that she has more encumbrances than Mrs McTavish, altho' she did say that she

was always terrified to look about her in case of seeing something disagreeable.
(35–36)

All the complexity of acknowledged and unacknowledged family ties within the fur trade appears in this long excerpt. Resonant with hushed silences and averted glances, the excerpt documents how, in this world, gender and class complicate the possibility of knowledge. As she returns to the "lived time" of the letter's composition, Hargrave's discursive attention shifts from Frances Simpson's recollection of an unpleasant encounter ten years previously to Frances Simpson's request for another story entirely. Apparently unbeknownst to Mrs. Simpson, the second story implicates her in precisely the kinds of "illegitimate" kinship relationships that she reports her friend Catherine McTavish struggling to accept.

Frances Simpson, that is, likely asked her question of James Hargrave innocently, not realizing that the same accident that killed John George McTavish's former wife's husband and children also killed the Governor's daughter by the first of his "country wives" and his daughter's husband, the man who had caused the accident (MacLeod 36n; Brown, *Strangers* 123). Hargrave's account of the subsequent conversation effectively underscores Frances Simpson's own awkward "otherness" within the shifting social universe of the fur trade. Profoundly lonely for the family and friends she had left behind in London, Frances Simpson's isolation was exacerbated both by her high status as the Governor's wife and by her husband's exaggerated efforts to insulate her, physically, from contact with the First Nations and mixed-blood wives of HBC officers (Brown, *Strangers* 129). "[George Simpson]," Brown speculates, "had developed some considerable prejudice, often expressed in racial terms, against natives of the country.... He was not anxious to have Frances associate with 'halfbreeds'.... He also probably hoped to shield her from knowledge of his earlier attachments to native women and from contact with them or their children" (130). Simpson's close scrutiny of his wife's existence (Galbraith, *Emperor* 124) and the care he took to circumscribe her life (Galbraith, *Emperor* 105, 112–13; Van Kirk 194)—ostensibly in order to protect her, but clearly also in order to protect himself—communicates unmistakable cultural and social messages about the status and sanctity of his "colonial wife" (Brownfoot 207). Frances symbolized, in her person, the change that Simpson had wreaked on fur-trade society. That he subsequently worked as hard as he did to keep her in effective social solitary confinement underscores how deeply fur-trade society had been ruptured by his marriage.

The passage quoted above powerfully and simultaneously foregrounds the complex interrelationship of acknowledged and unacknowledged legitimate, legitimated, and "illegitimate" kinship ties; and it gestures at how white men's sexual prerogatives literally created the intricate kinship network that characterized the Canadian northwest. It also presents a striking scene of original encounter, specifically the encounter between the former Mrs. McTavish and Mrs. George Simpson, the Governor's wife. In this female "contact zone" (Pratt 6–7), legitimate white wife-ness and wife-ness conveniently de-legitimized by British law encounter one another in a scene suffused by "radical inequality" (Pratt 6). "She says *she was a complete savage*," writes Hargrave, "with a *coarse* blue *sort of* woolen gown *without shape* & a *blanket* fastened around her neck" (35–36; emphasis added). In Hargrave's proprietary account, Frances Simpson represents the former Mrs. McTavish in the harshest light possible, as a version of the transgressive, "grotesque body" fundamentally scandalous to hegemonic, imperial dignity (Stallybrass and White 21–25) and to the scrupulously patrolled borders of the legitimate race (Henderson 17–18). Frances Simpson's terror, moreover, of "look[ing] about her," her refusal, in contemporary terms, to return the gaze of the mixed-blood wives and children of HBC men, acts metonymically for refusal on a larger scale: the refusal by those in the highest ranks of the HBC hierarchy to acknowledge the human and cultural consequences of shifting domestic policies.

According to Charles B. Davis, ventriloquism similarly deflects responsibility, specifically the "responsibility for committing speech acts from the actual human source" (148). Uncertain, like Susanna Moodie and Catharine Parr Traill, of her position as a colonial woman within normative patriarchal power relations (Gerson 10), Hargrave enters the fraught territory of HBC kinship claims by ventriloquizing Frances Simpson's version of "contact." In much the same way that Carole Gerson describes Moodie and Traill displacing anxiety onto their First Nations women friends (16), Hargrave deflects early anxiety about marital and maternal status—anxiety it would have been impossible for her to address overtly—into Frances Simpson's discursive world.

The possibility or impossibility of a speech act is, of course, profoundly determined by gender, social position, genre, and audience. "Where an individual speaks from affects both the meaning and truth of what she says...," Linda Martín Alcoff explains; "A speaker's...*social* location or social identity has an epistemically significant impact on that speaker's claims" (98; emphasis in text). From the work of Michel Foucault, moreover, we know that any speaker's social location is also a location in space and, hence, implicated in relations of power (252). In the next section, I examine the effect of social and spatial location on how and what Hargrave writes.

◆ "Here-there; now-then": negotiating space & position

HARGRAVE'S LETTERS from York Factory never stop lamenting her separation in time and space from her family. Surprisingly, however, they almost as frequently record her dislike of female company and her repeated desire for privacy. As James Hargrave's "incorporated wife," Letitia was clearly "first-lady" at York Factory, a subject position that required her to be physically, spatially, present to a certain class of visitors (MacLeod lvi, 70, 112, 127, 235; Payne 27–28; Callan 12–13). In this section of the essay, I examine how, within the unique space-times of epistolary discourse, she reflects the shifting society that she and everyone around and near her was negotiating.

Hargrave's extreme social and discursive visibility is dramatically and comically demonstrated in a letter that she writes to her mother a year and a half into her tenure at York Factory. Near the end of that letter, Hargrave describes York Factory "mess" patterns at different times of the year; "Willie" is her brother William, and she refers to conversations with him regularly throughout the letters. "On the 1st of June," she explains, "the gentlemen go over to the kitchen at the other side of the Fort, so that till 1st Octo[be]r, I have the whole house to myself & eat alone unless I expressly invite someone or when Mrs Evans, Cowley, or Ross are here...."[4] The ladies here appear to have prodigious appetites judging from those I have seen & Willie says they are all the same, high & low" (112). To that letter, she adds the following "N.B.":

> After finishing, I find that I was not guarded in the subject I chose for the end of my letter, & it would have been over the country that I had aspersed the appetite of the ladies. I hope this paper may be light enough to stand an envelope. It is always safest, as, if I am to believe all I hear, gossips are mightily anxious to get acquainted with my sentiments & notions of things & persons, & I know would not scruple to read my letter if they could. (112–13)

Hargrave records herself here dealing yet again with the possibility that information in a private letter might fall into public hands. This particular example also provides a glimpse into how Hargrave experiences and re-tales the literal, cultural, and metaphorical world around her. "The I of epistolary discourse," says Altman, "always situates [her]self vis-à-vis another.... To write a letter is to map one's coordinates— temporal, spatial, emotional, intellectual—in order to tell someone else where one is located at a particular time and how far one has traveled since the last writing" (119). Given her acute physical and social circumscription at York Factory and her equally acute longing for family, Hargrave is, surprisingly, far more likely to map coordinates that find her too *often* in the company of other women rather than too rarely (59, 70, 85, 206, 209, 222, 230–31, 232, 257).

Ironically, given the vengeance with which she values her privacy, Hargrave's personal space is dramatically invaded by a person whose presence British social protocol required: the personal servant no "lady" could be without (McBride 44; McClintock 79; Horn 17–18). Significant for this study is how often, after the Hargraves begin to have children, Hargrave ventriloquizes their nursemaid and her house servant, Mary Clarke. Clarke, who was likely in her mid-40s when she arrived at York Factory in 1843, had begun her service to the Mactavish family in Letitia

Hargrave's grandmother's home (MacLeod lxxviii). Well known to Hargrave's Mactavish relatives, Clarke provides a literal and discursive bridge between the "here" and the "there," the "now" and the "then" of Hargrave's letters. That Mary Clarke is also easy to mock is readily apparent. Indeed, soon after her arrival, Hargrave launches what will become years of ridicule at the servant's expense. Reporting to her family specifically on Clarke's safe arrival, for instance, Hargrave writes this gently sarcastic account of the older woman's self-aggrandizing description of her interactions with a distinguished fellow passenger, Joseph Burke, a British botanist known for his work in South Africa (MacLeod 161n):

> I felt very glad to see the old soul...but even yet, she is in a state of excitement & has not given me so much news as she might have done. She assured me she was sure Mr Burk had taken her for a lady and always called her Jane (Mr. Burk being a distinguished naturalist, by the by, must know a person's class, I suppose). "He said to me one day (he is an extraordinar discreet gentleman) Jane, might I beg of you to make me a pincushion to stick insects upon"—So I soon made him one... She went on to describe his admiration when she gave it to him. (161; emphasis in text)

However much she might mock Clarke, of course, Hargrave inadvertently acknowledges here her need for the servant's news: her need, that is, for conversation, dialogue, gossip, exchange.

Similarly ventriloquized accounts of Clarke characterize Hargrave's subsequent letters. In these accounts, Hargrave reiterates Clarke's general ignorance about the world; her obsequious deference to those she considered decisively high-class, her denigration of those she considers lower class, and what Hargrave represents as Clarke's explicit disrespect for *her*; Clarke's inability to meet Hargrave's standards; her avarice and miserliness; her relative ignorance about child rearing; and what appears to be at least mild anxiety on Hargrave's part about her children's attachment to the older woman.

Indeed, Hargrave's regular references to Clarke's shortcomings powerfully reinforce the letters' sense of immediacy and underscore the relationship between privacy, or the lack of privacy, and the production of discourse. On August 22, 1848, for instance, she writes, "I have cut off a slip (from this) containing an account of the nonsense that vexed & irritated me as I have not time to write another letter. It was...something Mary thought proper to tell me...far too absurd to be repeated, but at the time it unhinged me & I was made worse by Mary's cruelty" (233). Almost exactly two years later, on August 24, 1850, Hargrave ends an extended complaint about Clarke by explaining, "I would not have written you but she was tormenting me while I had the pen in my hand" (250).

Significantly, the letters' many references to Clarke reflect her explicit prejudices against particular groups of people, including, simultaneously, Irish, First Nations, and mixed-blood people and the English. "I tried to get Mary to face and be civil to them," Hargrave writes in the August 24, 1850 letter, referring to a couple who had come from London to be valet and lady's maid to the new Governor at Red River,

> but she refused point blank. "I hate to speak to the English. My sister that was in the Artillery said no flesh c[oul]d live in a barrack with them, they're a wheen taupies & thinks a great deal of themselves." So I had to look to their being attended to myself, & Mary takes to flight when she sees them approach, when she is out with the children. The best of it is, she harangues the valet & cross questions him as to his prospects & expectations when she gets hold of him apart from the ladies— (254)

This example foregrounds what had, by this time, become an issue of some tension between Hargrave and Clarke, specifically the latter's growing ambitions with respect to her place in the world, a characteristic desire among domestic servants in colonial contexts (Swaisland 168). "Mary Clarke has taken it into her head that she w[oul]d do well in a house of her own," Hargrave writes to her sister Flora two years earlier, "& she says she will get a gentleman's child whose father and mother are dead, & bring it up 'for a consideration'." She seems to think gentlemen's children so situated are abundant & to be had for the asking.... It is plain that she considers herself independent" (235).

Mary's subsequent flirtation with one of the HBC men at York exemplifies both the generality of her racial prejudice, her attention to the possibility of bettering her social position, and her awareness that pre-existing marriage patterns within fur-trade society might detract from the status she would otherwise assume by virtue of her skin colour. "George Lootit is pointed in his attention to Mary," Hargrave writes in August 1851 to her husband who was in Norway House for a council meeting,

> & has even got the length of intimating that it is his intention of leaving off smoking & taking a wife. Their flirtations being carried on with open doors between the nursery & me & Mary's not finding it necessary to mitigate her naturally loud voice I have the benefit of their conversations which, on Mary's side, consist entirely of invections against Orkney men and Indian women. (259–60)

Like the former Mrs. McTavish in the excerpt above, Mary Clarke is represented here as a version of the grotesque body, one whose excessive clamour—literally, her loud voice—intrudes unnecessarily into Hargrave's personal space and, by extension, into Hargrave's writing.

Indeed, Margaret Arnett MacLeod speculates that Hargrave mocks and complains about Mary Clarke as frequently as she does precisely because limited physical space so acutely exacerbated Clarke's foibles (cxv). By definition, of course, domestic servants occupy a liminal space characterized simultaneously by intimacy and social distance (Wright 436–37), a paradoxical space that critics name as the source of employers' often exaggerated sense of the threat their servants pose (McBride 52; Gallop 144–46; Stallybrass and White 138; Kirkwood 156–57). Here, within the limited physical space that protocol and status oblige her to share, Hargrave's own invective is directed, virtually exclusively, at her hapless servant.

Helen Buss's speculation about another high-ranking colonial wife's displacement of negative feelings onto *her* servant in her letters provides a useful frame for considering Hargrave's disparaging ventriloquial focus on Clarke. According to Buss, Elizabeth Simcoe, the wife of Upper Canada's first lieutenant-governor, employs a strategy of displacement that "while seeming to de-emphasize [Simcoe] and her feelings, draws attention to them. In fact...a special emphasis...is added, one that cues us to the alternate text of her account" (43). Buss's description of an alternate dynamic, especially in conjunction with theories of ventriloquism, offers a generative perspective on Hargrave's discursive choices. Virtually every student of ventriloquism remarks on the frequency with which the technique is used in situations of marked power difference (Reinhardt 84; Davis 145, 147; Connor 313–14; 404–7). Davis's claim, moreover, that ventriloquism enables the ventriloquist to occupy entirely other versions of self and reality (151) is peculiarly pertinent. Circumscribed as she is by the physical and cultural limitations of York Factory, Hargrave borrows the voice of a social inferior to articulate pent-up tensions and prejudices. In these extreme circumstances, Mary Clarke's may be the only voice with which a "lady" can express the unseemly, often overtly racist, sentiments that threaten, at times, to overwhelm her.

"White" women, according to Van Kirk, did not merely intrude into a society that had previously been limited to First Nations women, they actively promoted the growth of racial prejudice. "In a colony which offered the prospect of social mobility," she explains, "the desire for status and its material trappings was bound to be intense; in Rupert's Land, the increasing social rivalry which can be seen among the women was compounded by the question of race" (200). Mary Clarke's interest in bettering her social position, especially as that desire is inflected by her prejudice against First Nations and mixed-blood women—a class conveniently lower than her own (Swaisland 170)—dramatizes the dynamic that Van Kirk describes (217). It also exemplifies the way that Hargrave, whose social intercourse is severely circumscribed by the physical and geographical limitations of York Factory, uses other's voices to explore, discursively, the limits of a shifting social hierarchy. Hargrave, moreover, frequently appropriates voices that belong, in fact, to "others," people marginalized, to greater and lesser degrees, by the strictly monitored social rules of the fur-trade world. In the final section of this essay, I examine evidence of Hargrave's willingness to imagine and voice social and domestic realities far removed from her own.

◆ Voicing the contradictions of kinship claims

IF HARGRAVE'S RELATIONSHIP with Mary Clarke manifests the former's struggle with relative social positions, her early friendship with Harriet Vincent Gladman provides evidence of another version of ventriloquial self-broadening. This section begins by examining Hargrave's friendship with a woman who was explicitly negotiating kinship and legitimacy claims; it ends by examining how Hargrave's letters record the institutionally sanctioned and historically resonant de-constitution of what had been socially recognized family units.

Except for the friendships she maintained exclusively by letter, Hargrave's most significant acquaintance was with Harriet Vincent Gladman, the mixed-blood wife of George Gladman Jr., the only other officer stationed at York Factory when the Hargraves arrived from Scotland in 1840. Hargrave had to be guided into the friendship by Isobel Finlayson's assessment of the social circumstances, specifically, the rivetting fact that Hargrave and Mrs. Gladman would, when Mrs. Finlayson left for Red River, be "the only women" (read: the only euro-peanized women) at the Factory. "In [Mrs. Gladman]," MacLeod explains, "had Letitia but known it, she was meeting a member of the aristocracy of the country, the daughter and grand-daughter of early governors" (xliv).

Having become friendly with Mrs. Gladman, Hargrave includes numerous details of their conversations in her letters home, and, in the process, describes the domestic dangers that mixed-blood women like Mrs. Gladman and her mother faced. "Mrs. Gladman and I are getting very gracious," Hargrave writes to her own mother, three months after first meeting Mrs. Gladman, and continues:

> She favoured me with her history & that of her mother before her. Her father was partner in the other Co[mpan]y [i.e. the HBC before the union]. Her mother, his wife, as she considered herself, got a girl in to help her, who prevailed on her father to take her [as wife] too, so the first got indignant & left him....I wish I c[oul]d tell it as Mrs. Gladman did. Her mother suffered so much that she had to be bled on

the occasion— Her own story was as disastrous. Mr. Stewart...asked her father
for her when she was 12 years old. She was dragged out of her mother's room &
sent away with him. She declares that she never hated man [sic] as she did him, &
he beat and maltreated her till life was a burden.... After living with him 9 years,
he left her & the children & went to Canada, where he has been ever since. She
waited four years and then, "I went with Mr. Gladman." She always says, "When
I was sent with Mr. Stewart" & "When I went with Mr. Gladman"—She was
fairly married 3 years ago & sports a wedding ring. (82–83; emphasis in text)

By re-narrating Mrs. Gladman's story attentive to Mrs. Gladman's specific discursive choices and emphases, Hargrave foregrounds some of the domestic realities to which First Nations and mixed-blood women were peculiarly susceptible. A first threat was the possibility that their "husband" would take another "wife" and thereby jeopardize their relational status; a second was the ease with which they, as culturally and socially powerless females, might be "sent off" with whatever man desired them; a third was that their husband would simply abandon them.

Van Kirk describes how fur traders' adherence to the customs of the country was loosening throughout the nineteenth century (145–46) and how the shifting social hierarchy reflected an increasing prevalence of Victorian ideas. Ideas about female purity were especially dangerous because they attributed loose sexual morals to First Nations and mixed-blood women and, by the misogynist logic of Victorian morality, sanctioned men's sexual use of such women without either moral scruple or long-term responsibility for the women and any children their alliances might produce (Van Kirk 145–46, 159–60, 164–65). Women like Harriet Vincent Gladman and her mother were provoked by the unstable social structure to seek out the best possible social security, usually, though not always, guaranteed by church marriage (Van Kirk 240–41; Backhouse 9–28).

Mrs. Gladman's extensive connections throughout fur-trade society clearly foster Hargrave's passion for gossip and replicating voices. Mrs. Gladman specifically increases Hargrave's knowledge of events in the Red River colony, material which subsequently appears throughout the letters home. In the December 1840 letter to her mother excerpted above, for instance, Hargrave reiterates information from a conversation with Mrs. Gladman into which she intersperses details garnered earlier from Mrs. Simpson. That story propels her into one of her rare commentaries on the state of fur-trade society. In this excerpt, Dugald and Willie are Hargrave's brothers; James Bird is a former HBC Chief Factor who has retired to Red River; and John McLoughlen is Chief Factor in charge of the HBC's important Columbia Department (MacLeod 84n):

> When last in London [Uncle John] had his youngest daughter with him, 9 years old....Mrs Simpson said he spoiled her & she would not let him out of her sight....Dugald told Willie that all his cousins were equal to any white in every respect....The state of society seems shocking. Some people educate & make gentlemen of part of their family & leave the other savages. I had heard of Mr Bird at Red River & his dandified sons. One day while the boats were here, a common half breed came in to get orders for provisions for his boatmen. Mr H[argrave] called him Mr Bird to my amazement. This was one who had not been educated & while his father & brothers are Nobility at the Colony, he is a voyageur & sat at table with the house servants here. Dr MacLoughlen, one of our grandees at a great expense gave 2 of his sons a regular education in England & keeps the 3rd a common Indian. One of them had been for years at the Military College in Lon[do]n but they have both entered the Co[mpan]y's Service— I daresay the heathen is the happiest of them as the father is constantly upbraiding the others with the ransom they have cost him— (83–84)

In this extraordinary excerpt, Hargrave articulates precisely the fraught social realities of the fur-trade world and the disturbing fact that members of her own family actively transgress the newly rigid racial and social boundaries. Despite her apparent disapprobation of the behaviour she describes, however, Hargrave never engages either her brother Dugald's kinship claim on his mixed-blood cousins or his assertion that people she casually describes as "savages," "common halfbreeds," "common Indians," and "heathens" are "equal to any white."

It will, in fact, be almost three years before Hargrave makes her only explicit statement on the subject. In a September 1843 letter to her mother, she once again retails Red River gossip, focusing specifically on the rules governing the new school there, interspersing into her account Mrs. Gladman's opinions on the subject. It is the closest she ever comes to acknowledging the profound gender and race injustices in the system in which she is implicated. "They say," she writes of her Red River sources,

> that Mr. MacCallum's school is going to wreck. Children who have had duck, geese, & venison 3 times a day are supposed to suffer from breakfasts of milk & water with dry bread, severe floggings, confinement after any fault & the total want of the following meal....Then if the mothers are not legally married they are not allowed to see their children. This may be all very right, but it is fearfully cruel, for the poor unfortunate mothers did not know that there was any distinction & it is only within the last few years that any one was so married. Of course, had all the fathers refused, every one woman in the country w[oul]d have been no better than those that are represented to their own children as discreditable. The curious thing is that Mrs Glad[ma]n, who has had her own sorrows with a husband, & who literally was deserted by hers, yet she despises those who have been turned off, as much as any one & spoke with horror of 2 Miss MacKenzies who are at Mr. MacCallum's. Their father left the service & their mother & went into the American Fur Company some years ago. The 2 girls were sent to school & of course prohibited from having any intercourse with their mother who is in a miserable state of destitution. The poor creature sits in some concealment at MacCallum's with deer's head, or some such Indian delicacy ready cooked for her daughters, & they slip out & see her, & as she is almost naked they steal some of their own clothes & give them to her. This is a fearful fault & the young ladies suffer for it, as if any else could be looked for. Mrs Gladman reviles the poor ignorant Indian mother, but I think the father is a much more culpable character leaving children to be brought up by a starving woman who nevertheless w[oul]d be always kind to them. At 13 years old, taking them from her & placing them where they heard her called any thing but genteel cannot be a very good plan. (177–78)

Hargrave clearly distinguishes here between her own emotional and moral response to the story and Mrs. Gladman's. Mrs. Gladman, according to Hargrave, "despises those who have been turned off," "speaks with horror" at the MacKenzie daughters' breaking school rules, and "reviles" their cast-off mother. "*The curious thing is*," she emphasizes, underscoring Mrs. Gladman's own close brush with social infamy, "that Mrs Glad[ma]n... has had her own sorrows with a husband." "Mrs Gladman reviles the poor ignorant Indian mother," she insists further, "*but I think* the father is a much more culpable character" (emphasis added), articulating what she clearly considers her own, more fully moral, assessment of the situation.

More than three years after recounting without comment Frances Simpson's disapprobation of a woman similarly disenfranchised by HBC domestic politics, Hargrave stakes out specific moral territory here on the fraught question of legitimate kinship claims. The difference may equal precisely the difference in power between the Governor's wife, whose words apparently "speak for themselves," and the mixed-blood, but church-married, wife of a mid-ranking HBC officer. Or the difference may be a direct consequence of Hargrave's growing awareness of the lived realities of HBC domestic and social politics.

Ironically, of course, Hargrave's detailed, heartfelt, and justifiably indignant critique reveals how completely blinded she was to her own inadvertent role in the situation she describes. She astutely and appropriately lays the blame for Mrs. MacKenzie's deplorable state on Mr. MacKenzie, the fur-trade husband clearly versed in accepted domestic politics; Red River clergy, who had begun, by the early nineteenth century, to denounce domestic unions unsanctified by the church and to enact prohibitions like the ones Hargrave describes (Van Kirk 153ff); and sanctimonious Red River society at large. What she does not recognize is that her arrival in Rupert's Land, and the arrival of other British wives—most notably, Frances Simpson, Catherine McTavish, and Isobel Finlayson—in concert with George Simpson's deliberate exclusion of mixed-blood women from "the upper echelon of fur-trade society" (Van Kirk 207), radically reconfigured the world all fur-trade women would subsequently be required to negotiate. Inextricably implicated in a system that was enforcing increasingly harsh sanctions against individuals and groups rendered superfluous to the fur-trade world, Hargrave does, however, resolutely, and often inadvertently, mark her ability to see and think and write beyond the strict limitations of race and class.

◆

SEPARATED FROM HER FAMILY in Scotland by vast distances and the passage of many years, Hargrave writes letters home that regularly voice perspectives on the shifting social realities of HBC fur-trade life. Within the constraints of real-life epistolary, Hargrave's writing emerges powerfully marked by her predilection for mimicry and ventriloquism. Hargrave's letters are, that is, documents rich in fur-trade social history as well as an extraordinary repository of voices that describe and contest the cultural, racial, domestic, and gendered realities of the Canadian northwest. Resituating what Sara Mills calls the "lived experience of colonial life" (47) onto the page, Hargrave's records of fur-trade "trivia," like gossip in its best form, give voice to people, perspectives, and constructions of subjectivity that official histories typically suppress (Spacks 5, 15–16, 30). This paper has, for instance, presented only a small selection of the voices and perspectives that Hargrave's letters explore.

Hargrave was in Rupert's Land because George Simpson's domestic choices had turned fur-trade society inside out. Ironically, Hargrave could not be in Rupert's Land *except* as a witness to a social world negoti- ating its limits and boundaries, its sites, specifically, of familial inclusion and familial exclusion. Claims of kinship and affiliation— especially claims inflected by questions of race and ethnicity—profoundly and, indeed, sometimes violently, mark what was at stake in the domestic constitution of early Canada. "It may never be possible...to formulate...the story of relations between settler women and indige- nous women...as a unified metanarrative," Carole Gerson acknowledges. "Rather," she proposes, "stories of 'what really happened'...must be assembled from the fragments to be found in published and unpub- lished personal narratives" (17). Christine Welsh's account of her recent search for her "grandmothers" describes only too clearly how starkly First Nations and mixed-blood women have been erased from official, imperial HBC records (60–61). That we know anything at all about "what really happened" in a fur-trade world in radical social flux, that we can "recall" at least something about this bit of early Canada, is due, in part, to Letitia Mactavish Hargrave's unique, fragmented, richly other-voiced, epistolary record.

NOTES

1. All subsequent references to Mactavish Hargrave's letters are to this edition.
2. Mactavish Hargrave's letters reflect a much greater concern with fitting in as much writing as possible than with paragraphing, punctuation, or accurate pronoun references. I have, very occasionally, added explanatory or missing words to MacLeod's published transcriptions, all of which I indicate with square brackets.
3. John George had changed the spelling of his surname to correspond with that of his influential family member and fur-trade patron, Simon McTavish (MacLeod xxi).
4. The first two women were wives of British missionaries; the third was the former Mary McBeath of the Red River Settlement, who was married to Donald Ross, Chief Factor at Norway House.

The Knowledge of "Sex" and the Lattice of the Confessional

The Nun's Tales and Early North American Popular Discourse

JENNIFER BLAIR

...Lord Angelo is precise,
Stands at a guard with envy, scarce confesses
That his blood flows, or that his appetite
Is more to bread than stone.
 —Measure for Measure *(I.iii.50–53)*

THE ABOVE LINES appear as the epigraph to Matthew Lewis's *The Monk* (1796), a novel that has come to be regarded as the signal text for the study of the gothic genre. As William Veeder explains, "From the controversy over *The Monk* came the first tools for defining gothic fiction" (20), and I begin with a brief discussion of *The Monk* by way of fore-grounding my analysis of "nun's tales," the Lewis-inspired branch of monastic gothic that took hold of—and in some ways instated—literary popular culture in Canada and the United States in the early part of the nineteenth century. Like Lewis's *The Monk*, the North American nun's tales, of which the most famous is this continent's first "best-seller" *Awful Disclosures* (1836), are set in ostensibly alternative—predominantly Catholic—locales (*Awful Disclosures* is set in Montreal). Yet, as Carole Gerson has pointed out, while a nineteenth-century taste for the national romance saw several Canadian history and/or fiction writers look to Québec for material—its "settings, characters, and folklore associated with its antiquity and foreignness" (*Purer* 111)—the nun's tales are excep-

173

tional for their condemnation of Québec and its Catholic population.[1] Unlike the literature that makes use of Québec's "Old World" motifs with a benevolent nostalgia, the nun's tales' focus on religion "constituted another facet of Lower Canada's literary appeal by offering some English Canadian writers an opportunity to import the anti-Catholicism characteristic of much European gothic fiction" (Gerson, *Purer* 111). As Jenny Franchot adds, through the nun's tales (tales that would instigate such physical violences as the burning of the Ursuline convent in Boston in 1834), Protestant America sought to maintain links with its European origins while at the same time repudiating the "corruptions of Old World (principally Italian) Catholicism" (135). But as both Gerson and Franchot note, if this early instance of North American popular culture was the result of a desire to establish a certain cultural attachment to Europe combined with a national and religious distinctiveness, their overall legacy of achievement is more singular and less nuanced. First and foremost, these texts were written and circulated to generate a hatred of Catholicism including Catholic people, places, and institutions. They did so by telling the story, most often in the form of a first-person testimony, of an apparently "innocent" woman who is imprisoned in a convent and/or is sexually abused by priests, the latter occurring most often in the conveniently enclosed arena of the confessional.

And yet, to the extent that the settings of the nun's tales are displaced onto a Catholic nation or region, their religious focus may well serve as a disguise for anxieties regarding sexual citizenship and the circulation of information, both of which became newly meaningful, and acquired a new kind of cultural urgency, with the ascendance of popular literacy in North America brought by evangelical Protestantism. In other words, along with their anti-Catholic disapproval of what Maria Monk in *Awful Disclosures* terms "unreserved confession" (88),[2] these texts also voice a self-conscious concern with the evangelical Protestant movement and the potential unsolicited effects that Protestantism's otherwise exalted "private" confession might bring.

This chapter explores the nun's tales' efforts at placing restraints on the circulation of information—of sexual information in particular—by advocating for a certain scarcity of confessional utterances. However, and as I hope to show here, in this quest to demonstrate various forms of confessional restraint, they also inadvertently demonstrate confession's propensity for giving away more than the requisite guilt. In so doing, these nun's tales offer some important revelations of their own regarding the semantics of sexual repression and the production of gender difference in nineteenth-century North America.

◆ Scarce Confessions

AWFUL DISCLOSURES is as faithful as The Monk in its employment of gothic conventions. In fact it makes use of most of those listed in Eve Sedgwick's landmark text on the genre, The Coherence of Gothic Conventions: "the tyrannical older man with the piercing glance who is going to imprison and try to rape or murder [the hero and heroine]; the priesthood and monastic institutions; sleeplike and deathlike states; subterranean spaces and live burial; doubles; the discovery of obscured family ties; affinities between narrative and pictorial art; [and] possibilities of incest" (8). When it comes to delivering upon what Sedgwick identifies as the gothic promise to be "the great liberator of feeling" (Coherence 1), however, Awful Disclosures does so by aligning the liberation of feeling with a specifically Protestant promise of confession, where the confessing subject becomes "free" to disclose his or her guilt, not to a priest or an intermediary, but directly to God. Most important, the "feelings" of trepidation and horror typifying the gothic are rooted, in these monastic gothic texts, in a panic over the consequences of the distinct processes of confession. While they may pretend to locate trouble in the Catholic model of confession, the North American nun's tales, in fact, reveal a certain apprehension regarding the effectiveness of discourse as the medium through which the newly inaugurated "private individual" could express guilt, the jubilance of redemption, and eternal faith. As well, they express a certain discomfort with the way in which the confessing individual was thought to come to know him- or herself as part of an emergent, democratic collective through these confessions. Their identification of the Catholic confessional as the locus of evil and the source of emotional turmoil serves to displace this more secular concern over language and individual expression into a religious-theological domain.

Of course, from its sixteenth-century beginnings, Protestantism defined itself according to its mandate to make religion accessible to all worshippers by conducting services and printing the Bible in the vernacular of the people rather than in Latin. Under Protestantism, people were encouraged to read for themselves so that they did not have to depend upon a priest to interpret God's words. In England, John Wesley spearheaded the movement to make printed material available to the masses. In *The Methodist Book Concern: A Romance of History,* H.C. Jennings explains, "John Wesley was the first man to set the example for modern cheap prices with the idea that these prices might be sustained by large sales." His books were "surprisingly cheap," writes Jennings, and "they were brought within the reach of the poorest. They were sold by hundreds of thousands, and in this way the early Methodists became the most widely instructed Christians in the world of their time" (qtd in Pierce 3). Following Wesley, North American Protestants took to publishing and distributing cheap pamphlets of religious or other writings on related "worthy" subjects. The Ryerson Press, for example, was founded in York (Toronto) in 1829 to print a weekly newspaper called *The Christian Guardian.* According to Lorne Pierce's history of the press, from the "500 subscribers to *The Christian Guardian* the publishing concern grew until it issued hundreds of thousands of periodicals and a million books a year" (8). Combined with advancements in the technology of printing (see Sullivan 211), the Protestant interest in accessibility of the scriptures and the Methodists' industrious efforts at making printed texts available to the people led to popular literacy in North America. And it was the proliferation of print material that also made texts like *Awful Disclosures* possible—texts that seem to have little interest in furthering the Methodist missionary-style betterment of society, however much they may lay claim to it. What they *do* bring, however, is a "salvation" of perhaps an only slightly different sort: the pleasure of reading.

The nun's tales' prevailing concern that discourse is all too cooperative when it comes to mediating revelation runs counter to this Protestant movement for the "freedom of the Word." Instead, their preoccupation with the fearful possibility that confession, if unsuccessfully regulated, can reveal *too much* suggests a desire for the placing of limits on expression and communication. In this respect, the measurement and measurability of individual expression becomes another useful "tool," to use Veeder's term, for defining the gothic overtones of these and other monastic texts. It is little wonder, then, that *The Monk* begins by invoking Shakespeare's Lord Angelo and noting his remarkable capability to offer "scarce" confessions. As "scarce," Lord Angelo's confessions of his human desires are clearly "in demand," so to speak, in that others are aware of them (especially the scarcity of them) and that he delivers them with a spareness that describes the character of the confession itself as much as it does the matter of his confessions.[3] No doubt Lewis remembers Lord Angelo here not just as an ardently self-economizing individual, but also as someone whose so-called "precision" is to be undone only by his lust for a nun.[4] Like Lewis's Abbot Ambrosio, Lord Angelo's success depends upon the tight economic relationship between desire and self-control. Both of these figures—in some ways the gothic ancestors of the characters of the nun's tales—attempt (in vain) to withhold their carnal desires under the constraints placed on confession. As such, they are shown to be victims of a society which, as Foucault explains, "has ordered sex's difficult knowledge...around the slow surfacing of confidential statements" (*History* 63).

It is around the time of the *The Monk*'s publication that Foucault in *The History of Sexuality* identifies a "metamorphosis in literature"

> from a pleasure to be recounted and heard, centering on the heroic or marvelous narration of "trials" of bravery or sainthood, to a literature ordered according to the infinite task of extracting from the depths of oneself, in between the words, a truth which the very form of the confession holds out like a shimmering mirage. (59)

A nominal descendent of *The Monk*, the *Awful Disclosures of Maria Monk*, which is both a narrative of a woman's trials as well as a text that questions how evidence should be "extracted from the depths" of its narrator, straddles these two literary modes. With respect to the former (literature as the "narration of 'trials'"), Susan Griffin, one of only a handful of critics who has published on *Awful Disclosures*, addresses this text's judicial features, arguing that insofar as "her story and her self end up on trial," Monk's is a trial that ultimately proves "young women's incapacity to be trusted: [the nun's] testimony is essential to unveiling the truth, but it also proves her vulnerability and fallibility" (94, 104). Rebecca Sullivan extends this argument to point out that the nun's tales filtered this distrust of women through an associated distrust of North America's new and quickly developing urban environments. Sullivan offers the provocative suggestion that "the protagonist of *Awful Disclosures* was not Monk herself but Montreal and its environs" as if, in keeping with Foucault, the city becomes the hero through enduring such a trial (216). On the other side of Foucault's "transformation," however, Franchot, in a discussion of *Awful Disclosures* and Rebecca Reed's *Six Months In a Convent*, observes that Reed's "convent exposé ignores the etiquette of the belles lettres tradition to create a newly intimate voice of exploitation that produced legions of true believers" (147). The same could be said for *Awful Disclosures* which was published less than a year later.

My own discussion builds from Griffin's insistence, in the introduction to her recent book *Anti-Catholicism and Nineteenth-Century Fiction*, that "We cannot understand either the popularity or the uses of these narratives by ignoring the forms they take" (3). However, I take "form" much more literally than Griffin does in the sense that I am interested in the tension between the actual structure of the confessional described in these books and its metaphoric doubling in these tales—tales which not only describe but also take the form of an enclosure that gives way to a revelation.

While Foucault's theories of sexuality are well known, as Susan Bernstein notes, "less rigorous attention has been paid to his theory of confession" (2). Critics have recently become interested in the mechanics of confession, however, and what it was about the confessional that made it the focal point of anti-Catholic campaigns. Drawing in part from Bernstein, Griffin points out that the confessional figured as an evil substitute for the marriage bed, and, therefore, a significant threat to the national family, not just in Gothic literature but in British and American sensational fiction as well. As we have seen, Griffin argues that the nun's tales' distrust of the Catholic model of confession soon slides to become a distrust of women and women's testimony. My argument takes up this important issue of the relationship between gender and confession in North America, but it does so by first situating the nun's tales' trouble with Catholic confession in relation to the structures of discourse and of the architecture of the confessional itself, and then by looking to places where gender difference becomes meaningful according to these structures and/or their evident soundness. While Bernstein's illuminating analysis of women and confession in English Victorian literature critiques Foucault's panopticon and Freudian psychoanalysis for the ways in which both "intimate an invincible structure of power" (26) (she reads Freud and Foucault as offspring of Victorian confessional models), I look to these North American examples to find where the structures of confession may not have been so convincingly "invincible"—at least not yet. For, in these early examples of the nun's tales, "knowledge" and "sex" do not signify unquestionably, and accordingly "male" and "female" do not emerge as definitive, naturalized categories of knowing or as prerequisites for speaking. In other words, the various confessions in play in these texts—Protestant, Catholic, and/or those taking place in the arena of print culture—participate in, but do not finally bring about, what Foucault saw as confession's accomplishments in the nineteenth century. All in all, in the discussion that follows I explore how the confessional is figured as a threat to the sanctity of discourse to do the work of "extracting" and telling information about oneself, one's beliefs, and one's experiences.

Critical interest in the nun's tales is relatively recent, yet it is curious that what has yet to be explored in analyses of *Awful Disclosures* is the issue of disclosure itself, the conditions under which it operated and its social and literary effects. In approaching a text titled *Awful Disclosures*, a text for which sex is its most significant disclosure but which also must treat sex as its foremost unspeakable subject, not to mention a text exhibiting a paranoia about confession at every turn, it is helpful to begin with Foucault, in whose estimation "The confession was, and still remains, the general standard governing the production of the true discourse on sex" and for whom "Protestantism" is one of four factors implementing confession's "considerable transformation" (*History* 63).[5] At the same time, however, I will demonstrate that the nun's tales, as transcriptions of women's speech on the subject of sex, pressure Foucault's analysis of the repressive hypothesis precisely where *it* is most crucially lacking.

The nun's tales produce a scarcity of sexual knowledge by assisting sex's relegation to the private, even as they seek to make public certain illicit sexual liaisons. Part of the charge levied against the nuns and priests was that they dwelt in old world locales: convents, abbeys, hermitages, confessionals. These places were considered closed not just to sexual activity, but also to the reception of a discourse on sex, including sexual protocols that circulated in the social sphere and were increasingly considered necessary to a person's development as an individual. So, for instance, Lewis's Ambrosio, according to one of the Madrid noblemen, "is reported to be so strict an observer of chastity, that he knows not in what consists the difference of man and woman" (Lewis 11). Here, it is not only evident that Lewis and his readers were certainly no strangers to the constitutive relationship between private and public space and gender difference, but also that they subscribed to and actively reiterated the notion that gender difference, as part and parcel of what Foucault, Sedgwick and others term the "knowledge of sex," was threatened by enclosed spaces. And yet—and this is to build on the nun's tales' conflicting attitude towards disclosure I have so far suggested— even if openness were the key to the stability of a society stratified according to gender difference, this nascent genre and its community of "popular" readers were just as panicked by the prospect of such spaces becoming "open" to the flow of discourse as they were by the possibility of barriers overzealously inhibiting the circulation of sexual knowledge. In fact, the nun's tales' overriding concern regarding these socially and sexually sealed off institutions is with what happens when sex *does* trespass the sacred boundaries of the cloister. That it will is not merely an imagined possibility, for the nun's tales, operating in their own conveniently generous medium of fiction, manufacture this trespass themselves only to turn around and accuse the institution in question of allowing such an intrusion. Overall, their primary allegation is that regardless of how ordered and exacting these chaste locales may attempt and present themselves to be, they are unable to stop the diffusive spread of this contamination. To the ultimate discredit of these institutions, the structural and social designs of the cloister, especially the perforated lattice of the confessional, allow for too much sexual exchange. Projected here as a regime that fails because its own constitutive boundaries are too permeable, Catholicism is personified in characters like Monk and Ambrosio who did not properly police their own boundaries between their inward imaginations, desires, and feelings, and their outward behaviour. In this way, the nun's tales document the disciplinary encroachment on social discourse in the early nineteenth century when, as Vernon Rosario puts it, "sexuality became the cornerstone of explorations of individual subjectivity in both medical confessions and literary texts" (119). Yet, unlike Rousseau's *Confessions*—through which, by "telling all" with regard to his sexual experiences, as Rosario explains, Rousseau hoped to vindicate himself to his public—the nun's tales needed to speak of sex with a certain modesty. That is, they also had to keep their mention of sex scarce, if their narrators were to be socially redeemed.

Drawing from Foucault's claim that the "scientia sexualis" of "our civilization" is "confession," and that the "truthful confession was inscribed at the heart of the procedures of individualization by power" (*History* 58–59), the remainder of this chapter addresses what I consider to be two such "procedures of individualization" at work in *Awful Disclosures*. These "procedures" are the establishment of intimacy, and the localization of sexual knowledge into nameable sex acts and pleasures. In their implementation of such "procedures," *Awful Disclosures* and other nun's tales render sexual protocols without apparently speaking about sex, but also expose these protocols in such a way as to offer them up as cultural implements rather than natural predispositions. By the speaking and making sacred of intimate spaces, as well as sites and types of sex acts, the nun's tales work hard to inscribe impermeable psychic and physical boundaries around the diffusive and shifting notion of "sex." Insofar as they are confessional utterances themselves, however, and, therefore, victims of the confessional porousness they critique in the Catholic model, these Protestant texts give themselves away as not-quite-effective boundary keepers. In other words, "inscribed at heart" by confession, these texts are also, in a sense, haunted by it. Early North American Protestant evangelical discourse, whether *Awful Disclosures* and the other nun's tales or the Methodist sermons by influential ministers such as Egerton Ryerson and John Manly, is haunted by the fact that it might admit to the failure of its own will to power—the power to control the discursive field of sexual knowledge as well as to control its own utterances within this field. In other words, Protestantism worried that it might confess itself, so to speak, as failing in its own texts that otherwise profess a mastery of confession.

◆ **Awful Disclosures**

GIVEN THAT the nun's tales were so popular, it is surprising that a relatively small amount of scholarly attention has been paid to them. Critics have tended to focus on *Awful Disclosures*, and so we know more about its sources, authorship, production and distribution history, and overall reception, than we do about any other of the nun's tales. Ray Allen Billington was the first historian to pay serious attention to the text. As Maureen McCarthy points out, however, Billington devotes much of his analysis to the religious controversy behind the text without questioning "why the battle should take the form of a tale about an escaped nun, nor did he study the underlying or cultural factors shaping this controversy" (179–80). McCarthy focuses especially on these "cultural factors," filling in the major players and circumstances in this extraordinary episode in American history that has "not received the scholarly attention it merits" because it "is often seen as a ridiculous affair, an epiphenomenon, much less important than Jacksonian party politics or respectable reform efforts" (McCarthy 178–79). Her book-length study on the nun's tales seeks to show that "this affair was not marginal, but was part of mainstream American culture in the 1830s" (179). *Awful Disclosures* is currently available in print in a scholarly volume that also includes Reed's *Six Months in a Convent* edited and with an introduction by Nancy Lusignan Schultz. Apart from this academic readership, however, the text continues to be reprinted and circulated in anti-Catholic circles for the purposes of generating religious prejudice. Sullivan recalls, for example, the book's resurfacing "during John F. Kennedy's presidential campaign in 1961 and Pat Buchanan's nomination campaign during the 1995 Republican primaries" (215). Another significant contemporary development of the nun's tales occurs in Toni Morrison's 1998 novel *Paradise* in which the search of an Oklahoma convent to "expose its filth to the light" (these are Morrison's words from the opening of the novel) serves as a kind of critique, Schultz writes, of "the notion that nothing must be kept hidden, particularly from the male gaze" (Schultz xxvii).

What interests me most about this critical history of the text is the way in which a multitude of otherwise discrete classes of people, ideas, and nations cross in their engagement with *Awful Disclosures*. In other words, this book is itself evidence of a certain circulation and mobility of several factors, wired on a newly complex grid of social relations, as much as it is a story about this complex grid. Perhaps the contextual history of *Awful Disclosures*, if only generally, can be taken as typical of the history of the other nun's tales which are all similarly taken up with questions of social and discursive circulation.

Published in 1836 in New York City, *Awful Disclosures* is a first-person testimonial of a young Montreal Protestant woman named Maria Monk who attends the convent school of the Grey Nuns and eventually enters the "Black Nunnery" at the Hotel Dieu, where most of the "awful" action takes place.[6] While a novice she "heard from the mouths of the priests at confession what [she] cannot repeat, with treatment corresponding" (29); however, it is not until she is a nun that she experiences all of the horrors of the convent, including rape, torture, isolation, murders of babies born to nuns as a result of sexual abuse, and murders of nuns themselves. The scattered and temporally vague narrative recounts these and other atrocities, as well as the more ordinary events in the daily life of the convent. Some of the penances Monk and her colleagues must perform include kneeling on peas, walking on their knees through underground tunnels, kissing the floor and eating with ropes around their necks. One key character is "Mad Jane Ray," someone who, often taking Monk as her accomplice, schemes against the various oppressions of the convent. Together Ray and Monk speak out of turn, sneak into restricted areas, bastardize song lyrics, steal extra clothes, linen, and food, and play practical jokes on the nuns.

A conspicuous feature of the book is the architectural diagram of the convent's layout printed on both of its endpapers. In her Preface, Monk invites her readers to match this diagram with the actual convent as a way of authenticating her testimony:

> *Whoever shall explore the Hotel Dieu Nunnery, at Montreal, will find unquestionable evidence that the descriptions of the interior of that edifice, given in this book, were furnished by one familiar with them; for whatever alterations may be attempted, there are changes which no mason or carpenter can make and effectually conceal; and, therefore, there must be plentiful evidence in that institution of the truth of my description. (12–13)*

In the last few pages of the text Monk attempts a successful escape to save her unborn child. She flees to New York where she is harboured by Protestant ministers to whom she supposedly confesses these experiences and who, in turn, inscribe her testimony in book form.

Among these ministers, or "promoters" as McCarthy dubs them, those who likely "ghost-wrote" the book are: the Presbyterian minister John Jay Slocum; editor of the *Protestant Vindicator* William Craig Brownlee; the reverend, and supposed "real father" of Monk's baby, William K. Hoyt; a member of a prominent New England family, Theodore Dwight Jr., who was the nephew of the then President of Yale University and whose connection to the story "conferred upon it an air of respectability" (McCarthy 282); and, finally, another minister named George Bourne who worked as an itinerant preacher in Québec in the 1820s. Bourne is perhaps the most likely to have written *Awful Disclosures* since he had already published a convent novel set in Québec, *Lorette, the History of Louise, Daughter of a Canadian Nun* (1833), as well as the travel guide *The Picture of Quebec* (1830). Also among Bourne's publishing credits are a biography of John Wesley, an anthology of Protestant sermons and other religious writings, and an anthology of popular nonsense newspaper stories. If we understand, as Griffin does, the nun's tales to be evidence of Richard Hofstader's claim that "Anti-Catholicism has always been the pornography of the Puritan" (Hofstader 21, qtd in Griffin 99), then Bourne occupies an interesting authorial position as minister, newspaper publisher, and one of North America's first pornographers. On the other hand, as a text "jointly" authored by a minister (or several) and a woman, *Awful Disclosures* may also be taken for an early example of American sentimental fiction. Monk, however, was not at all the "Victorian Lady" authoress that is the subject of Ann Douglas's *The Feminization of American Culture*, but, instead, appears to have been a lower class woman from an illiterate family and community (the affidavits of her mother and Montreal locals are signed "her mark").[7]

Despite the work of these promoters, it was soon revealed that Monk had never set foot in a convent, let alone been imprisoned and abused in one, and had in fact been a prostitute in Montreal. The affidavits printed in a subsequent 1836 edition confirmed her imposture. In one of these, Monk's mother swears: "that when at the age of about seven years, she broke a slate pencil in her head; that since that time her mental faculties were deranged...that she could make the most ridiculous, but plausible stories...and that she was never in a nunnery" (217). Still, for approximately two years, Monk managed to keep company with respected Americans who argued for her veracity. The birth of Monk's second illegitimate child, however, distanced her from these connections. She was convicted of robbing a brothel client in the summer of 1849 and she died of cholera in a New York prison soon after.

Portions of Monk's story first appeared in the New York penny press, in a paper called the *Protestant Vindicator*, in November of 1835. John D. Stevens surmises that penny press readers included the "[t]housands of literate and ambitious clerks, bookkeepers, and junior partners [who] lived and worked within a few blocks of the waterfront" (20). The complete book version of *Awful Disclosures* was printed by Howe and Bates, a press set up by two partners of the respectable Harper and Row publishing house just, it seems, for this one occasion. That same year subsequent editions were published in Canada and in England. There were also several associated texts published which included refutations and counter-refutations of Monk's story, and general arguments against and in defense of Catholicism. Tagging onto the success of *Awful Disclosures*, a whole host of very similar nun's tales were published throughout the century. Of course, *Awful Disclosures* already followed the example of Lewis's *The Monk* as well as Diderot's *The Nun* (1796), and the North American examples of Reed's *Six Months in a Convent* and George Bourne's *Lorette*. But it was *Awful Disclosures*, an inexpensive 230-page pocket-sized book, that became the first North American bestseller. In Stevens's assessment, "By 1860 there had been twelve authorized printings and at least as many bootleg editions, with a combined circulation of perhaps 500,000" (35).

The commercial success of *Awful Disclosures* has also been attributed to a particular anti-Catholic sentiment prevailing in New England and New York at the time that was partly a consequence of Irish immigrants travelling to Canada and entering the United States by ship across the St. Lawrence (Billington, *Protestant* 34). By ushering this massive influx of cheap labourers into an already struggling employment market, Canada only added to its own already clouded reputation among Americans. Sullivan suggests that *Awful Disclosures* tapped into residual anti-Québec sentiments present in the United States that dated back to the American Revolution, renewing the attitude that "Lower Canada was viewed as the locus of all that could potentially go wrong in America" (204).

As a cultural artifact, *Awful Disclosures* is both product and vehicle of several circulations, from public perceptions of new immigration patterns to the new mass-consumption of print media that were affecting the social and economic life of early nineteenth-century North America. Against these forceful circuits of exchange, perhaps printed discourse appeared more amenable to a newly self-identified participating citizenry—at least it was another medium of circulation to which they had access. The nun's tales do evidence an avid interest in testing the governability of print, but their handle on discourse, as exhibited in the texts themselves through their appropriation of confession, could only ever be provisional.

◆ Intimate Confessions and Public Display

PROTESTANTISM'S SIGNAL DEPARTURE from Catholicism was its remodeling of confession as a private, inwardly located experience, an occasion in which the individual communicated directly with God through his or her "conscience." This newly privatized confession supposedly freed individuals to "speak" directly with God rather than only through the mediation of a priest. According to the nun's tales, however, Protestant confession was also preferable because it disallowed potentially improper intimate relations thought to occur frequently between priests and the innocent and unsuspecting confessants, especially women and boys. The Protestant convert, Father Chinquy, explained in *The Priest, the Woman and the Confessional* (1875) that the explicit charge falls against the priests who supposedly questioned confessants on sexual matters, thereby delivering sexual knowledge to them, tempting their desire, and even encouraging them to participate in sexual acts. Chinquy likens the Catholic confessional to the Indian custom of sati:

> For I do not exaggerate when I say that for many noble-hearted, well-educated, high-minded women to be forced to unveil their hearts before the eyes of a man, to open to him all the most sacred recesses of their souls, all the most sacred mysteries of their single or married life, to allow him to put to them questions which the most depraved woman would never consent to hear from her wildest seducer, is often more horrible and intolerable than to be tied on burning coals. (1)

Not only does Chinquy manage to vilify the convent by making a racialized association with Hindu sati, he also draws a parallel between the circulation of sexual information and a localized, religio-cultural ritual of exchange featuring the sacrifice of women. Chinquy's adoption of the nineteenth-century racist fascination with social practices in "other" British colonies notwithstanding, the attention to sacrifice is telling since Protestantism's apparently liberatory design did not entirely do away with sacrifice either. While the nun's tales depend upon a woman to speak about her sexual experiences, the end result is that they cast her off as somehow villainous for having had these experiences in the first place, and then also for contaminating public discourse by speaking about them.[8] This is the first of many examples where the nun's tales point to the terms of their own contradiction.

What most horrified Protestant readers about the imagined confessional liaison was that it introduced the supposedly "innocent" to a world of sexual exchange that constantly crossed rather than policed its boundaries. This includes, of course, the priests' putting questions of an alleged sexual nature to women, but sometimes the content of this exchange took a more palpable form. Chinquy's *The Priest...*reports that

> Under the bonds of secrecy, an educanda, of fine form and pleasing manners, and of a noble family, confided to me the fact of her having received, from the hands of her confessor, a very interesting book (as she described it), which related to the monastic life.... It proved to be the Monaca, by Dalembert [sic], a book, as we all know, filled with the most disgusting obscenity. (39)

Here Chinquy more than likely refers to Diderot's *The Nun* (English translation of "Monaca"), D'Alembert being Diderot's good friend and sometime co-author. Apparently, reading this book about the nun Suzanne, who is trapped in a convent where she receives not unwelcome sexual advances from the Mother Superior, brings Chinquy's "educanda" over into a world of sexual deviancy. In another revealing textual manifestation of illicit exchange, George Bourne's *Lorette* is the first-person-narrated product of two children born to a nun who had been raped by priests. In a sense, both *The Priest...*and *Lorette* depend upon the illicit exchanges that occur between priest and confessant—especially in a text like *Lorette* where these exchanges actually *conceive* their authors—if only to heroically extract them from the bounds of what was called "auricular confession" and deliver them to a mass audience in textual form. This literary debt to the confessional, however, was not an easy one to shake insofar as the tales display how confession serves as much to disrupt the course of Foucault's "procedures of individualization" as it does to carry it through. The Protestant call for a particularized, self-reflective "intimacy" to occur in the process of confession, a "private" intimacy between the individual and the "Spirit within," instead of the outward and more "public" intimacy between the confessant and the priest in the confessional, is, in fact, the site of one such disturbance.

Like Father Chinquy, *Awful Disclosures* also targets the Catholic confessional as an inherently improper space because, in its purposeful fostering of intimate conversations between a man and a woman, it lent itself too easily to sexual exchange:

> I shall not tell what was transacted at such times, under the pretence of confessing, and receiving absolution from sin: far more guilt was often incurred than pardoned; and crimes of a deep die were committed while trifling irregularities, in childish ceremonies, were treated as serious offences. I cannot persuade myself to speak plainly on such a subject, as I must offend the virtuous ear. I can only say, that suspicion cannot do any injustice to the priests, because their sins cannot be exaggerated. (124–25)

By figuring the confessional not just as a conveniently private place where sex occurs but, more specifically, as the locus of sexual "transaction," this text provides readers with ample opportunity to think through the possibilities for the circulation of sexual information as well as the possibilities for placing restrictions on it such that "guilt" and "pardon" would come out appropriately balanced. Accordingly, Monk's early description of the structure of the confessional takes issue explicitly with the site of transfer. As she explains (in rhyme no less) the novices "kneeled beside a fine wooden lattice work, which entirely separated the confessor from us, yet permitted us to place our faces almost to his ear, and nearly concealed his countenance from view, even when so near" (41). Clearly, these physical circumstances, allowing for close proximity, are what make the confessional so seductive. Monk continues: "I recollect how the priests used to recline their heads on one side, and often covered their faces with their handkerchiefs, while they heard me confess my sins, and put questions to me, which were often of the most improper and even revolting nature, naming crimes both unthought of, and inhuman" (Monk 41–42). Preceding the priests' verbal advances in this description, the various perforated separations—the lattice, the handkerchiefs—are the guilty instigators and enablers of the ensuing exchange. Not only are they ambiguous channels of communication, but the various partial screens feign "concealment" only to "permit" a sinister closeness. The permeable membranes of the wooden lattice and the handkerchief allow the transfer to be improperly multi-directional. Perhaps worst of all, the content exchanged may be untraceable as it travels through the apertures since, being of a sexual nature, it cannot be explicitly, as Foucault has said, "put into discourse" (*History* 11)—at least not by Monk who cannot "persuade" herself "to speak plainly on such a subject." At the same time, however, it cannot be kept *out* of discourse either. "To speak plainly" is a traumatic problem in these texts in the sense that the content of confession is always somewhat inseparable from the performative act of confessing. If the nun's tales articulate a panic about maintaining borders, it may well be the border between language and its objects that is of utmost concern.

After all, as part of the Protestant campaign, these texts took up the debate regarding what confession is and should be. In this respect, while Monk's accusations and the nun's tales' accusations are more generally based on malicious Protestant prejudice, their location of evil as a boundless, immeasurable exchange arises directly from Protestantism's preoccupation with the maintenance of borders. Specifically, they reference the Protestant interest in discrete interior and exterior spaces that functioned to sanctify and protect the conscience as the new site of confession. Following Wesley, Protestant ministers in both Canada and the United States preached to "awaken" the conscience.[9] Itself dependent on a spatial logic of interior and exterior, the conscience was understood to reside *within* every individual person. For Ryerson: "When a man's understanding is enlightened with the truths of the Gospel...his conscience is awakened, so that he turns from his sins and is humbled, abased, and ashamed before God on account of them" (*Wesleyan* 19). In the Preface to *Awful Disclosures*, Monk tells of her own similarly troubled conscience: "My feelings are frequently distressed and agitated, by the recollection of what I have passed through; and by night, and by day, I have little peace of mind, and few periods of calm and pleasing reflection" (12). Just as Monk hoped her confession would bring legal justice, her unmistakable appropriation of more respectable Protestant rhetoric here testifies to her accompanying wish for what Ryerson terms spiritual "justification":

> By justification, or pardon, or forgiveness, (which terms in the New Testament usually signify the same thing,) a sinner is exonerated from punishment and received into the Divine favour; by adoption and regeneration, he is taken into the family of God, and made a partaker of a filial and renewed Spirit: these blessings being usually, if not invariably, accompanied with an inward testimony or assurance of the Holy Spirit.... (Ryerson, Wesleyan 17)

Most important, at least in terms of the discussion here, is that this "inward testimony" was to be outwardly displayed. The Spirit, as a witness within, demonstrated the grace of God to the believer such that the believer could duplicate this "image" of God in his or her own outward behaviour. In one explanation of the ideal Protestant individual's "inward holiness as well as outward righteousness," Ryerson states: "Thus purity of life—embracing the whole circle of Christian virtues—is the estimation of purity of heart; and in proportion to our inward rectitude will be our outward obedience. When the heart is perfectly renewed 'in the image of God in righteousness and true holiness' then will we esteem 'all his precepts in all things to be right'" (Christians 14, 18; emphasis in text). Achieving this "outward righteousness" was crucial because, not only did newly converted individuals engage in a kind of intimacy with the spirit within, but also they entered into a kind of interpersonal intimacy with other members of the Protestant collective.[10] Protestant discourse emphasized the necessity of this collective community perhaps as much as it did the singular relationship between the believer and God. In his sermon titled The Nature, Origin, Progress, Present State, and Character of Wesleyan Methodism delivered in 1839, for example, John Manly preached the necessity of participating in "weekly class-meetings, in obedience to the Apostolic injunction we 'confess our faults, one to another, and pray one for another'...and, thus, like ancient fearers of God, speak often, to one another" (10). This "principle of 'voluntaryism,'" as Michael Gauvreau calls it, came with its own problems of separation in which the individual was to constantly work to maintain a proper division between his or her private and public selves (57). As with Lord Angelo, the body becomes as if inhabited by the wooden lattice. Here, the active "procedure of individualization" is the appropriate delimitation of the boundaries where the best of confessants not only distinguish between themselves and the "outside," but they must also show that they can maintain boundaries within. The properly self-governing individual must continually monitor what will pass through that lattice (and how quickly). In Protestant North America, then, in order to be as respected as Lord Angelo or Lewis's Ambrosio before their downfalls, a person had to "scarce confess" to his or her Protestant community.

This notion of a proper, voluntary, collective confession is especially relevant to *Awful Disclosures* given that Monk explicitly offers her text as a confession to a community of readers:

> As the period of my accouchment approached, I sometimes thought that I should not survive it; and then the recollection of the dreadful crimes I had witnessed in the nunnery would come upon me very powerfully, and I would think it a solemn duty to disclose them before I died. To have a knowledge of these things, and leave the world without making them known, appeared to me like a great sin: whenever I could divest myself of the impression made upon me, by the declarations and arguments of the Superior, nuns, and priests, of the duty of submitting to every thing, and the necessary holiness of whatever the latter did or required. (226–27)

Here, Monk describes herself as about to *give birth* to a confession that is the product of what took place in her previous Catholic confessions. Not only is the separation between subject and subject matter ambiguous here, but also the confession, figured as a foetus, can never be entirely voluntary since, at some point, she will have no choice about how much and how quickly it will be "born." Furthermore, as a "child," this confession, no matter how much it might respect Protestant doctrine, will always bear resemblance to its Catholic parentage. In general, the fact that the content of her confession is of a sexual nature causes Monk to engage in the most difficult of labours to get it right, so to speak, even though the impossibility of finally controlling its delivery guarantees that she will ultimately fail. For the time being, however, Monk must do her best to present this confession as the outward demonstration of her securely intimate, interior conscience.

As a result, the text bears the marks of one that withholds, that is modestly spare, that is appropriately economical in that it scarcely speaks of the sex it must tell. As such, it approximates a very specific kind of intimacy, determined both by how much it tells and what kind of relationship it solicits in the event of its measured telling. If, as Lauren Berlant observes, to "intimate is to communicate with the sparest of signs and gestures" while "intimacy also involves an aspiration for a narrative about something shared, a story about both oneself and others that will turn out in a particular way" ("Intimacy" 281), then passages such as the following should qualify Monk as an appropriately intimate member of the Protestant collective on both counts: "I am assured that the conduct of the priests in our Convent has never been exposed, and is not imagined by the people of the United States. This induces me to say what I do, notwithstanding the strong reasons I have to let it remain unknown. Still, I cannot force myself to speak on such subjects except in the most brief manner" (73). Implying a parallel here between forcing her own testimony of this incident and her experience of being forced into sex, Monk exhibits some control over the chain of exposures that runs through this passage—from her own exposure to the priests, to the exposure of their conduct, to the exposure of herself as a raped woman. Intimacy here, in keeping with Berlant's definition, has more to do with not-sharing than it does with the exchange of private information. In other words, it has to do with noting and producing the separation between the performative act of confessing and the material confessed.

So, while Monk may be destined to a Hester Prynne-like existence, displaying her guilt before her in the form of her child, in the meantime her expectant body—anticipating a delivery but as yet still harbouring a baby within, just as Monk harbours information about the history of her condition in her hesitancy to speak about it—is the "mantle" to be removed by Protestantism and its insistence that "every secret thing, however perpetrated in the loneliness of retirement or under the mantle of midnight, will be brought into judgment" (Ryerson, *Christians* 7). Remarkably, however, Monk harnesses discourse as another kind of mantle, one that is within her jurisdiction and one whose susceptibility to Protestantism's pursuit of revelation has important performative possibilities for her. In short, the autobiographical text, itself a kind of speaking body, does not betray her as easily or as finally as her physical body. As a verbal confession, *Awful Disclosures* is an obedient voicing of her refusal to confess everything, a refusal so conscious of its own parameters that it associates the speaking of confession with a force that is like being forced into sex. By presenting herself, in this way, as someone who possesses a fiercely withholding interior, analogous to possessing a will and ability to say "no" to sex and to speaking about it, Monk aspires to be a good Protestant confessant. The question is: *Can* her confession also put forth a kind of disobedience detached from the Protestant will and obedience of Monk?

As we have seen, the confessional works on the same principles Foucault finds in Bentham's panopticon, at least in the sense that the modern liberal subject becomes a figure for it, constantly maintaining the separation between an intimate interior conscience and the self-on-display. But as a supplement to the panopticon, the confessional, however, also takes over where Foucault (now famously) left off—that is, on the subject of gender. By formulating proper ways to speak about sexual abuse, Monk and the other nun-narrators highlight how this voluntary confession newly accredited by the North American Protestant evangelicals was different for men than it was for women. Therefore, the achievement of these texts may have little to do with their indications of whether or not this somewhat fantastic notion that sexual abuse frequently occurred in the Catholic confessional was the primary reason behind the transformation of confession—that is, the transformation from the auricular confession between confessant and priest to the individual's "private" confession to God whose effects were to be displayed publicly. By just raising this sexual abuse scenario as a possibility (however ridiculous) the nun's tales called attention to the more general and viable possibility that gender difference played a foundational role in this new mode of confession and the important religious and social transitions that came with it.

The general premise assumed by the newly emerging public culture of North America and legitimated by the principle of voluntary collective confession was that women were not to speak about sex. As Chinquy explains, "Everywhere woman feels that there are things which ought never to be told, as there are things which ought never to be done, in the presence of the God of holiness. She understands that, to recite the history of certain sins, even of thoughts, is not less shameful and criminal than to do them" (6). Nun's tales such as Monk's elucidate precisely the manner in which women could only speak about sex by disavowing it; that is, they could only speak their refusal to speak about sex. If women could only ever participate in a veiled, sparse confession with other believers, where whatever was said was meant to signal a much greater confession taking place within, then it is also possible that *everything* they said could be thought to reference the sexual. *Awful Disclosures* and the other nun's tales underscore the fact that women are sacrificed by discourse insofar as the repressive hypothesis—the way in which people in Western civilization both never speak about sex, and, conversely, speak about it all the time—only ever serves to disadvantage women by binding them to the sexual. Supposedly written by a woman, *Awful Disclosures* could not possibly speak about anything *other* than sex.

Perhaps the most significant relevance of the nun's tales in terms of contemporary literary studies is the unique way in which they underscore the limits of discursive analyses based on "the sex left unsaid." In fact, they seem to anticipate the frustration felt by critics, such as Sedgwick, who have only recently articulated their compelled attachment to "Foucault's 'repressive hypothesis' and his suggestion that there might be ways of thinking around it." This frustration arises from the realization that his "book was divided against itself in what it wanted from its broad, almost infinitely ramified and subtle critique of the repressive hypothesis" (*Touching* 9, 10). Similarly, Veeder launches his discussion of the connection between the gothic and pleasure by claiming that "Foucault's book-long argument functions finally to confirm, rather than to refute, the repression hypothesis, once we understand 'repression' to mean the identifying and policing of sexuality" (24). What the nun's tales make clear is that as long as repression also means that discourse produces the concealment of sex, it is women who both make possible, but also who are the most actively repressed under, this "identifying and policing of sexuality." What remains to be seen, then, is how the nun-narrators negotiated between the telling of their "own" secrets, and the confessing of the fact that these secrets were not entirely issued from "within" but were compelled and conveyed by a wide spectrum of publicly circulating discourses on sex. That is, in addition to the "sex that is disclosed" and the "sex left unsaid" there may well be confessions in these texts that have little to do with sex and little to do with intimacy, but the impossibility of separating confession from sex and intimacy—and their collective work of delivering the individual to the public eye—makes them difficult to see.

◆ Speaking of Pleasures

THE PROBLEM WITH the confessional, as it is often described in the nun's tales, was not necessarily so much that the priests took advantage of close quarters to abuse women, but, rather, that women could not handle the questions the priests put to them (sometimes apparently innocently in the name of helping them confess their sexual guilt). First, if single women—and especially nuns—were truly and properly ignorant of anything to do with sex, they would not be able to recognize the sexual content in what they heard from the priests. (Some characters, like The Monk's Ambrosio, enter the cloister as babies and, therefore, do not even have the experience of witnessing the gendered behaviour of their parents or of society at large.) If and when the women did recognize the priests' innuendos, however, it was thought that they would be tempted by this information and would ultimately engage in deviant thoughts and acts as if they simply could not help themselves. The nun's tales go so far as to identify certain specific sexual deviancies—masturbation, lesbianism, incest, as well as intergenerational and pre-marital

sex—to which confession, and/or Catholicism more generally, had supposedly led the most proper of women. The fact that it is possible to arrive
at this catalogue of deviancies from reading these texts indicates how
hard they work to individuate, and thus render identifiable (and deviant),
specific sex acts. What is more, part of this rendering deviant includes
classifying according to a specific alignment of qualities wherein difference is privileged over sameness. Of course, they also had to establish a
language that used inference and displacement to do so: to speak in
various disguises and yet still make known what constituted certain
improper sex. But as a procedure of individualization, the fact that
these individual sex acts were denominated by this new confessional
design dictates the inevitable emptying-out and display of the contents
of these containers of deviancy.

In this project the nun's tales were prolific. Diderot's *The Nun*, for
example, portrays a lesbian relationship. Even though its narrator appears
to be unaware that the activities in which she engages with her Mother
Superior are of a sexual nature, let alone an improper one, readers nevertheless will come away with the sense that we "know" something "more"
about what goes on between the two women than she does: i.e., readers
of the past several decades may make use of the term "lesbian" to describe
such activities. Similarly, *Awful Disclosures* hints at a kind of lesbianism
when Monk frequently gets into bed with Jane Ray at night. Later on in
the text she is pressured to sleep in the same room and eventually the
same bed as her Superior. To similar ends, Chinquy references and con-
demns masturbation when he notes on various occasions that a woman
can commit "polluted" acts of sexual deviancy in "single" life and when
"alone" (except for God's presence).[11]

Apart from lesbianism and masturbation, not to mention rape, the
sexual deviancy that frequently arises in the nun's tales is incest. The
incest plot in Julia Catherine Beckwith Hart's *St. Ursula's Convent* (1824),
for instance, is hatched in a long-past incident in which a wet-nurse
switches one infant for another. The restoring of Adelaide de St. Louis
and Louisa Dudley to their rightful families, and the necessary rearrange-
ment of marital engagements, solves all sorts of "who loves who" problems
that were previously complicated by close kinship ties.[12] Also caught up

in an incest plot, Bourne's *Lorette* takes the position that women will, somehow intuitively, not desire their blood-siblings even though confused circumstances (like ambivalent parentage and obliviously arranged marriages) will pressure them otherwise. Diganu and Louise meet by chance in "the head of the dell at Lorette" (12–13) and are betrothed when they find out (partly through the priests' and nuns' explanation of the matching tattoos on their heads) that they are brother and sister. But through their engagement they (apparently) do not desire to be with each other sexually. Diganu only proposes to Louise when there is speculation that the presence of a single woman in his household is improper, and when mysterious visitors begin to threaten to take her away:

> "No authority upon earth shall separate us—answered Diganu vehemently—if you will put yourself in my power to protect you, by becoming my wife."
> "Wife!—retorted Louise in extreme unfeigned surprise—I have loved you as a sister." (25)

Of course there is a different, legitimate "authority"—the prohibition against incest—that *will* separate them. In the book, however, the priests and nuns are the evil informants who force this otherwise helpful intervention into their naïvely incestuous plans. In their address of incest, both *Lorette* and *St. Ursula's Convent* imply that, because of the migrancy, ill-communication and warfare particular to colonial life, marriage required some kind of regulative authority. If this authority was to be taken out of the hands of priests, then it might well have to be repositioned elsewhere.

By visiting relatively improbable incest scenarios through fiction, the nun's tales issue a concerted warning against attraction based on resemblance and familial affinity—that is, against desire based on sameness rather than desire based on difference. Of course, this desire for the same is the principal deviancy of auto-eroticism and homosexuality as well. In this sense the nun's tales pledge an allegiance to the Malthusian couple so celebrated in nineteenth-century public discourse and which also served as ammunition against monastic life.[13] If the nuns were to be "freed" by Protestantism to act for themselves, they should then (so the argument goes) contribute to the collective through procreation. But the nun's tales never venture to propose or condemn specific social implications for the supposedly ruined women or near-ruined couple; instead, they remain content to provide a more or less open-ended forum for debating and delimiting what desire consists of, as well as what the discrepancies between sex and pleasure might be. In fact, these texts seem to worry over "pleasure" as a new category of concern. Like their late eighteenth-century French and American counterparts, the nun's tales treat pleasure "as a remarkable attribute, index of value, and denomination of selfhood" and serve as further evidence of Stephen Shapiro's suggestion that the pleasures of reading—and specifically popular reading— were associated with sexual pleasure. Shapiro's "The Moment of the Condom: Saint-Méry and Early American Print Sexuality," about a Philadelphia bookstore that sold literature as well as pornography and condoms, suggests that this self-denominating pleasure was invented partly through the "coming of the book" (131). While the threat of incest may have raised some important questions about pleasure and the limits of pleasure, it may also serve a structural function since it occupies, if not makes possible, not to mention suspect, the space of the secret. If the sexual transmissions alleged in these texts stand for the circulation and exchange of discourse, commerce, and women more generally, perhaps the secret of incest might stand for several possible secrecies that underlie and are necessary to desirous relations. Sedgwick identifies The Nun as an early text elaborating the process by which "a version of knowledge/sexuality [was] increasingly structured by its pointed cognitive *refusal* of sexuality between women, between men" and in which this same-sex desire became the "particular sexuality that was distinctively constituted *as* secrecy" (*Epistemology* 73). Of course, secrecy might also be another way to describe the fundamental intimacy of Protestant collective confession.

In their attention to sexual deviance, the nun's tales circle around an anxiety that, while displaced onto the Catholic church, seems to dwell more squarely in this new epistemological domain where Protestantism meets print culture. Protestant rhetoric sought to remove sexual knowledge from the jurisdiction of priests and place it in the imagined absolute privacy of the conscience, where it would be revealed only at the discretion of individual subjects. But in this new model where sex would not be spoken, at least not by women, how would sexual catastrophes be prevented? How would deviancies like lesbianism, masturbation, and rape be managed? How would it be known—how would *men* know—that such activities occurred? Finally, how could ordinary people organize their desires into good/bad, speakable/unspeakable, if they did not have a certain knowledge of sex? The texts themselves answer these questions as they are the medium communicating to all readers the information necessary to keep everyone in good order. As such, they follow in the late-eighteenth-century tradition of what Shapiro terms "print sexuality" which accomplished a "type-setting of new bodily sensations that developed a sense of the privileged liberal subject" (125). Further, they make the announcement that: "society has taken upon itself to solicit and hear the imparting of individual pleasures" (Foucault 63). In other words, the nun's tales themselves take over the duties of the priests, but in a way that is less obviously detrimental to women—though of course detrimental all the same, insofar as these texts seek to repossess women's right to speech and maintain gender difference.

As *women's confessions*, however, the nun's tales also manage to confess their authorial pre-condition of having been "ghost-written"—not just by certain minister-promoters, but also by a Protestant (male) discursive apparatus. Diderot's *The Nun* and *Awful Disclosures*, especially when taken as companion texts (although they were published forty years apart on opposite sides of the Atlantic) trace how the nun's tales' accomplished this secondary, unsolicited confession. However, while *The Nun* presents a narrative voice that distinguishes itself from its content, *Awful Disclosures* seeks to reconcile the two—that is, the confessional utterance and the matter confessed. Both texts, nonetheless, reproduce to the extent of hyperbole the restrictions placed on women's speech by their own new logic of confession, and in so doing they point to the artificiality of their own design. As a result, and contrary to the early nineteenth-century North American Protestant rhetoric to which *Awful Disclosures* ostensibly belongs, the alignments of print, sex, and women's speech are left remarkably un-negotiated.

Suzanne, in Diderot's *The Nun*, does not—or, perhaps, *will not*—acknowl-edge that her interactions with the Mother Superior have anything to do with sex even though her own first-person narration of them leaves readers without a doubt about the nature of their relationship. Current readers would call their relationship "lesbian," while eighteenth- and nineteenth-century readers would likewise recognize this relationship to be sexual, and improperly sexual, if not codify it as sexually deviant by use of another term. To exhibit such a disconnection between her physical sensations and her moral constitution is also to disregard the Protestant logistics of spiritual embodiment where all physical senses worked entirely in the service of the conscience. Ryerson argued that the conscience could be felt as certainly as any other sensation and was, therefore, as confirmable as any external, visible and physical worldly experience: "Does not our internal consciousness carry as strong a conviction of reality with it, as our external senses: our seeing, our hearing, or touching, or tasting, or smelling? Yes, when the love of God is shed abroad in our hearts by the Holy Ghost given unto us" (*Wesleyan* 20). The most important of the senses, for Ryerson, was the sense of sight, since it was by virtue of seeing and reflecting that each indi-vidual carried out his or her relationship with the conscience: "Vision absorbs conjecture, reasoning and faith; and dispels imperfection, doubt and error" (*Christians* 23). By this logic, if a person cannot not "see" the Spirit within, it is the result of faulty "vision" rather than spiritual vacancy, and, therefore, one's senses must be put in good working order. Also, vision was not simply a means by which information could be received; rather, vision delegated by "absorbing" and "dispelling" information. In this way, a person's body was entirely focused on the expression of the conscience, the outward demonstration that the Spirit was within. Accordingly, Suzanne's refusal to explicitly acknowledge sexual sensa-tions and sex acts indicates, on the one hand, a deficiency of spiritual recognition. But, on the other hand, Suzanne does take up a similar logic to Ryerson's if only to present a different way in which bodily sensations can (not) be marshaled to participate in the production and confirmation of the individual subject. Overall, both the sermons and the nun's tales testify to the fact that an individual's physical sensations were a cause for concern, and that they were a logical rallying point insofar as "proof" or "evidence" was thought to be found there. Suzanne, however, acknowledges this body-as-evidentiary site precisely with disavowal, insisting that her sensational experiences did not trigger in her an awareness of impropriety.

The primary matter of concern for Suzanne and Ryerson is the interaction between physical experience and the recognition of moral law. Of course, even to the religiously non-partisan reader, Suzanne's adamant naïveté will inevitably generate suspicion—after all, how could she possibly *not know*? How could she not know that what she was doing counted as sex—or, rather, deviant sex? Also, if Suzanne does not recognize her relationship as sexual or deviant, what compels her to speak about it? The nun's tales seem to pressure their narrators to reconcile themselves, as "speaking nuns," to a Lacanian subjective paradigm in which the speaking subject comes into being only by recognizing and submitting to a sexual prohibition. Judith Butler offers a useful summary of this paradigm in *Gender Trouble*:

> The Lacanian appropriation of Lévi-Stauss focuses on the prohibition against incest and the rule of exogamy in the reproduction of culture, where culture is understood primarily as a set of linguistic structures and significations. For Lacan, the Law which forbids the incestuous union between boy and mother initiates the structures of kinship, a series of highly regulated libidinal displacements that take place through language.... Speech emerges only upon the condition of dissatisfaction, where dissatisfaction is instituted through incestuous prohibition; the original jouissance is lost through the primary repression that founds the subject. (43)

Drawing from Freud as well, Butler extends the subjectifying prohibition against incest to include the prohibition against homosexuality, thus making the parallel between the characters of the nun's tales more clear.[14] While Diganu and Louise, and in fact whole texts like *Lorette* that are these characters' "speech," come into being by virtue of the "primary repression" of incest (the priests' and nuns' intervention into their wedding ceremony), characters like Suzanne likewise tell their story as the effect of a response to a similar (if not the same) prohibition against deviant sex. If Suzanne suits this model, however, it is by adamantly refusing to recognize and submit to this prohibition: all of her speech, like Monk's confessions of sexual abuse, is a refusal to put sex into discourse. As Sedgwick argues, Suzanne's "unknowing…insulates her from a consciousness that the most volatile of power negotiations is being conducted around and by herself. Is it any wonder that, far from passively *lacking* the knowledge that what is going on constitutes 'sexuality,' she actively and even lustily *repels* it?" ("Privilege" 38) In her explanation of events that "actively repel" both a knowledge of sex and the discursive mode of confession, Suzanne manages to expose not only herself, but also the specific condition of prohibition that governs her speech. Suzanne can speak insofar as she is aware of such prohibitions and chooses not to acknowledge them:

> Not only has she both seen and experienced orgasmic sensations with the Mother Superior, but she has repeatedly mused on whether they might be prohibited, how prohibited they might be, reasons why they might be prohibited; in the process of actively repelling sexual "knowledge," she has done a thorough survey of the territory where that "knowledge" might live, and only her refusal ever to allow anyone to attach a name to anything differentiates her state from that of the most deeply endued initiation. (Sedgwick, "Privilege" 45)

It may be nothing new to suggest that the possibilities of characters like Suzanne, characters who are legitimately ignorant of sex and who are, therefore, outside of the domain of surveillance, are what made Catholicism so conveniently despicable. What the nun's tales add to this observation, however, is that as long as there could be any speech, like Suzanne's testimony, that was not assimiliated into the discursive mode of confession, Protestantism would not have a handle on it either. Diderot's *The Nun* exploits that loophole of the Protestant private confession in ways that certainly influence *Awful Disclosures*, if only to point out the dangerous implications of disclosure fashioned in precisely this way—i.e., as the confession of a woman and, therefore, the quintessentially partial discourse that only exists by virtue of the fact of another and forever inaccessible utterance.

The questions that *The Nun* turns upon through Suzanne's sexual unknowing—i.e. *Where does sexual knowledge come from?* and *How forcefully does it make itself recognized?*—are very much present in *Awful Disclosures* as well. Yet, Monk cannot very believably feign sexual ignorance like Suzanne does because of the fact that, in her brief time away from the convent between her schooling and her entry as a novice, she gets married. By allowing for this highly implausible and disruptive detail within its plot, *Awful Disclosures* references *The Nun* even if only to make it clear that Maria Monk has no reason to be another Suzanne. Monk recounts having "been led into all those sins in consequence of my marriage, which I never had acknowledged, as it would cut me off from being admitted as a nun" (50) and this is the one secret she keeps, rather than offering it up for confession, when she receives her confirmation. Not only does she call attention, here, to the refusal-to-acknowledge strategy, but as well, there is an implicit parallel sketched between her refusal to acknowledge her sexual "sins" of marriage when she becomes a nun, and her refusal to speak of the sex she endured in the convent when she wishes to be accepted into the Protestant world. Even if she appears as a corrective to Suzanne, Monk shows that she recognizes Suzanne's discursive tactics and, though she does not follow them herself, she reproduces them for her readers.

In her refusal to "acknowledge" "all those sins," Monk differs from Reed, whose *Six Months in a Convent*, published in 1835, is Monk's direct precursor. When Reed, fed up with the advances she encounters in the confessional, and also fed up with not being able to talk about them with her friends, considers leaving the convent, she feels "a repugnance at the idea of returning to the world, supposing that many would believe me a person romantic and visionary, and inexperienced in the ways of the world, and therefore unfit for society" (149). The fact that Reed addresses this issue of sexual knowledge—and how it is transmitted between schoolgirls as well as between adults and children—is worthy of note, but what makes it especially telling is that being "inexperienced" can render a woman "unfit" for society. In other words, Reed's narrative may be the ultimate corrective to *The Nun* in its insistence that women find and lay claim to a knowledge of sex, rather than refuse it. It is only because Monk has acquired this knowledge legitimately through marriage that she avoids the double bind that troubles Reed, but that Suzanne uses to her advantage—that is, the double bind of being a good nun, who, therefore, does not know enough about sex to recognize it and make it intelligible in discourse, but who, at the same time, is compelled to speak. If Suzanne's response to the Lacanian inauguration of the speaking subject is somewhat backwards insofar as she recognizes the prohibition of a desire based on sameness only by refusing it, Monk's is as well: for Monk, however, it is marriage, rather than a prohibition, that gives her license to speak. If Suzanne's narrative is revolutionary because it recognizes the prohibition as a prohibition instead of as the voicing of a natural order of desire, then Monk's is too because it points to heterosexuality as the founding principle of this prohibition. Occurring at the beginning of this book rather than at the end, as it would in a comedy or a romance, marriage occupies the position of instigator rather than resolution of this text. In other words, rather than the imputed factors of Monk's naïveté or modesty, her fallibility as a woman, or the depravity of the priests, it is marriage that makes *Awful Disclosures*, as the narrative refusal to confess sexual experience, possible.

◆

IN EFFECT, my argument has been that Protestant discourse took on the responsibility of imparting sexual knowledge through the publication of nun's tales that, paradoxically, preached against this exchange of illicit information in almost the same form. By resorting to a "scientia sexualis" that its narrators could not have officially known, and attempting to fashion discourse as a confession, these tales confessed something else: their own authorial presence. In so doing they also confessed the perpetual incompletion of their attempt to manage the discourse of their individual subjects, especially the discourse of women. After all, while Protestantism sought to eliminate the confessional, it required a kind of replacement for the priest, something that would not only supply women with the knowledge they needed in order to make appropriate sexual choices, but also something that would do so in such a way as to maintain control over them. Since this circulation of information, and especially information about good sexual behaviour, was in the interests of Protestantism, the nun's tales can be read as self-congratulatory acknowledgements of the success of this circulation. The fantasy figured in all of these texts in which priests introduce sex to innocent women in the confessional—what Sedgwick terms "the increasingly pointed use or anticipation of (male) interdiction" ("Privilege" 44) or, as Monk writes, that which comes "from mouths of the priests at confession" (29)—was not eliminated by Protestantism. Instead, the Protestant movement, through its heralding of the private, only made the possibilities for interdiction greater by extending the confessional to every discursive occasion. Thus Protestants attempted to control the circulation of sexual knowledge with a new kind of comprehensiveness. By transferring confession to the private realm, to be shared with God and scarcely repeated in proper public intimacies, Protestantism did not necessarily relieve it from any and all mediation. Rather, it transferred confession's affiliations, so that sex and sexual difference became "mediated by publics," to borrow a phrase from Berlant and Michael Warner, where "publics" can include "'adult' markets for print" as well as "official national culture which depends upon a notion of privacy"—instead of priests—"to cloak its sexualization of the national membership" (547). Consequently, the sense of horror in these texts comes from the realization that when sex was "put into discourse" through this transformation of confession, in this case a transformation particular to Protestant evangelical North America, the makers and distributors of discourse would not be able to govern appropriately—not because of immorality or lack of faith, but because discourse itself was made unwieldy by virtue of its own confessional attributes. Billed as fuelling the early North American campaign against Catholicism, the panic of the nun's tales was in part a narcissistic one, rooted in aspirations to know and control the circulation of information and in the evident failure of Protestant rhetoric to intervene in all possible channels of communication.

NOTES

1. Gerson's examples of authors who draw from the apparent romance of Québec include: contributors to the *Literary Garland* Eliza Lanesford Cushing and her sister Harriet Vining Cheney, historical writers James LeMoine and Francis Parkman, and, later in the century, Charles G.D. Roberts and Gilbert Parker. Gerson also points out that William Kirby's *The Golden Dog* and Mrs. Ellen Ross's *Violet Keith* make use of the motifs of the convent exposé.

2. All direct quotations presented in this essay are taken from the original Howe and Bates edition. References to documents surrounding the case, such as affidavits, are taken from the revised edition.

3. The first sentence of *The Monk* is as follows: "Scarcely had the abbey-bell tolled for five minutes, and already was the church of Capuchins thronged with auditors." By repeating (a variation of) the word "scarce"—indeed, by selecting this as his own first word of the text—Lewis points to its significance in the epigraph as well as to the text as a whole. Not to go unnoticed is that scarcely refers to the lack of time, the immeasurable lack of time, that the bell needs to ring before the church is filled with an abundance of auditors.

4. Lord Angelo desires Isabella who is soon to take her final vows. He offers to stop her brother's execution in exchange for possessing her. The nature of his desire for her—Does he want to conquer her purity? Test her love for her brother? Exercise his own power?—is a question left unresolved in the play. A much more contemporary example of the persistence of this intrigue about the lives of nuns, if not the desire to possess them sexually, came up in a recent CBC radio report about calendar sales at Toronto's *World's Biggest Bookstore*. As it turns out, the store's best-selling 2004 calendar was one called *Nuns Having Fun*. These "nuns having fun" are, as I write this essay, being gazed upon daily, precisely as part of a person's self-organizing ritual of looking at the calendar, and, if sales indicate wide dissemination, then these images are more than any other subject thought worthy of regular consultation.

5. Foucault uses this catch-all term "Protestantism" to describe a religion that was, of course, immensely varied. In nineteenth-century Canada, the

Protestants included the Anglicans, led by Bishop John Strachan, who were often under attack by the Methodists—especially Egerton Ryerson—for attempting to keep the seat of power to a reserved few. Interestingly, the procedure of confession was an important matter of difference between Ryerson's and Strachan's views on religious practice—see Ryerson, *A Review*. In following from Foucault, I often use just the term "Protestantism" in this paper as the single descriptor for the movement and sentiment behind the nun's tales. This is partly in keeping with the writings of Methodist, Wesleyan and Presbyterian ministers in North America which claim that the differences between these factions are not as important as the distinction between them and the "Primitive Church" as Ryerson calls the Roman Catholic Church and in which he includes the Canadian Anglicans. In *A Review* Ryerson notes the "resemblance between congregations of the Church of England in Canada and the assemblies of ancient Christians" (28). See also Ryerson, *Christians* and Case.

6. The book is inaccurate in its understanding of the different convents and corresponding religious orders in Montreal—so much so that the end of the book contradicts its own explanation at the opening. Traditionally, "Black Nuns" refer to the Ursulines Order, a teaching order brought to Canada by Marie de l'Incarnation in 1639. *Awful Disclosures*, however, associates "The Black Nunnery" with Sister Bourgeoise, who was in fact the first Mother of the Grey Nuns. Furthermore, *Awful Disclosures* also confuses the "Black Nuns" with the Hospitallers, a nursing order that also wore black-coloured habits and which established the Hotel Dieu in Montreal.

7. Ann Douglas writes: "The Victorian lady and minister were joining, and changing, the literary scene.... Literature then, like television now, was in the early phase of intense self-consciousness characteristic of a new mass medium: the transactions between cultural buyer and seller, producer and consumer shaped both the content and the form. The American groups...showed an extraordinary degree, even by Victorian standards, of market-oriented alertness to their customers. They had a great deal in common with them" (8–9).

8. Kate Higginson's chapter in this volume addresses this phenomenon of women who must speak about sexual abuse, but who also risk inevitable punishment by doing so, in her analysis of a text in which two women write about their experiences of feminine vulnerability and/as rape when they are "captives" of the Cree during the North-West Rebellion. Higginson's comments on the history of rape law and trial proceedings in Canada offer some interesting context to my discussion here.

9. As Christie notes, most of the ministers in Canada were American-born: "Those very preachers who assertively set about reconstructing American social ideals along egalitarian and republican lines, extended the popular base of Methodism into the Canadas and the Maritimes. In doing so, they directly transplanted the ideology of equality and liberty into British North America, where their radical religious tenets found a sympathetic hearing among the American Loyalists who were largely common folk, small farmers and artisans" (28).

10. As Gauvreau explains: "troubling to the ancient regime equation of religious establishment and political loyalty was evangelicalism's rival concept of social order, based upon a voluntary sharing of the experience of faith. As Donald Mathews has explained, evangelical thought did have individualist implications, but equally important was the insistence on 'initiating the individual into a permanent, intimate relation with other people who shared the same experience and views.' The polarization was thus not between the individual and the community, but between the community of believers and the rest of the world. Social integration, for evangelicals, was not based upon hereditary custom, but upon the principle of 'voluntaryism,' a belief which implied not only the free association of equal individuals, but social participation and fellowship for the achievement of a common purpose.... And it was precisely the success of evangelicals, in the four decades after 1815, in establishing the 'voluntary' model of social relations in British North America that marks the decisive moment of transition from the culture of eighteenth century to the Victorian mental climate" (57).

11. See "Phantastical Pollutions: The Public Threat of Private Vice in France" by Vernon A. Rosario for the history of "pollution" as a reference to masturbation in the late-eighteenth century. In yet another instance, Chinquy imagines the "voice of God whispering into her ears, 'Is it not enough that thou has been guilty once, when alone, in My presence, without adding to thine iniquity, by allowing that man to know what should never have been revealed to him?'" (6)

12. Hart's 1824 text might be considered a uniquely North American precursor to the nun's tales that appeared a decade later. As "the country's earliest recorded work of fiction written by a native-born Canadian and published in book form in what is now Canada" (Lochhead xiiii), St. Ursula's Convent also attests to the importance of this genre for the history of novel-writing and reading in Canada that followed it.

13. In his Five years' residence in the Canadas... (1824) Edward Talbot writes: "It would certainly be most preposterous to encourage the formation of additional insulated societies of females, under solemn vows of perpetual celibacy, in

an infant colony which requires an increasing population to render it still more flourishing, and in which, it will afterwards be shewn, the fair sex fall much below their due proportion in point of number, and are therefore greatly enhanced in value" (74).

14. My argument loosely follows from Butler's suggestion that "This figuration of the paternal law as the inevitable and unknowable authority before which the sexed subject is bound to fail must be read for the theological impulse that motivates it as well as for the critique of theology that points beyond it" (57), although Butler is referring specifically to what she terms the "Old Testament God" and "those humiliated servants who offer their obedience without reward" (56) while the North American evangelical discourse is very much caught up in the New Testament promise of redemption in heaven in return for obedience on earth.

Writing (Canada) on the Body

Isolating the gene for "Canadian" in le petit cheval du fer?

ANNE MILNE

THE SUGGESTION that the heritage of early Canada is literally embodied in a domesticated animal was asserted in the enactment of Federal Bill S–22, *The National Horse of Canada Act*, in 2002. The Act recognizes "le cheval Canadien," also known as the "Canadian Horse," as uniquely Canadian, "an ideal symbol for all of Canada" ("Parliament endorses Calder's Bill"). The Canadian horse is thought to be an amalgam of French, Dutch and English breeds. Recent DNA analysis reveals that the Canadian "is genetically distinct from popular North American riding breeds" (Dohner 378). The longevity of the breed in Canada is connected to three ship- ments of about fourteen horses each sent to Québec by Louis XIV between 1665 and 1670. The breed is thought to have developed its unique char- acter in Canada as the result of the *habitant* agricultural practice of *l'abandon des animaux* by which animals were turned out during the winter to subsist by eating crop residues and foraging (Dohner 377).[1] As a result of natural selection, the breed developed the characteristic short stature, strong legs, versatility, gentle nature and the renowned hardiness that earned it its nickname—*le petit cheval du fer* (the little iron horse). As Vancouver Island breeder Richard West puts it, "I guess these horses say something about the Canadian character: We're tough, but we're gentle. They make a good symbol, don't they?" (Acker 6).

What Bill S–22 advocates, however, is not merely symbolic—it does not ask for an acknowledgement of the importance of this breed in Canadian history nor does it request that a Cornelius Krieghoff painting of the horse be hung in the Prime Minister's office or be reproduced on a stamp or coin. Rather, the bill demands that the breed itself be maintained, that the genome ascertained to comprise *le cheval Canadien* continue to be replicated. Distinct from other types of historical recovery, the recovery of the Canadian horse is not merely rhetorical; it is physical as well. Also, there is the implicit assumption of an established relationship between the genetic replication process and the maintenance of Canadian heritage. I would like to explore this legislated connection between genetics and heritage implied even if not fully analyzed or intended by this Act of Parliament. The attempt to convert a living subject into an abstract symbol, especially a symbol for a nation, can be interpreted as a violation. The act of troping or turning the animal into a national symbol is inherently hierarchical as the process necessarily subordinates the animal to the nation (as ideal, symbol, fact). If the process of symbol-generation (whether legislative or not) is violent, its potential for success becomes questionable, especially when measured against the integrity, subjectivity and cultural history of the horse itself. Undoubtedly, an animal's biological essence is compromised when it is appropriated for symbolic use. Human imagination is also circumscribed and held within the limited sphere of the attributed symbolic meaning. The use value of the symbol is privileged or exploited and schemes for raising capital based on this value lead to inflation and an obsessive focus on niche-marketing ventures. Some humans are entangled in this process too, and in this chapter I note that the abstraction of the Canadian horse as symbol is reflected in several Cornelius Krieghoff paintings that depict the Canadian horse actively engaged in *habitant* life in Lower Canada. I critically examine the tendency to read these paintings as documents of both human and animal history in the context of my contemporary discussion about replicating the genome of the Canadian horse as a means of both recalling and entrenching a specific version of this breed. If, as Donna Haraway suggests, twenty-first-century "literacy is about the kinship of the chip, gene, seed, bomb, lineage, ecosystem and database" (Haraway, *modest_witness* 2), linking molecular biology and heritage is a fundamental step towards taking (as Haraway has urged for many years now) "responsibility for the social relations of science and technology" (Haraway, "Cyborg" 181).

As Barry Commoner has pointed out, the assumption that an organism's genome "fully account[s] for its characteristic assemblage of inherited traits" is based on a false premise. That false premise stems from what Commoner suggests is a deliberate misreading of Francis Crick's "central dogma," a misreading that locates DNA as the "exclusive agent of inheritance in all things" (Commoner 39). Because most recent developments in the areas of molecular biology and genetics and specifically the massive (and massively funded) Human Genome Project are founded upon this DNA-supremacist paradigm, critiques that undermine the foundations of this work are vigorously marginalized by the scientific community. This, despite a large number of published articles that document the extensive failure of cloning or the failure of the Human Genome Project itself to convincingly prove that DNA has total control over inheritance.[2] Published research that documents the importance of alternative splicing and the vital, albeit mysterious, role that proteins and their amino acid sequences play in inheritance has also been neglected. There is momentum within the environmental activist community to alert the public to concerns generated by both the critique and its marginalisation. These concerns are especially true with regard to ethics and reproductive technologies. Other areas of concern are biotechnology and genetic engineering and how they affect food production. Activism in these areas has specifically focused on information campaigns against genetically modified organisms (GMOs). Typically, less public debate is taking place on issues that appear to have an impact on animals alone and on "soft" or seemingly irrelevant issues such as the relationship between genetics and culture.

In the spirit of extending this debate, I would like to consider some of these "soft" issues in relation to rare breed conservation discourses. While molecular biology, in all of its guises, tends to view the project of mapping life optimistically, I see it as a much more slippery and less certain task. For example, even in his dissent from the dominant view of DNA supremacy, Barry Commoner still considers whether inheritance as the cardinal and unique property of living things is "inherent in the complex chemical systems that comprise living matter" (Commoner and Athanasiou 10). Faced with the task of mapping the human or any genome, cultural critics might optimistically imagine the impossibility of the task as the beginning of inquiry and not as its failure. Rather than focus on how inheritance works, I prefer to ask why knowing how it works matters or why inheritance itself matters. The straightforward and mechanical answer is that the survival of any species depends on inheritance. At the molecular level, understanding how and why inheritance works enables intervention to ensure species survival and optimize species viability. The less straightforward answer, however, involves messier items such as imagination, national pride, commodity production, subjectivity and morality.

The current push to preserve rare breeds of domesticated animals creates a series of conundrums for ethicists and environmentalists. The urge to preserve acknowledges the importance of species diversity and bioregionalism to overall environmental health. However, the practice of rare breed regeneration often relies on genetic technologies that not only privilege DNA as the exclusive agent of inheritance, but that also tend to frame conservancy and heritage within a profitability paradigm. Older breeds are well-suited to alternative systems and appeal to the small subsistence farmer or small business farmer whose profit motive emphasizes quality and not quantity production. The qualities of the Canadian horse such as "hardiness, longevity, small size, docile nature, good mothering qualities, foraging abilities, ability to produce on poorer quality foodstuffs" (Dohner 6) are generally irrelevant to large producers. Where these qualities come to be of interest to the large producer is at the genetic level, especially as they affect selection, improvement and adaptation of animals. Rare breed conservancy advocates often speak in terms of a hierarchy of necessary and valuable genes, of "priceless" genetic potentials and of banking genes in the event of a "genetic emergency," a backhanded recognition of the treachery of monoculture and standardized breed management.[3] Discussion focuses on minimizing the damage done to breed stock because of inbreeding and promotes the banking of "unique" traits with an eye to creating synthetic animals should the need for these traits arise.[4] Embryos are blithely auctioned-off at Rare Breeds Canada annual meetings along with potted plants and fleeces ("Rare"). Biological research and practice tend to privilege a view of living creatures as fragmented, as a composite of genes and not as whole subjects (or even whole objects). As a result, genes, rather than the animal subject, all too often become the sole focus of discussion. Fragmentation and magnification direct the discussion regarding rare breeds towards privileging specific views.

All producers and geneticists, though, would agree that rare breeds hold keys to human survival. For large producers and geneticists, maintaining genetic diversity means that if monocultural production is threatened by disease, genes from rare breeds can be made available to create alternate breeds or hybrids resistant to that particular disease. Maintaining genetic diversity also plays into heritage discourses that emphasize a kind of nostalgia dependent on relived experiences of the past—historical sites or home farms, for example. The ephemeral arguments from niche marketers, subsistence farmers, philosophers and environmental ethicists mostly focus on the inextricable human-animal emotional bond and the spiritual value of diversity.[5] Another compelling but more difficult argument focuses on the animal's subjectivity, intrinsic value and the inevitable rights that stem from any recognition of that worth.

In the case of the Canadian horse, twentieth-century genetic technologies enable a valuing of, or an imagining of, Canadianness in the guise of a horse that has only recently left the critical list (defined by Rare Breeds Canada as having fewer than 200 breeding females). Imagination matters in this discussion of inheritance, shaping history and national character. The content of this imagining posits ephemeral qualities— toughness and gentleness—as inheritable. As well, it imagines a kinship, a line of inheritance based not on traditional biological inheritance but on a kind of transgenic inheritance that apparently encompasses all things Canadian, especially humans. As a kind of technology, kinship also creatively generates, as Donna Haraway has noted, "the material and semiotic effect of natural relationship" (Haraway, *modest_witness* 53). Not only is the image of the Canadian horse a comforting image of Canadianness that already fits in with some of our ideas about ourselves as a nation and a people, legislation compounds this illusion of a collective imagining. This imagining is fallible and illusory, appealing and persuasive. As "tough but gentle" allegedly conceptualizes the Canadian national character, it is like most criteria used to define nationhood: "as useless for the purposes of traveller's orientation as cloud-shapes are compared to landmarks [but] unusually convenient for propagandist and programmatic, as distinct from descriptive purposes" (Hobsbawm 6). The living body of the heritage horse concretizes that appealing image of nationhood. Technoscience, and particularly genetics, is necessary to create and recreate the living bodies of Canadian horses in the twenty-first century. This intervention, in what was historically an apparently natural process, creates a spillover effect in which the imperatives of several discourses—rare breed conservancy, genetics and nationalism—become muddled and may, without any critical examination, emerge to carry the veneer of natural processes that are then privileged and further replicated. The critical examination I am undertaking here includes a consideration of the legislative struggle for a national horse, the relationship between animals and place—especially what Janna Thompson calls "environment *as* cultural heritage" and how genetics conceives of and manages "rare" living bodies.

At first glance, the discourse about the Canadian horse appears to be somewhat different than that of other domesticated animals. Because, currently, Canadians neither rely on the horse as a transportation technology nor eat much horsemeat, the impetus to preserve the horse focuses on its heritage value and its potential as a symbol. In a sense, then, the horse's very uselessness within the capitalist agribusiness model saves it from the fate reserved for rare cattle, sheep, pig and poultry breeds, for the sustainability of these "useful" breeds is completely connected to either their commercial value or to their ability to contribute unique traits in the event that our genetically limited food supply requires their genetic contribution.[6] Despite this apparently reassuring lack of commercial interest in the Canadian horse, economic reasons did figure prominently in the choice of this breed as the National Horse of Canada.

Ontario Liberal MP for Dufferin-Peel-Wellington-Grey, Murray Calder, the originator of the private member's bill that became Bill S–22, is frank about the commercialism behind his promotion of the Canadian Horse. Calder notes that the "national" designation adds approximately

25% to the breed's resale value ("Feds"). He acknowledges that his tenacity in continuing to promote his bill despite two previous failed attempts reflects, in part, his loyalty to those constituents involved in the "vibrant equine industry" operating in his semi-rural riding northwest of Toronto ("Parliament"). Calder also fought efforts by both the federal Bloc Québecois and the Parti Québecois in Québec to have *le cheval Canadien* recognized as Québec's national horse.[7] Calder's determined fight for the national designation led him to change the horse's name from *Canadien* to Canadian in order to linguistically fashion a national importance and quell claims that the horse is indigenous only to Québec and primarily reflects Québec's heritage ("Feds").

Such economic motivations for the national designation also connect closely to ideologies of Canadian heritage that privilege particular regional, class and ethnic orientations. For example, the question of whether the Canadian is a Québecois or a national horse is not merely a stereotypical assertion of nationalist versus federalist rhetoric. The Québecois claim raises the very legitimate issue of regionalism—both socio-political-historical regionalism and bioregionalism. In a sense, the implicit recognition of biological diversity belies the notion of cohesive nationhood. On the other hand, biological diversity's insistence upon the interdependence of living things underpins the ideals of "One Dominion" and a cohesive nation-state. While Calder's victory has symbolic federalist overtones, the Canadian horse has no historical presence in Western Canada. The main claim to national status seems to lie in the fact that the Canadian horse had an established presence in the limited geographical area that was labeled "Canada" in the seventeenth century despite the fact that since then, and particularly since 1867, "Canada" has comprised regions that are vast and widely divergent from the lower St. Lawrence River area near Québec City. The claim for the Canadian as the national horse is paradoxical as well in the context of Lawrence Scanlan's suggestion that it was the British victory at Québec in 1759 and the process of nation-building under British rule that undermined the integrity of the breed through the importation of British breeds and the inability of the British to recognize the regional advantages of *le petit cheval du fer* (Scanlan 37). Reclaiming the breed now without considering the fact that definitions of early Canada are limited by ideologies of nationhood casts the Canadian horse in the role of historical revisionist pawn.

Some hints as to why we "need" a national horse now may come from Paul Webster's article "Who Stole Canadian History?"[8] Webster connects the recent interest in Canadian history by wealthy, corporate Canadians to initiatives such as those sponsored by *Historica*, The Charles R. Bronfman Foundation, and the Dominion Institute.[9] In his brief summary of Canadian history, Webster points out that the discipline changed in the late 1960s and 1970s from "a national history...as a story of conflict resolved" to one that fractured this unity through a focus on social themes (Webster 30). These new histories of, for example, women, immigrants, workers and/or aboriginals undermined the dominant history of unity. Webster surmises that the success of social history has fueled a backlash, funded by corporate Canada, which hopes to reestablish an image of a unified Canada by rewriting or resurrecting the national history. A quick look at the *Historica* and Dominion Institute websites reveals that both institutions embed this ideal into their mission statements. *Historica* introduces itself with the clear assertion that "Canada has a distinct and identifiable *national* character" (emphasis added). Bolstering this mission with military diction, *Historica* announces its intention to "arm" young people so that "they will be better equipped to achieve their potential as citizens well-qualified to guide Canada's future" ("About Historica"). Similarly, the Dominion Institute worries in its opening statement about "the erosion of a common memory in Canada" ("The Dominion Institute"). The Dominion Institute's strategy is to supply scores of survey data, which unfailingly indicate that Canadians are ignorant of their own history and thus create a need for the Institute's service. The presentation of survey data also implies a scientific impartiality to the work of the institute and masks many clearly partisan and ideological underpinnings.[10]

Webster's genealogy of the study of history in Canada may also explain why the Canadian horse was chosen over other breeds of historical significance. Indeed, the horse's name makes it the logical choice. Other contenders such as the Sable Island, Newfoundland, Lac La Croix or

Chilcotin breeds do not allow either in their names or in their current status for conceptualization beyond the regional. This is despite the fact that advocates for all of these breeds can make strong historical claims. The Sable Island breed is thought to have been stocked from horses left behind in the eighteenth century by the Acadians who were evicted to Louisiana.[11] Obviously, the breed's connection to the Acadian exodus and their relative isolation, which allowed them to breed and select naturally, lend them a uniqueness and a significant analogical role in mapping patterns of immigration, politics and oppression. But as they are less domesticated and have been less normalized within an agricultural paradigm than a horse such as the Canadian, they appear more limited in how they can represent Canada to Canadians, especially if the history of oppression and an assertion of identity politics are not currently popular modes of history-making.

The discussion concerning the Chilcotin wild horses in the Nemaiah Valley of British Columbia is similar, as it focuses on the bioregional issue of habitat preservation but goes further to link the preservation of the breed to the larger struggle to preserve a wilderness ecosystem under the threat of industrialization and deforestation. The image of wild horses has wide popular appeal, but also, by focusing public attention on preserving and maintaining the horse population, the ecosystem as a whole is protected, the traditional practices and the rights of the indigenous Xeni Gwet'in people are given voice and, finally, the need for legislative change is highlighted. While the wild horse image is easily transferable into symbolic meaning, the practical impossibility of creating a Chilcotin, which could be appropriated by the "vibrant equine industry" or, indeed, live anywhere else in Canada or the United States and maintain its identity, precludes its widespread conceptualization as a Canadian symbol. Canadianness, at least as it is manifested in the designation of the Canadian horse as the national horse, appears to admit and naturalize ideologies of purity in breeding standards to favour the capitalist agricultural model over a cultural model that would reject the perpetual generation of surplus value and the commodification of sentient beings as well as to question a hierarchy privileging nation-building over the preservation of richly historical bioregions.

This favouring of a progress model also makes it easy to understand why neither the Newfoundland pony nor the Lac La Croix pony has been promoted as a candidate for the National Horse of Canada. Because the Newfoundland pony has never been highly controlled, its gene pool is so varied that it has been difficult to establish breed standards. Though the Lac La Croix pony is a significant aboriginal pony rooted in French or Canadian horse stock and not bred from Spanish stock like virtually every other aboriginal horse in North America, the breed was neglected and even hunted as a nuisance animal until it was nearly extinct (Dohner 379). Not well-integrated within a formal market trading system and subject to an indigenous cultural practice of setting horses free when they were no longer needed, the Lac La Croix's story reiterates the privileging of genetic purity, formal pedigree and institutionalized monoculture. The neglect of the Lac La Croix pony demonstrates the lack of recognition of alternative cultural practices within nation-building exercises and, in the case of the National Horse of Canada, subsequent federal legislation.

Clearly then, the process of choosing a national horse foregrounds an assessment of its propagandistic and programmatic value. More than the other breed choices, the Canadian can simultaneously mask difference and serve as a unifying national symbol to promote a unique and distinct Canadian identity. Its manufacture in the twentieth century includes a folding of new categories of meaning into the animal body. The body of meaning that represents the heritage of early Québec and the Canadian as *habitant* horse must literally squeeze over and share space with a newly conceptualized version of the Canadian horse—one that can live anywhere (including the U.S.), participate in a "vibrant equine industry" and inhabit heritage sites even if that history must be massaged to extract new contexts and allow the Canadian horse to stand in as a kind of ubiquitous historical horse breed. This paradigm promotes the horse's portability and makes the ideological leap from portability to universality to nationalism. Rare breed conservancy does not fix domesticated animals to a particular bioregion, especially not the bioregion in which they developed their "unique" characteristics. Habitually ignoring the issue of place or rootedness for a heritage breed like the

Canadian horse enables and perpetuates the agribusiness viewpoint and entrenches the idea that animals are merely transportable commodities.[12] As transportable commodities, then, their heritage value must reside in their bodies. Breed management becomes the primary focus. Even the designation "rare breed" betrays these utilitarian and ideological biases. There is another argument, though, which asserts that despite the potential for the heritage animal to reside anywhere, the rare breed is inextricably tied to its generative bioregion.

Beyond regional and bioregional concerns, Québec breeders also worry about selling their breed stock outside of the province because they fear that this may bring about changes in the breed. This fear has blossomed into a full-blown dispute within the Canadian Horse Breeders Association. The "national horse" designation apparently does not guarantee the breed stock's stability. While the breed numbers for the traditional Canadian horse have improved since 1979, when there were only 400 Canadians, some enthusiastic supporters of the Canadian have curtailed their breeding programs because "there are too many horses and not enough buyers" (S. Reid, "Canada's" 1). A number of Canadian breeders are advocating changes to the breed to make the Canadian a more marketable twenty-first-century equine commodity. This desire for increased profitability operates in two ways. According to Alex Hayward, because "the Canadian bloodline throws desirable qualities in crossbreeding," it is sought out by breeders interested in enhancing their thoroughbred stock (S. Reid, "Taking" 2). In these cases, there would be no attempt to label or market the crosses as Canadian. However, some breeders are proposing to change registration standards in order to develop a new-style Canadian horse. Breeders feel that a larger horse standing 16 hands tall could be more marketable than the traditional Canadian at 14 hands. Yves Bernatchez of the l'Association Québecoise du cheval Canadien suggests that making such changes to the breed will "undermine [the Canadian's] best qualities, such as strength, soundness, stamina and easygoing temperament" and that profit motives need to be set aside in favour of preserving the "traditional" breed (S. Reid, "Taking" 2). As Ontario breeder Dave Pembroke adds, "if what they really want is a thoroughbred, then why don't they buy one? Why do they feel they have to change our little Canadien horse?" (S. Reid, "Taking" 2). This question is perhaps naïve when Murray Calder's economic motivations for the national designation are considered. Currently, breeders are wording their advertisements distinctly to read either "Canadian" or "traditional Canadian" so that prospective buyers are aware of which version of the Canadian they are purchasing. Clearly, for some, the national designation offers primarily an economic opportunity. Their interest in reclaiming a nearly lost Canadian heritage animal and whatever lost Canadian heritage comes along with(in) the animal does not go far beyond conceptualizing the horse as part of a niche-marketing strategy or isolating and integrating its attractive qualities into the larger horse population.

This, though, is not the first time the Canadian horse has been remade. Robert Leslie Jones notes that by the 1760s there was a lively trade in what he calls the French Canadian horse (Jones 136). Horses were traded into upstate New York for goods such as cheese and stockings. The Canadian's famed adaptability also drew it to the attention of West Indies traders and by the mid-1760s, large numbers of Canadians were shipped to sugar plantations in Jamaica, Haiti and Cuba. Canadians were also exported by United Empire Loyalists to Upper Canada where they provided a "solid foundation for the later development of the common horse of Upper Canada" (Jones 137). After the War of 1812, the trade in Canadians became so brisk that the breed was threatened. Because French Canadians did not geld their horses, stallions were particularly desirable and used for crossbreeding with common American stock (Jones 142). New varieties such as the Canadian Pacer, the Frencher (a Canadian-Thoroughbred cross) and the St. Lawrence (a Canadian-Clydesdale cross)[13] emerged at the expense of the French Canadian, which appeared to survive only in its comparatively pure form in Acadian communities and other communities that maintained a predominately French Canadian population. Even this community loyalty to the breed was threatened when, in the 1860s, American horse dealers started to come directly to the seigneuries to buy stock. Before Confederation, many in the agricultural community feared that the Canadian horse was in serious danger of extinction. There was no agreement, though, on how the breed could be revived. Some hoped to recover the best of the surviving stock and breed them to increase numbers. Others insisted that mongrelization created a crisis that could only be rectified through the importation of Percherons from France, which then could be crossed with the Canadians to simulate the original breed. Attempts to do this were not successful.[14] Finally, in 1886, a Stud book was established for the Canadian but this was not well managed either. It was not until 1913 that a formal breeding program was implemented at the Cap Rouge experimental station. The horses bred here through selection and inbreeding really constitute a new breed, yet the discourse around the national horse designation and legislation fails to illuminate this episode in the horse's history in favour of privileging its grander past: for example, Laird O'Brien, in his *Canadian Geographic* article calls it "A Horse Uniquely Ours From the King of France" and Alison Acker in *The Beaver* describes it as "a workhorse of New France [that] gallops into the present."

In part, domesticated breeds deemed "indigenous" or seen to have developed their unique characteristics in Canada have attracted attention because their "uniqueness" can be attributed to a natural selection directly connected to the Canadian landscape and the conditions for survival in early Canada. However, environmental and even social conditions for survival are not the same in all parts of Canada. To recognize the Canadian horse as the national horse and to elevate the designation to a symbolic or iconic level is a homogenizing gesture. Whereas rare breed conservancy advocates biological diversity as both a survival and a cultural imperative, the national designation is contradictory and mono-cultural—or, at the very least, hierarchical in its privileging of what is clearly a central Canadian breed adapted to very specific geographical conditions. Further, when Murray Calder proudly asserts the Canadian's claim to the national horse designation because "[l]ike our immigrants, it came from abroad but adapted itself to Canadian conditions" ("Despite"), he unconsciously and without malice underlines the normalization of colonialism within the Canadian psyche. In conservation biology circles, immigration adaptability is contentiously exemplified by the "immigration" of the zebra mussel or purple loosestrife into the Great Lakes region. These alien species invasions push "native plants and animals back, some towards extinction, and as a consequence global biological diversity steadily declines" (Wilson xix). To suggest that the horse existed and subsisted in Canada for several hundred years without considering its relationship-in-nature[15] and its place in an ecosystem is to misunderstand, diminish and decontextualize the Canadian horse, and lessen any understanding of its bioregion and especially the status of that bioregion before European settlement. This move is seemingly quite contrary to the attempt to honour the Canadian as an "indigenous" horse implied by the "national horse" designation.

The national horse designation also forces us to question agricultural practice as a prime feature of colonialism and it signals a real clash between natural selection and what Charles Darwin called artificial selection.[16] Because human survival in early Canada became inextricably tied to domesticated animals, it is understandable that the domesticated animal body has become a site for nostalgia.[17] The potential for the recovery of the human past through the animal body, though, must acknowledge several realities. One of these is that the body of the horse literally filters Canada's past even as it embodies it. It does this filtering because the whole idea of recreating the past in an animal body is illusory, just as illusory as the whole idea of conceptualizing nationhood in a symbol. Animal symbols appropriate a nostalgic view of the natural world—a view so askew from reality that they only serve to tell a chilling truth and underline the cynical malaise that more accurately describes global culture's sense of its "self-in-nature."[18] D.M.R. Bentley quotes Susanna Moodie to make this very point about early Canadian topographical poetry. Bentley notes little or no reference to "the hardships and loneliness of the pioneer experience" in poems with a romantic aesthetic that unrelentingly refuses to admit the existence of oppression in its drive to preserve beauty and reveal sublimity. Overall, the impulse to construct an illusory natural relationship between the Canadian horse as it trudged out its daily existence in early Canada and the Canadian horse as the iconic National Horse of Canada says a great deal about the human reluctance to admit or acknowledge both animal subjectivity and the relationship between both human and non-human subjectivity and habitat.

Several interesting aspects of my discussion are illuminated by Lawrence Scanlan's brief analysis of Cornelius Krieghoff's nineteenth-century paintings that depict the Canadian horse. Those of us researching the Canadian rely on Krieghoff's paintings as an important, perhaps even documentary, source of information on the horse, as early Canadian recollections of the horse are mostly a sparse and sketchy reassertion of its best-known qualities.[19] Scanlan comments on Krieghoff's interest in documenting *habitant* life by pointing out the Canadian horse's role as a class marker. The class distinction between the English who rode larger trotters and *habitants* who hitched Canadian horses to sledges for use in the transportation of both people and goods is clearly documented by Krieghoff. Daniel Francis has also established a link between Krieghoff's depictions of *habitants* and the infantilization of Québec to underline the ideological content embedded in seemingly innocent, charming representations. Francis's reading could be extended to suggest a similar idealization of the Canadian horse.

Beyond depictions of the Canadian as a workhorse, it is notable that all of Krieghoff's scenes involving the horse are winter scenes. This is typical of many of Krieghoff's *habitant* paintings and a sure indication that Krieghoff's representation of Québec life in the mid-nineteenth century is neither unbiased nor documentary.[20] In Krieghoff's paintings, the relationship between the *habitants* and horses appears manifestly utilitarian. *Bringing in the Deer* (c.1859), for example, depicts a tired Canadian just released from pulling a deer-laden sledge. While the corpse of the deer receives a great deal of attention, none of the seven human figures, nor the dog in the painting seem particularly interested in the horse, in feeding or watering it. One male figure carrying a stick walks beside the horse. In *Transporting Ice* (c.1847–50), a Canadian hauls a heavy sledge loaded with three huge chunks of ice up a hill. The *habitant* walks beside the sledge, holding the reins. His mouth is open as if in mid-shout and he holds a switch in the air like a drawn sword above the horse's back. In *The Upset Sleigh* (c.1856), another open-mouthed sleigh driver pulls on the reins to urge a fallen Canadian horse to right itself and the sleigh which has dumped its passengers, including a pig.[21] Finally, in *Bilking the Toll* (1859), three exuberant *habitants*, one brandishing a liquor bottle

FIGURE 8.1: *Cornelius Krieghoff (Canadian, 1815–1872), "Bringing in the Deer" (c.1859). Oil on canvas. 52.0 x 84.5 cm. The Thomson Collection, Art Gallery of Ontario.*

FIGURE 8.2: *Cornelius Krieghoff (Canadian, 1815–1872), "Transporting Ice" (c.1847–50). Oil on cardboard. 23 x 30 cm. Musée des beaux-arts du Québec. 59.605*

FIGURE 8.3: *Cornelius Krieghoff (Canadian, 1815–1872), "Off the Road—The Upset Sleigh" (c.1856). Oil on canvas. 33.9 x 54.7 cm. The Thomson Collection, Art Gallery of Ontario.*

FIGURE 8.4: *Cornelius Krieghoff (Canadian, 1815–1872), "Bilking the Toll" (1859). Oil on canvas. 43 x 63.5 cm. The Thomson Collection, Art Gallery of Ontario.*

and another thumbing his nose, fly through a tollgate on a Canadian-pulled sledge. Again, the driver brandishes a switch over the horse's back. Commenting on a similar painting, Scanlan underlines Krieghoff's class allegiances, allying him with the *habitants*.[22]

All of the examples cited above elucidate human class dynamics. Krieghoff preferred a particular vision or version of *habitant* life. His paintings contextualize the Canadian as a working horse within a working environment. There is no evident affection, no acts of kindness between horses and humans depicted in any of these paintings. Indeed, today we would characterize the depictions of whipping as unnecessarily violent and abusive.[23] Even by the nineteenth century, especially in England, cruelty to animals was increasingly a sign of uncultivated or lower class behaviour (see Thomas 143–50). Presumably, this class distinction existed in Lower Canada as well. Because the English tended to view themselves as distinctively kinder to animals than Europeans, the depiction of French habitants whipping, cursing and neglecting their animals may be intended to draw that distinction. Krieghoff's own apparent identification with the *habitants*, however, makes this less likely. More to the point perhaps is that in order to appeal to potential buyers, Krieghoff's paintings reveal a representation of an overall primitiveness with which Europeans liked to view the colonies. There is also a strong tone of quaintness inherent in each composition that belies the reality of winter survival for both horse and *habitant*. While Krieghoff's paintings are unsentimental, they are undoubtedly idealized and need to be contextualized within the market economy Krieghoff inhabited as a working painter. They also reflect how well-established the British were in the colony by this time. If Krieghoff had painted in the early seventeenth century, his representation of the relationship between *habitants* and horses would have been quite different. As Richard Colebrooke Harris notes, when horses were first introduced to the colony, the *habitants* delighted in them. They rode wildly, for pleasure, sneaking rides after midnight and did not use the horse for work. Later, the authorities, concerned that the *habitants* would lose useful winter warfare skills such as snowshoeing, imposed restrictions on when and where horses could travel. Restrictions also limited the number of horses a *habitant* could own (Harris 157).

This changing cultural context for the relationships between humans and horses in early Canada becomes an additional point for considering the status of the Canadian horse in twenty-first century Canada. This relationship could be, for example, understood through Calder's bill which effectively favours breeders who occupy a higher class position and have relationships to these horses that are very different from those that humans had with the horse in the seventeenth to nineteenth centuries. Alternatively, it could be understood in relation to the "quest" in the subtitle to Lawrence Scanlan's book *Little Horse of Iron: a Quest for the Canadian Horse,* a quest for a Canadian horse that he can own and with whom he can pursue a companionate relationship. Either of these approaches can be viewed pessimistically as decontextualizations or optimistically as re-contextualizations, but overall they imply that the animal body generally exists as an empty signifier. Meaning can be attributed to it at will and in the ways best suited to the inscriber of meaning. It is possible, for example, to align the seventeenth century with the twenty-first century by arguing that capitalism is simply a new form of utilitarianism. In the twenty-first century, the horse does not actually have to be useful, but at the same time it cannot resist commodification or deny its use value as a consumer entity, or as a kind of "text," a vessel for containing heritage, an overdetermined cultural product to be exchanged within a market economy.

In this respect, the historic site and the home farm where rare breeds are showcased can be seen in terms of a contemporary fetishizing of the early settler rather than reflecting a genuine interest in the animal. The propagation of rare breeds becomes a method for authenticating the site. The desire to reproduce an authentic past is a pedagogical and commercial tool. For example, Upper Canada Village's breeding program helps to appropriate the Canadian horse for Upper Canada—an example of a horse widely used in Upper Canada for about one hundred years. Nevertheless, the role that animals are asked to play is more than the equivalent of a long skirt and bonnet or breeches and a morning coat.

Viewed from an animal perspective, rare breeds propagation for use in the heritage site is like asking humans, in the cause of preserving Canadian history, to allow a great-great-grandmother to be cloned and kept gated within a designated heritage site in order to preserve the illusory accuracy and purity of "our" pioneer past.[24] Beyond the restrictiveness of this illusory historical existence, this heritage model also promotes a genetic purity that is seemingly attractive in an animal but abhorrent when extrapolated to the human dimension. As the line between human and animal particularly in the genetic context is increasingly blurred, surely this purity aspect of rare breed conservancy and breed management needs a broad ethical and political assessment.

While I am advocating for caution, I am not advocating against rare breed conservancy or heritage sites and home farms. Undoubtedly, the current interest in the Canadian horse has helped to save the breed from extinction. The breed's official designation with Rare Breeds Canada has moved from "critical" to "success" (in other words, it has been delisted). As well, the problems associated with inbreeding because of a limited reproductive base that often necessitates crossbreeding or gene banking do not appear to have surfaced with this breed. While re-contextualization changes the horse internally, the horse may effect beneficial changes externally. Overall, the Canadian horse's influence has been to raise awareness of endangered, vulnerable and rare species and of promoting overall biodiversity. Clearly, visits by urbanites to see rare breeds at home farms can provide education on biodiversity imperatives and endangered species. Janna Thompson refers to the "vivid experience" and "special value of being in the presence of objects made or used by people of the past" in her argument for valuing nature in the context of heritage conservation (Thompson 247). What I am concerned about, though, is that couching rare breed conservancy within the bounds of heritage preservation is a limiting and limited perspective that evades the question that should be at the centre of this discussion. That question is: How did we get to this point in the first place? Responding to this question is an essential task for ecocritical historical inquiry. Presumably, cultural and natural conditions in the past enabled the current conditions. The socio-political and economic conditions that have wiped out or nearly wiped out thousands of animal and plant species continue to create the monocultural monolith that is twenty-first-century agribusiness. Not only that, the contextless replication of seventeenth-century Canadian horses by, for example, rare breeders in the U.S., as well as home farms and national heritage sites, perpetuate and repeatedly marginalize discourses which are sensitive to and critical of the conditions that created its endangered status. To avoid facing these underlying factors, whether from a cultural studies base or within molecular biology, is to perpetuate further and future damage. To say that we only value the Canadian horse because it is implicated in recalling early Canada means that we have fully internalized a way of interpreting the horse that excludes alternate literacies and what Donna Haraway calls the "performative images that can be inhabited by figuration" (Haraway, *modest_witness* 11). In other words, since we know that the fixed meaning of the Canadian horse and the designation of a national horse of Canada are illusory, ideological, as well as anything but fixed, this should be an opportunity to enter and shape the conversation and the future of rare breeds. Ideally, this intervention involves placing rare breeds' conservancy within a biodiversity paradigm that promotes a bioregionalism genuinely grounded in local knowledges. The tendency continues to be to create illusory environmentalisms that obscure their underlying relationship to globalized monoculture.

Although, ultimately, humans are always speaking for the horse, when we attempt to understand him, we could begin with a more clear-headed reading of the early Canadian context for the Canadian horse. We could try, for example, reading the *habitant* as labouring-class and not as "happy husbandman" (see Barrell 59–60). Further, we could consider the *habitant* and horse in terms of their interlocking oppression. Such a reading might well bolster Québec's claim for the Canadian horse. But it would also reveal that, like the Canadian horse, *habitants* were dumped unromantically in Lower Canada to accelerate the pace of settlement and serve as military fodder already adapted to the harsh conditions.[25] Mostly urban poor, these *habitants* had little notion of agricultural practice in France much less in North America. The *habitants's* response to the new land was appropriate both in terms of their own experience and in terms of the conditions with which they were actually confronted. Farms, for example, were small because of the high price of labour needed to clear the land. The impulse to subsist rather than work to profit was appropriate since the market for agricultural goods was almost non-existent. As well, *habitants* found land speculation and employment in fishing and the fur trade more lucrative. It was often, according to Richard Colebrook Harris, only their fear of the Iroquois that kept them in one place (Harris 151). Seen from this perspective, *l'abandon des animaux* looks less like an agricultural strategy and more like its literal translation. As well, the notion that Janet Vorwald Dohner promotes of the domesticated horse enjoying an elevated status among animals; a degree of nobility, "a pampered animal linked with both mystical and actual power" (309) is irrelevant in the context of early Canada, especially if Krieghoff's scenes and the descriptions of the hard-working Canadian horse are in any way accurate. Recalling the subjectivity of the Canadian horse may elicit a rewriting of the horse as an alienated labourer with an unalienated relationship to the land. *L'abandon des animaux* shaped the Canadian horse in the paradoxical sense that the breed developed its characteristic traits at its most unmanaged and unsupervised moments. This is also true of the Sable Island pony, the Newfoundland pony, the Lac La Croix pony and the Chilcotin wild horse. All of the horses I have put forward as candidates for recalling early Canada tell a similar story: that without husbandry, they became who they are. Superimposing twenty-first century technologies on them at this point without ample discussion violates the horse and also the process of defining nationhood through the symbolic value created by the very creation of a national horse.

While environmental assessments increasingly take heritage into consideration and place is clearly acknowledged as possessing heritage value, morals and methods for assessing the environment's heritage value are still being formulated. The question of how a living animal subject or its genome can and should be assessed as a heritage *object* is a complicated problem. When this is extended to an imagined analogy between the animal and a national identity, there may be an opening or an invitation to discuss this animal/human amalgam as a cyborg identity that can be re-appropriated to shape change and enter into a conversation about genetic practices, ethics and economies. Another empowering paradigm is the feminist practice of "writing on the body." If agricultural practice continually writes on the animal body with stamps and brands and tags—all marks of ownership—and if the national horse designation can be viewed as another of those marks, resisting such marks of ownership means encouraging a new writing on the body, one generated from the speaking subject itself, as they say, from the horse's mouth.

NOTES

1. The horses apparently foraged on poplar bark as a way of supplementing their diet (Van Dusen). Robert Leslie Jones has also revealed that the horses would eat frozen fish if necessary (132).

2. Barry Commoner (2002) cites several highly credible sources for this, including: Wilmut, Schnieke et al. *Nature*. 385.6619 (1997): 810–13; Chan, Chong, et al. *Science*. 291 (2001): 309–12; Pursel, Pinkert et al. *Science*. 244.4910 (1989): 1281–88; Jaenisch and Wilmut. *Science* 291 (2001): 2552.

3. The "genetic emergency" is always contextualized with reference to human needs, usually as a public health concern regarding the stability and mainte-nance of the corporation-dominated food supply system.

4. The scientific community appears to privilege profitability and denies holism and the role of bioregionalism in shaping culture and context. In Michael M. Lohuis's discussion of the current situation facing the endan-gered Canadienne cattle breed, for example, he asserts that "many economic factors stand in the path of the breed's recovery as a feasible member of the commercial dairy population." Lohuis advocates improvement through the creation of synthetic cattle who would "offer breeders a more economical carrier for the genes they value" and provide "faster genetic progress" since it is not necessary to wait for the results of random mating trials (Lohuis 3).

5. See, for example, E.O. Wilson who warns that the "loss of diversity endan-gers not just the body but the spirit" (in Dohner 7).

6. For example, interest in recovering the Canadienne cow focuses on the shocking statistic that 90% of dairy products in Canada derive from a tiny base (maintained through artificial insemination and embryo transfer tech-

nologies) of approximately 12 Holstein studs (see Wagenaar). Another source suggests that 80% of cows are bred to 20 Holstein bull studs ("Whatever").

7. As its lengthy legislative history implies, the proposal of this legislation was not without its controversy. Nearly identical bills were tabled on the same day in the Québec legislature by Parti Québecois MP Solange Charest and federally by Calder.

8. Paul Hjartarson's essay "'Wedding' 'Native' Culture to the 'Modern' State: Frederick Alexcee and the Politics of 'Recalling Early Canada'" first drew my attention to Webster's article.

9. These corporately backed foundations aim to create a portrait of cohesive nationhood by revisiting and re-presenting Canadian history. *Historica* and the Dominion Institute have strong educational mandates. *Historica* provides programs and curricula directly to history teachers.

10. Translating this into rare-breed, DNA-speak, these "Canada genome projects" promise full disclosure, but genes deemed unnecessary are discarded. Which genes are maintained and selected to rescue the endangered nation-body depends, perhaps, on the ultimate goal or world view of the breeder.

11. Sable Island ponies have adapted specifically to their island ecosystem (in the Atlantic Ocean, 95 miles east of Nova Scotia). They are shaggy, strong and heavy, with an unusual gait and a rough ride (Dohner 373). Sable Island ponies are protected by regulations which limit access to Sable Island. While fundraising campaigns encourage all Canadians to help preserve the breed, the message always inextricably links the ponies to Sable Island. In the twentieth century, the identification of the preservation of the island and its horses as a symbol of the hardiness of Nova Scotians stands in sharp contrast to Joseph Howe's 1831 poem "Sable Island" which calls for the destruction of the island because of the large number of shipwrecks. Howe's recognition of the Sable Island "steed" (34) in the hours of "calm serenity" (32) and his call for Sable Island, in the guise of a lurking predator, to share Atlantis's fate and "[n]o longer crouch in thy dangerous lair, / But sunk far down beneath the 'whelming brine, / Known but to History's page—or in the poet's line" (124–26) underlines human-centred attitudes towards nature which would advocate for destroying a natural habitat because of its apparently adverse impact on humans.

12. Recall the tense few days in May 2003, while the sole BSE infected bull in Alberta was "traced" to its feedlot-of-origin.

13. Janet Vorwald Dohner identifies the St. Lawrence as a Canadian-thoroughbred cross (377).

14. Robert Leslie Jones suggests that the imported Percheron stock was not well-selected (153).

15. The self-in-nature (or relationship-in-nature) is an ecocritical appellation that acknowledges humans as an inextricable part of the landscape. As such, the term, replete with its hyphens, does not permit any distance between human and non-human nature. It is assumed, then, that such an attachment and engagement "in nature" encourages environmentally sensitive practices because the self-in-nature is fully implicated in the environment.

16. Many commentators suggest that domestication actually saved the horse. By 8000 B.C., according to Janet Vorwald Dohner, there were no wild horses left in Europe and few surviving horses at all, except on the Asian steppes (Dohner 304). Because horses were producers of milk, meat, hides and even manure, they were particularly valuable in areas where there were not a lot of cattle.

17. We readily remember, for example, the importance of animals in constructing stories of early Canada. For example, in *The Backwoods of Canada*, a text written for the potential British emigrant market, Catharine Parr Traill compellingly illustrates some of the challenges of settler life through the simultaneously amusing and frustrating tale of their yoke of oxen who

> not regarding the bush as pleasant as their former master's cleared pastures, or perhaps foreseeing some hard work to come early one morning, they took into their heads to ford the lake at the head of the rapids and march off.... At last we heard that they were twenty miles off, in a distant township, having made their way through bush and swamp, creek and lake, back to their former owner, with an instinct that supplied to them the want of roads and compass. (Traill 57)

18. Consider, for example, the "Roast Beef of old England" in the light of BSE or the level of knowledge and public activism regarding the real endangered status of the American eagle in symbol-hungry U.S. culture.

19. See Robert Leslie Jones for examples of early descriptions of the French Canadian horse.

20. It is certainly nostalgic in the light of Robert Leslie Jones's history of the French Canadian horse in the mid nineteeth century (283–84).

21. The pig depicted is likely a (now rare) spotted pig.

22. Krieghoff apparently (based on his own toll-bilking experience) liked this subject and painted thirty different versions of it. Scanlan adds that the British administered tolls were the bane of the *habitants* who could lose a sizable portion of their day's income at the gates (296).

23. Robert Leslie Jones notes that by the mid nineteenth century the French Canadian horse was popular as a roadster in Upper Canada in part because of its ability to "withstand a great deal of abuse" (147).

24. In her children's novel *Running out of Time* (1997), American author Margaret Peterson Haddix comes very close to making this same point. The thirteen-year-old girl at the centre of the plot believes she is part of a nineteenth-century pioneer family until, during a community diphtheria crisis, she learns that they are really living in the twentieth-century, imprisoned within a national historical site where their "authentic" nineteenth-century existence can be observed by tourists. Jessie's task, in the novel, is to escape from the site and bring twentieth-century technologies back to the community in order to save the lives of the children in the community, including one of her siblings. What she uncovers "outside" is an even more sinister plot: that the tourist site is only a front for a breeding experiment. By exposing the community to fatal diseases, the scientists behind the plot surmise that only the strong will survive and a first generation of hardy human breeding stock can be established.

25. Indeed, one of the factors that led to the rapid reduction of the Canadian horse population in the nineteenth century was that the horses valued for their toughness were imported in large numbers to the United States where they served as pack horses during the Civil War.

The Expatriate Origins of Canadian Literature

NICK MOUNT

CANADIAN LITERARY HISTORY typically dates the arrival of an English Canadian literature to the final decades of the nineteenth century. According to this nationalist narrative, the 1880s and 1890s saw the rise of Canada's first domestic poets and first internationally successful novelists, and with them the beginnings of a distinctively "Canadian" literature. But there is another narrative of this period in Canada's literary history, one recorded not by literary historians, but by Canadian and American census returns. In the 1880s and 1890s over a million Canadians left Canada for the United States, the greatest such emigration in any twenty-year period in Canadian history. By the turn of the century, Canadian-born residents in the United States numbered about 1.2 million—almost a quarter of Canada's total population at the time. With these emigrants went something approaching half of all working Canadian writers, most to the United States, and most of these to New York. Many became successful writers and public figures in their new markets, winning reputations ranging from recognition within their chosen literary culture to international fame. More important for Canadian literature, their successes encouraged the development of a domestic publishing industry and a domestic readership for imaginative writing. The boom in literary publishing in Canada from the late 1890s to the First World War has been well documented; less well known is that expatriate Canadian writers provided both the model and much of the content of this boom.

During the exodus, Canadians celebrated the achievements of their writers in exile, or at least of those who continued to identify as Canadian. But the expatriates' success proved their downfall: as the domestic literary scene gained momentum from their example, a rekindled literary nationalism dictated the celebration of a homemade Canadian literature and of its difference from other national literatures. Because Canadian critics followed the canonical precedent that a national literature must reflect its physical environment, many of the expatriates and most of their works were excluded from the literature they had themselves made possible. The topocentric axiom of national canon formation ensured that only those expatriate works that fit the increasingly refined sense of a Canadian literature grounded in the Canadian soil would survive, and that any works with too obviously foreign (especially urban American) settings, concerns, or influences would not. At the conference that prompted this collection, one question participants were asked to consider was how the search for an English Canadian literature might have marginalized the early works of women, First Nations, and African Canadian writers. Several of the resulting papers demonstrated that social as well as canonical forces impeded both access by these groups to traditional literary markets and critical recognition of alternative forms of literary expression. My own research suggests, however, that the largest single literary cohort left behind in the scramble to canonize an authentically Canadian literature were writers marginalized not by their gender or race, but by their decision to pursue their career elsewhere.[1]

Canadian census statistics give some idea of the size of the literary exodus. In 1881, the Department of Agriculture (then responsible for the census) reported the existence in Canada of 601 "artists and litterateurs." Ten years later, in the census of 1890–91, that number had slipped to 279. By the first year of the new century, just fifty-six Canadians—forty-one men and fifteen women—were identifying themselves as full-time authors. Of the hundreds of occupations abstracted from Canada's 1901 census for comparison in the following census, the only one to have attracted fewer adherents than literary work was the manufacturing of "fancy goods and notions."[2]

These numbers are probably not as dramatic as they appear. For one thing, the 1881 figure likely includes some of the country's full-time journalists, who do not show up as a separate profession until the census of 1890–91. For another, both the 1881 and 1890–91 figures almost certainly include an unspecified number of librarians, who were not reported separately until 1901. But even allowing for these and other differences between censuses, the figures still indicate a serious decline in the number of working Canadian authors in the last two decades of the century. The rate of that decline can only be estimated, but the census figures, together with the expatriation rate for better-known authors of the period, suggest a rate of about fifty per cent. (Of the forty-five English Canadian writers born before 1880 profiled in W.H. New's *Canadian Writers, 1890–1920*, for instance, twenty-two left Canada permanently or for an extended period.) Numbering the decline is more difficult: taking into account natural additions to the profession by birth or immigration, I would hazard the conservative estimate that between 1880 and 1900 upwards of two hundred Canadian writers either quit their profession or quit their country.

In part, Canada's writers left for the same reasons historians have offered to explain the larger exodus in which they participated. The economy of the period suffered a series of financial panics and outright depression. Droughts on the prairies forced farm foreclosures. High freight rates hurt existing businesses and discouraged new ones. Protective tariffs, ironically intended to foster the national economy and "retain in Canada thousands of our fellow-countrymen, now obliged to expatriate themselves in search of the employment denied them at home," ultimately forced Canadians to buy more expensive "Made in Canada" manufactured goods (Macdonald 854). Maritimers and Westerners, unhappy with the broken promises of Confederation, grumbled and talked of succession and annexation. Throughout all this, newspapers, friends and relatives told of jobs just a border away with better pay, better conditions, and better prospects. In sum, says one observer, the period "demanded a high price for being a Canadian and a great number chose not to pay" (Callwood 37). But for Canada's literary emigrants, there were additional incentives for the move. There must have been.

Even accepting the highest estimates, the national emigration rate over the 1880s and 1890s was under seventeen per cent, while the Canadian literary community was reduced over the same period by something approaching half its number.

Canadian censuses of this period do not record how many of these vanishing writers changed professions rather than left, or where those who left went. But American records provide some answers to these questions. In New York alone, eleven Canadian writers became prominent enough to merit entries in the first edition of *Who's Who in New York City and State*, published in 1904. Alongside the Astors and the Vanderbilts appear entries on Canadians Sophie Almon Hensley, Charles Brodie Patterson, Charles G.D. Roberts, and Ernest Thompson Seton, among others (Seton's entry fills almost two full columns, the same space accorded then president Theodore Roosevelt). That same year, Oscar Fay Adams's *Dictionary of American Authors* contained entries on over eighty Canadian-born authors then living in the United States.[3] And although too late to register the boom years of the Canadian literary emigration, the American census of 1910, the first to enumerate foreign-born workers by occupation, still recorded 93 Canadian-born authors and a further 570 editors and reporters (Truesdell 213).

The disappearance of these and other writers did not pass unnoticed in Canada. In the spring of 1893, a contributor to the Toronto *Week* complained that "More than one of our most prominent writers have left Canada permanently: in more fortunate climates they may find the soil and the atmosphere more congenial and more supporting..." (Libby). Ottawa poet Archibald Lampman made similar observations in his column in the next morning's *Globe*, noting the success of Grant Allen, Gilbert Parker, and Sara Jeannette Duncan in England, and of E.W. Thomson, Walter Blackburn Harte, and Bliss Carman in the United States. "They probably bring more honour to their country in the fields which they have chosen," Lampman wrote, "than they would if they had remained at home. Here their energies might have withered away in petty and fruitless occupations, and their talent have evaporated in the thin sluggishness of a colonial atmosphere."

More enthusiastic than Lampman's qualified approval (it is hard not to hear the bitterness of envy in the post office employee's voice) were several articles that appeared in the Canadian press by the expatriates themselves. In 1893, the *Dominion Illustrated Monthly* opened its May number with a contribution from Nova Scotia expatriate Sophie Almon Hensley on Canadian writers in New York. Canadians, wrote Hensley, boast of the work of their writers, but "we must not forget that there is a large number of writers, born Canadians, Canadians in heart, and hope, and ambition, who have been obliged to make their homes in other countries but who still assert their claim to be sons and daughters of Canada, and who should unquestionably come under the designation of Canadian writers" (195). Former University of Toronto student Frank L. Pollock contributed a detailed sketch to his alma mater's *Acta Victoriana* in April of 1899 on New York's "flourishing Canadian artistic colony," including portraits of its "chief," Charles G.D. Roberts, his brothers William and Theodore, and their cousin Bliss Carman (434, 436). Arthur Stringer's "Canadian Writers Who Are Winning Fame in New York," printed in the *Montreal Herald* in March of 1901, provided a more gossipy account of Canadian writers in the city. By his time, Stringer joked, Canadian writers were so common in New York that "New Yorkers have an idea that you can't throw a snowball in Canada without hitting a poet. When a New York editor has all the poetry he wants he hangs out a sign, 'No Canadians Admitted.' In the same way, when he runs short of verse, he swings out a placard with a red mitten on it."

With over 84,000 citizens of Canadian birth or parentage, Boston was by 1900 the third largest Canadian city, behind only Montreal and Toronto (Moffett 13). Both because of its historical ties to Canada (especially the Maritimes) and its reputation as literary America's elder statesman, the city attracted its own contingent of Canadian writers. Toronto journalist E.W. Thomson accepted an editorial position with the long-running *Youth's Companion* in 1891, writing home to Lampman that he was "nicely situated, with agreeable people in an agreeable city," and complaining only that Bostonians did not celebrate the Queen's birthday with enough zeal. Walter Blackburn Harte, a London-born immigrant to Toronto, lasted just three years before declaring literary success in Canada an impossibility and decamping for the States, becoming assistant editor of Boston's *New England Magazine* after a year of reporting work in New York. Hersilia Keays of Woodstock, Ontario, moved to Cambridge, Massachusetts, around 1897 and turned to fiction for a living, producing at least eight novels before her death. The Rev. William Benjamin King of Charlottetown, Prince Edward Island, elected to remain in Boston after retiring from his Cambridge ministry in 1900 and became (as Basil King) a best-selling novelist. Novelist Marshall Saunders deplored the Maritime migration to Boston, calling it "a huge pulp mill into which Nova Scotia throws many of her sons and daughters," but herself spent several years in the city before leaving in 1898 on an extended trip across America to her sister's home in California.[4] Bliss Carman worked in Boston for most of 1894–96, editing a new little magazine, the *Chap-Book*, and writing a weekly literary column for the *Boston Evening Transcript*. Like many other Canadian writers, he and his cousin Charles visited the city regularly throughout the 1890s and the first decade of the new century, placing manuscripts, looking for work, and meeting with their publishers.

Busy Chicago, especially strong in the 80s and 90s in the publishing and newspaper industries, drew more Canadian publishers and journalists than novelists and poets. After a lucrative career of pirating popular British and American authors (most famously, Mark Twain), Alexander and Robert Belford moved the headquarters of their Toronto publishing firm to Chicago around 1880 and became the largest publishers west of New York. George Doran quit his job with Toronto's Willard Tract Depository in 1892 for a position with Chicago's Fleming H. Revell and Company, rising to vice-president by age twenty-four. Fredericton native Slason Thompson arrived in Chicago via San Francisco and New York in 1880 as western agent for the Associated Press and thereafter occupied a dizzying number of editorial positions in the city, including co-founder and editor of the *Chicago Herald*, manager of the *Chicago Daily News*, founder and co-editor of the weekly *America*, and contributing editor for such dailies as the *Journal* and the *Evening Post*. Ontario journalist Eve Brodlique quit her position on the *London Advertiser* (for which she was Canada's first female parliamentary correspondent) and moved to Chicago around 1890, becoming a staff writer for the *Chicago Times-Herald*, arts reviewer for the *Times* and *Evening Post*, and president of the Chicago Women's Press Club. Constance Lindsay Skinner, a British Columbia writer who became a popular American historian, was the Chicago *Evening American*'s drama critic from 1908 to 1910. Poet and critic Thomas O'Hagan, another late arrival to the city, served as chief editor of the Catholic *New World* from 1910 to 1913 before returning to his native Toronto after more than twenty years of teaching and writing in the States.

In fewer numbers, Canadian writers also migrated to Baltimore, Detroit, Philadelphia, Cleveland, Seattle, and San Francisco. History recapitulated geography: Maritime writers moved in proportionally greater numbers to Boston, central Canadians to Chicago and New York, and so on westward, in diminishing numbers as the population decreased. A handful left the continent altogether. Nova Scotia journalist Daniel Logan, breaking regional tradition, migrated not to Boston but to Montreal and from there to the editor's desk at the *Honolulu Daily Bulletin*. Humorist Robert Barr originally left Toronto in 1876 for a position on the *Detroit Free Press*, but five years later his employers sent him to London to launch an English edition of the paper, and when the relationship ended Barr stayed. Like Barr, Ontario novelist Sara Jeannette Duncan left Canada for an American position on the *Washington Post* in 1885–86, but after a museum curator she met on her travels proposed to her, she married and settled in India. A frequent visitor to Great Britain and the northeastern United States, Montreal novelist Lily Dougall settled permanently in England in 1900. Ontario native Gilbert Parker, the most well known in his day of Canada's English expatriates, arrived in London via Australia as an unknown journalist in 1890; ten years later, the popularity of his novels and short stories helped elect him to a seat in the British Parliament.

Of all the literary centres of the English-speaking world in the last decades of the nineteenth century, New York City beckoned most brightly. By century's end New York was America's publisher, home to almost a thousand book publishing and printing firms. In these years, however, the primary medium for new writers and the mainstay for many established writers was not books but magazines, and here New York dominated the continent. Partly because of the size of its domestic market, and partly because the superior reputation and distribution of its major monthlies had by this time secured markets across the States and in Canada, New York was the undisputed leader of the magazine boom of the 1880s and 1890s. By 1900, the state was producing almost fifty million dollars annually in periodical sales, subscriptions, and advertising revenue—thirty million more than next ranked Pennsylvania, and nearly twice that of its own book and job business (Rossiter 1057, 1084). Literary historians are fond of dating New York's replacement of Boston as the literary centre of America from William Dean Howells's move from Boston to New York in 1891 to assume the editorship of John Brisben Walker's *Cosmopolitan* magazine. Such things no doubt matter, but what mattered more, to Howells as much as anyone, was New York's dominance over the industry that brought him to the city in the first place.

Canadian writers were neither ignorant of nor immune to the forces that brought Howells to New York. They saw the same publishers' imprints on the same books he did, read the same magazines with the same addresses on their mastheads, and in both their own and American periodicals followed the same literary currents and gossip from the city that Stringer called "the busiest literary market in the world." By far the largest single group of Canada's literary expatriates of the 1880s and 1890s made the same choice that Howells did, and the exodus of these years is mostly their story—the story of why they left Canada, of what they did in New York, and of what happened to them afterward. Its main cast numbers about two dozen, with walk-on parts by another dozen or so. All were English Canadians from the Maritimes, Québec, or Ontario. Most played multiple roles in this story: as members of the then relatively new profession of letters, they wrote in various genres for various audiences, and from one day to the next might also be editors, publishers, illustrators, lecturers, activists, or "metaphysicians."

Among the first of the Maritime arrivals in New York was Craven Langstroth Betts of Saint John, a poet, bookseller, and friend and patron of American poet Edwin Arlington Robinson. Charles Brodie Patterson of Pictou, Nova Scotia, became one of the American founders of the million-strong cult of the New Thought, and with two other Canadians in New York, metaphysician Ella Walton from Toronto and her third husband John Emery McLean from Orangeville, Ontario, ran a school, a publishing house, and two magazines devoted to the cult's teachings. Aspiring poet Sophie Almon Hensley of Windsor, Nova Scotia, arrived in New York in 1890 and there transformed herself into feminist activist Almon Hensley. That same year, Bliss Carman left Fredericton to take an editorial position on the New York *Independent*; seven years later, his cousin Charles joined him in the city as the assistant editor of the *Illustrated American*, bringing with him younger brothers William and Theodore and later his son Lloyd. Within a year of his arrival the eldest Roberts became a charter member of America's National Institute of Arts and Letters.

From Québec came Mary Elizabeth McOuat of Brownsburg, a staff writer for the *New York Recorder* in the 1890s and for the *Tribune* the following decade, and Acton Davies of St. Jean, who earned his reputation as drama critic for the *New York Evening Sun* for over twenty years, but his fifteen minutes of fame as the *Sun*'s unlikely correspondent in Cuba and Puerto Rico during the Spanish-American War of 1898. Easily the most famous Canadian writer in New York in the 80s and 90s, and one of the least well known today, was Granby's Palmer Cox, a humorist and illustrator who came to New York via San Francisco in the mid-70s and reinvented himself as "the Brownie Man," the creator of the fantasy world most popular with American children until L. Frank Baum sent Dorothy to Oz at the turn of the century. Arguably more infamous than famous, Montreal publisher John W. Lovell arrived in New York about the same time as Cox and by the early 90s had become known to the trade as "Book-a-Day Lovell," the largest, most aggressive publisher of cheap books in America.

Toronto, then as now the centre of publishing in Canada, was also the epicentre of the literary exodus. Especially hard hit was the city's fledgling *Saturday Night*, which could probably claim the title of the Canadian magazine most likely to be abandoned for an American paycheque. Two friends from the magazine's first years, humorist Peter McArthur and literary editor Duncan McKellar, left for New York in

1890 and 1891, respectively. The weekly's outdoors writer Edwyn Sandys left in 1891 to accept an editorial position on the New York sporting magazine *Outing*, and a year later its sometime society columnist Graeme Mercer Adam, the post-Confederation era's most tireless promoter of Canadian letters, left to work for his former partner John W. Lovell in New York.

Mary Bourchier Sanford, a humorist from Barrie, Ontario, arrived in New York the same year as McArthur and published her jokes and sketches in many of the same periodicals. In 1891, the success of Toronto lawyer Stinson Jarvis's first novel precipitated a career change and a move to New York, where Jarvis's upper-class Toronto recreations sustained additional careers as a yachting reporter, a drama critic, and an authority on psychic phenomena. By 1896 New York was home to Toronto naturalist Ernest Thompson Seton, author and illustrator of the animal stories that paid for a midtown studio overlooking Bryant Park and a hundred-acre country estate near Greenwich, Connecticut. The following year saw the arrival of Norman Duncan of Brantford, a former University of Toronto student whose first taste of literary success came with a series of stories about lower Manhattan's Syrian colony. By century's end three more University of Toronto students—Arthur McFarlane, Harvey O'Higgins, and Arthur Stringer—shared an attic in an old Fifth Avenue brownstone that, like the Robertses' family addresses, became a centre for Canadians in the city. McFarlane became a well-paid investigative journalist, a so-called muckraker, while O'Higgins won the title "prose laureate of the commonplace man" for his stories of New York's Irish community and Stringer broke onto the best-seller lists with fast-paced adventure novels about the city's criminal underworld.

There were, of course, other Canadians whose work has been lost in the unsigned columns of the city's dailies and weekend specials, or whose literary ambitions became careers in advertising, banking, or plumbing. The New York literary industry experienced an unprecedented boom in these years, the kind of prosperity that attracts many but rewards few and remembers even fewer. To the extent that it can be recreated, Canada's literary exodus is a story of remarkable successes, but there are failures in its silences.

An unjust history has left a better record of the failure that caused the exodus, the inability of post-Confederation Canada to sustain and thus retain its writers. The union of Britain's northern colonies in 1867 excited a burst of domestic literary energy, but as Graeme Mercer Adam later remarked, "the flush on its face ere long passed off," largely because the source of that energy was political need (for founding father Thomas D'Arcy McGee, a national literature was "a state and social necessity"), not a critical mass of writers and readers (Adam 221; McGee 6). The generation of Canadians who came of age in the 1880s and 1890s inherited a print culture virtually devoid of domestic models, and with substantial material impediments to domestic authorship, among them a publishing industry more intent on reprinting familiar English and American authors than encouraging new Canadian authors; inadequate copyright protection for books first published in Canada; higher postage rates for magazines shipped within Canada than imported into Canada; and, its writers claimed, a readership too preoccupied with economic progress to care about imaginative literature—about anything but "wheat, railroads and politics," as Walter Blackburn Harte fired back from exile.

Post-Confederation Canadians with an interest in fostering a domestic literature were acutely aware of and repeatedly lamented the problems specific to Canadian literary culture. To focus too closely on their complaints, however, is to lose sight of the full dimensions of that culture and therefore to misunderstand the conditions of authorship in late-nineteenth-century Canada. Traffic in literary goods and influences moved more freely across Canada's borders in this period than in any other, and like other forms of economic and intellectual traffic was especially fluid across the country's only land border. The problems confronting domestic literary production were real, but the domestic market was not the only option for Canadian writers of this generation: they also had access by mail or in person to the much larger American market, a market that by this time *included* Canada. Canadians had few home-grown literary models, but the flood of American magazines and American books into Canada provided models for them, models that had become features of a North American literary landscape. At a professional level, the decision by so many Canadian writers of these years to move to American cities was not about giving up one national literary culture for another; it was about moving from the margins to the centres of a continental literary culture. She was not entirely happy about it, but for Sara Jeannette Duncan in the summer of 1887 the literary predicament of her generation was clear: "The market for Canadian literary wares of all sorts is self-evidently New York, where the intellectual life of the continent is rapidly centralising."

The market Duncan described had consolidated its reach, not its products. A literature at the time of its production does not consist of anything like T.S. Eliot's "ideal order" of classic monuments, but is instead the highly diverse product of a constantly changing set of different artistic communities (15). These communities are rarely devoted to a single literary genre or confined to a single literary mode (fiction or non-fiction, realism or romance), or even to a single artistic medium. Their main organizing principles are content and sensibility: people who are interested in animal conservation write and read literature sympathetic to animals, but that interest ranges from factual studies of real animals to romantic stories of fictional animals, and is likely to include making, collecting, or just enjoying animal-sympathetic art in a variety of media. Each of these communities develops recognizable characteristics that help to promote it and that allow others to join by successfully reproducing those characteristics: if, in Eliot's day, you were interested in becoming a modern poet, you should have known better than to write poems about how happy daffodils made you feel. Eventually, those characteristics become entrenched and susceptible to challenge and revision, or to boredom, parody, and abandonment.

The American literary landscape of the 1880s and 1890s consisted of many such "cultures of letters," as their historian Richard H. Brodhead calls them. But what Brodhead calls American cultures of letters were actually North American cultures of letters, cultures based in the literary centres of the United States but with a transnational and in some cases transatlantic membership and audience. The northern reach of the American literary market ensured the visibility of these cultures in Canada, and therefore that Canadians could acquire, with the same facility as Americans, the familiarity required to reproduce their forms.

Some Canadian writers participated from a distance, sending their work to American magazines and publishers hospitable to their interests, but many took the next logical step and moved to the American centres of these literary cultures.

Canadian writers chose American cities in part for practical reasons such as cheaper travel than to destinations overseas, and in part for reasons of cultural affinity, the cumulative effect of a common geography, a common language, and increasingly, a common economy. But the main reason, of course, was more opportunity. Much more. The entire Canadian printing industry at the turn of the century was less than half the size of New York City's book and job business alone.[5] There is evidence to suggest, too, that Canadian writers were afforded not just more opportunity in America's publishing centres, but preferential opportunity. Then, as to some extent today, Americans cherished a romantic notion that Canada's unspoiled topography and more vigorous climate produced hardier, more dependable, more moral employees than those reared under relaxing southern skies. This stereotype probably influenced the appointment of Canadians to editorial positions on American magazines with an explicit focus on moral or physical well-being, such as Carman on the religious weekly *Independent*, Thomson on the juvenile *Youth's Companion*, or Sandys on the sporting magazine *Outing*. Certainly, the myth of the virile Canadian, together with the predilection of American editors of the day for poems, stories, and articles with a robust morality in an outdoors setting, created a disproportionately high acceptance rate for Canadians with American editors and publishers. One measure of this preference is the new best-seller lists in the New York and London *Bookman*, which reveal that between September 1900 and December 1902, Canadian-authored books accounted for ten per cent of the Toronto lists, just under seven per cent of the New York lists, and just one title on the London lists.[6]

The Canadian writers who moved to New York in this period joined American-based literary cultures, but they also formed their own social and professional communities within and across these cultures. Older arrivals like Lovell, Betts, and Halifax theology student turned dime-novel publisher, George Munro, joined the Canadian Club of New York, by 1887 occupying an ornately equipped four-story clubhouse on East Twenty-ninth Street and listing over four hundred resident and non-resident members (Fairchild 288). Younger, less solvent expatriates frequented cafés like Maria's spaghetti house on West Twelfth, the favourite of the city's Bohemian set, or Flouret's, a popular French restaurant at Eighteenth and Fifth. In working hours they met at each other's professional addresses, at the lower Broadway offices of Peter McArthur's *Truth*, or at Carman's office at the *Independent* five blocks north, or at what Roberts called "the down-town Canadian Club," the offices at 140 Fifth Avenue where Carman's friend and publisher Mitchell Kennerley managed the American interests of London publisher John Lane (qtd in Pollock 435). They gathered, too, at each other's homes, notably the East Fifty-eighth Street boarding-house that was the Robertses' first address in the city (just a few blocks from where Howells had landed, on West Fifty-ninth overlooking the Park), their next home on East Seventeenth, and the attic flat above Kennerley's offices where Stringer, McFarlane, and O'Higgins papered the walls with rejection letters and mixed drinks on credit for Carman, Roberts, McArthur, and other visitors to their "Chamber of a Thousand Sorrows" (Lauriston 32).

Here, in New York, Canadian writers formed their country's first professional literary communities. At these and other gathering places they shared setbacks and successes, read and discussed each other's work, exchanged literary gossip and argued about new literary trends. They helped each other into print, passing on tips about copy-hungry editors and warning about those slow with a paycheque. Most directly, they published each other's work in the magazines they edited, in McArthur's *Truth*, or in Carman's *Independent* and Sandys's *Outing*, or in Thomson's *Youth's Companion* and Harte's *New England Magazine* in Boston. And, crucially for some Canadian writers, they extended the reach of these communities beyond New York, using their positions and connections to promote and publish the work of Canadians still at home and in other literary centres.

These communities were not exclusively Canadian: professionally and socially they included American and transplanted English members, editors like Richard Watson Gilder of the *Century*, publishers like the

English-born Kennerley, mentors like the influential New York critic Edmund Clarence Stedman, and co-writers like Carman's companion in Vagabondia, the American poet Richard Hovey. However helped into print by Canadian friends, an extraordinary amount of the Canadian literature of this period would never have existed without American editors and publishers, all serving their own literary cultures. The fact that Arthur Stringer mixed milk-punches for Bliss Carman in a Fifth Avenue flat is, I think, of genuine importance to a revised literary history of Canada, but it does not negate the fact that Stringer wrote crime novels and Carman wrote poems about vagabonds. What those milk-punches reveal is that the common experience of exile brought together writers from villages, towns, and cities across central and eastern Canada. Ironically, but necessarily, it took moving to New York to fulfill the literary promise of Confederation. Here, for the first time, Canadian writers found literary-social communities composed primarily of other Canadians, in close proximity to a large and receptive market for their products, and with members who were proving it possible for a Canadian writer to earn a living and even fame from writing alone. For twenty-two-year-old Toronto writer Frank Pollock, a visitor in the winter of 1898–99 to the Robertses' busy rooms at 105 East Seventeenth, the effect of this combination of circumstances upon the city's colony of Canadian writers was "the most amazing *esprit de corps* imaginable" (434).

Its effect upon Canadian literature was equally dramatic. From the late 1890s to the First World War, Canadian literature experienced its own boom, a phenomenon that Ontario historian Lawrence Johnstone Burpee diagnosed in 1899 as "what promises to be the genuine and thorough awakening of the long dormant spirit of Canadian fiction" (754), and that the Canadian Institute for Historical Microreproductions has since quantified, more generally, as an increase in language and literature titles from nine per cent of its pre-1900 collection to twenty-five per cent of its collection from 1900 to 1920.[7] Canada's expatriate writers were directly responsible for much of this growth: they represented over half of the country's more prolific writers in these years, and all but a few of its best sellers. All five of the well-known novelists that prompted Burpee's prediction were expatriates. More important for

Canadian literature, the commercial and critical recognition the expatriates received from non-Canadian publishers, reviewers and readers helped to legitimize the writing, publishing, and reading of imaginative literature in Canada. In his *The Beginnings of the Book Trade in Canada*, publishing historian George L. Parker argues that the string of best-selling books by Canadian authors brought out in the late 1890s and early 1900s by William Briggs of Toronto "helped turn around the 'stigma' of a colonial book, and probably ensured that other books, with equal artistry and smaller sales, would be published" (237). Of the nine titles Parker instances as Briggs's decisive best-sellers, six were by expatriates.[8] Whatever else they might have achieved, the expatriates of the 1880s and 1890s had clearly provided a model for professional authorship in Canada. By their own work and by the example of that work, they did more than any other individual or group to lead Canada to a self-aware, self-sustaining, and eventually self-defining domestic literature.

At first, Canada thanked them. In the absence of a domestic literature most Canadian references to the expatriates proudly claimed their work as Canadian, usually by proudly claiming their authors as Canadian. But the arrival of a domestic literary scene renewed nationalist imperatives to celebrate its writers and to distinguish their work from other literatures, especially American. To meet these imperatives Canadian literary critics and historians used the same logic as their European and American predecessors. To be Canadian, they argued with increasing confidence, a work of literature must show the impact of the Canadian environment—the spirit of the soil, in one of their favourite figures. The consequence of this argument was the excision of many of the expatriates from the literature they had made possible. In 1896, the New Brunswick-born historian Thomas Guthrie Marquis defended Carman against a critical review in the New York *Bookman* by arguing that its (American) reviewer needed experience of the (Canadian) land to appreciate the poem he had found fault with. Seventeen years later, Marquis argued in English Canada's first comprehensive literary history that Carman and the other expatriates of his generation had "lost their Canadian colour and atmosphere and become a literary part of the country in which they have made their home" (588–89).

As the domestic literary scene gained momentum, and especially during the war years, those expatriates still known in Canada went though a period of neglect from which most never recovered. When Carman and Roberts returned to Canada in the 1920s, however, they were neither ignored nor dismissed as American or English writers; they were welcomed popularly and officially as conquering Canadian heroes, one crowned poet laureate and the other knighted. Carman and Roberts were welcomed home because they had succeeded where it has always mattered most to most Canadians, in the literary centres of the United States and England. To sacrifice home-grown celebrities to the nationalist demand for an indigenous literary tradition was too great a price to pay: Marquis may have thought the expatriates were no longer purely Canadian, but he included their books in his study all the same, because without them the short and humble story that he saw as Canada's literary history to date would have been shorter and humbler.

Over the long term, though, "Canadian colour" proved more important than commercial or critical success in deciding which of the expatriates would be repatriated, and which of their works. The principle that an authentic national literature reflects the special qualities of its homeland ensured, for instance, that Carman's nostalgic lyrics about his Maritime home, Seton's biographies of doomed animals, and Norman Duncan's stories about the hard life of a Newfoundland outport would become part of Canadian literature, and that Duncan's stories about the blending of cultures in Manhattan's Syrian quarter, Roberts's New York love poems, Stringer's racy urban crime novels, and any others that did not fit the developing perception of that literature, would not. In the end, the expatriates gave Canada more than a literature: they gave it a past in which critics could find both the Canada they wanted and the Canada they did not, a process of canonical construction that expressed itself in histories like Marquis's and that ultimately produced a recognized if perennially contested national literature. Very few of the expatriates were as enthusiastically reclaimed as Carman or Roberts. And yet, in outline, their story is typical: celebrated at home when they were needed, dismissed as not Canadian enough when they were not, and selectively repatriated and reinvented after their deaths as contributors, whether as founders or footnotes, to a discretely Canadian literary tradition.

In the last decades of the nineteenth century, powerful obstacles to a domestic literature together with powerful attractions to other literary centres caused most Canadian writers who mattered, and many who did not, to leave Canada, most for the United States, most of those for New York. As a profession, as the inspiration for a domestic literature, and as the groundwork of a national canon, Canadian literature began here: not in the backwoods of Ontario, not on the salt flats of New Brunswick, but in the cafés, publishing offices, and boarding-houses of late-nine-teenth-century New York.

NOTES

1. This essay attempts to pull together the main arguments of my research into Canada's literary exodus of the 1880s and 1890s. My forthcoming book discusses more fully than I can here the causes of the exodus, tells the stories of its principal figures, and argues their importance to the subsequent development of a domestic Canadian literature. The book is titled *When Canadian Literature Moved to New York*, and will be published by the University of Toronto Press in 2005.

2. Canada, *Census of Canada, 1880–81* 2: 316, *Census of Canada, 1890–91* 2: 189, *Occupations* 12, and *Fifth Census* 6: 4–5. These figures are summarised, with minor differences, in *Fifth Census* 6: 8–9.

3. Two caveats must be appended to Adams's number, the first upward and the second downward. First, like most works of its kind, his dictionary only lists authors of books; Canadian writers in the United States at this time who had only achieved periodical publication would not have been considered. Second, Adams does not distinguish between the kind or merit of a writer: to the *Dictionary*, Bliss Carman is an American author, and so is William Fletcher MacNutt, a Nova Scotia-born San Francisco physician who authored *Diseases of the Kidney and Bladder*. I suspect, though, that the forty or so Canadian-born professors, physicians, clergymen, etc. whom Adams includes as "authors" would be more than compensated for by those Canadian expatriates who had not yet achieved book publication or come to his attention.

4. · Marshall Saunders, "No Place Like Home," *Halifax Herald* 10 Aug. 1895, qtd. in Davies 246.

5. Canada, *Fifth Census* 6: 6–7; U.S., *Twelfth Census* 7: 13.

6. See Moffett 102–3. Widening Moffett's dates does not significantly change the results: my own search of the London *Bookman* between January 1895 and December 1902 turned up just three Canadian-authored books in the top six, Grant Allen's *The Woman Who Did* in March and April of 1895 and Gilbert Parker's *The Seats of the Mighty* in September of 1896 and *The Right of Way*, which Moffett missed, in November of 1901 (both Allen and Parker were by this time living in England).

7. The CIHM's 1900 to 1920 collection only includes Canadian imprints, but its pre-1900 collection includes titles published in Canada and titles written by Canadians but published elsewhere, the latter a large number because of the same impediments to domestic publication that caused the exodus. The percentage of language and literature titles among its pre-1900 collection of "Canadiana" is therefore artificially high, and the increase of these titles even greater than its figures indicate.

8. The Briggs titles were Thomson's *Old Man Savarin* (1895), *Walter Gibbs* (1896), and *Between Earth and Sky* (1897); Roberts's *The Forge in the Forest* (1897); W.A. Fraser's *The Eye of a God* (1899); Seton's *Two Little Savages* (1903); Stringer's *The Silver Poppy* (1903); Nellie McClung's *Sowing Seeds in Danny* (1908); and H.A. Cody's *The Frontiersman* (1910). All were first or simultaneously issued in the United States.

"Baptized with Tears and Sighs"

Sara Jeannette Duncan and the Rhetoric of Feminism

JANICE FIAMENGO

WRITING in the Toronto *Globe* on May 23, 1885, Sara Jeannette Duncan despaired of women ever achieving their intellectual and moral potential "so long as the newspapers complacently offer for our delectation— *pour les dames*—a column and a half of fashion points and wedding gossip" (6). Duncan is best known today as the author of polished social comedies about British imperialism, the fate of idealists, and the social forms that constrain human passions, but before she became a novelist, she was doing her part for the advancement of women as an iconoclastic young journalist, and she offered her readers a rich fare indeed. From 1885–88, Duncan took advantage of a boom in opportunities for women journalists to launch her public writing career. During this period, newspapers were becoming mass-circulating commercial ventures and needed women readers, and the writers who would attract them, to secure advertising revenue (Lang 31–36). After covering the New Orleans Cotton Centennial early in 1885 and then contributing freelance to the Toronto *Globe* over the summer, Duncan made her name when she was hired as literary editor of the *Washington Post* in October 1885, where she continued until June of the following year. On the basis of her U.S. credentials, Duncan was able to secure full-time employment at two major Canadian newspapers, the *Globe* (1886–87) and the Montreal *Star* (1887–88), and she became a regular contributor to the most prestigious Canadian weekly of the period, Goldwin Smith's *The Week* (1886–88). Even if she had not become a significant novelist later in her career, the writing of Canada's first full-time woman journalist would merit attention as a portrait of

North American society by an acutely observant young woman. That the journalism remains so little known despite her later achievements points to one of many significant gaps in early Canadian literary and social history.[1]

Although she was young and relatively inexperienced, Duncan established a name for herself quickly, becoming the first Canadian woman to declare in print her support for woman suffrage and one of the first Canadian women to work as a parliamentary correspondent during her time at the *Star*. Unlike most other female journalists of the 1880s, Duncan was not confined to a women's page of recipes, housekeeping tips, and social etiquette; although she wrote her share of "fashion points," she more often covered diverse and controversial subjects, attending women's conventions, visiting institutes for the destitute, interviewing professional women, reviewing serious literature, and reflecting on social problems. In her "Saunterings" column in *The Week*, for example, she took the entire field of human activity as her subject, reviewing the latest book on political economy (24 June 1886); assessing the social meaning of wealth in the United States (9 Sept. 1886); reporting on a Black Baptist service in Washington (18 Feb. 1886); and arguing against pay equity for women workers (2 Dec. 1886). As a literary critic, she was serious, exacting, and judicious; as a social critic, inclined to satire and frivolity. She seems to have had her say about nearly all of the pressing issues of her day in columns notable, as Thomas Tausky has observed, for their wit, buoyant self-confidence, and humour (*Selected* 2).

Feminist scholars Carole Gerson and Misao Dean have found much to interest them in the way that Duncan's fiction mocks and revises conventional narratives of womanhood,[2] and therefore it is surprising that the journalism, where Duncan engaged most explicitly with women's issues, has received so little consideration. What is often implicit in the novels is explicit in the journalism: a bold and challenging voice offering unorthodox opinions on women's nature and social role, and skewering social pieties wherever they offered themselves. Even more so than the novels, Duncan's journalism reveals the complexity and ambivalence of her feminist self-positioning, which ranged from measured support for suffrage to acid-tongued ridicule of feminist excess. Rarely in full sympathy with the claims of the women's movement, Duncan adopted a variety of dissenting and assenting postures, speaking by turns as a skeptic, rationalist, or coquette. As I hope to demonstrate in the pages that follow, each of her articles became the occasion for a virtuoso performance of rigorous non-alignment and affiliation; each was also a flamboyant demonstration of the young writer's rhetorical dexterity and wit. Through extensive irony, parody, self-contradiction, and ever shifting point of view, Duncan crafted a multi-voiced persona whose freedom and flexibility offer an illuminating window onto the Woman Question in the 1880s.

◆

A NUMBER OF SCHOLARS have remarked on "the charm of [Duncan's] prose style" (Tausky, *Selected* 2) and the intrinsic interest of her journalism. Tausky observes how "All of the many stylistic devices she used—abrupt beginnings, facetious circumlocutions, elaborate and unusual metaphors, rhetorical appeals to the reader—served to draw attention to the clever, lively, imaginative and unconventional character of the writer" (*Novelist* 41). Rae Goodwin's study of the journalism includes a chapter analyzing her style, noting especially her creation of a "fresh, clever and cultivated woman's disposition" (93) and her "manner of gay feminine imperiousness" (110). In her biography of Duncan, Marian Fowler refers to "her distinctive voice, arch and whimsical" (94) and her "decisive, opinionated, steely" persona (114). Dean also discusses Duncan's journalism as an important staging ground for ideas about women's independence and responsibility (*Different* 58–65). All agree that her witty and insouciant columns made her the provocative public voice of Canadian feminism in the 1880s.

Such insouciance, however, is apt to frustrate a twenty-first-century reader seeking a consistent critique of women's wrongs or a coherent position on emancipation from the woman who opened one of her columns for *The Week* (2 Sept. 1886) with a coy reference to "Those of us who are either actively or passively in favour of the progressive movement regarding women" (648). Duncan's own position was often elusive.

A column for the *Globe*, for example, announced the author's weariness with the subject of women's emancipation and quarrelled with the term itself. "I think most of us are very tired of hearing about the 'emancipation of women,'" Duncan began, and went on to consider the false implications of the call for liberty: "The term gives two false impressions, that the sex is in a condition of thralldom, and that it could accomplish its own liberation" (12 Aug. 1885, 3). Duncan's identification of women as "the sex" and her many "it" pronouns indicate her self-positioning at the beginning of the column as a neutral observer—both impartial and gender neutral—unimpaired by emotion or impatience.

As she developed the discussion, Duncan went on to scoff at the idea that women were oppressed and attacked the metaphor of slavery that some women employed to define their condition. If women were truly enslaved, she noted, they could do little to help themselves. But they were not and should recognize that they shared common interests with men: when men were convinced that women were ready for the responsibilities of suffrage, the privilege would be granted, and until then one of the best ways to prove their readiness was to abandon an irrational insistence on emancipation. "The convictions of men," Duncan notes condescendingly, "are the product of careful comparison and patient reasoning and observation from many sides, while ours spring forth, Minerva-like, born of the instant, ready armed, and because they are not immediately all potent, we wax wroth, some of us, and cry 'Emancipation!'" Here the pronouns have shifted to "we" and "us," but Duncan's sympathies remain firmly with men's caution and against women's unreasoning haste. Her use of epic terminology to describe women's convictions parodies the martial imagery so frequently found in women's narratives of political struggle, recasting righteous anger in mock-epic terms as a fuss over a largely imagined wrong.[3] Here, as elsewhere, Duncan expressed lofty disdain for the political immaturity, impatience, and exaggerated rhetoric she detected in some women's rights arguments.

In the same article, however, Duncan shifted to a more measured tone and endorsed suffrage unequivocally, claiming it to be a reasonable request indicative of women's desire for full citizenship. Decades before suffrage had become a socially acceptable cause, she stated her position without apology and returned to her quarrel with feminist rhetoric in order to recast the debate in terms of responsibility rather than freedom. "And now we ask the franchise," she concludes the column, "not by way of emancipation, as its intelligent exercise would certainly add another burden to the rest that have been laid upon us by our own solicitation.... Women's request for the ballot...is a simple declaration that the sex has reached that point of intelligence that will permit the useful exercise of a public spirit, and is desirous of accepting the duties and responsibilities and benefits that grow out of it" (*Globe*, 12 Aug. 1885, 3). Duncan preferred to depict suffrage as a burden women chose to shoulder rather than as a privilege they demanded. In emphasizing duties and responsibilities rather than rights, Duncan was employing a rhetorical strategy often linked with maternal feminism, the idea that women's capacity and responsibility to mother children and care for the home mandated their duty to mother the nation on a social level. Claiming moral legitimacy for their cause, maternal feminists consistently emphasized duty and responsibility over freedom, and here as elsewhere, Duncan proved her ability to make effective use of a widely sanctioned association between women and moral duty.

In the same column, Duncan rebutted an anti-suffrage argument by claiming the language of womanly duty for her own purposes, and she made her case by arguing vigorously within the terms set by her opponent, Gail Hamilton. Hamilton, whose real name was Abigail Dodge, was "America's best known woman journalist" (Fowler 98), and therefore a writer to whom the competitive Duncan paid attention. "The best point that Gail Hamilton makes against the extension of the suffrage to women," she observes, "is that while they have a right to vote, they have a higher right, based on the sacred first duty of motherhood, not to vote. This is wholly and extremely true, but with the addition of another and still higher right—the right of discretion as to whether they will or not" (*Globe*, 12 Aug. 1885, 3). The alacrity with which Duncan assented to Hamilton's assertion of women's "higher right" (one notes the conscious bombast of "wholly and extremely true"), only to invent "another and still higher right," reveals the ease and playfulness with which she could engage the language of moral duty for her own purposes.

Duncan was also, however, wary of maternal metaphors and often attacked them pointedly. In a *Globe* column for July 15, 1885, she cautioned that the maternal instinct so often celebrated by suffragists was irrelevant to public life, and in a statement that both affirmed and ironized clichés of femininity, she rejected the equation of home and state:

> Nothing is more unconsciously dramatic than a woman's outcry against a suffering which is often hers through no fault of her own; nothing more beautiful in all the dim world of abstractions than the intuitions with which she guards the hearth stone she has made sacred. But if she asks the ballot by virtue of her ability to sorrow eloquently or to know what is best for the baby, it seems to me that she will be sorely puzzled to know what to do with it when it is hers. (3)

Such careful redefinitions, ironic ambiguity, and acid disavowals revealed both her qualified acceptance of the language of womanly duty and her desire to maintain a careful rhetorical distance from other women's rights advocates of her day.

In other examples, desire for distance and consciousness of rhetorical strategy are even more marked. Reporting in the *Globe* (2 Oct. 1886) on a lecture at the Toronto Women's Medical College by Dr. Augusta Stowe Gullen, Canada's first licensed woman doctor, Duncan was impressed by the substance of the lecture but skeptical about the speaker's rhetorical choices, confessing herself compelled to deprecate the "rather elaborate sarcasm at the expense of the modern idea of 'chivalry'" (5). Moreover, Stowe Gullen's reliance on the figure of shackles to depict women's position annoyed her in the same way that the metaphor of slavery had done previously:

> It seems to me that in a community like this, where every advantage is not only willingly, but gladly accorded to women, the aggressive, satirical spirit is out of taste. It is effective anywhere, of course, but the effect is not wholly a pleasant one. Nor can I agree with the lecturer that there is any necessity in discussing the

"woman question" as it is in Canada, for the use of "shackles" as a figure of speech. It is my opinion that there are very few "shackled" women in our fair Dominion who do not hug their chains. (5)

Rhetorical exaggeration weakened feminist credibility, Duncan contended, and failed to address the Canadian situation honestly. The comments reveal Duncan's assessment of the rhetorical pitfalls that accompanied imprecise and emotional language.

Perhaps the most explicit attack on feminist rhetoric came in the same *Globe* article in which Duncan criticized maternal metaphors (15 July 1885). Identifying a familiar style of feminist address, Duncan expressed her impatience with the formulaic sentimentalism of much women's rights rhetoric and lamented the predictability and self-indulgence of some women's gatherings:

> *I do not attend a suffrage convention for the exercise of my emotions, and I confess I should like to go to a temperance meeting without running the risk of being called a "dear sister." Upon sober reflection, you know, nobody wants to adopt the sisterly relation to a lot of damp females of possibly questionable orthodoxy and unreceipted millinery bills. And when you sit in your place and wait for strong statement or trenchant ideas or promising plans, and Mrs. A. opens the deliberations by asserting with tears in her eyes that she is convinced this is a good work and ordered of the Lord, you feel she has not speeded it towards its consummation, and when Mrs. B. continues them by affectionately stating that her heart went out to Mrs. A., whom she never saw before, what can you do but wish it would stay out, and shut the door. (3)*

Adroit parody and *ad hominem* attack indicate Duncan's frustration with a meeting derailed by platitudes and emotionalism. In addition to demonstrating Duncan's cutting humour, these comments are interesting for a number of reasons. They suggest that as early as 1885 (at a time when the first Canadian suffrage organization was only three years old and many decades of campaigns, marches, petitions, and plebiscites lay ahead), a particular version of women's activism had already become an identifiable discourse, a matter of recognizable phrases, associations of ideas, forms of address, and metaphors (sisterhood, God's commission, purity, tears). It had accrued a symbology: a preferred style of clothing, of deportment, gesture, and inflection. One could stand outside of it, with irony, skepticism, and amusement, as Duncan did on this and other occasions. Her consciousness of the particular metaphors and symbols of evangelical feminism contradicts Mariana Valverde's assertion, in *The Age of Light, Soap, and Water* (1991), that such language was "invisible precisely because it was familiar.... The inconspicuous vehicle in which truths... were conveyed" (34).[4] On the contrary, as Duncan made clear, the rhetoric of suffrage was neither transparent nor uncontested.

Duncan's insistence that she was not a "sister" was meant to expose the clichéd metaphor that so grated on her sensibility and also to declare her ideological and social difference from these women. Her blunt appraisal of their likely habits and social position—their "questionable orthodoxy and unreceipted millinery bills"—reveals how deeply the dividing lines of class and religious affiliation marked the women's movement in the 1880s. Then, as now, the movement was emphatically heterogeneous. Duncan's reference to the "questionable orthodoxy" of the women at these meetings suggests, without clarifying, the significant and diverse religious underpinnings of nineteenth-century reform. Many leaders of women's organizations were evangelical Christians who affirmed God's presence in their work to prepare His kingdom on Earth.[5] These were the years in which audiences flocked to hear the passionate exhortations of evangelical leaders such as Letitia Youmans, founder of the Woman's Christian Temperance Union in Canada.[6] Other reformers were on the fringes of Christian belief or entirely outside of it—the theosophists, spiritualists, and free-thinkers celebrated as spiritual liberators in Flora MacDonald Denison's *Mary Melville: The Psychic* (1900).[7] Duncan might have placed either evangelicals or spiritualists in the category of "questionable orthodoxy." A moderate rather than evangelical Presbyterian, and a rationalist, Duncan preferred to base her claims to citizenship on self-restraint and intellectual rigour rather than spiritual fervour or womanly instinct.[8] In concluding the column, Duncan reminds her "sisters"—in ironic quotation marks—that "Political reform is not a matter of the simple assertion of desire to improve, howsoever baptized with tears and sighs that resolution may be. It is a long drawn battle where every resource of cool-headed intelligence is required" (3). Emotionalism and the sloppy rhetoric that was its sign had no place in her conception of political struggle.

Rhetorical and ideological distance are evident in another article Duncan wrote for *The Week* nearly a year later, entitled "Woman Suffragists in Council" (25 Mar. 1886), in which she satirized aspects of a suffrage convention she had attended in Washington, D.C. In particular, she targeted the element of compulsion she detected in this gathering of the faithful, an enforced conformity that irritated her independent spirit. Speaking of the receiving line of suffrage luminaries, she described how "From its genuflecting beginning to its undulating close, one was conscious of being confronted with a stern interrogation point, before which several pompadoured heretics felt constrained to announce fervent admiration for a cause which, up to that inquisitorial hour, they had amused themselves and their masculine attachments by prettily reviling" (261). The language of *heretic* and *inquisition* emphasizes Duncan's suspicion of compulsion both religious and feminist and enables her to question the sincerity of converts to the cause. Duncan was a convert herself, as she made clear in the article, but she could not forbear mocking the rhetorical excesses and occasional fakery of the movement.

Even so redoubtable a heroine as Susan B. Anthony, Quaker abolitionist, suffragist, and temperance activist (b. 1820)—probably at this time the most famous suffrage leader in the United States—came in for satirical treatment when Duncan parodied her penchant for religious metaphors. Noting Anthony's advanced age (she would have been about sixty-five years old) Duncan reflected on her retirement "from earthly scenes to that celestial democracy where, it is to be hoped, there are no invidious distinctions of the ballot...a world where all angels are free and equal, without even the disparity of trousers and skirts" (261). She also did not forbear to note Anthony's plainness, telling her readers (in a sentence that would later make an appearance in *The Imperialist*) that "Grace has done much more for her than nature has ever attempted"

(261). Duncan's mockery indicates that she was more than willing to puncture the pieties of the movement with which she warily aligned herself.

◆

DUNCAN'S OFTEN COMBATIVE relationship to the women's movement presents certain interpretive challenges for twenty-first-century readers trying to assess her irony and her allegiances. In light of the significant criticisms she leveled at the movement, how is Duncan's complex self-positioning to be understood? Given her penchant for scornful mockery as much as sober analysis, what are we to make of the slippery authorial "I"—both suffrage supporter and feminist antagonist—presented in these columns? Recent theorists of autobiography, drawing loosely on Judith Butler's theory of performativity,[9] have emphasized the performative nature of texts that present an autobiographical persona (Egan and Helms xv), and it seems accurate to understand Duncan's journalistic identity too as an ongoing textual performance, an effect rather than cause of her rhetorical dexterity and complex discursive choices. Like other women entering the public sphere through journalism in the 1880s, she was constructing a persona capable of arresting the attention and compelling the respect of a wide readership. As Marjory Lang has emphasized in her study of Canadian women journalists, the feminine persona of presswomen was a source of fascination for readers in the 1880s and 90s to the extent that women writers became "part of the newsmaking formula" (57). While many male reporters wrote anonymously, women writers, under their own or pen-names, became keenly scrutinized public commodities and had no choice but to be intensely aware of the personality their words projected. Agnes Maule Machar, who took the pen-name *Fidelis* to write on women's and labour issues from the 1870s to 90s, cloaked her radicalism in the immaculate garb of Christian idealism.[10] A few years after Duncan made her journalistic mark, Kit Coleman of *The Mail* became famous for her teasing and provocatively inconsistent feminine persona (Freeman 17–41). Then, as now, the public woman was neither entirely free nor hopelessly bound, as she endeavoured, within certain discursive constraints, to create a public identity.

One of the constraints the woman journalist encountered was the relatively conservative tenor of Canadian newspapers. As Lang explains, the newspaper of the 1880s was a man's world to which women were permitted entry only because their presence boosted sales; they were often treated condescendingly and regarded not as real reporters but as "accessories to the main process" (61). The majority of mainstream newspapers and weeklies kept a distance from, or were outright hostile to, the woman suffrage movement, with most editors stressing that women's priority, whatever they might contribute to the wider society, was to protect their femininity (Rutherford 177–78).[11] The Week, in particular, was an organ of the socially conservative Goldwin Smith, Canada's premier man of letters, with whom Duncan was on friendly terms. Smith's editorial pages consistently opposed progressive movements of the day, including the campaign to better the wages and working conditions of factory labourers, any expansion of the franchise, and the admission of women to institutions of higher learning. Such a firm editorial stance must have tempered Duncan's tone. On February 11, 1886, just a month prior to Duncan's column on the Washington women's convention, The Week weighed in against female suffrage with a classic conservative argument, urging the need for legislators to consider

> whether government is likely to be improved either for the men or for the women by putting it under the influence of feminine emotion. It is not a question of relative intelligence or virtue, in regard to which nobody denies the claim of the women, but whether political government is not the proper sphere of men, as domestic management is that of women, and whether mischief will not be done to both sexes by attempting to confound their parts in life.... Experience shows that those women who are the best representatives of their sex, and would be likely to make the best use of the franchise, listen to the voice of nature and keep aloof from the political arena, while those who throw themselves into public life...become political termagants, and do their sex incomparably more mischief, by impairing the grace and dignity of the female character in the eyes of the other sex, than they can do it good by any political reforms. (168)

Given this climate of resistance and hostility, it is not surprising that Duncan might distance herself from the type of woman and type of rhetorical claim that provoked her publisher's ire. Duncan may have been answering this editorial, or another like it, when, at the end of her article on the Washington suffrage conference, she commented dispassionately that "If legal justice to women means danger and detriment to society, the hypothesis should be made to appear in its most convincing aspect, lest in the fullness of time and the on-whirling progress of a civilization before which no barrier stands long it should become a fact" (The Week, 25 Mar. 1886, 261). The coolness and distance she establishes in this statement suggest Duncan's awareness of her multiple audiences.

Yet the extent to which Duncan's attacks on damp females and their unreasonable demands might be read as a distancing strategy is difficult to determine and reflects a more general problem of interpretation raised by women's public claims in this period. Ernest Forbes first raised the need for contextual readings in his detailed response to Carol Bacchi's Liberation Deferred (1983). In her revisionist history of the Canadian women's movement, Bacchi charged that the radical potential of the movement's origins was never realized; the movement failed because it did not challenge gender ideology in any thoroughgoing way. In response, Forbes countered that women's public statements about their suffrage and social reform goals could never be taken at face value. What looked like conservatism in many women's statements, he claimed, was really a pragmatic focus on achievable goals in the face of concerted opposition. Feminist activists by necessity "became experts at dissimulation and deference in a male-dominated society" (94). Forbes's argument is salutary in stressing the need for readers to be aware of the multiple rhetorical constraints and complex codes activated by women's political speech in this period. But there are problems, too, with reading everything as code for a more progressive feminist stance. The irritation, impatience, and dislike suggested by Duncan's reference to "damp females"—with its connotations not only of tearful excess but of the unseemly fact of the female body—seem too intense to be read as strategy alone. Rationality was crucial to Duncan's self-conception, which rested on her claims as a creative writer and witty intellectual. Her suspicion of emotional display, combined with class pride and keen awareness of conservative hostility, all likely played a role in provoking her lofty disdain.

The story might end here with Duncan tentatively defined as a certain kind of conservative feminist, a confident young upper-middle-class intellectual suspicious of organized reform movements and determined to retain favour with conservative editors. Yet there is much in the journalism to contradict any uniform view. As much as she turned an ironic and disparaging eye on official feminism, Duncan also employed her acerbic wit to attack the fortresses of public opinion, often radically and trenchantly. In the same article in *The Week* (25 Mar. 1886) in which she mocked women's rhetoric at the Washington suffrage convention, Duncan also defended the suffrage cause and charged that a hostile press failed to do it justice. "As to what I heard," she concludes the piece,

> *how shall I commit to this antagonistic page the heresy I heard! Indubitable facts, keen logic, unfaltering conclusions? All of that. Foolish bravado, unmeaning assertion, inconsequent reasoning? That, too; but may I be pardoned the auricular defect that caused these latter characteristics to dwindle into insignificance before the former! Is it surprising that where force and intelligence lead the way, impotence and ignorance will fall into line and be clamorous? Is it not a phase of every movement which history unfailingly repeats? And is it quite to be expected that a hostile press will disseminate the former and ignore the latter? (261)*

The silliness and wrong-headedness of some supporters of women's rights, Duncan averred, did not detract from the justice of their campaign. Dismissing as harmless the foolishness she had previously satirized, Duncan neatly shifted her metaphor (of heresy) and her perspective: now it is not feminism but the mainstream press that enforces a dogmatic orthodoxy; now it is not a giddy audience member but Duncan who feels compelled to ask pardon for the heresy of a different point of view; and the smooth rhetorical turn enables Duncan to make a serious criticism of journalistic bias, revealing her keen sense of the difficulties confronting women seeking freedom of opinion and action in a conservative society. Here as elsewhere, amused and even disdainful criticism of the women's movement did not prevent Duncan from defending its goals. Commitment to freedom of opinion and preference for rhetorical surprise are perhaps the only constants in the remarkably varied exploration Duncan conducted, over a two-year period in the *Globe* and *The Week*, into the nature and situation of women in her time. Writing as a woman (her pseudonym, Garth Grafton, was never a real disguise) about one of the great social questions of her day, she was by turns angry and dispassionate, provocative and conciliatory. Changing her line of attack as the situation seemed to invite, she was an unpredictable sometime-ally of the women's movement—and one whose propensity for a shifting point of view, frequent irreverence, and argumentative reversals suggests both intellectual breadth and an element of playful experimentation in the many discussions she devoted to the subject.

On one occasion, she employed bitter sarcasm to ridicule the argument that giving women the vote would undermine domestic stability. "Awful possibilities of coercion rise before the Governmental vision," she jeered in the *Globe* on May 23, 1885, "of meek Gretchen hastening to vote as her liege willeth, or henpecked Benedict fleeing to the polls with wrath and nameless threats in hot pursuit" (6). Parodying the claims of suffrage opponents in government, Duncan took direct aim at the logical flabbiness and irresponsible alarmism of anti-suffrage statements. In the very same column, however, flippant amusement was her refuge when she responded to *The Week*'s editorial disapproval of a new feminine fashion in gaudy hairpins, with a laughing rejoinder: "If we can't select our representatives you must at least give us choice in hairpins!" (6). On another occasion (*The Week*, 2 Sept. 1886), the elegant symmetry of her phrasing suggested an unshakeable poise and ability—at least ironically—to appreciate the traditional virtues of helpless femininity. "There is something very grand, very noble, very tender, in man's protection of woman because of her weakness and incompetence to protect herself," she proclaimed. "But the weakness and incompetence itself is not beautiful; and, at least in the eye of the law, I think we must be content to be as strong and competent as in us lies, sighing sometimes over the pages of some dusty old novel" (644). And on a third occasion

(*The Week*, 2 Dec. 1886), she claimed serenely, in discussing women's wages, that "If the music of the spheres were only truly pitched and sustained, the work of woman would always be within the sacred portals of home, and her reward the legal tender of love alone" (6).

Part of the puzzle and enjoyment of reading Duncan, as the above excerpts suggest, is deciphering her irony, deciding if and when her surface meaning is a reliable one. Irony is, as Linda Hutcheon explains, the ultimate mode of duplicity and doubleness, a potentially exclusionary and often ambiguous form of discourse. In the hands of a social satirist like Duncan, it could be a way of asserting and undermining with the same statement, of standing both inside and outside an argument. Always expressing at least "two meanings simultaneously" (Hutcheon 9), the ironic utterance points toward something unsaid that registers on the reader able to recognize the irony. Yet sometimes Duncan's ironic posture is difficult to read, as in the above comment about the ideal world in which no woman would work for wages. In a more fully developed example, Duncan devoted part of a *Globe* column to describing the traditional woman-of-years-gone-by to contrast the simple virtues and serenity of her life with the ambition and anxiety of the modern woman (12 Nov. 1886). She gives a nostalgic salute to the "gentle, ineffable repose" that one's grandmother gained from "knowing and doing her duty as wife, mother, and hostess" (6). Is Duncan's tongue firmly in her cheek as she trots out the clichés of domestic bliss? Is there a metaphorical wink to undermine her rosy-tinted portrait of this woman whose "whole existence was summed up in the prefix to her husband's name on her visiting cards" (6)? The piece seems to stand in opposition to all that Duncan has elsewhere written about women's moral obligation to exercise their abilities in public life, and yet it is not mere mockery.

Perhaps the irony is situational rather than verbal: nothing could more firmly signal the modern woman's break with her grandmother's generation than this sentimental (and transitory) indulgence in regret, this decorous tribute to a time irretrievably past. Non-ironic nostalgia may be more defiant than conservative, in this case, in its determination to cast a still powerful ideology as quaint and beautifully antique. It is hard to know what else to make of Duncan's (faux naïve?) assertion that "happiness is altogether relative, and can proceed from the parchment that covered jam jars, inscribed 'apricot,' as well as from the piece that contains the Latin words of your diploma" (6). In *A Different Point of View*, Dean makes a persuasive case for understanding Duncan's fictional irony as a trope to enhance a stable meaning rather than a mode of radical indeterminacy, but I would suggest that the irony of the journalism has a more deeply destabilizing function precisely because Duncan does not seek to create a stable point of view in her rapid-fire observations on the meanings of modern womanhood.

Ironic indeterminacy and lightning shifts in perspective were important for Duncan in providing a mobile stance from which to ridicule hypocrisy and wrong-headedness wherever she saw it, both in the rapidly forming orthodoxies of the women's movement and in her society's most dearly held convictions about women. Rhetorical subterfuge seems to have been a favoured strategy. Daring criticisms of social wrongs often appeared in her human interest pieces, the columns of observation and commentary that were not ostensibly about women's rights at all. Here she deployed a variety of modes of satiric address, her tone of voice ranging from amusement to outrage and often modulating between the two. In a column for the *Globe* of May 23, 1885, for example, Duncan reflected on women's habit of saying "I don't know," musing on what the irritating phrase really meant (6). The column begins as a Horatian satire on feminine habits of speech, light-hearted in tone, and develops gradually into a scathing reflection on a society that has thwarted women's ability to reason and to express themselves. In a similarly structured column for the *Globe* of July 15, 1885, Duncan lampooned women's tendency to use diminutive versions of their names. The impetus for the column was a book whose author, Duncan noted, was Mamie L. Hatchett (3). No matter how good the book is, Duncan asserts, nobody will take it seriously if the author insists on calling herself Mamie. The article's attack broadens to indict the societal infantilization of women and women's acquiescence in that infantilization.

Duncan's satire is often sharp and corrosive, as for example when she responds to condescending pronouncements about women in other serial publications. In response to a recommendation that women conceal their learning, her vituperation expresses itself in a string of rhetorical questions: "Are we to veil our indiscretion in venturing beyond the covers of the cookery book for fear of beguiling some unwary sister from her rightful contemplation of pickles and preserves, who might otherwise have developed into a housewife extraordinary! Or is it that some of us, having come short of the absolute stupidity required for perfect patient womanhood are to propitiate fate by trying to look as stupid as possible in deprecation of intelligence that is our misfortune and not our fault!" (*Globe*, 5 Aug. 1885, 3). Balancing such forthright attacks are cases where humour and irony combine to suggest a satiric approach rather than to articulate it directly. In a column for the *Globe* of September 8, 1886, Duncan reported on an exhibition of ladies' fancy work at a large fair, the sheer volume of which caused Duncan to confess herself overcome by a multitude of emotions she does not name (though one suspects that horrified sympathy is the predominant one). Her voice moves quickly between wonder, pity, mockery, and angry empathy as she reports on the extraordinary and pathetic investment of time, energy, and skill into the production of "Such acres of plush, and satin, and Berlin wool!" (4). Describing, with an attention bordering on compulsion, the array of "table scarfs and mantle drapes, tidies and wall pockets, toilet sets and knitted things, wall panels and China plaques" (4), Duncan emphasizes the ferocious energy of these women and suggests the pity of wasted lives.

At other times, social prejudice merits only contemptuous laughter. In a *Globe* piece published on August 23, 1886, Duncan interviews a woman doctor, ostensibly to see if her profession has damaged her femininity. A subject that might have provoked playful irony in a different context had a bitter edge given the resistance Ontario women had recently encountered in their pursuit of medical qualifications. In 1882–83, men in the medical school at Queen's University protested women's attendance at medical lectures, outraged at the indecency of the situation (Prentice et al. 161). Duncan makes no mention of this history, but her awareness of social opposition is evident in the deadpan earnestness with which she closely observes the woman's manner of dress, appearance, and mien. She is relieved to discover that the lady does not "stride" and is not "mannish"; the doctor is even, she is happy to note, rather maternal in her dealings with a small boy who has hurt his thumb. When Duncan ends the piece by asking her subject whether she was ever sorry to have chosen medicine rather than "something better suited to [her] feminine tastes and womanly predilections," a powerful laughter both derisive and affirmative rings out at the conclusion: "And will you believe it, she laughed at the idea—laughed at her feminine tastes and womanly predilections! Here's a state of things!" (*Globe*, 23 Aug. 1886, 4). Here, ironic laughter seems both to confirm and lighten feminist anger.

In launching her wide-ranging satiric assaults on unexamined orthodoxy and social injustice, Duncan must have found ironic double-voicing and shifting viewpoint to be powerful strategies in the service of a carefully waged guerilla war. Far from seeking to construct a unified feminist identity, she cultivated indirection, evasion, and laughing self-contradiction, strategies which, while at times threatening the coherence of her ethical stance, enabled both stinging attack and wary self-protection. In the same column in which she stated her support for woman suffrage as a sign of civic responsibility and intelligence (*Globe*, Aug. 12, 1885), she also indulged in some girlish frivolity, "confess[ing]" herself "not as much interested in it [voting] as the importance of the subject deserves" and objecting "to being supposed an elderly female with spectacles and side curls and an aversion to bangs" (3). Her Janus-faced approach allowed her to balance rational analysis of women's rights with a dose of feminine superficiality. Irritated by anti-feminist stereotypes of the elderly female with spectacles, her playful objection also confirms the stereotype's emotional force. In her article on the Washington suffrage convention (*The Week*, 25 Mar. 1886), Duncan interrupts her description of the proceedings to declare with mock solemnity that "It is a supreme moment in a woman's existence when she commits herself to suffrage for her sex. It marks the temporary and hard-won victory of her intelligence over her instinct" (261). The joke's evocation of a universal, biologically determined "woman" runs counter to Duncan's assertions of variety and intelligence in the movement. Such tonal shifts and playful contradictions were fundamental to Duncan's self-presentation.

Duncan's contradictory and multiple self-positioning suggests the need for reconsideration of the standard analytic categories through which the early Canadian women's movement has traditionally been understood. Her multiple ironies trouble the attempt to position her on the feminist spectrum, and the ease with which she adopted multiple positions calls into question the usefulness of accepted categories such as conservative or progressive. As Duncan said of the suffrage supporter, "She is not homogeneous; she differs from her sister as radically as it is possible for people with a common purpose to differ" (*The Week*, 26 Mar. 1886, 261)—and Duncan most certainly embodied the diversity she named.

To some extent, such contradictory self-positioning developed out of the personal circumstances and material conditions of her writing at this time, such that rhetorical strategy cannot be separated from the medium that fostered it. As a journalist, Duncan was producing her material quickly, filling column inches to meet deadlines at various papers. The work was fatiguing and the demand to come up with new material and perspectives daunting in a society consumed by ephemera; the nature of newspaper writing meant that one's labours rarely had any lasting impact. Moreover, Duncan was a very young woman at the time she was making her mark, not yet twenty-five when hired at the *Globe*, her best novels still two decades in the future. These two circumstances combined—Duncan's youth and the ephemeral nature of newspaper publication—may have helped to make this a period of experimentation for Duncan, a time when she tried on and discarded a variety of voices, identities, and platforms.

Without the need to achieve a consistent or stable point of view, she was free to move between positions, to take them on as literary and political exercises, perhaps in a form of impersonation or ventriloquism, certainly in a deliberate act of self-fashioning. Her multiple self-positioning enabled her to be provocative without being offensive; to canvas radical feminist ideas without appearing doctrinaire; to present herself as a serious intellectual without seeming dour or unfeminine. Describing the individual personalities of the women she encountered at the Washington convention, she noted that one of them, she was sure, "would have flirted strategically in its [the movement's] favour" (261), and Duncan too liked to flirt. In refusing a single, coherent feminist position from which to speak, Duncan risked charges of flippancy and self-contradiction in order to insist on the multi-dimensionality of her public self. That newspaper writing allowed her the freedom to make and unmake her narrative persona, to occupy a variety of ideological positions, suggests the importance of this form of writing both as literary apprenticeship for Duncan and as a significant feminist staging ground in its own right.

While some feminist commentators have understood ideological contradictions in early Canadian women's writing to be a problem and a limitation, with Dean noting of Duncan's era, for example, that "feminist movements in Canada were plagued by ideological contradiction" (*Different* 59), the case of Duncan strongly suggests that ideological contradictions could be not a plague but a source of strength, a condition of multiplicity that enabled at least as much as it disabled. In occupying many rhetorical positions, Duncan could move easily between female, feminist, and universal/male speaking positions, questioning assumptions about all three and exploring the question of women's social position with a remarkable boldness. She could attack without having to be on the defensive because she did not definitively occupy one position; her rhetorical mobility opened up a space of critique, challenge and invention that never bogged down in self-justification. Duncan's success in this regard suggests that more attention should be paid to nineteenth-century periodical literature for its production of a variety of provocative forms of cultural intervention. Given the centrality of the newspaper as a mass-market medium in the late nineteenth century and the appearance of a significant number of women journalists at that time, such investigation is long overdue.

◆

THIS DISCUSSION has looked at only a small number of the hundreds of articles Duncan wrote during her years as a journalist. Such a small sampling, with its focus on the Woman Question, only begins to suggest the range and enormous intellectual energy of her output as a young writer finding her public voice. Her engagements with Canadian and American national character, with Canada's literary and cultural development, with race and empire, and with manifold aspects of social relations are all equally complex and provocative, and opportunities abound for research into this rich mine of cultural information.

Yet because Duncan—skeptical feminist, elitist, imperialist—so often falls outside of the approved narratives of ideologically oriented criticism, her work poses multiple challenges for contemporary critics. The entry on Duncan in W.H. New's *Encyclopedia of Literature in Canada* (2002) concludes with a reference to the discomfort her work seems to produce. Summing up Duncan's critical stature, Neil ten Kortenaar notes the failure of her Anglo-Indian fiction to generate the post-colonial interest that might have been expected, and his remarks might apply equally well to the reception of her feminist journalism: "Part of the difficulty in reading Duncan, the colonial imperialist who wrote from a position outside all centres and all communities, may be that few readers, then or now, can comfortably join her there" (322). The characterization is apt, and I am struck by ten Kortenaar's suggestion that much current critical investigation relies on an ideologically "comfortable" relationship between critic and subject, in which criticism becomes the arena where the political credentials of both scholar and subject are put forward for scrutiny and judgement. The prickly, ironic, and elitist Duncan has always been a dubious candidate for such an exercise.

Feminist criticism in particular has devoted a considerable amount of energy to assessing early Canadian women writers against an evolving ideal of subversion, resistance, and liberation. The feminist recovery project in Canada began in celebration of heroic foremothers and has wrestled for the past decade with the racism, class consciousness, and other ideological failings of these historical figures. Defensible and perhaps necessary as these preoccupations have been, both idealization and disavowal have a tendency to skew our critical emphasis, leading to responses of deference and moral righteousness—all critics of good conscience will approve or deplore the following!—that too often become critical ends in themselves.[12] Writing of another disciplinary context, Rod Preece has recently criticized what he calls "Advocacy Scholarship," research and writing that promote political objectives. The desire to side with the oppressed is a laudatory one, Preece affirms, but it almost inevitably leads to "a greater concern for representation than intellectual impartiality, an attempt at which is an absolute necessity for all sound thought" (22). While it would clearly be impossible *not* to read Duncan through twenty-first-century eyes, I believe that our work is more useful when political judgment is not our guiding principle and when we pay more attention to the writer's contexts than to our own.

Unfortunately, not a great deal is known about how Duncan's journalism was received by the province she once called, famously, "one great camp of the Philistines" (30 Sept. 1886, 707). Certainly, she was widely read. Readers' letters, asking or dispensing advice and proffering opinions, were frequently published in her columns for the *Globe*, often contributing to drawn-out debates on such matters as dress reform, modern marriage, and the wearing of ladies' hats at the theatre. Duncan took pleasure in teasing her correspondents for infelicities of expression and logic, and readers appealed to her authority with an affectionate combination of deference and raillery. Her readership was not exclusively female, as Duncan enjoyed pointing out; one woman reader in the *Globe* reported that her husband "always reads Woman's World immediately after the Political Intelligence" (1 Nov. 1886, 6). Like other female journalistic pioneers, Duncan earned a loyal readership because she created a fascinating persona that was acknowledged by her peers. In his memoir of a prominent life as a journalist and cultural arbiter, Hector Charlesworth credited Duncan with single-handedly creating the "fame" of the *Globe*'s women's department (89), and according to Lang, she "had become such a celebrity by 1888 that her movements were reported by other journalists" (41). Her wit, inventiveness, and acerbity earned her a significant place in Canadian journalism in her own time, and make for a fresh and provocative challenge to scholars today.

1. I am indebted to Thomas Tausky for first bringing Duncan's journalism to my attention in *Sara Jeannette Duncan: Selected Journalism* (1978). My paper deals with a few of the articles in Tausky's collection but also includes material that he omitted because of space constraints. Finding Duncan's newspaper articles has been made relatively easy by the painstaking groundwork laid by Rae Goodwin in her Master's thesis (1964); her extensive annotated bibliography traces the majority of articles Duncan published before leaving Canada on her world tour in 1888.

2. See especially Dean's "'You may imagine my feelings'" (1990) and Gerson's "Wild Colonial Girls" (1995).

3. See, for example, the metaphor of temperance as a war employed by Letitia Youmans in her autobiography. Youmans frequently referred to a battlefield in which all women and men of conscience were called to take up arms in the struggle for the soul of the nation.

4. See especially Valverde's chapter entitled "The Work of Allegory," in which she urges social historians to pay attention to the discourse of reform. Valverde's was the first Canadian study of the period 1880–1920 to consider language in detail, but her conclusion—that social activists were largely unconscious of their rhetorics—not entirely accurate.

5. For an illuminating discussion of the significant differences between evangelical and moderate strands of nineteenth-century Christianity, see John Webster Grant's *A Profusion of Spires* (1988), especially 170–220.

6. See Sharon Anne Cook for a discussion of WCTU support for woman suffrage as early as the 1870s (99–102).

7. *Mary Melville* (1900) is a fictionalized biography of the author's sister, whose unusual life and mysterious death confirmed the suffragist author's belief in spirit communication.

8. She was frequently hostile to religious enthusiasm in her columns, reporting with asperity on the Methodist revivalism sweeping Ottawa in the spring of 1888 and relishing the opportunity to enumerate the preacher's shortcomings (*The Week*, 1 Mar. 1888).

9. This theory was first and most clearly developed in *Gender Trouble* (1990).

10. For an overview of Machar's theology and social concerns, see Ramsay Cook 186–91.

11. Rutherford sums up Canadian newspapers' editorial stance as follows: "Woman, it seemed, should be man's helpmate (and few, indeed, were the editors who would give her a greater stature) in the community at large as well as in the family" (178).

12. For a related argument, see Nick Mount's "In Praise of Talking Dogs" (1998), which refers to the paucity of evaluative criticism of early Canadian literature and the predominance of cultural and ideological studies, with their "largely implicit political praise or censure" (78).

The Search for a Livable Past

Frye, Crawford, and the Healing Link

CECILY DEVEREUX

I mean by form the shaping principle of the individual poem, which is derived from the shaping principles of poetry itself. Of these latter the most important is metaphor, and metaphor, in its radical form, is a statement of identity: this is that, A is B. Metaphor is at its purest and most primitive in myth, where we have immediate and total identifications.

—Northrop Frye, "Preface to an Uncollected Anthology"

[W]hile metaphors can be abused in many different ways, the most serious and interesting danger is that a given metaphor or its allegorical extension may be transformed into myth.

—Douglas Berggren, "The Use and Abuse of Metaphor"

One does not obliterate a native culture with impunity, however, no matter how alien it may seem.

—Northrop Frye, "Criticism and Environment"

ISABELLA VALANCY CRAWFORD'S POEM *Malcolm's Katie: A Love Story* seems to have first appeared in print in 1884, in the self-published and hugely unsuccessful collection, *Old Spookses' Pass, Malcolm's Katie, and Other Poems*. It is a long poem of 1279 lines of blank verse narrative with interspersed lyrics, in the manner of Tennyson's 1847 poem, "The Princess."[1] Although the poem's first appearance proved to be so unrewarding both financially and professionally for Crawford, it has enjoyed a fairly solid canonicity, beginning not while she was alive—she died in impecunious ill health at the age of thirty-seven in 1887—but not long after her death, and more than a decade before it appeared in the significant, if contentious, 1905 volume, *The Collected Poems of Isabella Valancy Crawford*, edited by John Garvin and with an introductory note by Crawford's slightly younger contemporary, Ethelwyn Wetherald (1857–1940).[2] Although Garvin's book would be the first, and still is the only, collection of Crawford's poetry, his work was not so much recuperative as organizational. By 1905 Crawford and at least some part of *Malcolm's Katie* had figured in virtually every major national anthology or study of literature in Canada, at least since the early collection by W.D. Lighthall, *Songs of the Great Dominion*, which appeared in 1889. Lighthall, who observes that Crawford's "work [was] scarcely noticed in her native country" (450), excerpts two longish sections of *Malcolm's Katie* in his book, published only two years after she had died; he also includes the "canoe" lyric of Part 1 and the song of the axe from Part 4.[3] In fact, of the seven poems by Crawford in *Songs of the Great Dominion*, four are taken from *Malcolm's Katie*.

The print status of the poem has continued into the twentieth century. Since 1905, all or part of *Malcolm's Katie* has been reproduced in numerous anthologies, most recently, in its entirety, in Carole Gerson and Gwendolyn Davies's *Canadian Poetry: From the Beginnings Through the First World War* (McClelland and Stewart, 1994). The text used in the Gerson and Davies volume, and which now represents the standard text of *Malcolm's Katie*, is that of D.M.R. Bentley's Canadian Poetry Press (CPP) edition of 1987, the first with comprehensive notes and apparatus. This edition of the poem (also included in Bentley's 1993 CPP anthology, *Early Long Poems on Canada*), has been extremely important in marking Crawford's place in nineteenth-century English Canadian literary culture, and in situating her best-known poem in relation to the long and ongoing tradition of narrative poetry in English Canada. It has, moreover, foregrounded the position of *Malcolm's Katie* as what is still the only long narrative poem by a nineteenth-century English Canadian woman that has canonical—

or even print—status, and as one of the best-known and most widely discussed long narrative poems of any period in Canada.

In 1986, in an investigation of what he described as "Seven Myths About Canadian Literature," Don Precosky noted and deplored what he saw then as a growing and regrettable critical focus on Crawford. Precosky objected to "the tremendous vogue which [she] has recently enjoyed," and argued against the "misconception," as he put it, that "*Malcolm's Katie* is a great poem" (94).[4] Although Precosky has made some interesting points about the critical reception of Crawford in the 1970s and 80s and about the poem, it seems to me that the real question that needs to be asked about *Malcolm's Katie* is not why readers see it as a "great" poem (since not every reader has), but what it is that makes it matter, and why it continues to circulate in the way that it does, as an important document—to revert for a moment to Dorothy Livesay's well-known argument about the long poem in Canada as a "documentary" genre[5]— of English Canadian settlement and of late nineteenth-century emergent nationalism. The question, in other words, is not why readers see it as "great," but what they see of themselves and their national history in it.

In fact, *Malcolm's Katie* has a curious mystique in the canon of early English Canadian literature. Generally recognized as a poem that is doing what many early long poems on Canada are arguably doing— constructing a narrative of settler history within a conventional discourse of colonization, empire, and incipient nation—*Malcolm's Katie* has also been seen to be doing something more. Northrop Frye, who imputed considerable value to *Malcolm's Katie* as a key text of Canadian settler literature, and who returned to the poem repeatedly in his writing on Canada, articulated this duality most clearly in his 1956 essay, "Preface to an Uncollected Anthology," where he suggested that, in *Malcolm's Katie*, and particularly in

the long mythopoeic passage...beginning "The South Wind laid his moccasins aside," we see how the poet is, first, taming the landscape imaginatively, as settlement tames it physically, by animating the lifeless scene with humanized figures, and, second, integrating the literary tradition of the country by deliber-

ately re-establishing the broken cultural link with Indian civilization.... (Bush Garden 181)

In other words, for Frye, Crawford's poem is engaged both in settler writing's usual work of "colonization by text"—overwriting and domesticating indigeneity, encoding place with new referents, filling the colony's putative empty space—and in another kind of work, effectively overwriting the work of colonization's overwriting. In nineteenth-century English Canadian poetry, for Frye at any rate, only *Malcolm's Katie* manages simultaneously to colonize and to "integrate" colonial society with an indigenous, pre-colonial past; to constitute a pre-colonial past, in effect, within the cultural memory of the settlers.

It is tempting to see Frye's reading of Crawford's healing work as an index primarily of gender ideologies that pertain as much to the post-World War II period in which Frye is writing about *Malcolm's Katie* as to the late nineteenth-century imperial context within which Crawford produced the poem. It is conventional still in the twenty-first century to imagine that men destroy and women heal, that men are naturally aggressive and that women are naturally care-givers. It is also still conventional in English Canadian literary history to categorize men's and women's settler writing along the lines of colonial agency: men do the physical and intellectual work of colonization and settlement; women make homes and communities, reaching out, after a time, to invite the indigenous peoples displaced by masculine colonization into the social formations that have overwritten their own, trying to build a national family along the lines of the microcosmic domestic space they manage inside the home. Read along this axis of gender ideologies, *Malcolm's Katie* is doing what women's work is understood to undertake in the context of colonial space.

While it is clear, however, that gender is a factor in Frye's take on Crawford, whom he elsewhere somewhat dismissively describes as "an intelligent and industrious female songbird of the kind who filled so many anthologies in the [nineteenth] century" (*Bush Garden* 149), the question of the ideologies underpinning these essentializing binarisms is beyond the scope of this paper. What I am concerned with here are the questions of how it is possible to see *Malcolm's Katie* performing a work of healing and what are the implications of the valuing of the poem according to this work. It will be evident that Frye's statement about the poem in the 1956 essay is highly ambivalent in its representation of a broken link with "Indian" civilization, and that it does not specify whose link is broken and for which constituency the link is re-established. It is not clear, moreover, what exactly is a broken *cultural* link and how it is different from a broken social or political link; and it is not absolutely clear how *Malcolm's Katie* does what Frye suggests it does, and how this work helps us to understand the circulation of this poem and other national narratives in English Canada. This paper reconsiders *Malcolm's Katie* in light of Frye's assessment, in terms of what "mythopoesis" is and does for Frye and of the extent to which this poem's "mythopoesis" can be understood to constitute in any way cultural healing of the kind Frye imagines, with the objective of understanding the continued canonical "value" of Crawford's poem and the work that it has done and continues to do as a nation-building text and an English Canadian narrative of origin.

Malcolm's Katie is all about settlement. It is, even for its time, a fairly conventional romance of settlement, constructed around a recognizable account of clearing the land and overthrowing malign influence on the work of colonization, concluding with the two young lovers, Max Gordon and Katie Graem, united and productive, sitting with their child at the centre of their prosperous farm. Although the poem is quite well known, in order to make a point about its work and the way it is functionalized in critical treatments such as Frye's, it would be useful to revisit the narrative here and map its progression. The poem begins at the moment of betrothal. Max, "[p]oor soldier of the axe" (1.24), has given Katie a little ring he has made from the first coin he ever earned ("sacred coin—first well-priz'd wage/ For boyish labour, kept thro' many years" [1.3–4]). Before he can claim Katie as his next "prize," however, Max must go and make himself into a man—a productive land-owning man— in the manner of Katie's father, Malcolm Graem. Malcolm, the patriarch of the title's possessive, is "[a] mighty man,/ Self-hewn from rock, remaining rock through all" (1.56–57): he has, in other words, formed himself into the powerful patriarch and landowner that he is by his own hand and through his own work. Indeed, as Max reminds Katie, Malcolm had yoked himself with his brother Reuben "to the new plough" to clear their first field (1.75–81). Malcolm, it is pointed out, has come from "poverty" (1.74) to what Max describes as "[o]utspreading circles of increasing gold" (1.110), and he has made that transition heroically. He deserves his rewards, it is suggested, because "[h]e work'd for all" (1.68): both Max and Katie agree on this point. Malcolm's opposition to the union of the two, while it is bemoaned, is thus not questioned. Max is not yet able to claim as his the woman who remains the father's object, "Malcolm's Katie," the "little daughter heir/ Who must not wed the owner of an axe,/ Who owns naught else but some dim, dusky woods/ In a far land" (1.112–15). He will therefore go and do the work he has to do—knight-like—to bring the romance to its happy conclusion.

Max, it is clear, *does* have property, but it is as yet "naught," woods, rather than farm, "far" from the centres of settlement. Max's—and *Malcolm's Katie*'s—is the logic of post-1769 settlement of colonial space in Canada, or what is now Canada: that the land was not being "used" by its Native inhabitants, and therefore was entirely "naught," the *terra nullius* or empty space into which settlers naturally (evolution), necessarily (progress), and rightfully (empire and land acquisition) moved. Max must make the land into something meaningful—habitable, in other words, and profitable for the white settler, a part of the imperial enterprise, signifying within imperial discourse—before he can marry Katie; he has to do what Malcolm has done for his property. It is implicit in the poem that Max's task and his story are not unique, and will not be as long as there is a frontier of wilderness to claim. The pattern has been established, notably by Katie's father, whose initials "M.G." appear on the logs from which he has wrested his wealth, and whose own patriarchal status thus mirrors Max's own. Malcolm Graem and Max Gordon are both working for the same "sacred coin"; they are figures in the same story, told again here for the younger man precisely to show that it *is* an ongoing narrative. This story is a familiar capitalist myth of the "new world," where the possibility of economic and social self-fashioning is widely propagandized from the beginning of the nineteenth century, or of the industrial revolution, at any rate, when Anglo-imperial principles of class become less hereditary and more dependent on ideas of hard work and opportunities taken. This is the primary "freedom" of the "new world" for European emigrants: it appears to offer an escape from ancestral systems of economic and social oppression, while providing a space that is still "within" the "old world" because it is imperial. Max and Malcolm both make themselves into men on these terms.

Max goes off to the woods—identified as *his* woods, it is important to observe—where he cuts down trees to convert the land to agricultural and domestic space. As in many nineteenth-century texts, this work is represented in epic and heroic terms: Max does battle with the trees and "slays" them. In the process, he begins to transform the wilderness into a "livable" space and himself into a man, inside and out: "His young soul grew and shew'd a virile front,/ Full muscl'd and large statur'd, like his flesh" (2.172–73). Max, now an antecedent of the late twentieth-century image of the successful man who has both property and time to take care of his body, is muscular and manly on the outside, because he also is on the inside.

The point is made again, as it was with the mirror-image initials "M.G.," that Max, in thus emerging in and from his body, through its "conflict" with the soil, as a new man is not alone. "It was not all his own," we are told, "the axe-stirr'd waste" (2.191):

> In these new days men spread about the earth
> With wings at heel—and now the settler hears,
> While yet his axe rings on the primal woods,
> The shrieks of engines rushing o'er the wastes;
> Nor parts his kind to hew his fortunes out.
> And as one drop glides down the unknown rock
> And the bright-threaded stream leaps after it
> With welded billions, so the settler finds
> His solitary footsteps beaten out,
> With the quick rush of panting, human waves
> Upheav'd by throbs of angry poverty,

> And driven by keen blasts of hunger, from
> Their native strands—so stern, so dark, so dear! (2.192–204)

The long section of Part 2 in which Crawford summarizes the process of settlement, and in which this passage cited above appears, is crucial to the way the poem is positioned on the question of colonization. First, the point is made that settlement is an effect of necessity: the settlers have been driven from "[t]heir native strands" by "poverty" and "hunger." This point is a familiar one by the 1880s in narratives of settlement and especially in long narrative poems. Oliver Goldsmith made it much earlier in the century, in his long narrative poem, *The Rising Village* (1825); Alexander McLachlan made it in *The Emigrant* (1861).[6] But it is significant because so much of what will be understood in Canada for a century and a half, at least, about colonization and the rights and responsibilities of settlers will pivot on the idea of necessity as the impetus for settlement: colonization in Canada, that is, is represented in relation to a self-preserving impulse in the face of poverty and want, an impulse that is collective in its emergence and that directs attention to a collective outcome of benefit for the community (the Anglo-imperial "race" and the empire) through the betterment of the individual. Related to this idea in the familiar settler narrative of the nineteenth century is the second key point of this passage, the notion of colonization as a means not only to the productivity of the land, but to the physical improvement of the colonists. Max (Canadian-born) is a sturdy lad from the outset, but there are others introduced in this section that is so concerned with embedding the story of Max and Katie in a proliferating, repeating narrative of settlement as progress. There are many men, we are to see, who begin in colonial space as effeminized weaklings, are converted by the work of their own hands in settlement into strong, muscled, healthy, *manly* men who do not work for another but for themselves, as landowners and potential patriarchs, and who, through their self-focused work, actually work harder to build the nation, as and of themselves. This process is represented as natural, framed in the poem within a vocabulary of growth and nature that aligns the processes of colonization and progress—the poem's linear impetus—with a cyclical and endlessly renewed pattern of seasonal growth and change. Thus "roses of Plenty" bloom in the cheeks of the once pale and unhealthy "wife and children" (2.219–20) and "shanties gr[o]w...amid the blacken'd stumps" (2. 210–11). Similarly, the weak man grows, as we have already seen Max doing, into a settler:

> The pallid clerk look'd on his blister'd palms
> And sigh'd and smil'd, but girded up his loins
> And found new vigour as he felt new hope.
> The lab'rer with train'd muscles, grim and grave,
> Look'd at the ground and wonder'd in his soul,
> What joyous anguish stirr'd his darken'd heart,
> At the mere look of the familiar soil,
> And found his answer in the words—"Mine own!" (1.222–29)

In addition to being configured as a work of nature, or perhaps to emphasize its putative naturalness, colonization is an erotic act here, a performance of gendered sexual power.

The erotics of colonization are not unique to *Malcolm's Katie*, of course. There are countless examples of what might be understood as the spontaneous overflow of powerful colonial feeling in nineteenth-century English Canadian writing and after. The best-known example may be Frye's frequently noted delineation of the movement of settlement in English Canada as a "gigantic east-to-west thrust" (219). The many representations of men made manly as they make the land habitable through a work that is impelled by the desire to own it function not so much as an affirmation of manhood than as a precondition for colonization, as they indicate that this manliness is an *effect* of colonization. The man, that is, is a product of the imperial context, and he earns his right, as he grows his muscles through hard work, to be where he is. These are imperialist and capitalist erotics, in which the outcome of the production of labour justifies it, and in which masculinity is constructed in relation to wealth and property, power, and sexual and commercial productivity. *Malcolm's Katie* does not counter the fundamental structure of capitalist patriarchal progress, nor does it meddle in any significant way with the ideology of the self-made man as the epitome of masculinity. It thus cannot be understood to be anti-colonial or anti-imperial (both of which positions many readers have argued the poem takes): it repeats and valorizes as heroic the colonial and imperial narrative of the simultaneous construction of self and place, resulting in economic growth for both the individual and the empire that the settler represents and supports with colonial labour.

Although the primary contest in the poem takes place between the settler-man and the land—again, a conventional enough motif in colonial narrative—the central conflict occurs between the newly manly Max and the "wooer" Alfred, who appears on the domestic scene while Max is away clearing his homestead. Alfred is not particularly manly; certainly he is not manly inside and out, as Max is. At one level Alfred is best understood in terms of nineteenth-century colonial representations of the sissyish Englishman (Alfred has "Saxon-gilded locks") who thinks he is smarter than the colonial man, but who is bested by him in the proofs of masculinity—winning the girl, most obviously, in what are often obviously phallic contests (sword fights, battles with or over sticks and trees, log rolling), but also losing the battle with nature, which, in nineteenth- and early twentieth-century English Canadian narrative, sometimes turns settlers into men, but sometimes does not.[7] Alfred, although he has a "great chest" (3.232), does not have manliness in store for him. Alfred is bad, like many other opportunist Englishmen of nineteenth-century English Canadian writing (Audley Sternfield in Rosanna Leprohon's *Antoinette de Mirecourt* [1864], for example): he does not love Katie (3.92), but only "her father's riches" (3.122). He wants the capital without the work that makes it, according to *Malcolm's Katie*, meaningful and "sacred"; he is not a "good" colonialist, like Max and many others, who are represented as engaging in a struggle with the land for its and their and the community's improvement and gain.

Although Katie resists his advances, Alfred manages to gain a foothold on the paternal hearth by saving her from being crushed by her father's logs—symbol, as has often been pointed out, of Malcolm's patriarchal power. Katie has been leaping barefoot over the logs on the river, and has fallen; Alfred pulls her out of the water by her hair, an act that, in relation to the phallic logs, suggests his perceived right to Katie as a sexual commodity: women's hair, bound, unbound, in disarray, is a familiar trope of female sexual condition, and Alfred has a strong grip on her in terms of what it is that makes her valuable as an object of patriarchal exchange—or so it appears. Although Alfred's action seems to him to offer a certain right to ownership of this symbol of Malcolm's patriarchal power (*Malcolm's Katie*), Katie resists this directing of the story and remains true to Max. Nothing daunted, Alfred, who wants his prize, goes to find Max in the woods. First, he attempts to make him believe that his work of nation-building is pointless. In his frequently cited "nihilist" speech, Alfred argues against the value and efficacy of colonial nation-building: empires do not last, he argues; "Naught is immortal save immortal—Death!" (4.136). But Alfred's anti-imperial commentary does not serve as the ideological basis for the poem as a whole. Although the poem *does* question this category of empire-building (plunder, rapine, self-serving exploitation of resources), the fact that it is Alfred who actually represents this category ironically undermines his own apparently anti-imperial rhetoric. Empire-building, it is implicit in the narrative, if not in Alfred's speech to Max, is not so bad, as long as it is done for the purposes of the development of the individual as a member of a disempowered community, and as long as the engagement with the colonial land can be figured in terms of mutual benefit.

Already, then, emptied of force by Alfred's contradictory position— saying that he opposes what it is he actually does—this part of his argument has little impact on Max. It is his *second* false point—that Katie now loves him instead of Max—which hits the mark. Max, although freshly "virile," is suddenly unmanned when he lets his faith in Katie falter: his arm is "wither'd in its strength" (4.173). In his weakened state, a tree falls on him and pins him to the ground. Alfred leaves Max to die, and returns to Katie, telling her first that Max has married an Indian woman, "comelier than her kind" (5.105), from which union there is already a "child with yellow locks, / And lake-like eyes of mystic Indian brown" (5.106–7). Because Katie refuses to believe him, he changes his story, telling her that Max is "dead. I heard his last, loud cry, / 'O Kate!'

ring thro' the woods; in truth I did" (6.84–85). Katie faints; Alfred snatches her up, Wacousta-like, and indicates that he will throw her into the water, if he cannot have her (6.104–11).[8] Max appears from the woods and rescues Katie; the logs get Alfred (6.127), emblems of the patriarchal hand intervening at the right moment. Nonetheless, Alfred does survive. He repents (he "woke/ To sorrow for his sins" [7.9–10]), and his bad behaviour is redeemed in the naming of Max and Katie's first-born son "Alfred, as the seal of pardon set" (7.8). The story ends with the patriarchal family unit gathered together in Max's fresh space, a settler paradise that is described by Katie as *not* Eden but something better. "I would not change," she declares at the end of the poem,

> *these wild and rocking woods,*
> *Dotted by little homes of unbark'd trees,*
> *Where dwell the fleers from the waves of want,—*
> *For the smooth sward of selfish Eden bowers,*
> *Nor—Max for Adam, if I knew my mind!" (7.36–40)*

As was the case with the earlier framing of the growth of the settler as an effect of work in colonial space, colonization is presented as desirable and natural. In Katie's conclusion, the land itself, the "woods and plains" "[b]eck[on] pale starvelings with their fresh, green hands" (7.33).

The narrative is thus set up as a settler story, embedded in a familiar fantasy of capitalist patriarchal self-fashioning, a love story that is a romance of production, the individual's heroic transformation of the useless and resistant soil to "[o]utspreading circles of increasing gold," an image of proliferating commodity value. According to this story, settler right to these "outspreading circles" inheres in the class necessity produced by industrial capitalism, and in the offering of the land—by itself—as refuge. The colonists in this story begin as an identity-less, dispossessed, disempowered collective—or potentially, like Max, of that category. They make themselves into subjects—landowning, empowered, self-identified to the point where they can score their own initials on their own logs—in the mutually rewarding process of clearing the land to which they have been beckoned.

As I have suggested, *Malcolm's Katie* is a conventional settler narrative, reproducing and reaffirming the range of familiar nineteenth-century colonial ideology. Where, then, is the "re-establishing of the broken cultural link with Indian civilization" and what makes this poem "mythopoeic" rather than simply "nation-building"? In Frye's assessment, it is not in fact in the nation-building narrative *per se* that the poem's mythopoesis and thus its cultural and national value are located: it is Crawford's embedding of her narrative in aboriginal representations of the land and the seasons. "[T[he 'South Wind' passage from *Malcolm's Katie*," he writes,

> is only the most famous example of the most remarkable mythopoeic imagination in Canadian poetry. [Crawford] puts her myth in an Indian form, which reminds us of the resemblance between white and Indian legendary heroes in the New World, between Paul Bunyan and Davy Crockett on the one hand and Glooscap on the other. The white myths are not necessarily imitated from the Indian ones, but they may have sprung from an unconscious feeling that the primitive myth expressed the imaginative impact of the country as more artificial literature could never do. (Bush Garden 149–50)

According to Frye, the key passages of *Malcolm's Katie* as a national poem on these terms are the "Indian" representations that link the sections of the narrative.

Most of the seven parts of the poem begin with some framing of the white settlers on the land in relation to images of aboriginality, and while the narrative itself does not engage with or represent aboriginal people except in two fleeting references (the "half-breed" boy helping Max clear the land, the comely wife Alfred invents for Max), it is built around a system of "Indian" images, its linear narrative of progress embedded in a vocabulary of a cyclical and indigenous system of seasonal change and growth, and the "artifice" of colonization in the "authenticity" of nature. The image that begins Part 4, for instance, is that of the North Wind as a warrior brave, whose actions metaphorically represent the onset of winter: he emerges from his "far wigwam" to "rush[...] with war-cry down the steep ravines," to "wrestl[e] with the giants of the woods"—that is, the trees—to "beat" the water to "death," to "sm[i]te the "tall reeds to the harden'd earth," and so on. The onset of winter is represented *as if* in aboriginal discourse of seasonal change, and *as if* what happens in the transition from fall to winter has a parallel in aboriginal culture. The "Indian" in these images, as they are deployed in the poem, becomes the land, not necessarily in a way that acknowledges a historical non-industrial relationship of first peoples with a homeland, but in a colonial metaphor, a trope that configures the project of displacement and settlement by connecting and distancing—"Indian" *as* land and not *on* it, white settler as doing what "Indians" do—or would do, if they were "there." But, in this poem, at any rate, they are not. What *is* "there" is an idea of spiritual essence and a portable, usable vocabulary of indigeneity.

As I have suggested, in the case of the North Wind passage, as in the South Wind passage cited earlier, Crawford uses Native images as metaphors for seasonal change. These metaphors are fundamental to the work the poem is doing for settler culture, primarily because they appear to establish the healing link Frye sees in the South Wind passage and the poem's mythopoesis. But the value of the metaphors lies in the relationship they establish between the white settler and what is "natural." Everything the settler—notably Max—does on the land has a counterpart in nature, "Indian" nature. His battle with the trees parallels the conflict between the North Wind and the trees in Part 4: the North Wind "wrestl[es] with the giants of the woods" (4.3); Max, a little later, is shown to "sm[i]te the snow-weigh'd tree" (4.53) that he will subsequently "slay." His "smiting" echoes the North Wind's, and this echo is a crucial indication of the extent to which the poem undertakes to show how Max's work—clearing the land with an axe—is *like* the work of winter—natural, and, while temporarily destructive, ultimately part of a cycle. (The axe, for instance, is "moon-like" [2.153].)

It is important to note that Max is not in conflict with the North Wind; rather, both he and the North Wind are in conflict with the trees. This parallelism simultaneously aboriginalizes the settler's process of clearing the land and displaces the conflict between settler and Native that had been the basis of earlier narratives, such as Goldsmith's *Rising*

Village. It becomes possible for Max to *become* aboriginal, because he is doing the same thing the "Indian" wind is doing. It also becomes possible for what is aboriginal in human terms *not* to be connected to this system, but to be separated from it. It is important, in other words, that the images be understood metaphorically, rather than metonymically: there is no contiguity established between First Nations people and the aboriginalized system of representation.[9] The contiguity is established, as Frye makes clear, between the settler and the system, the settler and the place.

Aboriginality becomes, then, in *Malcolm's Katie*, not a cultural identification, but an essentialized commodity or, perhaps, a kind of cultural capital: hard work will get it, just as it also makes you manly and rich. It is a right of belonging. It does not, for Crawford, as it does not for Frye, necessarily have anything to do with First Nations people, who are all but absent from the narrative, and whose future in this nation is not part of the story's projection. The story thus *reaffirms* the "broken link with Indian civilization" *for* "Indian civilization," its metaphors not connecting aboriginal peoples to the poem's present, but displacing them from it. It does not fill colonial space with aboriginal people, but affirms their absence, "repeopling" colonial space with metaphorical representations whose value pertains to the settler culture. Its mythopoesis is that of the white settler nation, and its healing is directed at the settler culture, who, through myth, can be restored to a precolonial wholeness, a "process" Terry Goldie has described in settler writing that "includes an implied transformation of the Other nation, the indigenous, into an extension of the self nation" (49). It is, that is, the white settler whose rupture is being addressed, and the settler culture that is seen to have been separated from *its* national past, a past not of the diasporic community in its imperial homelands, but of the colonial nation-space itself.

What has been "broken," it is thus suggested, is not the historical aboriginal "link" to the land, but the settlers' "cultural link with Indian civilization" or the land's past. "Indian civilization" here represents not the actuality of displaced aboriginal culture, but the settlers' cultural memory of aboriginality and intimate connection with a space in formation—their own unremembered prehistory that is, implicitly, embodied and performed by aboriginal culture. "Indian civilization," for Frye, in this passage at any rate, represents the forgotten past of the modern society, its memories of itself in an earlier social formation. This imagined rupture of the settler from an unremembered past needs to be healed, not to restore aboriginal culture to its place on the land, or to bring aboriginal and settler cultures into a functional alignment, but to establish the logic of the settler culture's emplacement in colonial space. What, then, needs to be recovered, or in the case of "the literary tradition of the country" and particularly its national narrative, "integrated," is the cultural "primitiveness" that the settler diaspora no longer knows. The way to get "there"—to that condition of imagined historical wholeness—is through mythopoesis.

Mythopoesis is a central concept for Frye in his criticism of English Canadian literary production and particularly of English Canadian poetry, where he situates "the identifying of subject and object, [as] the primary imaginative act of literary creation" *Bush Garden* 244). (Fiction, he suggests, written for a mass market, can more easily "seek refuge in conventional social formulas" than can poetry [244].) In Frye's writing on Canadian poetry, a poem's "mythopoeic qualities" serve as the measure of its place and value in the Canadian canon and of its broad use to the nation. By "mythopoeic qualities" in this context, Frye says in the 1956 essay, he is referring to "the qualities in Canadian poetry that illustrate the poet's response to the specific environment that we call approximately Canada, [something, he suggests, that] is easiest to see...when the poetry is mythical in content as well as form" (180)—thus his favouring of *Malcolm's Katie*. What is important to recognize in Frye's categorizing of poetry according to its "mythopoeic qualities" is his positioning of this material—writing that responds to the immediate environment—in relation to an idea of the nation as emergent, in formation, and *new*. What is *mythopoeic* pertains to "myth-making" or the "creation of myths" and to what is "productive of myths" (OED), myths understood here as "traditional stor[ies], typically involving supernatural beings or forces, which embod[y] and provide an explanation, aetiology, or justification for something such as the early history of a society, a religious belief or ritual, or a natural phenomenon" (OED).

Mythopoesis—or the "making or construction of myths" (OED)—happens where, it is implicit in Frye's writing, at any rate, no myths exist for at least one geopolitical constituency—or at least none that provide a usable and unified narrative of emplacement and historical development as a people in a particular location. It is not, after all, necessary to "make" myths where myths already circulate, unless those myths counter the narrative of a new people, or unless the point is to overwrite and to selectively reconfigure existing myths as a crucial part of a new narrative and a new mythology. Mythopoeic poetry in Frye's writing on Canada is thus the new poetry of a new people who have found themselves without a functional set of myths connecting them to a new land. This notion is a familiar one in Canadian writing and literary history, articulated for instance in Douglas LePan's famous characterization of Canada as "a country without a mythology," a concept to which Frye returned repeatedly in his writing.[10]

But there is more to the mythopoeic. For Frye, as for other critics of the mid-twentieth century, mythopoesis is a term that denotes not only a "[d]eliberate and conscious myth-making [but] a writer's return to the primitive habit of non-logical anthropormorphization and ritual-ization" (Seymour-Smith 556). In other words, mythopoesis is the imagined "return" of "humans" to their own earlier social and cultural forma-tions, through the "deliberate and conscious" *use* of "primitive" myths. These myths, it is suggested, do not belong to culturally specific groups, but are universal, authorless, cultureless. They are "human."

The "primitive" lets those who are putatively beyond the "primi-tive"—i.e., in the discourse of progress, white people, people from industrialized nations—imagine that they see something originary and self-referential in it, enabling what Goldie has described as "a return to a whole, before the 'abstraction and splitting' of civilized life" (36). Native cultures do this for settler cultures: by failing to "advance," they preserve the condition of early "man," enabling the "modern" society to see itself as it was in its "primitive" formations. The "return" to "the primitive" is a fundamental act of colonization, and a primary gesture of imperialism: it is an act of self-constructing nostalgia (*you* are what *we* were until *we* became too sophisticated to see), and *we* reclaim that anachronistic space because it is "universal" (*you* too will become like *us*). It is "authentic" because it is not sophisticated enough to dissemble, not so distant from the originary moment that it has become mystified.

Malcolm's Katie is favoured by Frye because it does what, in his view, settler literature in general does. White settler culture "uses" or "integrates" aboriginal myths, as in this poem, not to represent aboriginal experience but eighteenth- and nineteenth-century settler experience in narratives of beginning, origin, of being first peoples, and making the land into an inhabited space. What is overwritten in the myth of origin and the conversion of the land from wilderness to productive, livable space is the actual history of the transfer of the land to the emergent patriarch—for Malcolm Graem as for Max and for the pallid clerk: the absence of aboriginal peoples *on* the land is the salient feature of the poem. Colonization and imperial expansion are here represented as a benevolent outsourcing, the dispersal of landless, hopeless, impoverished, working-class peoples at the centre of the empire to land and the prospect of growth, prosperity and self-hood. This is the conventional propaganda of colonization at the end of the nineteenth century. At one level, and on these terms, *Malcolm's Katie* is an ideological land claim, an argument for the right of the settler to own land because what he does with it benefits himself and "humanity." It is supported with apparent references to First Nations engagement in the affirmation of these rights, both in the aboriginalizing of the settler, and in the representation of the first peoples as "here," in the "form" of the spirit of the land, and a circulating system of metaphors that connect the settler to his own "primitive" self—beginning, belonging. This, then, is the "danger" to which Berggren refers: these metaphors can be, and arguably, for Frye, are transformed into myth through the kind of immediate and total identification Frye describes: A *is* B; settler *is* aboriginal.

What matters for Frye, then, is that *Malcolm's Katie* restores or creates what can be understood as national unity though text, and specifically through a narrative, that brings the settler past into conjunction with pre-colonial history, establishing a continuum not of aboriginal and settler relations, but of settler history in English Canada, and over-writing aboriginal displacement by refiguring aboriginality in and of the land—without actual First Nations people—and, profoundly, in and of the white settler. *Malcolm's Katie*, because it is all about settlement in nineteenth-century Canada, is, as Frye recognizes for much early writing on Canada, about the obliteration of Native culture. Both *Malcolm's Katie* and Frye's assessment of it foreground a major problem in settler cultures— the impulse to find and to represent what is best understood as a "livable" past in text and, ultimately, through the preservation and valuation of certain early English Canadian narratives of origin such as Crawford's, in cultural memory.

NOTES

1. The connections between *Malcolm's Katie* and *The Princess* have been made before. See D.M.R. Bentley, Introduction xx and n. 57 (lv–lvi); see also "'Repetition with a Vengeance': 'Imitations' of Tennyson in the Poetry of Isabella Valancy Crawford," Cecily Devereux (PhD, York U, 1995).

2. As has been noted before, Garvin's *Collected Poems* is not a complete represen-tation of Crawford's poetry. Nancy Johnston has compellingly delineated Garvin's editorial involvement in producing a particular kind of poet; see her MA thesis, "Garvin's Crawford" (York U).

3. Lighthall may be the first to call this lyric the "Song of the Axe," the title under which it often appears in anthologies.

4. See, for instance, Robin Mathews, "'Malcolm's Katie': Love, Wealth, and Nation Building" and Ann Yeoman, "Towards a Native Mythology: The Poetry of Isabella Valency [sic] Crawford." Mathews suggests that Crawford has "employed Indian lore and imagery with richness and evident sympathy" (49); Yeomans argues that, "It is not until the poetry of Isabella Valancy Crawford that there appears to have been any serious attempt at the creation of a purely native mythology, or language of symbols" (40).

5. See Livesay, "The Documentary Poem: A Canadian Genre," *Contexts in Canadian Criticism*. Ed. Eli Mandel. (Chicago and London: U of Chicago P, 1971), 267–81.

6. See Goldsmith, who refers to those who left "far behind their native plain,/ [...] In search of wealth, of freedom, and of ease!" (*The Rising Village* 49–52) and Alexander McLachlan: "Many from their homes had fled,/ For they had denied them bread" (*The Emigrant* 2.5–6).

7. This is a favourite motif of Nellie McClung, for instance; see her early story "Babette," as well as her novella *The Black Creek Stopping House* and the novel *The Second Chance*.

8. In a scene at the end of John Richardson's *Wacousta, or, The Prophecy; A Tale of the Canadas* (1832), Wacousta, a Cornish man who has been living in Canada as a First Nations warrior, holds aloft the body of an abducted Englishwoman, Clara de Haldimar. See *Wacousta* (Ottawa: Carleton UP, 1990) 534–35.

9. See, for instance, Gilbert D. Chaitin, who has made this point in *The Encyclopedia of Contemporary Literary Theory*: "Metonymy...indicates relations among signs based on external *contiguity*; metaphor refers to relations of internal *similarity*" (589).

10. See LePan's 1948 poem, "A Country Without a Mythology," *The Wounded Prince*, 1948.

12

Colonial Phantasms

Aboriginality and "The Family"
in the Photographic Archive

J.V. EMBERLEY

LIKE OTHER BIOGRAPHICAL TEXTS, the photographic family album tells a story, a narrative of familial and familiar relations, of filiations that blend and develop over time, that start off small and grow bigger and bigger with each passing day, year, and generation. The family portrait is sometimes the product of a formal event, a holiday, a staged production in the studio, an accident of time and place, and other moments that are made to stand for one's auto-visual-biography. The images themselves are framed by the formal limits of the eye of the camera and then reframed by how they are situated in relation to other images and texts, or to the places in which they are located or found. Further to the formal frame of the photograph and its material location are the socio-historical contexts which, writes Mieke Bal, "limit the possible meanings" of the image—the meanings that emerge in the act of reading and spill out chaotically and randomly onto the page (x). The family album is a particular visual frame of representation and the subject of Jo Spence and Patricia Holland's edited volume *Family Snaps: The Meaning of Domestic Images*. This important book in photographic studies stages the instability of meaning in the family album by compiling a series of essays, interventions, and explorations that denaturalize the formal and contextual assumptions that create and re-create this seemingly transparent and innocent genre. The book stages various acts of *reframing* in order to rupture the family portrait out of its apparent coherency, its predictability and familiarity. As Holland writes in her introduction, "Blurring the boundaries between personal reminiscence, cultural comment and

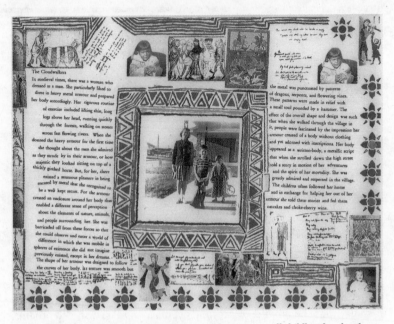

FIGURE 12.1: *"My sister, my brother, my self in a Time I call childhood and a Place I call home." J. Emberley. Original Artwork, 1999.*

social history, paying attention to the overlap between history and fantasy, using popular entertainment, reading official histories between the lines and against the grain, these exploratory styles fit easily with the *bricolage* and loose ends of the family album" (9). The family album is perhaps not as secure a site of meaning as we would like to believe. Throughout the family album, the spectator is confronted by the familiarity of faces and names but their unmistakable differences as well. The chatter, the noise, and the conversations around the images sometimes contradict memories and experiences. Uneasiness and ambivalence rise up as one tries to align subjective memory with the exterior image and stabilize the relationship between meaning and event; thus the spectator is confronted with the difficulty of keeping still the significance of the image even if it remains so on the page. Sometimes the image becomes dislocated, even lost, but leaves its shadow-mark nevertheless. Resistance erupts within the family album's disposition of truth.

IN AN AUTOBIOGRAPHICAL SKETCH titled "Biography of a Dress," the Caribbean writer Jamaica Kincaid tells a story about a yellow smocked dress that was made by her mother for her second birthday. The dress was made because Kincaid's mother wanted to have her photographed in this dress for her birthday. One of the meanings attributed to this dress by Kincaid's mother lay in its value for this photographic representation. For Kincaid this is a painful memory because in rethinking it through her body, she realizes that her mother was trying to reconstruct an image of Jamaica as a white child. This is how Kincaid remembers this experience:

> My skin was not the colour of cream in the process of spoiling, my hair was not the texture of silk and the colour of flax, my eyes did not gleam like blue jewels in a crown, the afternoons in which I sat watching my mother make me this dress were not cool, and verdant lawns and pastures and hills and dales did not stretch out before me; but it was the picture of such a girl at two years old—a girl whose skin was the colour of cream in the process of spoiling, whose hair was the texture of silk and the colour of flax, a girl whose eyes gleamed like blue jewels in a crown, a girl whose afternoons (and morning and nights) were cool, and before whom stretched verdant lawns and pastures and hills and dales—that my mother saw, a picture on an almanac advertising a particularly fine and scented soap (a soap she could not afford to buy then but I can now), and this picture of this girl wearing a yellow dress with smocking on the front bodice perhaps created in my mother the desire to have a daughter who looked like that or perhaps created the desire in my mother to try and make the daughter she already had look like that. (96–97)

The image of a white, blond and blue-eyed girl in an advertising image powerfully shaped the meaning of being female, feminine and civilized for Kincaid's mother. Kincaid's narrative elaborates the meanings of femininity, not only in a gendered inscriptional space connected to the world of appearances, clothing, and hygiene but in a racialized inscriptional space in which the body, the colour of skin, hair, eyes, and even the so-called beauty of natural scenery are also seen to be part of the meanings attributed to a European and colonial definition of civilization and white femininity. It is interesting that Kincaid calls this story a "Biography of a Dress" and not, for example, an "Autobiography of my second birthday." The emphasis on the dress, the advertising image and photographic images, draws attention to the object, and not the subject, of the gaze. It is as if Kincaid is remembering the way in which her child's body was being treated as if it were an object too, something that could be or should be changed like a dress.

Origin stories in the discourse of fashion assume that skin colour and clothing belong equally to the world of appearances; to be fashionable, to be feminine, and hence, female, is to be able to change oneself into a white, middle-class woman. Books on fashion often begin with the example of body painting or tattooing as an original instance of "fashion" or "bodily adornment." Elizabeth Wilson begins her book *Adorned in Dreams: Fashion and Modernity* with a sixteenth-century watercolour of a Native American woman by the British painter John White, titled "A Woman of Florida" (4). This representation of an indigenous woman is underscored by Wilson's caption "The widespread human desire to change the human body: in this case by body painting or tatooing" (5). Skin becomes like clothing, a site of exhibition and display. In the figure of the white, middle-class woman, however, the colour of her skin remains transparent. It is the brown, black, non-white "spoiled" skin colour that is on display like an article of clothing. Kincaid dramatizes this inversion of dress and skin colour by foregrounding the yellow dress, the object of her subjective experience. Kincaid's "Biography of a Dress" is a *petit recit* that disrupts the colonial gaze and its phantasmatic production of aboriginal female difference.

◆

IN THIS ESSAY I am interested in confronting the colonial photographic archive and how it organizes my reception and knowledge of a general cultural formation known as "the Aboriginal family." To this end, I will discuss two very different archival sources: one, an electronic database affiliated with the Royal Museum of British Columbia in Victoria, B.C. (and available online through a B.C. government archival web service) and, the other, a photographic collection of a notable female bourgeois traveller of the Canadian northwest at the beginning of the twentieth century, Mary T.S. Schäffer, held in the Whyte Museum in Banff, Alberta. My "confrontation" with these archives produced a series of strategic moves through various forms of spectatorship involving a mixture of resistance and ambivalence which led eventually to a position of eye/I witness. My study of these archives and, especially, my readings of some selected images is intended to be neither programmatic nor methodologically definitive; rather, they are constitutive of a process of resignification designed to open up the complexity of such images as well as demonstrate the instability of meaning that exists between words and images, including my own, in the specific contexts of colonization and decolonization.

◆

IN THE FOLLOWING PASSAGE from Ralph Ellison's novel, *Invisible Man*, the Invisible Man, the narrator, who is also in this case a witness, describes the residue produced on the sidewalk by the eviction of an elderly black couple from their home in Harlem:

> I turned aside and looked at the clutter of household objects which the two men continued to pile on the walk. And as the crowd pushed me I looked down to see looking out of an oval frame a portrait of the old couple when young, seeing the sad, stiff dignity of the faces there; feeling strange memories awakening that began an echoing in my head like that of a hysterical voice stuttering in a dark street.... And in a basket I saw a straightening comb, switches of false hair, a curling iron, a card with silvery letters against a background of dark red velvet, reading "God Bless Our Home"...I watched the white men put down a basket in which I saw a whiskey bottle filled with rock candy and camphor, a small Ethiopian flag, a faded tintype of Abraham Lincoln, and the smiling image of a Hollywood star torn from a magazine. And on a pillow several badly cracked

pieces of delicate china, a commemorative plate celebrating the St. Louis World's
Fair. (271)

In the several pages Ellison devotes to this eviction narrative, the reader, along with the invisible narrator, becomes implicated in the scene, a witness to the utter despair and angst felt by the dislocation of everyday objects and their expulsion from the "comfort of home." The catalogue of objects reads like an unruly archeological archive, its troubling effect due to the fact that these objects represent a symbolic displacement of the surplus of emotional life that inhabits the dank and dusky odour of everyday living. In the final instance, of course, these dispossessed objects represent the lives of the couple evicted from their home. While white men toss cheap commodities and personal artifacts onto the street, the Invisible Man feels nauseated; his stomach turns as personal and historical memories of racism and slavery collide with each other and the present:

> *In my hand I held three lapsed life insurance policies with perforated seals*
> *stamped "Void": a yellowing newspaper portrait of a huge black man with the*
> *caption: Marcus Garvey Deported...and my finger closed upon something resting*
> *in a frozen footstep: a fragile paper, coming apart with age, written in black ink*
> *grown yellow. I read: FREE PAPERS.* Be it known to all men that my negro,
> Primus Provo, has been freed by me this sixth day of August, 1859.
> Signed: John Samuels. Macon... *I folded it quickly... (272)*

In this dramatic scene of eviction and dislocation, the humble artifacts of personal life become a public museum of everyday living and the reader along with the narrator becomes an intrusive spectator to the disruptive force of personal experience invading the public sphere. The increasing porosity between the private sphere of accumulation and the public domain of commodity exchange and jurisprudence destabilizes the ordinary significance attached to these objects. The mixture of things haphazardly thrown on the sidewalk represents a wild profusion of the real and the imaginary, the concrete and the ephemeral, the present and the memorial, people and things. These everyday things signify world historical events, slavery, exile, deportation, and eviction and they become, in the narrator's words, textualized by "remembered words,... linked verbal echoes, [and] images heard even when not listening at home" (273). This dangerous mixture of history and everyday living, of words, people and things, threatens to break up the epistemic and geo-political borders between the so-called higher spheres—the Nation, Empire, governance, leaders, policies—and everyday life with its mundane matters of domesticity, sentiment, childhood, sexuality, and household labour.

◆

RESISTANCE on the part of the spectator may range from psychoanalytical disavowal to a kind of political action, from the fear of interrogating family photos too closely for what they may reveal about personal experiences, histories and memories, to a politics of resistance toward the use and abuse of personal images in struggles for power and domination. Adeola Solanke, in her postcolonial critique of photographic representations of her parents and grandparents in Nigeria, writes that "[t]he *images* representing the public soul of pre-colonial Africa are themselves in need of independence" (138). Resistance often leads to a process of resignification in which the photographic "text," its visual, coded and written dimensions, offer up opportunities for redefinition and the production of other meanings. Marianne Hirsch points out that "[g]etting beneath the surface or around the frame of conventional family photographs can make space for resistances or revisions of social roles and positions in vastly different cultural contexts—of conventions upheld through photographic practice" (193). Thus the spectator can experience and participate in negotiating several forms of resistance and resignification: resistance to the evidentiary claims and referential power of the photographic family portrait and ambivalence toward the use, or abuse, of the family portrait in official historical accounts. In the historical contexts of colonization and imperialism, slavery and diaspora, the tensions between the spectator and the family photograph are further complicated by the discontinuous, yet mutually related, intersections of the personal and the political.

In the idealized version of the middle-class photographic family album, photos are organized according to a developmental sequence characteristic of an oedipal narrative about the growth of the family from its marital beginnings by civil or religious contract to compulsory child-bearing, from the original heterosexual couple to the multiple lineages of genealogical descent. In the public archive, however, family portraits are ruptured from the seemingly normal and natural domain of everyday domestic life. In the case of the digital archive in the Royal Museum of British Columbia, images of family portraits are scanned into computer databases. The web site offers a number of prescribed subject headings as well as providing the viewer with the opportunity to search their own. I click the subject heading "Family Groups." What comes forth is a disparate set of images, images that lack the familiar teleological framing of the family album. These images occupy a different representational space that, in turn, delimits the image and transforms it into a discrete space of representation.

Questions such as how this new electronic organization of family photographs transforms the meanings ascribed to the family portrait, what new techniques of *framing* emerge in this context and how they reframe or limit the possibilities of readings, and how the spectator reads intertextually for "the family portrait" within the family portrait— where conflicts arise between the perception of the proper family, its possible historical significance, and its lived realities—require an approach that can situate the formal limits of mechanical reproduction in relation to the contextual limits of the family photograph (i.e., its all too easily taken-for-granted socio-historical framework). Such a dialectical materialist approach is necessary in order to understand how images become *representative* in colonial history; what, indeed, it is that they represent or are made to represent. Further to the question of representability are the epistemic principles, systematicities, methodologies, and disciplines that organize the possible reading(s) of the family photographic image.

When examining the digital archive at the Royal Museum of British Columbia in April of 2003, I click on the prescribed subject heading, "Family Groups" and the database produces 620 matches. I am given the option to choose up to nine images at a time in order to construct a "Contact Sheet," a visual grid containing nine boxes. The visual grid simulates a classificatory paradigm of intelligibility. The symmetry of the frames—their formal regularity—creates the illusion that some essential unity transcending time and place links these distinct images. In part, this formal iterability produces, both materially and ideologically, the supposed universality of "the family."

In the traditional family album, the sequential narrative is never "uncomplicated," as Marianne Hirsch puts it. She writes, it "does not forget to reassert its boundaries of difference at certain strategic moments." So too, a content analysis of the 620 matches reveals a principle of inclusivity and the deployment of "diversity" as familiarity (47). The category, Family Groups, succeeds in creating certain anxieties of belonging while it also establishes its apparent "universality" by demonstrating the scope of its existence. As if the computer database were mimicking the representational logic of the famous 1955 Museum of Modern Art exhibition titled *The Family of Man*, curated by Edward Steichen, in which hundreds of family photos were displayed precisely in order to exemplify *diversity* as a family-oriented objective, my content analysis of the digital archive revealed nothing surprising. Of the 620 matches, there were four "Indian Families," one "Chinese Family" and one "Japanese Canadian Family" displayed in the first 150 entries, most of which consisted, as did the following 250 images, of white middle-class families. Several "Indian Families" appeared in the early 400s range and mid-500s range, approximately thirty in all. A couple more of a Chinese Family and Japanese Family appeared along with a few photos of orphanages at the end of the numerical list, including one of Chinese children called the Oriental Home Family. There was one black family, number 612 (out of 620). The purpose of this web site, owned and operated by the provincial government, is ostensibly for a "public" interested in examining family genealogies. This is how the Royal Museum remains accountable to its provincial tax-payers.

If the placements of these images have anything to tell us, it is that the assumed spectatorship for this database is predominantly white middle-class and "English." The rules that govern cataloguing procedures for the Library of Congress, for example, explicitly state that initial entries will be most representative of the subject heading in question, and those entries that are "other" are included at the end. The instances of "visible minority-ness" or visible difference that can be determined through identity-signifiers such as bodies and clothes reinforce Englishness as a code of normativity in relation to which visible difference could only signify a desire to mimic the same. Some "differences," however, are not containable in the same way but become incorporated into the colonial archive by way of "Other" hegemonic practices. For example, some images include within the "family group" governesses and farm labourers, those whose links to the family are based on class, gender, and "race" hierarchies of labour exploitation and oppression.

For all the differences signified within these photos, I would suggest that it is difficult to unpack the power dynamics between and among the categories of "men" and "women," "parents" and "children" within the institution of the nuclear family. Such an examination reveals that patriarchal governance is a constitutive feature of its "familiarity." It is not the case, of course, that patriarchal gender relations are universal and global; rather, they are made to appear universal across cultures, so that the presentation of a "Japanese Family" or an "Aboriginal Family" is framed by its conformity not just to the photographic conventions of "the family portrait" but to its colonial governing practices and relations of patriarchal power.

Those relations and practices of power also include the universalizing of "the family" in terms of its "whiteness" and "Englishness," specifically linked to the bodies of white, bourgeois women as noted by Anne McClintock and others. Thus, it is important to interrogate closely the naturalization of "the family" in the photographic portrait as something that occurs due to the representation of colonial patriarchal alliances across national boundaries *and* racialized gender codes of alterity and difference. These intersecting representations of sameness and difference, identity and alterity, in the family portrait are entirely constitutive of a

FIGURE 12.2:
"Harold Alfred and family."
Alert Bay, B.C. [n.d.].
British Columbia Archives
(E–07422).

FIGURE 12.3:
"Bear Lake Tom and Family."
Photographer: Frank C.
Swannell, 1880–1969.
British Columbia Archives
(I–33192).

FIGURE 12.4:
"Lord and Lady Aberdeen with
their children, and Miss
Witterman, governess," [1895].
British Columbia Archives
(C–08539).

Contact Sheet

FIGURE 12.5:
"Ahousat. Chief Ketla
and Family."
British Columbia Archives
(B–01072).

FIGURE 12.6:
"William Ketlo and Family,
Nechako Road."
By Frank Swannell, [1912].
British Columbia Archives
(G–03877).

FIGURE 12.7:
"Japanese Family, Victoria."
[circa 1900].
British Columbia Archives
(C–07918).

FIGURE 12.8:
"East Indian (Sikh) farm
labourers and members of the
Burrell Family." [190—].
British Columbia Archives
(B–06052).

FIGURE 12.9:
"Robinson with his family." [n.d.].
British Columbia Archives
(B–01278).

colonial web of power and its many governing practices and modes of representational classification.

The archival assemblage of family portraits produces and reproduces, as it does on the actual computer screen, a normative grid of intelligibility, a set of conventions by which it is possible to understand the very meaning of the family through its composition, the positioning of bodies, their physicality and their arrangement vis-à-vis each other. The constitutive elements of the family appear to be engraved in stone, immutable, and transparent. W.H.R. Rivers, in what is acknowledged to be a seminal work in early twentieth-century anthropological studies of kinship and social organization, writes in his *Genealogical Method of Anthropological Inquiry*: "I begin with the method of collecting the pedigrees which furnish the basis of the method. The first point to be attended to is that, owing to the great difference between the systems of relationship of savage and civilized peoples, it is desirable to use as few terms denoting kinship as possible, and complete pedigrees can be obtained when the terms are limited to the following: father, mother, child, husband and wife" (97). The components of the family are delineated as universal precisely because they can be applied to both "savage and civilized peoples" regardless of the "great difference between the systems of relationship." The universality Rivers attributes to such terminology belongs, however, to an established discourse in which the European bourgeois family figures as *the* representative, and hence, universal family structure. This so-called universality is achieved, in part, by the reproducibility of the image and the discursive iterability of a particular set of codes: father, mother, child, husband and wife. These codes, the product of mechanical reproduction and technical classification, must also, however, be mobilized within particular orders of regularity created, historically and politically, by the oppositional logics of colonial power. Thus, each photo in the B.C. digital archive can be enlarged and isolated from the set so as to study or make contact with its own particular order of regularity: the mobilization of dualities such as nature/artifice and civilization/savagery and the use of differential signs and figures, including but not limited to, the Orient, aboriginality and femininity.

FIGURE 12.10: *"Lord Aberdeen." [circa 1896]. British Columbia Archives* (F–04996).

In this image titled simply "Lord Aberdeen," the bodies circle around the figure of the mother, the biological core at the centre of its surrounding filiations; and yet, the circle is disrupted by a vertical line cut by the figures of the mother and father. One child, the youngest, still touches his mother's body. It is by virtue of his status as the youngest that he is still allowed to occupy this proximity to the mother's body—and such proximity to the maternal figure signifies his place as the last born. The eldest son stands beside his father. The eldest daughter places her hand on the middle boy's shoulder, suturing the bond between brother and sister. There exists in this visual field a series of relations that are gendered, generational and geopolitical. The clothing of the male children in traditional Scottish kilts connotes the colonial link to Empire and the role of Scotland's indigenous elite in carrying out the duties and obligations of the Empire in the Canadian colonial context. There is the luxurious texture of velvet in the women's clothes, the silk bow around the dog's neck, the oriental carpet and the painted backdrop of a sculptured staircase ornament and candelabra. The delicate folds of the lace collars and trim on the women's clothing contrast with the large crimped folds of the boys' white vests made from a heavier cotton or linen fabric. The starched upright collar against the sturdy tweed suit marks the evolutionary power of the male upright body, standing tall and erect, his eyes gazing off into the distance as if he were envisioning something important and not staring at the bland wall of a photographic studio. In his essay "The Suit and the Photograph," John Berger examined the visual discontinuity of European peasants dressed in bourgeois male clothing. He coined the phrase *sedentary power* to describe the symbolic value of the suit: "Almost anonymous as a uniform, it was the first ruling costume to idealize purely *sedentary* power. The power of the administrator and conference table" (38). Similarly, in *Three Guineas*, Virginia Woolf noted how other forms of male attire connoted symbolic power, especially military uniforms and the fur-trimmed gowns worn by magistrates or university professors at Oxford and Cambridge (184). Lord Aberdeen's ruling status in the family and in the colony as Governor General of Canada from 1893–1898 is represented in the photograph in the way his clothes are differentiated from those of the women and the children, who appear in feminine artifice or traditional costume. Only Lord Aberdeen appears to be dressed in his normal and perfectly natural everyday clothes.

The conventions of the staged family portrait perform their own kind of sedentary power—the posed and self-imposed immobility of bodies in a spatio-temporal dimension signifying the solid immutability of "the white bourgeois family," its patriarchal rule, racial supremacy and centrality to colonial governance. But such symbolic powers are also achieved in the representational space of this photograph through the oppositional logic of artifice/nature and tradition/primitivism. Thus, it is the power of feminine artifice signified by the luxurious clothing, the painted Oriental backdrop, the bourgeois woman's feminine beauty and the staging of the bodies along with the traditional costume worn by the boys that naturalizes Lord Aberdeen's status and position of colonial authority. In the constantly shifting borders between nature and artifice in imperial and colonial contexts, here femininity re-presents artifice and deception in opposition to nature, the bearer of truth, brute fact, and authenticity. In this colonial context, symbolic powers are naturalized and nature itself becomes the passive repository of all that must be made to stand outside the colonial spheres of influence, authority, and power. Thus, the location of feminine artifice in colonial space functions as a particular technique of power designed to differentiate nature, the wild, the frontier, and the bush from bourgeois civilization. It also works to uphold "bourgeois civilization" as the proper domain for the bourgeois mother. Lady Ishbel Aberdeen was the first President of the newly-founded National Council of Women of Canada (1897). This organization and others have come to represent for feminist historiography a form of "maternal feminism" in Canada's history of (white, middle-class) women. In this case, the National Council of Women of Canada, following in the footsteps of the American organization of the same name, was built upon the philanthropic heritage of bourgeois women and their concern for the "underprivileged" such as women prisoners, women factory workers and women immigrants. Such organizations also served to establish and maintain the hegemony of colonial state power in Canada, a point I will return to with the photographic work of Mary Schäffer.

The micropolitical dimension of body-powers consisting of posture, clothing, surrounding furniture, objects and landscape as well as the spatial coordination of bodies in relation to one another represent some of the clues that make it possible to trace the contested meanings of familial ideology in colonial space. The staging of the family scene in photographic images produces these body-powers, and the image of "the family," in turn, becomes a representational effect of such micropolitical powers.

FIGURE 12.11: *"Group picture with Indian Family." (n.d.). British Columbia Archives (D–03411).*

Within the representational space of the bourgeois colonial family portrait emerges, then, this figure of the civilized family. But it is not only the iterability of these images that brings the figure of the bourgeois colonial family into view in this archival collection; it is also the fact that among all these images of the wealthy colonial elite of Victoria, British Columbia, some images appear to stand out in stark contrast to the majority, such as the image with the caption "Group picture with Indian Family."

The picture is blurry, taken outdoors on a river bank. It contains an array of women and children, its sameness or regularity contained by the woman/child configuration, its difference by the lack of any male figures, not to mention the anomalous figure of the white child to the far right. This image is differentiated from the preceding ones in its representation of the "Other": the poor and the uncivilized, non-bourgeois family. Now, the preceding images take on a new mode of signification as representative of cultural, racial, and heterosexual supremacy; thus, the bourgeois family is enlisted in the pictographic colonial archive as an agent of imperial and patriarchal conquest.

The double axis of sameness and difference, apparent in the materiality of mechanical reproduction and its ideological codification, does the hegemonic cultural work necessary in British colonization in late nineteenth- and early twentieth-century Canada to (1) regulate gender, class and "race" relations within the colonial bourgeois family; (2) establish the white colonial bourgeois family as a global phenomenon; and (3) create practices of looking and knowing that teach "imperial spectatorship," the sanctioned knowledge with which to identify who is civilized and who is not.

◆ **Madonnas Roughing it in the Bush**

MARY T. SCHÄFFER is the author of the early twentieth-century travelogue *Old Indian Trails: Incidents of Camp and Trail Life, Covering Two Years' Exploration through the Rocky Mountains of Canada* (1911). Her account contains photographs she took of two expeditions carried out with her companion Mary W. Adams in 1907 and 1908. The following photograph appears in her book and has been popularized on a contemporary postcard. It is available at major tourist sites in Alberta, including Banff, where the Whyte Museum, which holds Schäffer's archive, is located.

Schäffer's representation of the so-called Aboriginal Family in this image, which I will return to, and others reveal her particular fascination with an important feature of the so-called Aboriginal Family, the mother/child configuration. Indeed, Schäffer took many photos of what she herself called "the Indian Madonna." The iterability of this figure crossed the religious as well as the anthropological frontiers of the bourgeois family, framing First Nations kinship relations within the figural limits of the Christian bourgeois family. Before discussing her work in greater detail I want first to situate it within a colonial geography of the maternal body.

The all too familiar "feminization" of colonial space made it possible for bourgeois women to find a very specific location in the colonial project.

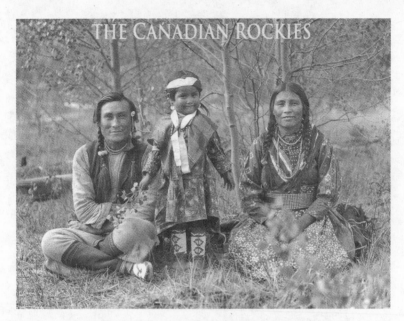

FIGURE 12.12: *"Samson Beaver and his Family"* (postcard description).

FIGURE 12.13: *"Sampson Beaver, His Squaw, and Little Frances Louise"* [1907]. *Photographer: Mary Schäffer, (Caption in* Old Indian Trails*). Whyte Museum of the Canadian Rockies (V.527 PS–5).*

Colonial space could easily become a site of intense identification with the oppressed. Thus the philanthropic ideal of the bourgeois woman, who always appears grammatically in the singular due to her individuality and uniqueness as compared to the working masses, tribes, or Natives, permitted "her" the opportunity to regulate her identity in a paternalistic guise. The British woman's journal, *The Imperial Colonialist* (1902–1927), was created so as to provide female working-class domestic and factory labour to the colonies, especially New Zealand, Palestine, and Canada in the early twentieth century. The philanthropic work of English bourgeois women contributed to colonial governance and was a particularly gendered strategy that allowed such women to transfer their skills in the management of the home and children to colonial space.

The history of British bourgeois women travellers in the nineteenth and twentieth centuries suggests that colonial travel for leisure or business offered these women the opportunity to realize an unprecedented freedom from the confines of domesticity and access to new and interesting knowledge and experience, and to new and different relations of power. Colonization opened up travel to bourgeois women; it also, however, brought new problems in gender and sexual relations: new alliances between colonial and indigenous male elites, new objects of sexual desire for colonial men and women, and new relations of power within the bourgeois home between husbands, wives, youth and servants—in short, it gave rise to a new sexual politics in the colonial bourgeois household. Given the tenuous situation of bourgeois women's hold on their physical-material existence in the nineteenth and early twentieth century, for which they depended on husbands, fathers, or brothers, the newly emerging sexual and gender alliances between men were, needless to say, threatening, and thus a catalyst to further secure bourgeois hegemony through the support and involvement of bourgeois women in the colonial civilizing mission—most notably through the figure of Christian motherhood.

In the geohistorical trilectics of space, body, and power, the figure of the Aboriginal Mother came to occupy a significant place for the colonial bourgeois woman. Her body stands at the juncture of a multitude of colonial practices and representations that sought to regulate and dominate the lives of First Nations people territorially, administratively, governmentally, and economically. First Nations mothers suffered the real effects of colonial policies. Their sexuality and bodies were subject to regulations for the purposes of establishing and reaffirming racial purity and patriarchal governance in the family—its rule of women and children. The Canadian *Indian Act* (1876), including those amendments made up until 1951, as well as other nineteenth-century Canadian legislation, enabled colonial powers to exercise control over the "species-body," a body that was the bio-political agent of demographic control, racial regulation, the supply of physical labour power, the role of the bourgeois citizen and the constitution of the nation (Emberley 68–71). As I argue in "The Bourgeois Family, Aboriginal Women, and Colonial Governance in Canada," the historical fact of the gender distribution of responsibilities, jobs, and duties in gatherer/hunter social formations was appropriated and reframed as a division between the domestic and civil spheres, the private and the public, the personal and the political (64–65). This repositioning of First Nations gender relations reconfigured the power dynamics between First Nations men and women, the jobs assigned to their bodies and the spaces they occupied.

As the Aboriginal "poster family," Schäffer's image of Sam[p]son Beaver and his family conforms to the Universal familial configuration. Sam[p]son Beaver is the head of his family and in both Schäffer's caption as well as the one attached to the postcard, it is only his name and that of the child that appear. The mother, Leah Sampson, is referred to, possessively and derogatorily, as "His Squaw." The caption situates Sam[p]son Beaver as the patriarchal father, as if this representation were the most natural of social formations: either it is the family itself that conforms to nature or it is the (ab)original family in nature, the always already origins of the European bourgeois family, that is depicted. Interestingly their clothes combine European styles: dresses for women and the little girl, pants and vest for the man. They wear jewelry and beaded moccasins.

Nature is circumscribed in Schäffer's narrative by aesthetic interests: "I often wonder when passing an Indian camp-ground, be it ancient

FIGURE 12.14: *"Frances Louise Beaver." Photographer: Mary Schäffer [1907], Whyte Museum of the Canadian Rockies (V.527 PS–4).*

or modern, if ever for an instant the natural beauty of a location consciously appeals to them. I have seen not one but many of their camps and seldom or never have they failed to be artistic in their setting, and this one was no exception" (174). Nature is so natural to the Indian that its artistic possibilities remain unconscious or go unnoticed. So, too, is the Aboriginal family a product of nature's raw materiality and not its artificially understood "natural beauty." Little Frances Louise is not the only child of Sam[p]son and Leah Beaver. She is one of many but, importantly, she is Schäffer's favourite:

She had been my little favorite when last we were among the Indians, accepting my advances with a sweet baby womanliness quite unlike the other children, for which I had rewarded her by presenting her with a doll I had constructed from an old table-napkin stuffed with newspaper, and whose features were made visible to the naked eye by the judicious use of a lead-pencil. Necessity constructed that doll, love blinded the little mother's eyes to any imperfections, and the gift gave me a spot of my own in the memory of the forest baby; to call her name was to introduce myself. (175)

Little Frances Louise is nature's mythical "forest baby," a wild child tamed into domesticity and motherhood with the introduction of a make-shift doll and bourgeois feminine sentimentality in her appropriate emotional response to Schäffer's "advances." But nature's rough earthliness, its ultimate savagery, is hard to shake off: "In an instant her little face appeared at the tepee-flap, just as solemn, just as sweet, and just as dirty as ever." Hygiene is central to the civilizing process of bourgeois domesticity: "She turned and spoke to some one inside, and in a moment out came three smiling, dirty squaws, who looked as though wash-days were not over numerous...." Indian women represent the "essence" of nature—raw, dirty and animalistic: "Such grimy paws, but such shapely ones they were, so small and dainty, with tapering fingers, that their white sister, bending from her saddle, envied them" (176).

The "essence" of a feminized nature is a class-conscious stereotype of the labouring woman, a figure that Schäffer's text takes for granted. Her figuration of the aboriginal woman in the guise of the bourgeois woman of vanity, however, is constructed with ironic pleasure and deployed to counter the male stereotype of "the sullen, stupid Indian":

When I hear those "who know," speak of the sullen, stupid Indian, I wish they could have been on hand the afternoon the white squaws visited the red ones with their cameras. There were no men to disturb the peace, the women quickly caught our ideas, entered the spirit of the game, and with musical laughter and little giggles, allowed themselves to be hauled about and pushed and posed in a fashion to turn an artist green with envy. The children forgot their rabbit-like shyness, and copied their elders in posing for us...Yahe-Weha [Stoney name for

FIGURE 12.15: "*The Indian Madonna.*" Photographer: Mary Schäffer [1907], *Whyte Museum of the Canadian Rockies (V.527 PS–51).*

Schäffer that means Mountain Woman] might photograph to her heart's content.
She had promised pictures the year before, and had kept the promise, and she
might have as many photographs now as she wanted.

   Personal experience has shown me that the Indian has the vanity of his white
brethren, but he is not going to pose for nothing. I have no belief in their supersti-
tious dread of photography, at least so far as the Plains Indians are concerned; it
is simply a matter of fair trade. (176, 178)

"The Indian Madonna" appears at this point in Schäffer's text (181).

Schäffer further challenges the image of the sullen and stupid Indian in her remark: "it is so hard to associate jokes with Indians whom most of us have only met in books." Not only does she challenge this myth, she also makes fun of her own missionary zeal in attempting to reorient male/female relations among the Indians:

Beginning, I said: "Silas, do you really let your squaw saddle and pack your horses?" "Sure." (How well he had learned English!) "And let her fix the tepee-poles and put up the tepee?" "Yes." "And get the wood, and cook, and tan the skins?" "Yes, sure!" (He was growing impatient at so much quizzing.) The time seemed ripe for some missionary work which was perceptibly needed along more lines than one, and every one else had stopped to listen. "Now, Silas," I said impressively, "you should be like the white men, you should do the work for your squaw. We do not put up our tepees or pack our horses or cut the wood, our men do that." Taking his pipe from his mouth and inspecting me from head to foot leisurely, he said, "You lazy!"

The missionary effort went to the floor with a bang and every one burst out laughing (at the missionary, of course) and she only recovered herself enough to say, "And what do you do while your squaw works?" "This," and he folded his arms, closed his eyes, and puffed away at his pipe. But the rest of them need not have laughed, his look of contempt had swept round and included every man who had so demeaned himself as to be placed in such straits by a woman. (180, 181)

Schäffer's photograph of Sampson, Leah and Francis Louise Beaver appears in the interstices of this text. Thus, her commentary on acceptable gender-labour relations is also constructed in the image of the proper Aboriginal bourgeois family.[1]

Constitutive to the proper Aboriginal bourgeois family is the ideal relationship between Mother and Child. For Schäffer that ideal representation is the Christian image of Madonna and Child that not only appears in her travelogue *Old Indian Trails*, as noted above, but is a remarkable feature of her larger photographic archive, as well as that of other notable photographers of the West such as Byron Harmon, which contains many more such images, such as the following:

FIGURE 12.16: *"Indian Woman with Papoose." Photographer: Mary Schäffer [1908], Whyte Museum of the Canadian Rockies (V.527 PS–705).*

FIGURE 12.17: *"Indian Woman and Child." Photographer: Byron Harmon [1913], Whyte Museum of the Canadian Rockies (V.439 PS–352).*

Schäffer's photographs of the Aboriginal family in Nature self-consciously follow the Rousseauian ideal of the noble savage as head of the First Family. This Aboriginal family, the First Family, the Primitive Family, constitutes a particular enlightenment deployment against which an emerging bourgeois and patriarchal family was to define itself. It was also the mythical foundation of European civilization's unidentified past time and yet, ironically, still in existence in the colonies of contemporary nineteenth-century Europe. Against this mythical construction stands the historical formation of the nineteenth-century bourgeois family. This latter family belongs to the realm of historical truth whereas the (ab)original family belongs to the realm of myth. If the primitive family is born of nature and the natural world of flesh, and procreation, then the bourgeois family is the product of artifice, commodity formation, and femininity; both, however, are apparently based in patriarchal lines of descent.

In the following commentary on the Schäffer postcard, Lucy Lippard attempts to counteract this "naturalization" of the Aboriginal Family:

> For all its socially enforced static quality, and for all I've read into it, Mary Schäffer's photograph of Sampson, Leah, and Frances Louise Beaver is "merely" the image of an ephemeral moment. I am first and foremost touched by its peace and freshness. I can feel the ground and grass, warm and damp beneath the people sitting "here" in an Indian summer after disaster had struck but before almost all was lost. Despite years of critical analysis, seeing is still believing to some extent—as those who control the dominant culture (and those who ban it from Native contexts) know all too well. In works like this one, some of the barriers are down, or invisible, and we have the illusion of seeing for ourselves, the way we never would see for ourselves, which is what communication is about. (43)

Writing from the position of the non-aboriginal spectator, Lippard's experience of *disalienation* with the image unfortunately re-creates another moment of alienation in the form of an historical blindness to the reality of colonization as a radically violent event that obliterated one history by creating another. In another critical work on early North American photography, Laura Wexler examines, among other things, a series of photographs by the late nineteenth-century American portrait photographer, Gertude Käsebier. Käsebier is well known for her photographs of what Wexler calls "white motherhood," especially images of her own daughter and granddaughter. Wexler argues that in Käsebier's images of the mother/child configuration, the white bourgeois female photographer takes on the role of *"universal* mother" bringing forth the birth of domestic civilization through her photographic reproduction (188). Wexler's discussion of Käsebier's images also focuses on her portraits of male Sioux leadership. These two distinct aspects of Käsebier's work serve to demonstrate her failure, according to Wexler, to acknowledge the Aboriginal mother and to use her photographic work as a way of building alliances between "white" and Native American women: "Everything that Käsebier felt about herself and her own daughter and 'white' motherhood in general depended upon the fact that for Käsebier, and for the culture she represented, *Indian* motherhood could have no similar heritage" (206). Wexler concludes that Käsebier's work and that of similar middle-class female photographers of this time signal that "the defeat of cross-racial empathy is the ultimate failure of these women's work. They might have risen to the occasion as women in political alliance with the 'Other,' and who knows what visions they might then have shared, but they decided as photographers instead to interpret the occasion according to the wishes of the strongmen of empire" (208). In addressing how the colonial bourgeois family and its reproduction of mother/child relations were deeply enmeshed in the codes of aboriginality, Wexler nevertheless assumes, mistakenly, that the mother/child configuration of bourgeois civilization is a transcultural model. I have no quarrel with Wexler's call for political alliances between First Nations and non-First Nations women; however Schäffer's representations of Indian motherhood which contain their own particular fantasy of cross-cultural female homosociality, should at least alert cultural critics to how the institution and representation of "the family" can function as a mode of colonial power and governance in order to regulate and alter First Nations political and social relations through the body of the Aboriginal Mother. Representations of colonial and aboriginal male elites created the illusion of "cross-cultural" male homosociality, which is accurately described as a form of complicity among men produced by the conjoined patriarchal oppression of women. One way in which First Nations women were divested of their social and political power was through criticism directed toward the labouring aboriginal female body, "the squaw," a body that needed to be radically subjected to a gendered and racialized process of *embourgeoisement* in order to render it feminine, infantile, vulnerable, and powerless.

An additional problem with Wexler's analysis is that she privileges the visual object and its diachronic four-century-long production of the image of the Virgin Mary and Child in several media, a history already discussed, as Wexler notes, by Julia Kristeva in her essay "Motherhood According to Giovanni Bellini" (Kristeva 180). Rather than locating this image in the differing historical and geopolitical contexts of European nation and colony, Wexler deploys the image itself as a visual universal equivalent, put up for exchange in a chromatic-based notion of "whiteness" in a Western symbolic economy. It is more important, I argue, to track the links between the meaning production and institutional locations of such images, whether they be religious, educational, racial or *familial*. This means recognizing "the family" during this period of time as an institutional apparatus within which and through which colonial power amassed both knowledge and representation in the North American context. What is at stake, therefore, is not achieving "cross-cultural empathy" based on the apparent universal equivalency of the figure of mother and child, nor attempting to demonstrate such empathy through a disalienated experience with the image as in Lippard's case, but a careful exploration of the use of such images as part of the techniques of power designed to institutionalize subjects of representation for the purposes of subjugating them as economically as possible. With the rise of film and photography, the deployment of a representational, rather than a physical or epistemic, mode of violence became increasingly possible and cost-effective.

In the nineteenth century the rhetoric of civilization dominated the production and reception of European images of a so-called primitive existence in the colonies. Civilization and Empire were key formations built upon a representational violence that served to regulate the bourgeois family and produce a representation of it as normal, natural, and different from its other, the Aboriginal Family. Borrowing from the work of Edward Soja in the field of spatial studies, I have constructed the following three related spatializations of representational violence:

1. *Spatial practices of violence: Locations*
2. *Spatial representations of violence: Discursive, Textual, Epistemic, Corporeal and Visual*
3. *Spaces of representational violence: The Family Portrait*

On one level we can say that violence often takes place in particular locations, circumscribed by real material boundaries, such as the house, the school yard, the urban street or the war zone. The spatial practice of violence in these particular locations is rendered visible or invisible depending on covert or overt strategies of legitimation. The spectacle of war and street violence is a visible practice designed to be a "show of force." The violence of sexism and racism in the school yard or the home is generally covert and surreptitious, its dangers to the perpetrator as well as the victim often result in focusing the public's attention on the agent of violence. The known dangers of military, domestic, and pedagogical violence are perceived through the concrete and empirical spaces they occupy. Thus, the physicality of violence is itself localized and located within an experiential and perceived dimension, a known place.

Articulated to the spatial practices of violence are spatial representations of violence conceived in discourses of resistance and oppression that work to delimit the very meaning of violence as well as the places in which violence occurs. This is the realm of an epistemology of violence and the study of knowledges, signs, codes, representations, and practices about violence. For example, the study of *violence against women* is encoded by multiple terms used to decipher the specificity of gendered violence: domestic violence, sexual abuse, wife battering, youth violence, the violent school girl, rural violence, pornography, family violence, intimate violence in families, abused children, and lesbian battering. Media studies in representations of violence in comic books, television programs and films, for example, interrogate the border between real and imagined violence from the assumption that however complex such a relationship is, fundamentally, these forms of violence are interrelated in deterministic and causal ways.

The organization of knowledge can itself be a mode of representational violence such as the way the Royal British Columbia Museum arranges certain images under the heading "Family Groups" and others under the heading "Indian Family Portrait." There is no category for Colonial Family Portrait or Non-Indian Family Portrait. How subjects are categorized and organized and what forms of regularity emerge from the types of classifications used constitute spatial modes of epistemic violence.

The third configuration combines real spatial practices of violence and the spatial representations of violence. There is no known catalogue of the spaces of representational violence from which to draw a series of examples. What characterizes these spaces are discontinuities and marks of difference that rupture the image from its context and intervene in the space between reception and meaning so that resignification becomes not only possible but necessary.

In her essay "Writing as Witness," Beth Brant defines witnessing with respect to First Nations epistemology and spectatorship as an act of historical remembering that leads to renewal. Remembering involves a sense of vision that "is not just a perception of what is possible, it is a window to the knowledge of what *has* happened and what *is* happening.... Witness to what has been and what is to be. Knowing what has transpired and dreaming of what will come. Listening to the stories brought to us by other beings. Renewing ourselves in the midst of chaos" (72, 74). Part of that renewal takes place in response to the violence done to kinship relations in colonial governance.

Domicide, write J. Douglas Porteous and Sandra E. Smith, may result in:

the destruction of a place of attachment and refuge; loss of security and ownership; restrictions on freedom; partial loss of identity and a radical de-centring from place, family, and community. There may be a loss of historical connection;

FIGURE 12.18 : "*Tea in the garden at Pentrelew, 1201 Fort Street; the four children.*"
[1897], British Columbia Archives (F–06877).

FIGURE 12.19 : "*Stoney Children, Banff Indian Days, 1929.*" Photographer
Unknown, Whyte Museum of the Canadian Rockies (V.701/LC–369 1929). Tom Wilson,
in the Stetson, was an originator of the Banff Festival.

a weakening of roots; and partial erasure of the sources of memory, dreams, nostalgia, and ideals. If home has multiple, complex meanings that are interwoven, then so does domicide.... What is lost is not only the physical place, but the emotional essence of home—aspects of personal self-identity. (63)

The violence of colonial domicide was achieved through legislation such as the *Indian Advancement Act* (1884), which called for the forced removal of children from their homes and the *Indian Act and Amendments,* which implemented residential schooling during the 1920s (see Treaties and Historical Research Centre in *Indian Acts and Amendments*). This legislative violence also sought to regulate First Nation's women's marital and sexual relationships and exclude status First Nation's women from political governance. Other aspects of colonial domicide include the foster parenting of First Nation's children by non-Aboriginal families. The current focus by First Nations, Métis and Inuit women's political organizations on decolonizing domestic and sexual violence within First Nations families indicates yet another important area of concern in the struggle against domicide. Knowing this history is part of the process of "witnessing."

What would it mean to become an eye/I witness to the colonial photographic archive, to move from the spectator examining how the colonial archive classifies "the family" in the service of normalizing and naturalizing the bourgeois family through its *aboriginal* genealogy to becoming a witness to First Nations' histories of residential schooling, for example, its effect on First Nations children, its dismantling of kinship relations, and how children were exposed to cultural genocide and sexual abuse?

To "unlearn" as a non-Native and to be a witness to colonial history, as I am attempting to do here, is to learn to speak to that history of representational violence by making visible the *mechanisms* (i.e., the technologies and classificatory techniques of representation) that produce it. This is a two-fold process that, in the case of this essay, has involved, firstly, addressing cultural materials which might have had little or no significance for the historical record and may even be perceived to have no aesthetic or truth value, such as photographs of the Aboriginal Family and, secondly, declassifying these photographs from their bourgeois genealogical framing in the Royal Museum's database and from the Christian, familial, mother/child imperative in Schäffer's archive by re-situating them in the discontinuous, however mutually related, context of the legislative violence of the Canadian state. This dual process of resignification responds to the cultural genocide outlined by Gerald McMaster in his study of a residential school photograph, "Colonial Alchemy: Reading the Boarding School Experience," in which he writes that

> the participation of the churches in European imperialism has contributed immensely to alcoholism, family breakdown, and numerous other problems that torment Native communities across Canada and the United States. Today the boarding school is all but nonexistent in its original form—that is, administered by religious denominations for the sole purpose of conversion and assimilation. Many of Canada's original boarding school buildings exist, some still operating as schools, albeit usually Indian-controlled.... With so many repulsive stories about boarding school experience emerging from native communities all across Canada and the United States, it would be more appropriate to turn them into historical sites, comparable to Alcatraz and Auschwitz, as reminders of the legalized atrocities of [wo/man] against [wo/man]. (85)

Resignification discloses colonial representational and epistemic violence as neither inevitable nor immutable but as constitutive realities of historical contestation. Through the act of eye/I witnessing the history of colonial representational violence is transformed from a sign of subjugation into a renewed site of resistance.

1.   Further to this point, it is worth considering Duncan Campbell Scott's poem, "The Onondaga Madonna" published in *Labor and the Angel*.

> *The Onondaga Madonna*
>
> *She stands full-throated and with careless pose,*
> *This woman of a weird and waning race,*
> *The tragic savage lurking in her face,*
> *Where all her pagan passion burns and glows;*
> *Her blood is mingled with her ancient foes,*
> *And thrills with war and wildness in her veins;*
> *Her rebel lips are dabbled with the stains*
> *Of feuds and forays and her father's woes.*
>
> *And closer in the shawl about her breast,*
> *The latest promise of her nation's doom,*
> *Paler than she her baby clings and lies,*
> *The primal warrior gleaming from his eyes;*
> *He sulks, and burdened with his infant gloom,*
> *He draws he heavy brows and will not rest.*

The title of Scott's volume of poetry gestures toward that nineteenth-century staple of feminine domesticity, the Angel in the House, juxtaposed to the figure of labouring aboriginal women in "The Onondaga Madonna." Such a gesture situates Scott's image of the Onondaga Madonna within the colonial gendering of First Nations woman's bodies. Such bodies were made to represent a "savage" nature, sexually and physically, as distinct from the proper body of civilization, the European female bourgeois body.

Bibliography

"About Historica." *Historica.* 12 August 2003.
   <http://www.histori.ca/foundation/about.jsp>

Abrams, M.H. *A Glossary of Literary Terms.* 6th ed. New York: Harcourt, 1993.

Achard, Eugène, ed. *Jacques et Marie: Souvenirs d'un peuple dispersé.* 1865. Montréal:
   Librairie Générale, 1944.

Acker, Alison. "A Noble Canadian: the Workhorse of New France Gallops into the
   Present." *The Beaver* 77.1 (Feb/Mar 1997): 4–6.

Adam, G. Mercer. "An Outline History of Canadian Literature." *An Abridged History of
   Canada.* By William H. Withrow. Toronto: Briggs, 1887. 179–232.

Adams, John Coldwell. *Sir Charles God Damn: The Life of Sir Charles G.D. Roberts.* Toronto,
   U of Toronto P, 1986.

Adams, Oscar Fay. *A Dictionary of American Authors.* 5th ed. Boston: Houghton, 1904.

Agamben, Giorgio. *The Coming Community.* Trans. Michael Hardt. Minneapolis: U of
   Minnesota P, 1993.

Alcoff, Linda Martín. "The Problem of Speaking for Others." *Who Can Speak?
   Authority and Critical Identity.* Ed. Judith Roof and Robyn Wiegman. Urbana: U
   of Illinois P, 1995. 97–119.

Alpers, Paul. *What is Pastoral?* Chicago: U of Chicago P, 1996.

Altman, Janet Gurkin. *Epistolarity: Approaches to a Form.* Columbus: Ohio State UP,
   1982.

Anderson, Benedict. *Imagined Communities: Reflections on the Origin and Spread of
   Nationalism.* 2nd ed. London: Verso, 1991.

Aravamudan, Srinivas. *Tropicopolitans: Colonialism and Agency, 1688–1804.* Durham:
   Duke UP, 1999.

Ashcroft, Bill, Gareth Griffiths and Helen Tiffin. *Key Concepts in Post-Colonial Studies.*
   London: Routledge, 1998.

Aubert de Gaspé, Philippe. *Les Anciens Canadiens.* 1863. Ed. Maurice Lemire.
   Montréal: Fides, 1994.

——. *Canadians of Old: A Romance*. Trans. Jane Brierley. Montreal: Véhicule, 1996.

——. *Le Chercheur de trésors, ou, L'influence d'un livre*. 1837. Québec: Brousseau, 1878.

Bacchi, Carol Lee. *Liberation Deferred? The Ideas of the English-Canadian Suffragists, 1877–1918*. Toronto: U of Toronto P, 1983.

Backhouse, Constance. "First Nations' Laws and European Perspectives." *Petticoats and Prejudice: Women and Law in Nineteenth-Century Canada*. Toronto: The Osgoode Society/Women's P, 1991. 9–28.

——. *Petticoats and Prejudice: Women and Law in Nineteenth-century Canada*. Toronto: Published for the Osgoode Society by Women's Press, 1991.

Bakhtin, Mikhail. *The Dialogic Imagination: Four Essays*. Trans. Caryl Emerson and Michael Holquist. Ed. Michael Holquist. Austin: U of Texas P, 1981.

Bal, Mieke. "Reading art?" *Generations and Geographies in the Visual Arts*. Ed. Griselda Pollock. New York: Routledge, 1996. 25–41.

Balfour, Ian. "The Sublime of the Nation." Paper delivered at McMaster University, March 1996.

Balibar, Etienne. "The Nation Form: History and Ideology." *Race, Nation, Class: Ambiguous Identities*. Trans. Chris Turner. London: Verso, 1991. 37–68.

Bannerji, Himani. "On the Dark Side of the Nation: Politics of Multiculturalism and the State of Canada." *The Dark Side of the Nation: Essays on Multiculturalism, Nationalism, and Gender*. Toronto: Canadian Scholar's Press, 2000. 87–124.

Banting, Pamela. "The Archive as a Literary Genre: Some Theoretical Speculations." *Archivaria* 23 (1986–87): 119–22.

Barbeau, Marius. "The Canadian Northwest: Theme for Modern Painters." *The American Magazine of Art* XXIV.5 (1932): 331–38.

——. "Frederick Alexie, A Primitive." *Canadian Review of Music and Art* 3.11–12 (1945): 19–22.

Barrell, John. *The Dark Side of the Landscape: The Rural Poor in English Painting, 1730–1840*. Cambridge: Cambridge UP, 1980.

Barton, David and Nigel Hall, eds. *Letter Writing as a Social Practice*. Amsterdam: John Benjamins, 2000.

Bate, Jonathan. "Poetry and Biodiversity." *Writing the Environment: Ecocriticism and Literature*. Eds. Richard Kerridge and Neil Sammells. London: Zed Books, 1998. 53–70.

Bazerman, Charles. "Letters and the Social Grounding of Differentiated Genres." In Barton and Hall, eds. 15–29.

Bear, Perry. "Alexcee, Freddie." *St. James Guide to Native North American Artists*. Ed. Roger Matuz. Detroit: St. James Press, 1998. 10–11.

Beattie, Judith Hudson and Helen M. Buss, eds. *Undelivered Letters to Hudson's Bay Company Men on the Northwest Coast of America, 1830–57*. Vancouver: U of British Columbia P, 2003.

Beeton, Isabella. *The Book of Household Management...* 1861. London: Jonathan Cape, 1968.

Benson, Adolph B., ed. *Peter Kalm's Travels in North America: The English Version of 1770.* 2 vols. New York: Dover, 1937.

Bentley, D.M.R. "Breaking the 'Cake of Custom': The Atlantic Crossing as Rubicon for Female Emigrants to Canada?" *Re(Dis)covering our Foremothers: Nineteenth-Century Canadian Women Writers.* Ed. Lorraine McMullen. Ottawa: U of Ottawa P, 1990. 91–122.

———. *The Confederation Group of Canadian Poets, 1880–1897.* Toronto: U of Toronto P, 2004.

———. ed. *Early Long Poems on Canada.* London, ON: Canadian Poetry Press, 1994.

———. "Thomas Moore's Construction of Upper Canada in the 'Ballad Stanzas'." *Canadian Poetry* 35 (Fall/Winter 1994). <http://www.arts.uwo.ca/english/canadianpoetry/cpjrn/vol35/bentley.htm>

Berger, Carl. "Introduction." *Imperialism & Nationalism 1884–1914: A Conflict in Canadian Thought.* Ed. Carl Berger. Toronto: Copp Clark, 1969. 1–5.

———. "The True North Strong and Free." *Interpreting Canada's Past.* Vol 2. Ed. J.M. Bumstead. Toronto: Oxford UP, 1986. 157–73.

Berger, John. "The Suit and the Photograph." *About Looking.* New York: Pantheon Books, 1980. 27–36.

Berggren, Douglas. "The Use and Abuse of Metaphor, I and II." *Review of Metaphysics* 16 (1962–1963): 237–258, 450–472.

Berlant, Lauren. "Intimacy: A Special Issue." *Intimacy.* Spec. Issue of *Critical Inquiry.* 24 (1998): 281–88.

———, and Michael Warner. "Sex in Public." *Intimacy.* Spec. Issue of *Critical Inquiry* 24 (1998): 547–66.

Bernstein, Susan David. *Confessional Subjects: Revelation of Gender and Power in Victorian Literature and Culture.* Chapel Hill: U of North Carolina P, 1991.

Besner, Neil. "What Resides in the Question, 'Is Canada Postcolonial?'" Moss, ed. 40–48.

Bhabha, Homi K. "DissemiNation: Time, Narrative, and the Margins of the Modern Nation." *Narration and Nation.* Ed. Homi K. Bhabha. London and New York: Routledge, 1990. 291–322.

"Big Bear's Captives... Their Story Told By Themselves..." *Globe* (25 June 1885): 2.

Billington, Ray Allen. *The Protestant Crusade 1800–1860: A Study of the Origins of American Nativism.* Gloucester, Mass.: Peter Smith, 1963.

———. Introduction. *Awful Disclosures of the Hotel Dieu Nunnery.* 1836. Rpt., Hamden, CT: Archon Books, 1962.

Birney, Earl. "Can.Lit." *An Anthology of Canadian Literature in English*. Revised and abridged edition. Eds. Russell Brown, Donna Bennet and Nathalie Cooke. Toronto, Oxford UP, 1990. 296.

Bliss, Michael. "Privatizing the Mind: The Sundering of Canadian History, the Sundering of Canada." *Journal of Canadian Studies* 26.4 (Winter 1991–92): 5–17.

———. "Teaching Canadian National History." Address at "Giving the Future a Past" Conference, Association for Canadian Studies, Winnipeg, 20 October 2001. *Canadian Social Studies* 36. 2 (Winter 2002). <http://www.quasar.ualberta.ca/css/Css_36_2/ ARteaching_canadian_national_history.htm>.

Blodgett, E.D. *Five-Part Invention: A History of Literary History in Canada*. Toronto: U of Toronto P, 2003.

Boire, Gary. "Canadian (Tw)ink: Surviving the White Outs." *Essays on Canadian Writing* 35 (Winter 1987): 1–16.

Boucherville, Georges Boucher de. *Une de perdue, deux de trouvées*. 1864–65. Montréal: Sénécal, 1874.

Bourassa, Napoléon. *Jacques et Marie: Souvenir d'un peuple dispersé*. 1865. Montréal: Fides, 1976.

———. "Quelques réflexions critiques à propos de l'art association of Montreal." *Revue canadienne* 1.3 (1864): 170–82.

Bourdieu, Pierre. *The Field of Cultural Production: Essays on Art and Literature*. Ed. and introd. Randal Johnson. New York: Columbia UP, 1993.

Bourne, George. *Lorette, the History of Louise, Daughter of a Canadian Nun: Exhibiting the Interior of Female Convents*. New York: Wm. A. Mercein, 1833.

———. *Picture of Quebec and Its Vicinity*. Rev. ed. Quebec: P. & W. Ruthven, 1831.

Bragg, Rick, and Jessica Lynch. *I Am a Soldier, Too: The Jessica Lynch Story*. New York: Alfred A. Knopf, 2003.

Brah, Avtar. *Cartographies of Diaspora: Contesting Identities*. London: Routledge, 1996.

Brant, Beth. *Writing as Witness: Essays and Talk*. Toronto: Women's Press, 1994.

Brierley, Jane, trans. *Canadians of Old*. By Philippe Aubert de Gaspé, père. Montréal: Véhicule, 1996.

Brodhead, Richard H. *Cultures of Letters: Scenes of Reading and Writing in Nineteenth-Century America*. Chicago: U of Chicago P, 1993.

Brown, Jennifer S.H. "Changing Views of Fur Trade Marriage and Domesticity: James Hargrave, His Colleagues, and 'The Sex'." *The Western Canadian Journal of Anthropology* 6.3 (1976): 92–105.

———. *Strangers in Blood: Fur Trade Company Families in Indian Country*. Vancouver: U of British Columbia P, 1980.

Brownfoot, Janice N. "Memsahibs in Colonial Malaya: A Study of European Wives in a British Colony and Protectorate 1900–1940." In Callan and Ardener, eds. 86–210.

Brydon, Diana. "Canada and Postcolonialism: Questions, Inventories, and Futures." Moss, ed. 49–77.

———. "Introduction: Reading Postcoloniality, Reading Canada." *Essays on Canadian Writing* 56 (Fall 1995): 1–19.

———. "It's Time for a New Set of Questions." *Essays on Canadian Writing* 71 (Fall 2000): 14–25.

Burley, Edith I. *Servants of the Honourable Company: Work, Discipline, and Conflict in the Hudson's Bay Company, 1770–1870.* Toronto: Oxford UP, 1997.

Burpee, Lawrence J. "Recent Canadian Fiction." *Forum* [New York] Aug. 1899: 752–60.

Buss, Helen M. *Mapping Our Selves: Canadian Women's Autobiography in English.* Montreal and Kingston: McGill-Queen's UP, 1993.

Butler, Judith. *Gender Trouble: Feminism and the Subversion of Identity.* New York: Routledge, 1990.

Calhoun, Craig. *Nationalism.* Concepts in Social Thought. Series Ed. Frank Parkin. Minneapolis: U of Minnesota P, 1997.

Callan, Hilary. "Introduction." In Callan and Ardener, eds. 1–26.

———, and Shirley Ardener, eds. *The Incorporated Wife.* London: Croom Helm, 1984.

Callwood, June. *The Naughty Nineties, 1890–1900.* Canada's Illustrated Heritage Series. Toronto: Natural Science of Canada, 1977.

Campbell, William Wilfred. "Ode to Canada" (1896). *William Wilfred Campbell: Selected Poetry and Essays.* Waterloo: Wilfred Laurier UP, 1987. 57–59.

Canada. Census and Statistics Office. *Fifth Census of Canada, 1911.* 6 vols. Ottawa: Parmelee (vols. 1–3) and Taché (vols. 4–6), 1912–15.

———. *Census of Canada, 1890–91.* 4 vols. Ottawa: Dawson, 1893–97.

———. Dept. of Agriculture. *Census of Canada, 1880–81.* 4 vols. Ottawa: Maclean, Roger, 1882–85.

———. *Occupations of the People.* Bulletin 11 of the 1901 Census. Ottawa: Parmelee, 1910.

"Canadian Art History to be Made in Ottawa." Review of the *Exhibition of Canadian West Coast Art—Native and Modern. Ottawa Citizen.* 2 December 1927.

Canadian Institute for Historical Microreproductions. "CIHM Progress Report." *Facsimile* 13 (May 1995): 16.

Carter, Adam. "Namelessness, Irony, and National Character in Contemporary Canadian Criticism and the Critical Tradition." *Studies in Canadian Literature* 28.1 (2003): 5–25.

Carter, Sarah. "'Captured Women': A Re-examination of the Stories of Theresa Delaney and Theresa Gowanlock." *Two Months in the Camp of Big Bear: The Life and Adventures of Theresa Gowanlock and Theresa Delaney.* Ed. Sarah Carter. Regina: Canadian Plains Research Center, 1999. vii–xxxviii.

——. *Capturing Women: The Manipulation of Cultural Imagery in Canada's West.* Montreal and Kingston, ON: McGill-Queen's UP, 1997.

Case, William. *Jubilee Sermon Delivered at the Request of and Before the Wesleyan Canada Conference.* Toronto: G.R. Sanderson, 1855.

Charlesworth, Hector. *Candid Chronicles: Leaves from the Note Book of a Canadian Journalist.* Toronto: Macmillan, 1925.

Cheah, Pheng. "Spectral Nationality: The Living-On [sur-vie] of the Postcolonial Nation in Neocolonial Globalization." *Becomings: Explorations in Time, Memory, and Futures.* Ed. Elizabeth Grosz. Ithaca: Cornell UP, 1999. 176–200.

"Chilcotin Wild Horse Sanctuary." *Friends of the Nemaiah Valley.* 17 March 2005. <http://www/fonv.ca/articles/wildhorses.html>.

Chinquy, Charles. *The Priest, The Woman and the Confessional.* Montreal: F. E.Grafton, 1875.

Christie, Nancy. "'In These Times of Democratic Rage and Delusion': Popular Religion and the Challenge to the Established Order 1760–1815." *The Canadian Protestant Experience 1760–1990.* Ed. George Rawlyk. Burlington, ON: Welch, 1990. 9–47.

Clark, David. L. "Monstrosity, Illegibility, Denegation: De Man, bp Nichol, and the Resistance of Postmodernism." *Monster Theory: Reading Culture.* Ed. Jeffrey Cohen. Minneapolis: U of Minnesota P, 1996. 40–71.

Clarke, George Elliott. Introduction. *Eyeing the North Star: Directions in African-Canadian Literature.* Toronto: McClelland and Stewart, 1997. xi–xxviii.

——. *Odysseys Home: Mapping African-Canadian Literature.* Toronto: U of Toronto P, 2002.

Cohen, Robin. *Global Diasporas: An Introduction.* London: University College London, 1997.

Cohen, William A. *Sex Scandal: The Private Parts of Victorian Fiction.* Durham: Duke UP, 1996.

Cole, Douglas. *Captured Heritage: The Scramble for Northwest Coast Artifacts.* Seattle and London: U of Washington P, 1985.

Coleman, Daniel. "Immigration, Nation, and the Canadian Allegory of Manly Maturation." *Essays on Canadian Writing* 61 (1997): 84–103.

Commoner, Barry. "Unravelling the DNA Myth." *Harper's Magazine* February 2002: 39–47.

——, and Andreas Athanasiou. "A Work in Progress." *Critical Genetics Project.* 20 February 2003. <http://www.criticalgenetics.org>.

Conan, Laure (i.e. Félicité Angers). À l'oeuvre et à l'épreuve. Québec: Darveau, 1891.

Connor, Steven. Dumbstruck: A Cultural History of Ventriloquism. Oxford: Oxford UP, 2000.

Cook, Ramsay. The Regenerators: Social Criticism in Late Victorian English Canada. Toronto: U of Toronto P, 1985.

Cook, Sharon Anne. Through Sunshine and Shadow: The Woman's Christian Temperance Union, Evangelicalism, and Reform in Ontario, 1874–1930. Montreal and Kingston: McGill-Queen's UP, 1995.

Crawford, Isabella Valancy. Malcolm's Katie. 1884. Ed. D.M.R. Bentley. London, ON: Canadian Poetry Press, 1987.

———. The Halton Boys. Ed. Frank M. Tierney. Ottawa: Borealis, 1979.

———. Hugh and Ion. Ed. Glenn Clever. Ottawa, Borealis, 1977.

———. Collected Poems of Isabella Valancy Crawford. Ed. John Garvin. 1905. Intro. James Reaney. Toronto: U of Toronto P, 1972.

———. Old Spookses' Pass, Malcolm's Katie and Other Poems. 1884.

Crean, Susan. The Laughing One: A Journal to Emily Carr. Toronto: HarperFlamingoCanada, 2001.

Culler, Jonathan. "Apostrophe." The Pursuit of Signs. Ithaca: Cornel UP, 1981. 135–44.

"Cultural apartheid in the digital Age." McGill Reporter February 11, 1999.

Dandurand, Albert. Le Roman canadien-français. Montréal: Lévesque, 1937.

Darling, David and Douglas Cole. "Totem Pole Restoration on the Skeena, 1925–30: An Early Exercise in Heritage Conservation." BC Studies 47 (1980): 29–48.

Davidoff, Leonore. Worlds Between: Historical Perspectives on Gender & Class. New York: Routledge, 1995.

Davies, Barrie. "'We Hold A Vaster Empire Than Has Been': Canadian Literature and the Canadian Empire." Studies in Canadian Literature 14.1 (1989): 18–29.

Davies, Gwendolyn. "The Literary 'New Woman' and Social Activism in Maritime Literature, 1880–1920." Separate Spheres: Women's Worlds in the 19th-Century Maritimes. Ed. Janet Guildford and Suzanne Morton. Fredericton, NB: Acadiensis, 1994. 233–50.

Davis, Charles B. "Reading the Ventriloquist's Lips: The Performance Genre behind the Metaphor." The Drama Review 42.4 (1998): 133–56.

Dean, Misao. A Different Point of View: Sara Jeannette Duncan. Montreal and Kingston: McGill-Queen's UP, 1991.

———. Practising Femininity: Domestic Realism and the Performance of Gender in Early Canadian Fiction. Toronto: U of Toronto P, 1998.

———. "'You may imagine my feelings': Reading Sara Jeannette Duncan's Challenge to Narrative." Re(Dis)covering Our Foremothers: Nineteenth-Century Canadian Women Writers. Ed. Lorraine McMullen. Ottawa: U of Ottawa P, 1990. 187–97.

Decker, William Merrill. *Epistolary Practices: Letter Writing in America Before Telecommunications*. Chapel Hill: U of North Carolina P, 1998.

Deguise, Charles. *Le Cap au diable*. 1863. Montréal: Sénécal, 1980.

De Man, Paul. *The Rhetoric of Romanticism,* New York, Columbia UP, 1984.

———. *The Resistance to Theory*. Minneapolis: U of Minnesota P, 1986.

Dempsey, Hugh A. *Big Bear: The End of Freedom*. Vancouver: Douglas and McIntyre, 1984.

Denison, Flora MacDonald. *Mary Melville: The Psychic*. Toronto: Austin, 1900.

Derounian-Stodola, Kathryn Zabelle and James Levernier. *The Indian Captivity Narrative, 1550–1900*. New York: Twayne, 1993.

Derrida, Jacques. "The Onto-Theology of National-Humanism (Prolegomena to a Hypothesis)." *Oxford Literary Review* 14:1–2 (1992): 3–24.

"Despite a few 'nays,' MPs voted Tuesday to recognize the Canadian Horse as the Country's Official National Horse." *Canadian Press Newswire*, April 23, 2002.

Devereux, Cecily. "'The Maiden Tribute' and the Rise of the White Slave in the Nineteenth Century: The Making of an Imperial Construct." *Victorian Review* 26:2 (Summer 2001): 1–23.

Dickason, Olive Patricia. *Canada's First Nations: A History of Founding Peoples from the Earliest Times*. 3rd ed. Toronto: Oxford UP, 2002.

———. *The Myth of the Savage and the Beginnings of French Colonialism in the Americas*. Edmonton: U of Alberta P, 1984.

Diderot, Denis. *The Nun*. Trans. Leonard Tancock. London: Penguin, 1974.

Ditz, Toby L. "Formative Ventures: Eighteenth-Century Commercial Letters and the Articulation of Experience." In Earle, ed. 59–78.

Dohner, Janet Vorwald. *The Encyclopedia of Historic and Endangered Livestock and Poultry Breeds*. New Haven: Yale UP, 2001.

"The Dominion Institute: Memory, Democracy, Identity." *The Dominion Institute*. 11 August 2003. <http://www.dominion.ca/English/home.html>.

Douglas, Ann. *The Feminization of American Culture*. New York: Alfred A Knopf, 1977.

Douglas, Mary. *Purity and Danger: An Analysis of Concepts of Pollution and Taboo*. London: Routledge and Kegan Paul, 1966.

Drummond, Henry William. "The Habitant's Jubilee Ode." *The Habitant and Other French Canadian Poems*. New York: Puntnam, 1903.

Dubinsky, Karen. *Improper Advances: Rape and Heterosexual Conflict in Ontario, 1880–1929*. Chicago: U of Chicago P, 1993.

Duffy, Dennis. *Sounding the Iceberg: An Essay on Canadian Historical Novels*. Toronto: ECW, 1986.

Duncan, Carol. "Art Museums and the Ritual of Citizenship." *Exhibiting Cultures: The Poetics and Politics of Museum Display*. Washington: Smithsonian Institution P, 1991. 88–103.

————. *Civilizing Rituals: Inside Public Art Museums*. London: Routledge, 1995.

Duncan, Sara Jeannette. "American Influence on Canadian Thought." *Week* [Toronto] 7 July 1887: 518.

————. *The Imperialist*. 1904. Toronto: McClelland and Stewart, 1990.

Durrans, Brian. "The future of ethnographic exhibitions." *Zeitschrift für Ethnologie* 118 (1993): 125–39.

Düttmann, Alexander García. *Between Cultures: Tensions in the Struggle for Recognition*. New York: Verso, 2000.

Earle, Rebecca, ed. *Epistolary Selves: Letters and Letter-writers, 1600–1945*. Aldershot: Ashgate, 1999.

Early, L. R. "Myth and Prejudice in Kirby, Richardson, and Parker." *Canadian Literature* 81 (Summer 1979): 24–36.

Egan, Susanna and Gabriele Helms. "Autobiography and Changing Identities: Introduction." *Biography* 24.1 (Winter 2001): ix–xx.

Eliot, T. S. "Tradition and the Individual Talent." 1917. *Selected Essays, 1917–1932*. London: Faber, 1932. 13–22.

Ellison, Ralph. *Invisible Man*. New York: Modern Library, 1952.

Emberley, Julia. "The Bourgeois Family, Aboriginal Women, and Colonial Governance in Canada: A Study in Feminist Historical and Cultural Materialism." *Signs: Journal of Women in Culture and Society* 27.1 (Autumn, 2001): 59–85.

Empson, William. *Some Versions of Pastoral*. New York: New Directions, 1974.

Etherington, Norman. "Natal's Black Rape Scare of the 1870s." *Journal of Southern African Studies* 15:1 (1988): 36–53.

Ettin, Andrew V. *Literature and the Pastoral*. New Haven: Yale UP, 1984.

Eviatar, Daphne. "The Press and Private Lynch." *The Nation* (19 June 2003). <http://www.thenation.com/doc.mhtml%3Fi=20030707&s=eviatar>.

Fairchild, G. M. "The Canadian Club." *Canadian Leaves; History, Art, Science, Literature, Commerce: A Series of New Papers Read Before the Canadian Club of New York*. Ed. Fairchild. New York: Thompson, 1887. 283–89.

"Feds and Québec Trot Toward Horse Legislation [to Make Canadian Horse an Official Symbol]." *Canadian Press Newswire*, December 2, 1999.

Findlay, Len. "Is Canada a Postcolonial Country?" Moss, ed. 297–99.

Fletcher, Angus. *Allegory: The Theory of a Symbolic Mode*. Ithaca: Cornell UP, 1964.

Forbes, Ernest R. *Challenging the Regional Stereotype: Essays on the 20th Century Maritimes*. Fredericton: Acadiensis P, 1989.

Foucault, Michel. *The Birth of the Clinic: An Archaeology of Medical Perception*. Trans. A.M. Sheridan Smith. New York: Vintage Books, 1975.

————. *The History of Sexuality*. Vol. 1. Trans. Robert Hurley. New York: Vintage, 1978.

————. "Space, Power, Knowledge." *The Foucault Reader*. Ed. Paul Rabinow. New York: Pantheon, 1984. 239–56.

————. "What is an Author?" *Language, Counter-Memory, Practice: Selected Essays and Interviews*. Ed. Donald F. Bouchard. Trans. Donald F. Bouchard and Sherry Simon. Ithaca: Cornell UP, 1977. 113–38.

Fowler, Marian. *Redney: A Life of Sara Jeannette Duncan*. Toronto: Anansi, 1983.

Franchot, Jenny. *Roads to Rome: The Antebellum Protestant Encounter with Catholicism*. Berkeley: U of California P, 1994.

Francis, Daniel. *The Imaginary Indian: The Image of the Indian in Canadian Culture*. Vancouver: Arsenal Pulp Press, 1992.

————. *National Dreams: Myth, Memory and Canadian History*. Vancouver: Arsenal Pulp Press, 1997.

Francis, R. Douglas. *Images of the West: Changing Perceptions of the Prairies, 1690–1960*. Saskatoon: Western Producer Prairie Books, 1989.

Freeman, Barbara M. *Kit's Kingdom: The Journalism of Kathleen Blake Coleman*. Ottawa: Carleton UP, 1989.

Frye, Northrop. *Anatomy of Criticism: Four Essays*. Princeton: Princeton UP, 1957.

————. *The Bush Garden: Essays on the Canadian Imagination*. 1971. Intro. Linda Hutcheon. Toronto: Anansi, 1995.

————. "Conclusion to a *Literary History of Canada*." 1965. *The Bush Garden: Essays on the Canadian Imagination*. Toronto: Anansi, 1971, 1995. 213–51.

————. *The Modern Century*. New ed. Toronto: Oxford UP, 1990.

————. *Northrop Frye on Canada*. Ed. Jean O'Grady and David Staines. *Collected Works of Northrop Frye*. vol. 12. Toronto: U of Toronto P, 2003.

————. *The Secular Scripture: A Study of the Structure of Romance*. Cambridge: Harvard UP, 1976.

Galbraith, John S. *The Hudson's Bay Company as an Imperial Factor, 1821–1869*. Berkeley: U of California P, 1957.

————. *The Little Emperor: Governor Simpson of the Hudson's Bay Company*. Toronto: Macmillan, 1976.

————. Introduction. *London Correspondence Inward from Sir George Simpson 1841–42*. Ed. Glyndwr Williams. London: Hudson's Bay Record Society, 1973. xi–lviii.

Gallop, Jane. *The Daughter's Seduction: Feminism and Psychoanalysis*. Ithaca: Cornell UP, 1982.

Gartrell, Beverley. "Colonial Wives: Villains or Victims?" In Callan and Ardener, eds. 165–85.

Garvin, John. "A Word from the Editor." *Collected Poems of Isabella Valancy Crawford*. 1–4.

Gauvreau, Michael. "Protestantism Transformed: Personal Piety and the Evangelical Social Vision, 1815–1867." *The Canadian Protestant Experience 1760–1990.* Rawlyk, ed. 48–97.

Genand, J.A., trans. *Antoinette de Mirecourt, ou, mariage secret et chagrins cachés*. By Mrs. Leprohon. Montréal: Beauchemin, 1865.

———, trans. *Armand Durand, ou, La promesse accomplie.* By Mrs. Leprohon. Montréal: Beauchemin, 1869.

Gerson, Carole. "Nobler Savages: Representations of Native Women in the Writings of Susanna Moodie and Catharine Parr Traill." *Journal of Canadian Studies* 32.2 (Summer 1997): 5–21.

———. *A Purer Taste: The Writing and Reading of Fiction in English in Nineteenth-Century Canada.* Toronto: U of Toronto P, 1989.

———. "Wild Colonial Girls: New Women of the Empire, 1883–1901." *Journal of Commonwealth and Postcolonial Studies* 3.1 (Fall 1995): 61–77.

———, and Gwendolyn Davies. *Canadian Poetry: From the Beginnings Through the First World War.* Toronto: McClelland and Stewart, 1994.

Glazerbrook, G.P. de T. "Introduction." *The Hargrave Correspondence 1821–1843.* Toronto: Champlain Society, 1938. xv–xxvi.

Godard, Barbara. "Notes from the Cultural Field: Canadian Literature from Identity to Hybridity." *Essays on Canadian Writing* 72 (Winter 2000): 209–47.

Goldie, Terry. *Fear and Temptation: The Image of the Indigene in Canadian, Australian, and New Zealand Literatures.* Kingston and Montreal: McGill-Queen's UP, 1989.

Goldsmith, Elizabeth C., ed. *Writing the Female Voice: Essays on Epistolary Literature.* Boston: Northeastern UP, 1989.

Goldsmith, Oliver. *The Rising Village.* 1825. Bentley 195–216.

Goodwin, Rae E. "The Early Journalism of Sara Jeannette Duncan with a chapter of Biography." Master's thesis. U of Toronto, 1964.

Gowanlock, Theresa and Theresa Delaney. *Two Months in the Camp of Big Bear: The Life and Adventures of Theresa Gowanlock and Theresa Delaney.* Parkdale, ON: Times Office, 1885.

———. *Two Months in the Camp of Big Bear: The Life and Adventures of Theresa Gowanlock and Theresa Delaney.* 1885. Ed. Sarah Carter. Regina: Canadian Plains Research Center, 1999.

———. *Two Months in the Camp of Big Bear: The Life and Adventures of Theresa Gowanlock and Theresa Delaney.* 1885. Garland Library of Narratives of North American Indian Captivities. Vol. 95. New York: Garland Publishers, 1976.

———. *Two Months in the Camp of Big Bear: The Life and Adventures of Theresa Gowanlock and Theresa Delaney.* 1885. CIHM Microfiche 30360–62. Ottawa: CIHM, 1982.

———. *Two Months in the Camp of Big Bear: The Life and Adventures of Theresa Gowanlock and Theresa Delaney.* 1885. *Early Canadiana Online.* Canadian Institute for Historical

Microreproductions. 15 June 2004.
<http://www.canadiana.org/ECO/mtq?id=543f11e60b&doc=30361>.

———. *Two Months in the Camp of Big Bear: The Life and Adventures of Theresa Gowanlock and Theresa Delaney*. 1885. Peel Bibliography on Microfiche. Microfiche #819. Ottawa: National Library of Canada, 1977.

———. *Two Months in the Camp of Big Bear: The Life and Adventures of Theresa Gowanlock and Theresa Delaney*. 1885. Project Gutenberg. Etext # 6604. 15 June 2004. <http://www.gutenberg.net/etext/6604>.

Granatstein, J.L. *Who Killed Canadian History?* Toronto: HarperCollins, 1998.

Grant, John Webster. *A Profusion of Spires: Religion in Nineteenth-Century Ontario*. Toronto: U of Toronto P, 1988.

Grauer, Lalage. "Two Months in the Camp of Big Bear: The Life and Adventures of Theresa Gowanlock and Theresa Delaney." *Women's Writing and the Literary Institution*. Edmonton: Research Institute for Comparative Literature, 1992. 127–38.

Griffin, Susan M. "Awful Disclosures: Women's Evidence in the Escaped Nun's Tale." *PMLA* (1996): 93–107.

———. *Anti-Catholicism and Nineteenth-Century Fiction*. New York: Cambridge UP, 2004.

Grutman, Rainier. *Des Langues qui résonnent: L'hétérolinguisme au XIXe siècle québécois*. Montréal: Fides, 1997.

Ha, Tu Thanh, Rhéal Séguin, Louise Gagnon and Canadian Press. "Outside Police Called to Patrol Kanesatake." *Globe and Mail* 6 May 2004: A9.

Haddix, Margaret Peterson. *Running Out of Time*. New York: Aladdin, 1997.

Haliburton, R.G. *The Men of the North and Their Place in History: A Lecture*. Montreal: John Lovell: 1869.

Haliburton, Thomas Chandler. *An Historical and Statistical Account of Nova Scotia*. Halifax: Howe, 1829.

Haraway, Donna J. "A Cyborg Manifesto." *Simians, Cyborgs and Women: The Reinvention of Nature*. New York, Routledge, 1991. 149–81.

———. *modest_witness@second_millenium.com: Feminism & Technoscience*. New York: Routledge, 1997.

Harper, J. Russell. *Krieghoff*. Toronto: Key Porter, 1999.

Harris, Richard Colebrook. *The Seigneural System in Early Canada*. Quebéc: Les Presses de L'Université Laval, 1966.

Hart, Julia Catherine Beckwith Hart. *St. Ursula's Convent or The Nun of Canada, Containing Scenes from Real Life*. Ed. Douglas G. Lochhhead. Ottawa: Carleton UP, 1991.

Harte, Walter Blackburn. "A Literary Mecca." *Literary World* [London]. Excerpted in "Literary and Personal Gossip." *Week* [Toronto] 12 Feb. 1892: 172.

Hasselberg, Ylva. "Letters, Social Networks and the Embedded Economy in Sweden: Some Remarks on the Swedish Bourgeoisie, 1800–1850." In Earle, ed. 95–107.

Hatch, Ronald. "Narrative Development in the Canadian Historical Novel." *Canadian Literature* 110 (Fall 1986): 79–96.

Hawker, Ronald William. "Frederick Alexie: Euro-Canadian Discussions of a First Nations' Artist." *The Canadian Journal of Native Studies* XI.2 (1991): 229–52.

Hayne, David M. "Literary Translation in Nineteenth-Century Canada." *Translation in Canadian Literature*. Ed. Camille R. la Bossière. Ottawa: U of Ottawa P, 1983. 35–46.

Heble, Ajay. "Sounds of Change: Dissonance, History, and Cultural Listening." *Essays on Canadian Writing* 71 (Fall 2000): 26–36.

Henderson, Jennifer. *Settler Feminism and Race Making in Canada*. Toronto: U of Toronto P, 2003.

Hensley, Sophie Almon. "Canadian Writers in New York." *Dominion Illustrated Monthly* May 1893: 195–204.

Higgins, Lynn A. and Brenda R. Silver. "Introduction: Rereading Rape." *Rape and Representation*. New York: Columbia UP, 1991. 1–11.

Higginson, Kate. "'The fact of blood that was the cause of so much pain': The Raced Female Body and the Discourse of *Peuplement* in Rudy Wiebe's *The Temptations of Big Bear* and *The Scorched-Wood People*." *Essays on Canadian Writing* 72 (Spring 2001): 172–90.

Hirsch, Marianne. *Family Frames: Photography, Narrative and Postmemior*. Cambridge: Harvard UP, 1997.

Ho, S.K., E.E. Lister, and S.P. Touchburn. "An Overview of Canadian Farm Animal Genetic Resources Conservation and its Associated Biotechnological Approaches." *Canadian Foundation for the Conservation of Farm Animal Genetic Resources*. 1997. 1 April 2005.
<http://www.cfagrf.com/overview.html>.

Hobsbawm, E. J. *Nations and Nationalism since 1780: Programme, Myth, Reality*. 2nd ed. Cambridge: Cambridge UP, 1992.

Hofstader, Richard. *"The Paranoid Style in American Politics" and Other Essays*. 1965. Chicago: U of Chicago P, 1979.

Horn, Pamela. *The Rise and Fall of the Victorian Servant*. Stroud: Allan Sutton, 1986.

Howe, Joseph. "Sable Island." 1831. *Representative Poetry Online*. 23 April 2003.
<http://eir.library.utoronto.ca/rpo/display/poem1067.html>.

Hoy, Helen. *How Should I Read These? Native Women Writers in Canada*. Toronto: U of Toronto P, 2001.

Hughes, Stuart. *The Frog Lake "Massacre": Personal Perspectives on Ethnic Conflict*. Toronto: McClelland and Stewart, 1976.

Hutcheon, Linda. *Splitting Images: Contemporary Canadian Ironies*. Toronto: Oxford UP, 1991.

Ignatieff, Michael. *Blood and Belonging: Journeys into the New Nationalism*. Toronto: Penguin, 1993.

The Imperial Colonialist. London, 1902–1927.

Inness, Sherrie A. "'An Act of Severe Duty': Emigration and Class Ideology in Susanna Moodie's *Roughing It in the Bush*." *Imperial Objects: Essays on Victorian Women's Emigration and the Unauthorized Imperial Experience*. Ed. Rita Kranidis. New York: Twayne, 1998. 190–210.

International Council of Women of Canada Online. 1 April 2005. <http:/www.ncwc.ca/aboutUs_history.html>.

Jameson, Anna Brownell. *Winter Studies and Summer Rambles in Canada*. 1838. Toronto: McClelland and Stewart, 1990.

Jameson, Fredric. *Marxism and Form*. Princeton: Princeton UP, 1971.

———. *The Political Unconscious: Narrative as a Socially Symbolic Act*. Ithaca: Cornell UP, 1981.

Jackel, Susan. Introduction. *A Flannel Shirt and Liberty: British Emigrant Gentlewomen in the Canadian West, 1880–1914*. Vancouver: U British Columbia P, 1982.

Jennings, Clotilda. *The White Rose in Acadia; and Autumn in Nova Scotia*. Halifax: James Bowes, 1855.

"Jessica Lynch 'raped' in Iraq: U.S. soldier Jessica Lynch was Raped During Captivity in Iraq, According to a New Biography quoted by U.S. Media." *BBC NEWS*. 6 November 2003. <http://news.bbc.co.uk/go/pr/fr/-/1/hi/world/americas/3248021.stm>.

Johnson, Barbara. "Anthropomorphism in Lyric and Law." *Material Events: Paul de Man and the Afterlife of Theory*. Ed Tom Cohen et al. Minneapolis: U of Minnesota P, 2001.

Johnston, Anna and Alan Lawson. "Settler Colonies." *A Companion to Postcolonial Studies*. Ed. Henry Schwarz and Sangeeta Ray. Oxford: Blackwell Publishers, 2000. 360–76.

Jones, Robert Leslie. "The Old French-Canadian Horse: Its History in Canada and the United States." *The Canadian Historical Review* 28.2 (1947): 125–55.

Jump, John. *The Ode*. London: Methuen, 1974.

Kauffman, Linda. *Discourses of Desire: Gender, Genre, and Epistolary Fictions*. Ithaca: Cornell UP, 1986.

Kealey, Linda. Introduction. *"A Not Unreasonable Claim": Women and Reform in Canada, 1880s–1920s*. Ed. Linda Kealey. Toronto: The Women's Press, 1979. 1–15.

Kelly, Fanny. *Narrative of My Captivity Among the Sioux Indians*. Toronto: Maclear and Co. 1872.

Kertzer, Jonathan. "Destiny into Chance: S.J. Duncan's *The Imperialist* and the Perils of Nation Building." *Studies in Canadian Literature* 24.2 (1999): 1–34.

——. *Worrying the Nation: Imagining a National Literature in English Canada*. Toronto: U of Toronto P, 1998.

Kincaid, Jamaica. "Biography of a Dress." *Grand Street* 11.3 (1992): 93–100.

Kirby, William. *The Golden Dog: A Romance of the Days of Louis Quinze in Quebec*. New York: Lovell, 1877.

Kirkwood, Deborah. "Settler Wives in Southern Rhodesia: A Case Study." In Callan and Ardener, eds. 143–64.

Klinck, Carl F. *Giving Canada a Literary History: A Memoir by Carl F. Klinck*. Ed. Sandra Djwa. Ottawa: Carlton UP for the University of Western Ontario, 1991.

Krell, David Farrell. *Intimations of Mortality: Time, Truth, and Finitude in Heideggers's Thinking of Being*. University Park, PA : Pennsylvania State UP, 1986.

Kristeva, Julia. "Motherhood According to Giovanni Bellini." *Desire in Language: A Semiotic Approach to Literature and Art*. Ed. Leon S. Roudiez. New York: Columbia University Press, 1980.

Lampman, Archibald. "At the Mermaid Inn." *Globe* [Toronto] 4 Mar. 1893: 6.

Lang, Ian. "The French Connection–CGIL Update 2000." *Centre for the Genetic Improvement Of Livestock*. 15 January 2003. <http://cgil.uoguelph.ca/pub/Update2000/FrenchConnection.htm>.

Lang, Marjory. *Women Who Made the News: Female Journalists in Canada, 1880–1945*. Montreal and Kingston: McGill-Queen's UP, 1999.

Laurent, Albert. *L'Épopée tragique, roman canadien*. Montréal: Beauchemin, 1956.

Lauriston, Victor. "Three Musketeers of the Pen in New York of the Nineties." *Saturday Night* 12 Jan. 1946: 32–33.

Laver, Ross. "Lynton (Red) Wilson: 'We're Losing our Sense of How Great this Country Is.'" *Maclean's*. Toronto Edition. 112.50 (13 Dec. 1999): 78.

Lawson, Alan. "Postcolonial Theory and the "Settler" Subject." *Testing the Limits: Postcolonial Theories and Canadian Literatures. Essays on Canadian Writing* 56 (1995): 20–36.

Lecker, Robert. "Where Is Here Now?" *Essays on Canadian Writing* 71 (Fall 2000): 6–13.

Lefebvre de Bellefeuille, Joseph-Édouard, trans. *Le manoir de Villerai: roman historique canadien sous la domination française*. By Mrs. Leprohon. Montréal: Plinguet, 1861.

Léger, Antoine-J. *Elle et lui, idylle tragique du peuple acadien*. Moncton: Évangeline, 1940.

Léger, Jules. *Le Canada français et son expression littéraire*. Paris: Nizet et Bastard, 1938.

Le May, Pamphile, trans. *Le Chien d'or: légende canadienne*. By William Kirby. Montréal: Étendard, 1884.

Lemire, Maurice. *Formation de l'imaginaire littéraire au Québéc (1764–1867)*. Montréal: Hexagone, 1993.

———. *Les Grands Thèmes nationalistes du roman historique canadien- français*. Québec: PUL, 1970.

LeMoine, J.M. *Maple Leaves*. Fourth Series. Quebec: Augustin Coté, 1873.

Le Moine, Roger. *Napoléon Bourassa: L'homme et l'artiste*. Montréal: Fides, 1977.

Leprohon, Mrs. (Rosanna Eleanor). *Antoinette de Mirecourt; or, Secret Marrying and Secret Sorrowing*. Montréal: Lovell, 1864.

———. *Antoinette de Mirecourt*. 1864. Ed. John C. Stockdale. Ottawa: Carleton UP, 1989, 1995.

———. *Armand Durand, or, A Promise Fulfilled*. 1868. Montréal: Beauchemin, 1892.

———. *The Manor House of De Villerai*. 1859–60. rpt. *Journal of Canadian Fiction* No. 34.

Lesperance, John Talon. *The Bastonnais. Tale of the American Invasion of Canada in 1775–76*. Toronto: Belford, 1877.

Lessard, Marie. "Narration et écriture de l'histoire: paradigme narratif de la chute et du salut et recits de conquête." *Textual Studies in Canada* 5 (1994): 84–94.

Lewis, Matthew. *The Monk*. 1796. New York: Random House, 2002.

Libby, M. F. "Canadian Literature." *Week* [Toronto] 3 Mar. 1893: 318.

Lighthall, William Douw. Introduction. *Songs of the Great Dominion*. 1889. Toronto: Coles, 1971. xxi–xxxvii.

Lippard, Lucy, ed. *Partial Recall: Photographs of Native North Americans*. New York: The New Press, 1992.

Livesay, Dorothy. "The Documentary Poem: A Canadian Genre." *Contexts in Canadian Criticism*. Ed. Eli Mandel. Chicago and London: U of Chicago P, 1971. 267–81.

Lochhead, Douglas G. Introduction. *St. Ursula's Convent or The Nun of Canada, Containing Scenes from Real Life*. Ottawa: Carleton UP, 1991. xvii–xli.

Lohuis, Michael M. "Breeding Strategies Useful in Genetic Conservation." *Centre for Genetic Improvement of Livestock*. 1997. 1 April 2005. <http://cgil.uoguelph.ca/pub/mmlpapers/conserve.htm>.

Longfellow, Henry Wadsworth. *Evangeline*. 1846. Toronto: Briggs, 1908.

Lukács, Georg. *The Historical Novel*. 1962. Trans. Hannah and Stanley Mitchell. Lincoln: U Nebraska P, 1983.

Macdonald, John A. *Commons Debates, 5th Sess., 3rd Parliament*. Vol. 1. Ottawa: House of Commons, 7 Mar. 1878.

Mackay, J. *Quebec Hill; or, Canadian Scenery. A Poem. In Two Parts*. 1797. Ed. D.M.R. Bentley. London: Canadian Poetry Press, 1988.

MacLeod, Margaret Arnett, ed. *The Letters of Letitia Hargrave*. Toronto: Champlain Society, 1947. Facsimile ed. New York: Greenwood, 1969.

Maillet, Antonine. *Pélagie-la-Charette*. 1969. Paris: Francopoche, 1990.

Manly, John G. *The Nature, Origin, Progress, Present State, and Character of Wesleyan Methodism, A Sermon Preached at Picton, Upper Canada, on Friday the 25th October, 1839....* Kingston: Bentley, 1840.

Maracle, Lee. "*Ka-Nata.*" *Bent Box*. Penticton, BC: Theytus Books, 2000. 107–12.

Marmette, Joseph. *Charles et Éva*. 1866. Montréal: Lumen, 1954.

——. *François de Bienville, scènes de la vie canadienne au XVIIe siècle*. 1870. Montréal: Beauchemin, 1883.

——. *L'Intendant Bigot*. Montréal: Desbarats, 1872.

Marquis, T. G. "Crude Criticism." *Week* [Toronto] 6 Mar. 1896: 350–51.

——. "English-Canadian Literature." *Canada and Its Provinces*. Gen. ed. Adam Shortt and Arthur G. Doughty. Vol. 12. Toronto: Glasgow, Brook, 1914. 493–589.

Matas, Robert. "Are B.C.'s Wild Steeds a Rare and Noble Breed?" *The Globe and Mail*. 17 May 2002. <http://vancouverplus.workopolis.com/servlet/News/fast-track/20020517/UHORSN?section=bc>.

Mathews, Robin. "'Malcolm's Katie': Love, Wealth, and Nation Building." *Studies in Canadian Literature* 2 (1977): 49–60.

Mazel, David. "American Literary Environmentalism as Domestic Orientalism." *The Ecocriticism Reader: Landmarks in Literary Ecology*. Eds. Cheryll Glotfelty and Harold Fromm. Athens: U of Georgia P, 1995. 137–46.

McBride, Theresa. "'As the Twig is Bent': the Victorian Nanny." *The Victorian Family: Structure and Stresses*. Ed. Anthony S. Wohl. London: Croom Helm, 1978. 44–58.

McCaig, JoAnn. *Reading In: Alice Munro's Archives*. Waterloo: Wilfred Laurier UP, 2000.

McCarthy, Maureen. *The Rescue of True Womanhood: Convents and Anti-Catholicism in 1830s America*. Diss. Rutgers U, 1996.

McClintock, Anne. *Imperial Leather: Race, Gender and Sexuality in the Colonial Contest*. New York: Routledge, 1995.

McClung, Nellie L. *Clearing in the West: My Own Story*. Toronto: Thomas Allen, 1935.

——. *In Times Like These*. 1915. Introd. Veronica Strong-Boag. Toronto: U of Toronto P, 1972.

McCrory, Wayne. "Preliminary Conservation Assessment of the Rainshadow Wild Horse Ecosystem." March 2002. *Friends of the Nemaiah Valley*, <http://www.fonv.ca/research/mccroy_summary.PDF>.

McCullough, Michael. "Less is MOA: For busy pilgrims, a stripped-down tour of UBC's famous Museum of Anthropology." *Western Living*, March 1998: 11–14.

McGee, Thomas D'Arcy. "The Mental Outfit of the New Dominion." *Montreal Gazette* 5 Nov. 1867. Ottawa: CIHM microfiche, 1981.

McKay, Ian. "The Liberal Order Framework: A Prospectus for a Reconnaissance of Canadian History." *The Canadian Historical Review* 81.4 (December 2000): 617–45.

McKillop, A.B. "Who Killed Canadian History? A View From the Trenches."
Canadian Historical Review 80.2 (1999): 269–99.

McLachlan, Alexander. *The Emigrant*. 1861. Bentley, ed. 451–506.

McMaster, Gerald. "Colonial Alchemy: Reading the Boarding School Experience."
Partial Recall: Photographs of Native North Americans. Ed. Lucy R. Lippard. New
York: the New Press, 1992. 76–87.

Merk, Frederick. "Introduction to the Revised Edition: The Strategy of Monopoly."
Fur Trade and Empire: George Simpson's Journal. Rev. ed. Cambridge, Massachusetts:
Harvard UP, 1968. xi–xxxi.

Metro Morning. "World's Biggest Bookstore." CBC Radio One. 18 Nov. 2003.

Mills, Sara. "Knowledge, Gender, and Empire." *Writing Women and Space: Colonial and
Postcolonial Geographies*. Ed. Alison Blunt and Gillian Rose. New York: Guilford
P, 1994. 29–50.

Mitchell, Tom. "'The Manufacture of Souls of Good Quality': Winnipeg's 1919
National Conference on Canadian Citizenship, English Canadian
Nationalism, and the New Order After the Great War." *Journal of Canadian
Studies* 31.4 (1996–97): 5–28.

Moffett, Samuel E. *The Americanization of Canada*. 1907. Toronto: U of Toronto P, 1972.

Monk, Maria. *Awful Disclosures of Maria Monk: As Exhibited in a Narrative of Her Sufferings
During a Residence of Five Years as a Novice, and Two Years as a Black Nun, in the Hotel Dieu
Nunnery at Montreal*. New York: Howe and Bates, 1836.

———. *Awful Disclosures by Maria Monk of the Hotel Dieu Nunnery of Montreal*. Rev. ed. New
York: privately printed, 1836.

Monture-Angus, Patricia. *Journeying Forward: Dreaming First Nations Independence*.
Halifax: Fernwood, 1999.

"More Indian Outrages." *The Toronto World*. 20 May 1885: 1.

Morton, Arthur S. *Sir George Simpson, Overseas Governor of the Hudson's Bay Company: A Pen
Picture of a Man of Action*. Toronto: Dent and Sons, 1944.

Morton, Desmond. *Rebellions in Canada*. Toronto: Grolier, 1979.

Moss, Laura, ed. *Is Canada Postcolonial?: Unsettling Canadian Literature*. Waterloo:
Wilfrid Laurier UP, 2003.

Mount, Nick. "In Praise of Talking Dogs: The Study and Teaching of Early
Canada's Canonless Canon." *Essays on Canadian Writing* 63 (Spring 1998): 76–98.

Mukherjee, Arun P. "Canadian Nationalism, Canadian Literature, and Racial
Minority Women." *Essays on Canadian Writing* 56 (Fall 1995): 78–95.

Mulvaney, Charles P. *The History of the North-West Rebellion of 1885*. 1885. Toronto:
Coles, 1971.

Murphy, Rex. "The Standoff at Kanesatake." *The National: CBC News*. 8 June 2004.
<http://www.cbc.ca/national/rex/rex_040116.html>.

Murray, Heather. *Come, Bright Improvement! The Literary Societies of Nineteenth-Century Ontario*. Toronto: U of Toronto P, 2002.

Nairn, Tom. *Faces of Nationalism: Janus Revisited*. London and New York: Verso, 1997.

Namias, June. *White Captives: Gender and Ethnicity on the American Frontier*. U of North Carolina P, 1993.

National Gallery of Canada. Catalogue of the *Exhibition of Canadian West Coast Art—Native and Modern*. Ottawa: National Gallery of Canada, 1927.

New, W. H., ed. *Canadian Writers, 1890–1920*. Vol. 92 of *Dictionary of Literary Biography*. Detroit: Gale, 1990.

"The Newfoundland Pony: A Heritage Animal. *The Newfoundland Pony Society (NPS)*. Publication AP028, 12 October 1999.

Northey, Margot. *The Haunted Wilderness: The Gothic and the Grotesque in Canadian Fiction*. Toronto: U of Toronto P, 1976.

O'Brien, Laird. "A Horse Uniquely Ours From the King of France." *Canadian Geographic* (Feb/Mar. 1991): 76–81.

P de S***. *L'Acadien Baptiste Gaudet*. *Courrier de Saint-Hyacinthe*, July 28–Aug 25, 1863.

Pacey, Desmond, ed. *The Collected Poems of Sir Charles G.D. Roberts*. Wolfville, NS: Wombat Press, 1985.

———. *Creative Writing in Canada: A Short History of English-Canadian Literature*. Toronto: Ryerson, 1952.

Pache, Walter. "English-Canadian Fiction and the Pastoral Tradition." *Canadian Literature* 85 (1980): 15–28.

Palmer, Bryan D. "Of Silences and Trenches: A Dissident View of Granatstein's Meaning." *Canadian Historical Review* 80.4 (Dec. 1999): 676–86.

Parker, George L. *The Beginnings of the Book Trade in Canada*. Toronto: U of Toronto P, 1985.

Parkman, Francis. *Pioneers of France in the New World: France and England in North America*. 1865. Boston: Little, Brown, 1922.

"Parliament endorses Calder's bill on Canadian horse." *Member of Parliament Murray Calder Dufferin-Peel-Wellington-Grey*. 15 January 2003. <http://www.murray-calder.ca/news/2002%20releases/horse190202.htm>.

Paxton, Nancy. "Mobilizing Chivalry: Rape in British Novels about the Indian Uprising of 1857." *Victorian Studies* 36. 1 (Fall 1992): 2–30.

———. *Writing Under the Raj: Gender, Race, and Rape in the British Colonial Imagination, 1830–1947*. New Brunswick, NJ: Rutgers UP, 1999.

Payne, Michael. *"The Most Respectable Place in the Territory": Everyday Life in Hudson's Bay Company Service: York Factory, 1788–1870*. Ottawa: Minister of the Environment, 1989.

Pederson, Diana. "Providing a Woman's Conscience: The YWCA, Female Evangelicalism, and the Girl in the City, 1870–1930." *Canadian Women: A Reader*.

Eds. Paula Bourne, Alison Prentice, Gail Cuthbert Brandt, Beth Light, and Naomi Black. Toronto: Harcourt Brace, 1996. 194–210.

Pennee, Donna Palmateer. "Après Frye, rien? Pas du tout!" *New Contexts of Canadian Criticism*. Eds. Ajay Heble, Donna Palmateer Pennee, J.R. Struthers. Peterborough, ON: Broadview, 1997. 202–19.

———. "Looking Elsewhere for Answers to the Postcolonial Question: From Literary Studies to State Policy in Canada." Moss, ed. 78–94.

Pennée, Georgiana M., trans. *Canadians of Old*. By Philippe Aubert de Gaspé. Québec: Desbarats, 1864.

Peterman, Michael. "Writing and Culture in Nineteenth-Century Canada." *Journal of Canadian Studies*. Special Issue on *Writing and Culture in Nineteenth-Century Canada*. 32.2 (Summer 1997): 3–4, 208.

Piché, Aristide, trans. *Les Bastonnais*. By John Talon Lesperance. Montréal: Beauchemin, 1896.

Pierce, Lorne. *The House of Ryerson 1829–1954.* Toronto: Ryerson, 1954.

Podruchny, Carolyn. "Festivities, Fortitude, and Fraternalism: Fur Trade Masculinity." *New Faces of the Fur Trade: Selected Papers of the Seventh North American Fur Trade Conference*. Ed. Jo-Anne Fiske, Susan Sleeper-Smith, and William Wicken. East Lansing: Michigan State UP, 1998. 31–52.

Pollock, Frank L. "Canadian Writers in New York." *Acta Victoriana* [Victoria College, University of Toronto] Apr. 1899: 434–39.

Pomeroy, E.M. *Sir Charles G.D. Roberts: A Biography*. Toronto: Ryerson, 1943.

Poovey, Mary. *Making a Social Body: British Cultural Formation, 1830–1864*. Chicago: U of Chicago P, 1995.

Porteous, J. Douglas, and Sandra E. Smith. *Domicide: The Global Destruction of Home*. Montreal: McGill-Queen's UP, 2001.

Potter, Mitch. "The real 'Saving Pte. Lynch': Iraqi medical staff tell a different story than U.S. military. 'We all became friends with her, we liked her so much'." *Toronto Star* (4 May 2003). A1, A7.

Pratt, Mary Louise. *Imperial Eyes: Travel Writing and Transculturation*. London: Routledge, 1992.

———. "Scratches on the Face of the Country; or, What Mr. Barrow Saw in the Land of the Bushmen." *"Race," Writing, and Difference*. Ed. Henry Louis Gates, Jr. Chicago: U of Chicago P, 1986. 138–62.

Precosky, Don. "Seven Myths About Canadian Literature." *Studies in Canadian Literature* 11.1 (1986): 86–95.

Preece, Rod. *Animals and Nature: Cultural Myths, Cultural Realities*. Vancouver: U of British Columbia P, 1999.

Prentice, Alison et al. *Canadian Women: A History*. Toronto: Harcourt Brace Jovanovich, 1988.

Rajan, Tilottama. "Introduction: Imagining History." Special Issue *Imagining History. PMLA* 118.3 (2003): 427–35.

Rameau de Saint-Père, Edme. *La France aux colonies*. Paris: Jouby, 1859.

"Rare Breeds Canada Annual General Meetings" and "Rare Breeds Canada Priority List of Animals."*Rare Breeds Canada*. 1 April 2005.

    <http://www.rarebreedscanada.ca/priority.htm>.

Raudsepp, Enn. "Patriotism & Class Interest in *Les Anciens Canadiens*." *Journal of Canadian Fiction* 30 (1984): 106–13.

"RCMP to patrol troubled Kanesatake." *Globe and Mail* 5 May 2004: Online edition.

Readings, Bill. *The University in Ruins*. Cambridge: Harvard UP, 1996.

Redfield, Marc. *The Politics of Aesthetics: Nationalism, Gender, Romanticism*. Stanford: Stanford UP, 2003.

Reed, Rebecca. *Six Months In a Convent*. Schultz, ed. *Veil of Fear: Nineteenth-Century Convent Tales by Rebecca Reed and Maria Monk*. West Lafayette, Indiana: NotaBell Books, Purdue UP, 1999. 49–186.

Reid, Dennis. *Krieghoff: Images of Canada*. Toronto: Douglas and McIntyre, 1999.

Reid, Sue. "Canada's Little Iron Horse Inspires Passion and Controversy." *The Lanark Era*. 15 January 2003.

    <http://www3.sympatico.ca/mapleridge/Articles.html>.

———. "Taking the 'little' out of Canada's Little Iron Horse." *The Lanark Era*. 15 January 2003. <http://www3.sympatico.ca/mapleridge/Articles.html>.

Reinhardt, Mark. "Who Speaks for Margaret Garner? Slavery, Silence, and the Politics of Ventriloquism." *Critical Inquiry* 29.1 (Fall 2002): 81–119.

"Reward for Service: Each North-West Volunteer to Have 320 Acres of Land." *Globe* (13 July 1885): 2.

Richardson, John. *Wacousta, Or; The Prophecy: A Tale of the Canadas*. 1832. Ed. Douglas Cronk. Ottawa: Carleton UP, 1987.

Rivers, W.H.R. *Kinship and Social Organization: Together with 'The Genealogical Method of Anthropological Enquiry'*. New York: Athlone P, U of London, 1968.

Roberts, Sir Charles G.D. "Canada" (1885). *The Collected Poems of Sir Charles G.D. Roberts*. Ed. Desmond Pacey. Wolfville NS: Wombat Press, 1985. 85–86.

———. "Collect for Dominion Day" (1885). *The Collected Poems of Sir Charles G.D. Roberts*. Ed. Desmond Pacey. Wolfville NS: Wombat Press, 1985. 89.

———. "An Ode for the Canadian Confederacy" (1885). *The Collected Poems of Sir Charles G.D. Roberts*. Ed. Desmond Pacey. Wolfville NS: Wombat Press, 1985. 90.

———. Foreword. *Flying Colours*. Ed. Sir Charles G.D. Roberts. Toronto: Ryerson, 1942: vii–viii.

———. trans. *Canadians of Old*. By Philippe Aubert de Gaspé, père. New York: Appleton, 1890.

Rosario, Vernon A. "Phantastical Pollutions: The Public Threat of Private Vice in France." *Solitary Pleasures: The History, Literary and Artistic Discourses of Autoeroticism.* Eds. Paula Bennett and Vernon A. Rosario. New York: Routledge, 1995. 101–30.

Rossiter, William S. "Printing and Publishing." *Twelfth Census of the United States, Taken in the Year 1900.* Vol. 9. Washington: U.S. Census Office, 1902. 1037–1119.

Rothman, Claire, trans. *The Influence of a Book.* By Philippe Aubert de Gaspé, fils. Montréal: Davies, 1993.

Rushdie, Salman. "The Empire Writes Back With a Vengeance." *The Times* 3 July 1982: 8.

Russell, Edmund. "Evolutionary History: Prospectus for a New Field." *Environmental History* 8 (April 2003): 204–28.

Rutherford, Paul. *A Victorian Authority: The Daily Press in Late Nineteenth-Century Canada.* Toronto: U of Toronto P, 1982.

Ryerson, Egerton. *Christians on Earth and in Heaven: The Substance of A Discourse, delivered in the Adelaide Street Wesleyan-Methodist Church, Toronto, on Sabbath Evening, Oct. 29th, 1848.* Toronto: W. M. Book Room, 1848.

———. *Doctrines and Discipline of the Methodist Episcopal Church in Canada.* York: E. Ryerson and F. Metcalf, 1829.

———. *A Review of a Sermon, Preached by Hon. and Rev. John Strachan D .D. York U.C. 3rd of July 1825, on the Death of the Late Lord Bishop of Quebec, by a Methodist Preacher.* York, 1825.

———. *Wesleyan Methodism in Upper Canada, A Sermon Preached Before the Conference of Ministers of the Wesleyan-Methodist Church in Canada. City of Toronto, June 18th, 1837.* Toronto: Conference Office, 1837.

"Sable Island: A Story of Survival." 23 April 2003. <http://collection.ic.gc.ca/sableisland/english_en/index_en.htm>.

Saul, John Ralston. "Canada: John Ralston Saul Speaks Out on What it Means to be a Canadian." *Chapter One: The Members' Almanac,* Winter 1999–2000: 4–5.

———. *Reflections of a Siamese Twin: Canada at the End of the Twentieth Century.* Toronto: Viking, 1997.

———. "Think Outside the Box." *The Globe and Mail.* 11 March 2003: A13.

"Saved from Danger: Brave young Jessica Lynch survives captivity—and torture—to become hero of the Iraqi war." *People Magazine* (21 April 2003): cover, 54–59.

Saxby, Jessie M. "Women Wanted." 1890. *A Flannel Shirt and Liberty: British Emigrant Gentlewomen in the Canadian West, 1880–1914.* Vancouver: U British Columbia P, 1982. 66–76.

Scanlan, Lawrence. *Little Horse of Iron: a Quest for the Canadian Horse.* Toronto: Random House, 2001.

Schäffer, Mary T.S. *Old Indian Trails: Incidents of Camp and Trail Life, Covering Two Years' Exploration Through the Rocky Mountains of Canada.* Toronto: William Briggs, 1911.

Schultz, Nancy Lusignan. Introduction. *A Veil of Fear: Nineteenth-Century Convent Tales by Rebecca Read and Maria Monk*. Ed. Schultz. West Lafayette, IN: NotaBell-Purdue UP, 1999. vii–xxxiii.

Scott, Duncan Campbell. "Fragment of an Ode to Canada" (1911). *The Emergence of the Muse: Major Canadian Poets from Crawford to Pratt*. Toronto: Oxford UP, 1993. 232–33.

———. *Labor and the Angel*. Boston: Copeland and Day, 1898.

Scott, F.R. "The Canadian Authors Meet." 1927. *An Anthology of Canadian Literature in English*. Revised and Abridged Edition. Ed Russell Brown. Toronto: Oxford UP, 1990. 272.

———. "Laurentian Shield." 1954. *An Anthology of Canadian Literature in English*. Revised and Abridged Edition. Ed Russell Brown. Toronto: Oxford UP, 1990. 276–77.

Sedgwick, Eve Kosofsky. *The Coherence of Gothic Conventions*. Rev. ed. New York: Arno Press, 1980.

———. *Epistemology of the Closet*. Berkeley: U of California P, 1990.

———. "Privilege of Unknowing: Diderot's *The Nun*." *Tendencies*. Durham: Duke UP, 1993. 23–51.

———. "Shame and Performativity: Henry James's New York Edition Prefaces." *Henry James's New York Edition: The Construction of Authorship*. Ed. David McWhirter. Stanford: Stanford UP, 1995. 206–39.

———. *Touching Feeling*. Durham: Duke UP, 2003.

Seymour-Smith, Martin. "Mythopoeia." *The Fontana Dictionary of Modern Thought*. 2nd ed. Ed. Allan Bullock, Oliver Stallybrass, and Stephen Trombley. London: Fontana, 1988. 556.

Shadbolt, Doris. *Emily Carr*. Vancouver and Toronto: Douglas and McIntyre, 1990.

Shadd, Mary A. *A Plea for Emigration or, Notes of Canada West*. 1852. Ed. Richard Almonte. Toronto: Mercury, 1998.

Shakespeare, William. *Measure for Measure*. Ed. N. W. Bawcutt. Oxford: Oxford UP, 1991.

Shapiro, Stephen. "The Moment of the Condom: Saint-Méry and Early American Print Sexuality." *Pioneering North America. Mediators of European Culture and Literature*. Wurzburg, Germany: Konigshausen and Neumann, 2000. 122–35.

Sharpe, Jenny. *Allegories of Empire: The Figure of Woman in the Colonial Text*. Minneapolis: U of Minnesota P, 1993.

Shaw, Harry E. *The Forms of Historical Fiction: Sir Walter Scott and His Successors*. Ithaca: Cornell UP, 1983.

Shek, Ben-Zion. *French-Canadian & Québécois Novels*. New York: Oxford UP, 1991.

Simmons, Deidre. "Frederick Alexcee, Indian Artist (c. 1857–1944)." *The Journal of Canadian Art History* XIV.2 (1992): 83–92.

Smith, Sidonie. *A Poetics of Women's Autobiography: Marginality and the Fictions of Self-Representation*. Bloomington: Indiana UP, 1987.

Soja, Edward W. *Thirdspace: Journeys to Los Angeles and Other Real-and-Imagined Places*. Cambridge, Mass.: Blackwell, 1996.

Solanke, Adeola. "Complex, Not Confused." *Family Snaps: The Meanings of Domestic Photography*. Eds. Jo Spence and Patricia Holland. London: Virago, 1991.

Sorfleet, John Robert. "Fiction and the Fall of New France: William Kirby vs. Gilbert Parker." *Journal of Canadian Fiction* 2.3 (Summer 1973): 132–46.

Spacks, Patricia Meyer. *Gossip*. Chicago: U of Chicago P, 1986.

Spence, Jo, and Patricia Holland, eds. *Family Snaps: The Meanings of Domestic Photography.* London: Virago, 1991.

Stallybrass, Peter and Allon White. *The Politics and Poetics of Transgression*. Ithaca, NY: Cornell UP, 1986.

Starowicz, Mark. *Making History: The Remarkable Story Behind "Canada: A People's Story."* Toronto: McClelland and Stewart, 2003.

Steedman, Carolyn. "A Woman Writing a Letter." In Earle, ed. 111–33.

Stevens, John D. *Sensationalism and the New York Press*. New York: Columbia UP, 1991.

Stevenson, Winona. "Colonialism and First Nations Women in Canada." *Scratching the Surface: Canadian Anti-Racist Feminist Thought*. Eds. Enakshi Dua and Angela Robertson. Toronto: Women's Press: 1999. 49–80.

Stonechild, Blair and Bill Waiser. *Loyal till Death: Indians and the North-West Rebellion*. Calgary: Fifth House, 1997.

Strange, Carolyn. *Toronto's Girl Problem: The Perils and Pleasures of the City, 1880–1930*. Toronto: U of Toronto P, 1995.

Stratford, Philip. *Bibliography of Canadian Books in Translation: French to English and English to French*. Ottawa: HRCC, 1977.

Stringer, Arthur. "Canadian Writers Who Are Winning Fame in New York." *Montreal Herald* 2 March 1901: 11.

Sullivan, Rebecca. "A Wayward from the Wilderness: Maria Monk's *Awful Disclosures* and the Feminization of Lower Canada in the Nineteenth Century." *Essays on Canadian Writing* 67 (1997): 201–22.

Swaisland, Cecillie. "Female Migration and Social Mobility: British Female Domestic Servants to South Africa, 1860–1914." *Migrant Women: Crossing Boundaries and Changing Identities*. Ed.Gina Buijs. Oxford: Berg, 1993. 161–78.

Talbot, Edward Allen. *Five Years' Residence in the Canadas: Including a Tour Through Part of the United States of America, in the Year 1823*. London: Longman, Hurst, Rees, Orme, Brown and Green, 1824.

Taschereau-Fortier, Mme. Alexandre. *Les Orphelins de Grand-Pré*. 1931. Montréal: Lévesque, 1932.

Tausky, Thomas E. *Sara Jeannette Duncan: Novelist of Empire*. Port Credit: P.D. Meany,
1980.

———. *Sara Jeannette Duncan: Selected Journalism*. Ottawa: Tecumseh P, 1978.

Taylor, Charles. "Institutions in National Life." *Reconciling the Solitudes: Essays on
Canadian Federalism and Nationalism*. Ed. Guy Laforest. Montreal: McGill-
Queen's UP, 1993. 120–34.

———. "The Politics of Recognition." 1995. Rpt. in *New Contexts of Canadian Criticism*.
Eds. Ajay Heble, Donna Palmateer Pennee and J.R. (Tim) Struthers.
Peterborough: Broadview, 1997. 98–131.

Ten Kortenaar, Neil. "Sara Jeannette Duncan." *Encyclopedia of Literature in Canada*.
Toronto: U of Toronto P, 2002. 320–23.

Thomas, Keith. *Man and the Natural World: Changing Attitudes in England 1500–1800*.
London: Penguin, 1984.

Thompson, Janna. "Environment as Cultural Heritage." *Environmental Ethics* 22
(2000): 241–58.

Thomson, E. W. "To Archibald Lampman." [May 1891?] and 24 May 1892. *The Letters
of Edward William Thomson to Archibald Lampman (1891–1897)*. Ed. Arthur S.
Bourinot. Ottawa: Bourinot, 1957. 3, 7.

Tippett, Maria. *Emily Carr: A Biography*. Toronto: Oxford UP, 1979.

Traill, Catharine Parr. *The Backwoods of Canada*. 1836. Toronto: McClelland and
Stewart, 1966.

———. *The Canadian Settler's Guide*. 1855. Vancouver: Alcuin Society, 1971.

Treaties and Historical Research Center. *Indian Acts and Amendments*. 2nd ed.
Ottawa: Research Branch, Corporate Policy. Department of Indian and
Northern Affairs, Canada, 1981.

Truesdell, Leon E. *The Canadian Born in the United States: An Analysis of the Statistics of the
Canadian Element in the Population of the United States, 1850 to 1930*. New Haven: Yale
UP, 1943.

United States. Census Office. *Twelfth Census of the United States, Taken in the Year 1900*. 10
vols. and supplements. Washington: U.S. Census Office, 1901–03.

Valverde, Mariana. *The Age of Light, Soap, and Water: Moral Reform in English Canada,
1885–1925*. Toronto: McClelland and Stewart, 1991.

———. "'When the Mother of the Race Is Free': Race, Reproduction, and
Sexuality in First-Wave Feminism." *Gender Conflicts: New Essays in Women's History*.
Eds. Franca Iacovetta and Mariana Valverde. Toronto: U of Toronto P, 1992.
2–25.

Van Dusen, Tom. "The Proud Canadian." *Ontario Farmer*. 15 January 2004.
<http://www3.sympatico.ca/mapleridge/Articles.html>.

Van Kirk, Sylvia. *"Many Tender Ties": Women in Fur-Trade Society, 1670–1870*. Winnipeg:
Watson and Dwyer, 1980.

Veeder, William. "The Nurture of the Gothic, or How Can a Text Be Both Popular and Subversive?" *American Gothic: New Interventions in a National Narrative*. Eds. Robert K. Martin and Eric Savoy. Iowa City: U of Iowa P, 1998. 20–39.

Viau, Robert. *Les Grands Dérangements: La déportation des Acadiens en littératures acadienne, québécoise et française*. Beauport, Qc.: MNH, 1997.

Wagenaar, Norman. "Barnyard Diversity: Pulling our Farms Friends Away from the Brink." *Earthkeeper* (Dec. 1994): 25–28.

Walcott, Rinaldo. *Black Like Who?: Writing Black Canada*. 2nd Rev. Ed. Toronto: Insomniac Press, 2003.

Walker, Fred. "Flying His Own Colours: The Patriotic Poetry of Sir Charles G.D. Roberts." *Journal of Canadian Poetry* 3.2 (1981): 48–54.

Warkentin, Germaine, ed. *Canadian Exploration Literature: An Anthology*. Toronto: Oxford UP, 1993.

Warkentin, Germaine, and Heather Murray. "Introduction: Reading the Discourse of Early Canada." *Canadian Literature*. Special Issue entitled *Discourse in Early Canada*. 131 (Winter 1991): 7–13.

Watson, Scott. "The Modernist Past of Lawrence Paul Yuxweluptun's Landscape Allegories." *Lawrence Paul Yuxweluptun: Born to Live and Die on Your Colonialist Reservations*. Vancouver: Morris and Helen Belkin Art Gallery, University of British Columbia, 1995. 60–71.

Webster, Paul. "Who Stole Canadian History? (Just Why are Canada's Corporate Giants Pouring Money into Foundations and Projects Promoting the Subject.) *This Magazine* 3 (Mar./Apr. 2000): 28–31.

Welsh, Christine. "Women in the Shadows: Reclaiming a Métis Heritage." *New Contexts of Canadian Criticism*. In Heble, Pennee, and Struthers, eds. 56–66.

Wente, Margaret. "Women at War: time to rethink?" *Globe and Mail* (29 Mar 2003): A21.

Wetherald, Ethelwyn. Introduction. *Collected Poems of Isabella Valancy Crawford*. 15–29.

Wexler, Laura. *Tender Violence: Domestic Visions in an Age of U.S. Imperialism*. Chapel Hill: U of North Carolina P, 2000.

"Whatever Happened to All Our Breeds?" *Canadian Foundation for the Conservation of Farm Animal Genetic Resources (cfcfagr)*. 7 May 2001. <http://www.cfagrf.com/pamphlet.html>.

"What Women Say of the Canadian North-West." 1886. *A Flannel Shirt and Liberty: British Emigrant Gentlewomen in the Canadian West, 1880–1914*. Vancouver: U British Columbia P, 1982. 31–65.

Who's Who in New York City and State. New York: Hammersly, 1904.

"Wild Horses May Outrun Wildfires." *CBC News British Columbia*. 7 August 2003. <http://vancouver.cbc.ca/regional/servlet/view?filename=bc_horses20020807>.

Williams, Catherine R. *The Neutral French: or the Exiles of Nova Scotia*. Providence: The
 Author, 1841.

Williams, Raymond. *Marxism and Literature*. Oxford: Oxford UP, 1977.

———. "The Future of Cultural Studies." *The Politics of Modernism: Against the New
 Conformists*. London: Verso, 1989.

Wilson, Edward O. *The Diversity of Life*. 2nd edition. New York: Norton, 1999.

Wilson, Elizabeth. *Adorned in Dreams: Fashion and Modernity*. London: Virago, 1985.

Wolin, Richard. *Walter Benjamin: An Aesthetic of Redemption*. New York: Columbia UP,
 1982.

Woodward, Garth. "Brittany: Beetlemania in a Wild-horse Haven." *Ecoforestry*
 (Summer 2002). 17 March 2005.
 <http:www.fonv.ca/articles/beetlemania.html>.

———. "Shadow over the Brittany Triangle." *Ecoforestry* 16:1 (2001): 5–9.

Woolf, Virginia. *Three Guineas*. In *A Room of One's Own/Three Guineas*. Notes and Intro.
 Michele Barrett. Toronto: Penguin, 1993.

Wordsworth, William. "Preface to the *Lyrical Ballads*." *The Critical Tradition: Classic Texts
 and Contemporary Trends*. 2nd ed. Ed. David Richter. New York: Bedford/St
 Martin's, 1998. 302–15.

Wright, Julia McNair. "Mistresses and Servants." *The Complete Home: An Encyclopedia
 of Domestic Life and Affairs*. Brantford, ON: Bradley, Garretson and Company,
 1879. 436–59.

Yeoman, Ann. "Towards a Native Mythology: The Poetry of Isabella Valency [sic]
 Crawford." *Canadian Literature* 52 (1972): 39–47.

Youmans, Letitia. *Campaign Echoes: The Autobiography of Mrs. Letitia Youmans, the Pioneer of
 the White Ribbon Movement in Canada*. Toronto: William Briggs, 1893.

Young, Robert J.C. *Colonial Desire: Hybridity in Theory, Culture and Race*. London:
 Routledge, 1995.

Zaremba, Eve, ed. *Privilege of Sex: A Century of Canadian Women*. Toronto: Anansi, 1974.

Zemans, Joyce. "Establishing the Canon: Nationhood, Identity and the National
 Gallery's First Reproduction Programme of Canadian Art." *Journal of Canadian
 Art History* XVI.2 (1995): 7–35.

FIGURE 1.1: *Frederick Alexcee, Baptismal Font, Tsimshian, 1886. Wood and paint, 82.5 cm height x 62.5 cm depth x 60.6 cm width. Courtesy UBC Museum of Anthropology, Vancouver, Canada.*

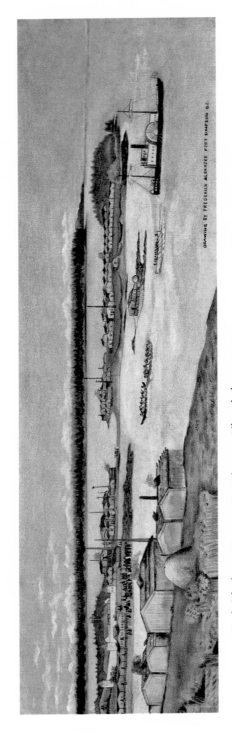

FIGURE 1.5: *Frederick Alexcee, Beaver at Port Simpson. Oil on cloth, 43 × 137 cm.*

Wellcome Institute Library, London, England.

FIGURE 8.1: *Cornelius Krieghoff (Canadian, 1815–1872), "Bringing in the Deer" (c.1859). Oil on canvas. 52.0 x 84.5 cm. The Thomson Collection, Art Gallery of Ontario.*

FIGURE 8.2: *Cornelius Krieghoff (Canadian, 1815–1872), "Transporting Ice" (c.1847–50). Oil on cardboard. 23 x 30 cm. Musée des beaux-arts du Québec. 59.605*

FIGURE 8.3: *Cornelius Krieghoff (Canadian, 1815–1872), "Off the Road— The Upset Sleigh" (c.1856). Oil on canvas. 33.9 x 54.7 cm. The Thomson Collection, Art Gallery of Ontario.*

FIGURE 8.4: *Cornelius Krieghoff (Canadian, 1815–1872), "Bilking the Toll" (1859). Oil on canvas. 43 x 63.5 cm. The Thomson Collection, Art Gallery of Ontario.*

FIGURE 12.1: *"My sister, my brother, my self in a Time I call childhood and a Place I call home."* J. Emberley. Original Artwork, 1999.

FIGURE 12.12: *"Samson Beaver and his Family" (postcard description).*

FIGURE 12.13: *"Sampson Beaver, His Squaw, and Little Frances Louise" [1907].*
Photographer: Mary Schäffer, (Caption in Old Indian Trails). *Whyte Museum of the*
Canadian Rockies (V.527 PS–5).

FIGURE 12.15: *"The Indian Madonna." Photographer: Mary Schäffer [1907],*
Whyte Museum of the Canadian Rockies (V.527 PS–51).

FIGURE 12.16: *"Indian Woman with Papoose." Photographer: Mary Schäffer [1908], Whyte Museum of the Canadian Rockies (V.527 PS–705).*

FIGURE 12.17: *"Indian Woman and Child." Photographer: Byron Harmon [1913], Whyte Museum of the Canadian Rockies (V.439 PS–352).*

Contributors

JENNIFER BLAIR is a doctoral student in the Department of English and Cultural Studies at McMaster. Her dissertation looks at the relationship between architecture and literature in nineteenth-century North America.

ANDREA CABAJSKY is an Assistant Professor of Comparative Canadian Literature at l'Université de Moncton. She teaches and does research in English and French Canadian literature, as well as in gender and postcolonial studies. Her research focuses on the literary history of nationalism in Canada and Britain in the Romantic and Victorian periods. Her current research project examines the intersections between literary translation, print culture, and national identity in early Canada.

ADAM CARTER is an Associate Professor in the Department of English at the University of Lethbridge where he teaches Critical Theory and Canadian Literature. His current research interests concern the intersections of aesthetics, tropology and nationalism in theoretical and literary texts.

DANIEL COLEMAN holds the Canada Research Chair in Critical Race and Ethnicity Studies in the Department of English and Cultural Studies at McMaster University. He has published *Masculine Migrations: Reading the Postcolonial Male in "New Canadian" Narratives* (1998) and *The Scent of Eucalyptus: A Missionary Childhood in Ethiopia* (2003), as well as articles and has guest edited special issues of journals. His monograph entitled *White Civility: The Literary Project of English Canada* is forthcoming with the University of Toronto Press.

CECILY DEVEREUX is an Associate Professor in the Department of English at the University of Alberta, specializing in English Canadian women's writing of the late nineteenth and early twentieth centuries, with particular reference to women's writing on gender and empire. She recently published an edition of L.M. Montgomery's *Anne of Green Gables* (Broadview Press, 2004), and a book-length study, *Growing a Race: Nellie L. McClung and the Fiction of Eugenic Feminism* (McGill-Queen's UP, 2005) is forthcoming.

J.V. EMBERLEY is Associate Professor of Women's Literature and Feminist Theory in the English Department of the University of Western Ontario. She is the author of *Thresholds of Difference: Native Women's Writing, Feminist Critique, and Postcolonial Theory*, *The Cultural Politics of Fur* and other writings on gender, race, sexuality and the class culture of colonization and decolonization. She is currently working on *Representational Violence and Phantasms of Aboriginality in "the family" of De/Colonization*.

JANICE FIAMENGO is an Assistant Professor of English at the University of Ottawa. She has published articles on nineteenth- and twentieth-century Canadian authors in such journals as *Canadian Literature*, *Journal of Canadian Studies* and *Essays on Canadian Writing*, and is at present writing a monograph on the rhetorical strategies of early Canadian women writers and social activists.

CAROLE GERSON is a Professor in the Department of English at Simon Fraser University. She has published extensively on early Canadian literature, with a focus on women writers, and is currently co-editor of volume III of *History of the Book in Canada / Histoire du livre et de l'édition au Canada*.

KATE HIGGINSON is pursuing a PhD in Canadian Literature and Culture at McMaster University. Her research interests include visual representation (especially photography), and issues of gender and indigeneity; her dissertation will trace a literary and visual history of captivity and confinement in Canadian and First Nations narratives.

PAUL HJARTARSON, a Professor of English at the University of Alberta, writes and teaches primarily in the area of Canadian literature and culture. His most recent book, edited with Tracy Kulba, is *The Politics of Cultural Mediation: Baroness Elsa von Freytag-Loringhoven and Felix Paul Greve* (Alberta/CRCL, 2003). His essay for this volume is a part of a larger study of Canadian cultural nationalism in the 1920s.

ANNE MILNE is an Assistant Professor with the Centre for Leadership in Learning at McMaster University. Her research focuses on representations of animals and the labouring classes in eighteenth-century British texts. Recent articles have appeared in *ISLE (Interdisciplinary Studies in Literature and Environment)* and *The Scottish Studies Review*. Her entry on "Ecocriticism" appears in the second edition of *The Johns Hopkins Guide to Literary Theory and Criticism*.

NICK MOUNT is Assistant Professor of English at the University of Toronto. The author of essays and reviews in *ECW*, *CNQ*, *Time & Society*, etc., his current research includes a forthcoming book from the University of Toronto Press on the migration of Canadian writers to New York in the 1880s and 1890s (*When Canadian Literature Moved to New York*) and a book-length study of Canadian literature's long engagement with the idea of America.

ROBERT DAVID STACEY recently received his PhD in Canadian literature from York University. Though he has presented papers and published on a number of topics in the Canadian literatures, the focus of his current research is on the uses of the pastoral in Canadian historical fiction.

KATHLEEN VENEMA is an Assistant Professor in the Department of English at the University of Winnipeg, where she teaches Canadian literature. She has published in a variety of journals, most recently in *Mosaic*. Her current research examines textual constructions of femininity, masculinity, identity, place, and home in nineteenth-century Hudson's Bay Company letters. She is also interested in the relationships between Canadian historiographical literary texts and their (usually) non-literary antecedents.

LORRAINE YORK, a Professor of English at McMaster University, recently published *Rethinking Women's Collaborative Writing* (U of Toronto P, 2002) and is finishing a study of Canadian literary celebrity. Her next project analyzes the relations between celebrity and notions of acceptable citizenship.

Index

Note: *Bold page numbers indicate photo captions.*

class. *See* social class

classification

    in art/anthropology displays, 25–28, 30

    in photography archives, 304–5, 308–12, **311**, 330, 332

Cleomati's poem on NW Rebellion in *Two Months*, 45

clothing

    in photography: Aboriginal/colonial family portraits, 320; colonial family portrait (Aberdeens), **313**, 313–16; fashion and race (Kincaid), 303–4

    power of male attire (Woolf), 314

    sedentary power (Berger), 314–15

    tattooing and body painting as bodily adornment, 304

Cody, H.A., 255n8

Cohen, Robin, on diasporic myth, 85

Cole, Douglas, on collection of First Nations artifacts, 25

Coleman, Daniel, 143n1

Coleman, Kit, as female journalist, 266

"Collect for Dominion Day" (Roberts), 142

colonialism and imperialism

    Acadian diaspora and anti-imperialism (*Jacques et Marie*), 73–74, 82–86, 90n12

    anti-imperialism (*Malcolm's Katie*), 291

    colonialism and rape scares in captivity narratives, 35–38, **36**, 40–43

    Confederation poets and, 120–21

    erotics of colonization (Frye), 289

    in fur-trade society (*See* fur-trade society)

    naturalization of colonization (*Malcolm's Katie*), 288–89, 292–93, 298–99

    in photography (*See* photography)

    simultaneous construction of colonial self and place, 288–91

    tropes for, gluttony/imperialism (*Jacques et Marie*), 82–83, 90n12

colonial wives. *See* fur-trade society

Commoner, Barry, on genomes, 213

confederation, as term of fragmentation, 132–33

Confederation poets

    critical reception, 117–18, 121–22

    See also odes, national

Conservative Party

    U.S. free trade as rape of Miss Canada (poster), 35–38, **36**, 64, 69

Cook, Sharon Anne, 279n6

country wives. *See* fur-trade society

Cox, Palmer, as expatriate writer, 245

Crawford, Isabella Valancy

    life of, 120–21, 282

    works: *Collected Poems*, 282; *Old Spookses' Pass, Malcolm's Katie, and Other Poems*, 281; See also *Malcolm's Katie: A Love Story* (Crawford)

Crean, Susan, on land claims litigation funding, 27

Cree people. *See* Big Bear, Frog Lake camp (Cree and Métis); First Nations

Culler, Jonathan, conventions of the ode, 122, 123

cultural studies

    archives for research, xlii–xlvi

role of formation (Williams), 8

See also "Recalling Early Canada:
Reading the Political in
Literary and Cultural
Production" conference,
Hamilton (June 2003)

Cushing, Eliza Lanesford, 207n1

Davies, Acton, as expatriate writer,
245

Davies, Barrie, on Confederation
poets, 120

Davies, Gwendolyn, 282

Davis, Charles B., ventriloquism,
158, 164

Dean, Misao
feminine manual labour, 72
on Sara Jeannette Duncan, 258,
272, 276

death and loss. See mourning and
nationalism

de Gaspé, Philippe-Joseph Aubert. See
Aubert de Gaspé, Philippe-
Joseph

DeGuise, Charles, Le Cap au diable, 88n1

Delaney, Theresa. See Two Months in
the Camp of Big Bear (Gowanlock
and Delaney)

de Man, Paul
on anthropomorphism, 129–31,
134, 143n4
impossibility of closure, 136–39
on odes and elegies, 119
prosopopoeia, 136–37, 139

Denison, Flora MacDonald, Mary
Melville, 264

Derrida, Jacques
on nationalism and ghosts, 136,
140
phonologocentrism, 132

Devereux, Cecily
captivity narratives, 42, 69, 70
on Malcolm's Katie, xxxviii, 281–300

Devon (rapper), xxvi

Diamond Jubilee of Confederation, 23

diaspora, 85–86

Dictionary of American Authors (1904), 240

Diderot, Denis, The Nun, 186, 188, 197,
199–205

Dinesen, Isak, "The Caryatides,"
xxxix–xl

DNA and genomes, 213

Dodge, Abigail (Gail Hamilton), 261

Dohner, Janet Vorwald, 232, 234n13,
235n16

domestic life
in captivity narratives (See Two
Months in the Camp of Big Bear
(Gowanlock and Delaney))
in fur-trade society (See Hargrave,
Letitia Mactavish)
spectatorship: public/private
spheres (Ellison), 305–7
See also clothing; photography

Dominion Illustrated Monthly, 241

The Dominion Institute
historical initiatives, 8–9, 218
members of, 12

Doran, George, as expatriate, 242

Dougall, Lily, as expatriate writer,
243

Douglas, Ann, 185, 208n7

Douglas, Mary, domestic manual
labour, 47

Dragland, Stan, 32n4

Drummond, William Henry, "The
Habitant's Jubilee Ode," 117,
143n3

Dubinsky, Karen
legal history of rape, 59

on sexual assault, 57

Duffy, Dennis, *Sounding the Iceberg*, 75–76

Duncan, Carol, on art museums, 2, 4, 23

Duncan, Norman, as expatriate writer, 246, 253

Duncan, Sara Jeannette, 257–80
  as journalist: articles other than woman's movement, 258, 273; career in U.S. and England, 240, 243, 248, 257; firsts in journalism, 257–58
  critical interest and reception, xx, 257, 258, 266–67, 276–78
  fiction by, 258, 277
  life of, 257–58, 264, 269, 275–76
  pseudonym [Garth Grafton], 270
  style of: multi-voiced persona, 259–65, 268–70, 274–76; non-alignment and shifts, 259–65, 270–72; rhetorical questions, 273; satire, parody and irony, 258–60, 263, 265, 270–75
  on woman's movement: on "damp females," 263, 268–69; on gender differences, 260; her stated position on suffrage, 258, 259, 261, 265; on maternal feminists, 261–63; metaphors, 260, 262–65, 279n3; on suffrage, 269, 275; on Susan B. Anthony, 265–66
  on women's convention in Wash. D.C. (1886), 263, 265, 269, 274–76
  works (articles, columns): in *Globe*, 257, 260–65, 270–74, 278; in Montreal *Star*, 257, 258; in *Washington Post*, 257; in *The*

Week, 257, 258, 259, 265, 267–71, 275

Düttmann, Alexander García, identity and recognition, xxxvii

Dwight, Theodore, Jr., *Awful Disclosures*, 184

Early, Leonard, on Kirby's *Golden Dog*, 106

Early Canadiana Online, xv

Early Long Poems on Canada, 282

economic issues
  capitalism in settlement narratives (*Malcolm's Katie*), 288–90, 292, 298
  free trade as rape of Miss Canada (poster), 35–38, **36,** 64, 69
  in *The Golden Dog*, 97–98
  pensions for published authors, 37, 43–44, 61
  "redundant woman" problem, 52–55
  rhetoric of debt and payment, 50–52

education and citizenship initiatives
  goals for, 8–12, 22–23, 218
  political crises as impetus for, 5–6, 22–23
  post-WWI conditions and, 19–23

Elle et lui (Léger), 90n9

Ellison, Ralph, *Invisible Man*
  domestic artifacts and spectatorship, 305–7

Emberley, J.V.
  on aboriginality and families in photographic archives, xliii, 301–34
  "Bourgeois Family, Aboriginal Women, and Colonial Governance," 320

country wives: church marriages and, 166, 168–69; colonial wives and, 155–59; Gladman as, 165–70; power of, 166, 168; Simpson as role model, 147–49, 158

HBC/NWC amalgamation effects, 155

instability of family definition, 152–53

knowledge limitations in, 157, 158

mixed-blood children: colonial/country wives and, 148–49, 155–59; Hargrave on treatment of, 167–69

mixed-blood wives: Gladman as officer's wife, 165–70; not as "mothers of the race," 46–50; powerlessness of, 166, 168–69

social systems: race and colonial/country wives and children, 146–49, 155–59, 170–71; racial prejudice and injustices, 162–64, 167–69; regulation by Simpson, 154, 157, 170

See also Hargrave, Letitia Mactavish; Hudson's Bay Company; Simpson, George

Garneau, François-Xavier, *L'Histoire du Canada,* 87

Garvin, John, *Collected Poems of Isabella Valancy Crawford,* 282

Gaspé, Philippe-Joseph Aubert de. *See* Aubert de Gaspé, Philippe-Joseph

Gauvreau, Michael, 191–92, 209n10

gender

and colonial female travellers, 319

and nationalism: femininity and idylls, 83–85, 87; gendering of patriotic duty, 84; gendering of sense of time, 84–85

of nation as single subject (national odes): limits of (Frye and de Man), 128–31; masculinity of, 129–31, 135–36, 143n4; race, gender and class, 121, 125–27

in photography: colonial family portrait (Aberdeens), **313,** 313–16

and representational violence (Soja), 329–30

roles in settlement narratives, 284

See also females and femininity; First Nations; fur-trade society; males and masculinity; women's movement

genetics. *See* Canadian Horse (*le cheval Canadien*)

genres and modalities, 92–94

Gerson, Carole

on anti-Catholicism in nun's tales, 173–74

on anxiety displacement to First Nations women, 52, 159

on Jennings' *White Rose,* 88n1

on knowing about fur-trade society, 170

on literacy rates, xxxii–xxxiii

on *Malcolm's Katie,* 282

on Sara Jeannette Duncan, 258

Gilder, Richard Watson, 250

Gladman, Harriet Vincent

as mixed-blood country wife, 165–70

Glenbow Museum, Calgary, 29

Hargrave, Letitia Mactavish
letters: audience for, 153, 160;
gossip in letters, 149–51, 161,
166, 170; self-censorship,
154–55, 160, 162; style, 171n2;
subject matters, 145–46, 160;
time and space dislocations,
152, 159–64
life as colonial wife, 145, 147–49,
155, 159–61, 170–71
life with servants, 160–64, 168
ventriloquism in letters: as
multiple stories, 156, 170; as
voices of others, 146, 150–51,
160–61; on McTavish's country
family, 155–56, 158–59; on old
Mrs. Simpson, 154; power
relations and, 152, 164;
Simcoe's use of, 163–64
works (letters): on dining
customs, 159–60; on gender
and racial injustices, 167–69;
on gossip, 149–50; on Harriet
Gladman, 165–66; on a hostess
in Stromness, 150; on London,
England, 145–46; on Mary
Clarke (servant), 160–64; on
McTavish's colonial wife and
his country children, 155–56;
on old Mrs. Simpson, 153–54;
on servants, 150–51; on a
teacher travelling to Red
River, 150; on treatment of
mixed-blood children, 167–69
Hargrave, William and Dugald
(brothers of Letitia), 159–60,
167
Harmon, Byron
Aboriginal mother/child photographs, 324, **325**

Harris, Lawren, 19, 23
Harris, Richard Colebrooke, 228, 232
Hart, Julia Catherine Beckwith, *St.
Ursula's Convent, or The Nun of
Canada*, xxxix–xl, 197, 198,
209n12
Harte, Walter Blackburn, as expa-
triate writer, 240, 241–42
Hatchett, Mamie L., 272
Hawker, Ronald, on Alexcee, 28–30
Hayward, Alex, 221
HBC. *See* Hudson's Bay Company
Henderson, Jennifer, captivity narra-
tives, 42, 71n4, 72n10
Hensley, Sophie Almon, as expatriate
writer, 240, 241, 245
Heritage Fairs, Heritage Teacher
Institutes, Heritage Minutes,
Heritage YouthLinks, 9
Higgins, Lynn, inscription and
erasure of rape, 56
Higginson, Kate
on captivity narratives and femi-
nine vulnerability,
xxviii–xxix, xlii, 35–72, 208n8
Hinduism
custom of sati, 187
Hirsch, Marianne, framing photo-
graphs, 307, 309
Historica, education and citizenship
initiatives, 9, 218, 234n9
historical fiction
allegory and, 91–97, 102–6, 113–15
comparative treatment of
French/English fiction, 74–76
See also *The Golden Dog* (Kirby);
Jacques et Marie (Bourassa); *Les
Anciens Canadiens* (Aubert de
Gaspé)

historic sites and home farms
    (horses), 215, 229–33
history of Canada
    as settler-invader nation,
        xxix–xxxi, 6, 15–16, 20, 27,
        30–32
    Canada, indigenous derivation of
        name, xxx
    citizenship and history education
        (*See* education and citizenship
        initiatives)
    classification systems: in
        art/anthropology, 25–28, 30;
        as privileging of nation-state,
        xxi; in photography archives,
        304–5, 308–12, **311**, 330, 332
    colonialism and imperialism (*See*
        colonialism and imperialism)
    critical questions, xiii–xiv, xviii,
        xxi–xxii; critique of nation-
        alism, xxii; global issues,
        xxii; inclusions/exclusions,
        xxviii–xxix, xxxvi, 10–11;
        local/national/outer-national
        forces, xxvi–xxvii, xxviii; poli-
        tics of recognition,
        xxxv–xxxvii; representation of
        constituencies, xxviii–xxix;
        tropes to regulate and
        organize, xxviii–xxix
    emigration (*See* United States,
        expatriate Canadian writers)
    French Canadians (*See* French
        Canadians)
    literacy and readers (*See* literacy
        and readers)
    nationalism (*See* nation-states and
        nationalism)
    research on: archives, xlii–xlvi;
        archives and cultural studies,

xlv; authorship (Foucault),
    xlv–xlvi; resources for
    research, xiv–xv, 42; transla-
    tions of early texts, 73–76
views of history: alterity of
    near/far, xxxix–xl; alterity of
    past/present, xvii–xx,
    xxxvii–xxxviii, 40; as linear
    progress, xix–xx, 38, 40, 82,
    297–99; as nation-building
    work, xv–xvii; centralist views
    of (Bliss/Granatstein), xv–xvii,
    9–10, 218; mourning as linear
    return, xix–xx; Saul on mono-
    lithic/nonmonolithic
    nation-states, 13–14; Saul on
    three pillars of Canada, 12,
    14–19; selection of usable
    pasts, xvi–xvii, xviii, 5; social
    (specific/local) views of,
    xv–xvii; traditions as pre-
    shaped present (Williams),
    4–5
*A History of English-Canadian Literature to
    Confederation* (1920) (Baker),
    xix
Hjartarson, Paul
    on native culture and the modern
        state, xliii, 1–34
Hofstader, Richard, 185
Holland, Patricia, photographic
    studies, 301–2
home farms and historic sites
    (horses), 215, 229–33
Hotel Dieu, Montreal, 183–84, 208n6
Hovey, Richard, 251
Howe, Joseph, "Sable Island," 234n11
Howells, William Dean, 244
Hoy, Helen, xxii
Hoyt, William K., *Awful Disclosures*, 184

Lafontaine, Louis-Hippolyte, 13, 14, 15

Lampman, Archibald, on expatriate writers, 240–41

land claims. *See* First Nations

Lang, Marjory, on female journalists, 266, 278

Laurent, Albert, *Épopée tragique*, 90n9

Lawson, Alan, settler-invader colonies, 6, 15–16

Le Cap au diable (DeGuise), 88n1

Léger, Antoine-J., *Elle et lui*, 90n9

Lemire, Maurice
    on Aubert de Gaspé's *Les Anciens Canadiens*, 107–8, 109–10
    on historical fiction, 76
    on Kirby's novels, 101

LeMoine, J.M., *Maple Leaves*, 105, 207n1

Le Moine, Roger, 79, 86–87, 88n1, 90n14

LePan, Douglas, Canada and mythology, 297

le petit cheval du fer (the little iron horse), 211
    See also Canadian Horse (*le cheval Canadien*)

Leprohon, Rosanna, 75, 76, 89n4, 290

Les Anciens Canadiens (Aubert de Gaspé), 75, 91–116
    as escapist fiction, 92, 95–96, 115n5
    historical allegory, 91–92, 107–15
    historical romance conventions, 91–92　.
    idyll as social ideal, 95–97, 110–11
    incomplete structures, 112–15
    life of Aubert de Gaspé, 115n5–6
    modalities and genres, 92–95

narrative: double plot, 107–10, 113; episodic, 107, 109; of reconciliation, 112–13

pastoral romance conventions, 90n12, 106–8

publication, reception and translations, 75, 89n5, 91, 114

social class and "prince and pauper" narratives, 108–10

tone of, 106

tropes: dwellings/past of New France, 110–11; family life/political compromise, 112–13

Les Orphelins (Taschereau-Fortier), 90n9

Lesperance, John Talon, *The Bastonnais*, 75, 76, 89n4, 89n6

Lessard, Marie, 95

Les Têtes à Papineau (Godbout), 13

letters
    as multi-form genre, 152
    business letters by HBC employees, 146
    critical interest in, 146, 147, 152
    gender of writer, 146, 152
    public/private boundaries, 152–53
    self-censorship in, 154–55, 160, 162
    time and space confusions, 152, 159–64
    See also Hargrave, Letitia Mactavish

Lewis, Matthew, *The Monk*
    confession, 192
    gender difference in, 180
    publication and reception, 173, 186
    sexual knowledge, 196

transgression of sexual bound-
aries, 181
See also nun's tales
L'Histoire du Canada (Garneau), 87
Liberal Party
free trade policy as rape of Miss
Canada (1891), 35–38, **36**, 64, 69
librarians
statistics on expatriate
Canadians, 239
Lighthall, W.D., *Songs of the Great
Dominion*
on "Canada," 121–22
Crawford's *Malcolm's Katie*, 282,
299n3
Lippard, Lucy, on naturalization of
Aboriginal family, 326
Lismer, Arthur, 23
literacy and readers
alterity of near/far, xxxix–xl
cautions against reading, xl–xli
Gerson on, xxxii–xxxiii
literary clubs and classes of
readers, xxxii–xxxiii, xxxviii,
xli
Protestantism and expansion of
print culture, 176
readers past and present,
xxxiii–xxxviii
reading/sexual pleasures, 176,
177, 199–200
secrets and discoveries, xxxix–xl
texts as all discursive materials,
xxxv–xxxvi
See also letters
literary history
comparative treatment of
French/English historical
fiction, 74–76

recognition of "Canadian" literature, xxxvi
translations, 73–76, 88, 89n4–6
The Literary History of Canada, xviii, xxii
literature in English
canon formation, 237, 238, 241,
283
nationalism: exclusion of expatri-
ates, 238
See also novels in English; poetry
in English
Livesay, Dorothy, on long poems, 283
Logan, Daniel, as expatriate journalist, 243
Lohuis, Michael M., 233n4
London, England
expatriate writers in, 240, 243
Letitia Hargrave on, 145–46
Longfellow, Henry Wadsworth,
Evangeline, 88n1
Lorette, the History of Louise (Bourne), xl,
184, 186, 188, 198
Lovell, John W., as expatriate
publisher, 245, 246, 249
Lukács, Georg, historical romance,
94, 110
Lynch, Jessica, captivity narrative in
Iraq War (2003), 37, 38, 40,
65–70, **66**

MacDonald, Sir John A.
Conservative Party campaign
poster, 35, **36,** 38, 69
maternal feminism in *Grip* illus-
trations, 38, **39**
Machar, Agnes Maule, as female
journalist, 266, 279n10
Maclean, Norman, on definition of
an ode, 121

MacLennan, Hugh, *Two Solitudes*, 113

MacLeod, Margaret Arnett, 163

Mactavish, Letitia. *See* Hargrave, Letitia Mactavish

magazines. *See* journalism

"The Maiden Tribute of Modern Babylon" (Stead), 56–57

Maillet, Antonine, *Pélagie-la-Charette*, 90n9

Malcolm's Katie (Crawford), 281–300

    aboriginality: as agent of cultural healing, 284–85, 294–99; "Indian" representations, 291–99; and *terra nullius*, 284, 286, 298–99; trope of Indians as land, 294–95, 298

    as settlement narrative: aboriginalizing of settler, 294–96, 298–99; naturalization of colonization, 288–89, 292–93, 298–99; necessity of immigration, 288, 298; simultaneous construction of self and place, 288–91

    capitalism in, 286–90, 292

    Frye on: broken links with "Indian" culture, xxxviii, 283–85, 293–99; Crawford as "female songbird," 284; erotics of colonization, 289; metaphor as identity, 281; mythopoesis, 285, 293–99

    gender: female commodification, 291; manly colonial body, 287–91; patriarchal power, 290–92; sissified gentlemen, 289–92

    metaphors and tropes: metaphor as identity (Frye), 298; metaphors as myths

(Berggren), 298; trope of Indians as land, 294–95, 298

    plot of, as settlement narrative, 285–92

    publication and reception, 281–84

    rhetoric of connectedness, xxxviii

    social class mobility, 287, 298

males and masculinity

    Duncan on gender differences, 260

    in nation as single subject (national odes), 130–31, 135–36, 143n4

    patriarchal systems in photography, 310, **313**, 313–16, 320

    representational violence (Soja), 329–30

    in settlement narratives (*Malcolm's Katie*): gender roles, 284; manly colonial body, 287–91; patriarchal power, 290–92; sissified gentlemen, 289–92

Manguel, Alberto, xxxiv

Manly, John, as influential minister, 182, 191

Maracle, Lee

    "Ka-Nata," xxx–xxxi

Marquis, Thomas Guthrie, 252–53

maternal feminism

    infantilization of MacDonald in *Grip*, 38, **39**

Mathews, Donald, 209n10

Mathews, Robin, 299n4

McArthur, Peter, as expatriate, 245–46, 250

McCaig, JoAnn, on Alice Munro, xliv

McCarthy, Maureen, nun's tales, 182

McClintock, Anne

    gender roles in nationalist discourses, 135–36, 310

on manual domestic work, 47

temporality and gender, 84

McClung, Nellie, 255n8, 300n7

on captivity narrative of
Gowanlock and Delaney, 63–64

McCullough, Michael, on Alexcee's
baptismal font, 1–2

McFarlane, Arthur, as expatriate
writer, 246, 250

McGee, Thomas D'Arcy, xxv,
xxxii–xxxiii, 247

McKay, Ian, xxviii

McKellar, Duncan, as expatriate,
245–46

McKillop, A.B., on citizenship, 10

McLachlan, Alexander, *The Emigrant*,
288

McLean, John Emery, 245

McLellan, Anne, xxiii–xxiv

McLoughlen, John, 167

McMaster, Gerald, residential school
photographs, 333

McMullen, Lorraine, on literacy,
xxxiv

McOuat, Mary Elizabeth, as expatriate writer, 245

McTavish, Catherine Turner (wife of
John George McTavish), as
colonial wife, 155–59, 169

McTavish, John George
country/colonial marriages and
children, 155–58

Memory Project, 9

metaphors
Berggren on metaphors and
myths, 281, 298

Frye on metaphor as statement of
identity, 281

and metonymy, 281, 298, 300n9

in settlement narratives (*Malcolm's
Katie*): "Indians" as land, 294,
298

in women's movement rhetoric:
inquisition and heresy, 265,
269; maternal, 38, **39**, 262;
religious, 265; sisterhood, 264;
slavery, 260, 262–63; war, 260,
279n3

See also tropes

Métis. *See* Big Bear, Frog Lake camp
(Cree and Métis); fur-trade
society; North-West Rebellion

metonymy, 281, 298, 300n9

Mills, Sara, fur-trade society, 170,
171n3

Milne, Anne
on the National Horse of Canada,
xxviii, xlii, 211–36

Miss Canada
U.S. free trade as rape of (poster),
35–38, **36**, 64, 69

Mitchell, Tom, on labour movements, 21–22

modalities, theories of, 92–94

Mohawk people
Oka Crisis (1990), xxiii–xxiv, xxvi

Monk, Maria
See Awful Disclosures of Maria Monk

The Monk (Lewis). *See* Lewis,
Matthew, *The Monk*

Montreal, Québec
in *Awful Disclosures*, 178, 183–85,
208n6

Monture-Angus, Patricia, xxiv

Moodie, Susanna, 52, 159, 224

Morrison, Toni, *Paradise*, 183

Mount, Nick
on expatriate origins of Canadian
literature, xxix, xxxvi, 237–56

mourning and nationalism
    Anderson on, 118, 126, 140, 142,
        143
    communication technologies,
        140–41
    First Nations kinship relations
        (Brant), 330, 332
    Gray's Elegy in Kirby's *Golden Dog*,
        115n4
    idyllic temporality as antithetical
        to linear history, 82
    literary forms (odes and elegies):
        in national odes and elegies,
        118–19, 139–42; prosopopoeia
        (de Man), 136–37, 139
    mourning as return in linear
        history, xix–xx
    in nation as single subject
        (national odes): gendered divi-
        sion and living/dead, 135–36;
        impossibility of closure (de
        Man), 136–38
    Redfield on, 118, 137, 140–43
    WWI war memorials, 23
Mukherjee, Arun, nationalism and
    diversity, xxi, xxxi
Munro, George, 249
Murphy, Rex, xxiii–xxiv
Murray, Heather
    on literacy, xxxiii–xxxiv,
        xxxvii–xxxviii, xxxix
Museum of Anthropology (MOA),
    University of B.C., 1–2
museums and heritage sites
    as zones for living and dead
        culture, 24
    for defining identity, 23
    heritage sites and home farms
        (Canadian Horse), 215, 229–33

    See also Museum of Anthropology
        (MOA), University of B.C.;
        Royal Museum of B.C.,
        Victoria, B.C.; Whyte
        Museum of Canadian Rockies
mythopoesis (Frye), 285, 296–99

Namias, June, captivity narratives,
    43
nation-states and nationalism
    Aboriginal cultures: as reminder
        of diversity, xxiii–xxiv; First
        Nations as term of resistance,
        xxiii; settler-invader colonies
        and, xxix–xxxi, 6, 15–16, 20,
        27, 30–32
    "Canadacentric" modes of study,
        xxii
    gendering of patriotic duty, 84
    nationalism: exclusion of diver-
        sity, xxi–xxii; "foundational
        myths" (Francis), 10–11;
        ideology of diversity,
        xxxi–xxxii; nation as moti-
        vated construction, xxviii;
        significance of contexts for,
        xxii
    nation-states: as field of cultural
        production, xxvi–xxvii; early
        "braces" of nationhood, xxvii;
        and globalization, xii, xxv,
        xxvii; monolithic/nonmono-
        lithic nation-states (Saul),
        13–14; nation as unit of
        analysis, xxvii
    temporality and gender, 84–85
    traditions: as pre-shaped present
        (Williams), 4–5; patriotic
        rituals for unity, 119; use of

nun's tales
anti-Catholicism, 174, 178, 183, 185, 186, 206–7
as contemporary popular culture, 207n4
confessionals as settings: accessibility as threat, 181; anxieties over, 178–79; as place of abuse, 174
confessional utterances: anxieties over, 174–79, 182
physical sensations as concern, 201–2
Protestantism: evangelical movements, 174; and print culture, 199–200; Ryerson and, xl–xli, 182, 190–91, 201–2, 208n5
publication and reception: in Canada and United States, 173; critical interest, 179, 182; reading/sexual pleasures, 176, 177, 199–200
sexual deviancies; incest, 175, 196–202; lesbianism, 197–201; masturbation, 196–97, 200, 209n11
sexual information: anxiety about circulation, 174–75, 199–207; as unspeakable subject, 179–82, 181
See also *Awful Disclosures of Maria Monk;* Bourne, George, Lewis, Matthew, *The Monk; Six Months in a Convent; St. Ursula's Convent, or The Nun of Canada*

Objects and Expressions (Museum of Anthropology), 2
O'Brien, Laird, 223

"O Canada"
as national anthem, 117, 118
"O Child of Nations" (Roberts)
as alternate title for "Canada," 122
See also "Canada" (Roberts)
"An Ode for the Canadian Confederacy" (Roberts), 117–44
as national ode, 118–19
confederacy as term of fragmentation, 132–33
land as symbol, 131, 132
mourning and nationalism in, 139–43
North-West Rebellion and, 120, 132–34, 140
poetic form, 121, 131, 136–37, 139
publication and reception, 117, 120, 131
trope of nation as single subject, 119; biography of nation (Anderson), 124–25, 131; limits of (Frye and de Man), 128–31, 134; masculine agency and feminine body, 134–36; race, gender and class, 129–31; sleeping/awakening, 122, 131, 134, 143n1; voice and face, 132–34, 137–39
odes, national, 117–44
apostrophes: to nation, 122–23; parodies of, 118; prosopopoeia (de Man), 136–37, 139
as national imagining, 118
critical interest in, 117–18
history in, 122, 132–34, 142–43
land as nation, 122, 123, 131, 132
traditional forms, 121–22
See also "Canada" (Roberts); "An Ode for the Canadian Confederacy" (Roberts)

O'Hagan, Thomas, as expatriate writer, 243

O'Higgins, Harvey, as expatriate writer, 246, 250

Oka Crisis (1990), xxiii–xxiv, xxvi

Old Indian Trails (Schäffer), 317, 324

Old Spookses' Pass, Malcolm's Katie, and Other Poems (Crawford), 281

Ontario
  audience for *Two Months*, 44, 45, 56, 72n9
  expatriate writers from Toronto, 245–46
  Klinck on literary studies of, xix

On the Face of the Waters (Steele), 56

orientalism, in national odes, 141–42

Pacey, Desmond, on historical romance, 96

Pache, Walter, 95–96

Papineau, Louis-Joseph, 74

Parker, George L., 252

Parker, Gilbert, as expatriate, 240, 243, 255n6

Parkin, Sir George, 120

Parkman, Francis, 207n1

Passages to Canada, 9

pastoral modes, xx, xxix, 92–94, 115n5
  conventions, 106–8
  incomplete processes, 111–15
  See also *The Golden Dog* (Kirby); *Les Anciens Canadiens* (Aubert de Gaspé)

patriarchal structures. *See* males and masculinity

Patterson, Charles Brodie, as expatriate writer, 240, 244–45

Pélagie-la-Charette (Maillet), 90n9

Pembroke, Dave, 221–22

Pennee, Donna Palmateer, xxviii

Peterman, Michael, xiii–xiv, xvii, xx

peuplement (Foucault), 71n6

photography, 301–34
  archives: classification systems, 304–5, 308–12, **311**, 330, 332; electronic database (Royal Museum of B.C.), 305, 308–12, **311**, 330, 332; First Nations portraits, **316**, 316–17; race and class, 309–12, **311**, 316–17
  bourgeois family as universal, 309–10, 312, 316–17, 320, 327–28
  framing and reframing: family albums, 301–2, 308–9; history as usable past, xvi; public archives, 308
  Kincaid on fashion, race and photography, 303–4
  memory and, 302–4
  naturalization of families, 310, 315, 326
  portraits: colonial family portrait (Aberdeens), **313**, 313–16; exhibition of diversity (Steichen), 309; family portraits, 301; resistance and resignification, 307–8; white motherhood (Käsebier), 327
  representational violence (Soja), 329–30
  sedentary power (Berger), 314–15
  spectatorship: public/private spheres (Ellison), 305–7; resistance and resignification, 307–8, 332–33
  See also Schäffer, Mary T.S.

Phrygian modes, 90n13

The Picture of Quebec (Bourne), 184–85

Pierce, Lorne, 176

socialism and post-WWI citizenship initiatives, 19–22

Soja, Edward, spatial studies, 329–30

Solanke, Adeola, 307

"Song of the Axe," 299n3

See also *Malcolm's Katie* (Crawford)

Songs of the Great Dominion (Lighthall), 121–22, 282, 299n3

Sorfleet. J.R., on Kirby's *Golden Dog*, 115n3

Sounding the Iceberg (Duffy), 75–76

Spacks, Patricia Meyer, 150

Spence, Jo, on photography, 301

St. Ursula's Convent, or The Nun of Canada (Hart), 197, 198, 209n12

Stacey, Robert David
    on Kirby's *Golden Dog* and Aubert de Gaspé's *Les Anciens Canadiens*, xx, 91–116

Star (Montreal), 257, 258

Starowicz, Mark, on society's memory, 8, 32n3

Stead, W.T., "The Maiden Tribute of Modern Babylon," 56–57, 69

Stedman, Edmund Clarence, 251

Steele, Flora Annie, *On the Face of the Waters*, 56

Steichen, Edward, *Family of Man* exhibition, 309

Stevens, John D., 185

Stevenson, Winona, 48, **49**

Stoney people, **331**

Stowe Gullen, Augusta, 262–63

Strachan, Bishop John, 208n5

Stratford, Philip, *Bibliography of Canadian Books in Translation* (1977), 74–75

Stringer, Arthur
    as expatriate writer, 241, 246, 250, 251, 253

suffrage, women's. *See* women's movement

Sullivan, Rebecca, on *Awful Disclosures*, 178, 183, 186

Talbot, Edward, 209n13

Taschereau-Fortier, Madame Alexandre, *Les Orphelins*, 90n9

Tausky, Thomas, on Sara Jeannette Duncan, 258, 259, 279n1

Taylor, Charles
    on multiple options, 114
    politics of recognition, xxxv–xxxvii

temporality
    Bakhtin's idyllic chronotrope, 81
    history as Gordian knot of mythic past, 85
    McClintock on time and gender, 84
    time and space confusions in letters, 152, 159–64

ten Kortenaar, Neil, on Sara Jeannette Duncan, 277

Tennyson, Alfred Lord, "The Princess," 281

The Christian Guardian, 176

The Mail, 266

The Week
    conservatism of, 120, 267–68
    Duncan as journalist for, 257, 258, 259, 265, 267–71, 275
    on expatriate writers, 240

Thompson, Janna, 216, 230

Thompson, Slason, as expatriate writer, 242

Thomson, E.W., as expatriate writer, 240, 241, 249, 255n8

Three Guineas (Woolf), 314

Toronto, Ontario
expatriate writers from, 245–46
Jamaican-Torontonians, xxvi
See also Art Gallery of Toronto
Traill, Catharine Parr, 50, 52, 72n9,
159
Back Woods of Canada, 235n17
travellers, female colonial, 319
See also Schäffer, Mary T.S.
tropes
definitions, 80
metonymy and historical
processes, 114
typology in lyric poetry, 119, 129
of uncertainty in pastoral modes,
94
use to regulate and organize,
xxviii–xxix
See also metaphors; tropes of
nation
tropes of nation
definitions, typology and uses:
definitions, 80; typology in
lyric poetry, 119, 129; use to
regulate and organize,
xxviii–xxix
metonymy and historical
processes, 114
nation as animal:
carnivores/British imperialism, 82; lion's
brood/Canada, 122
nation as dwelling:
dwellings/past of New France
(*Golden Dog*), 91, 98–101, 104–6;
dwellings/past of New France
(*Les Anciens Canadiens*), 110–11
nation as family: as trope, 119;
broken family/broken culture
(*Jacques et Marie*), 73, 79, 84,

87–88, 90n9; family life/polit-
ical compromise, 112–13;
marriage/cultural union of
First Nations and settler-
invader culture (Saul), 17–18,
30; marriage/cultural union
of French/English (*Jacques et
Marie*), 87–88; nation/family
(*Golden Dog*), 92; parent/child
(Britain/Canada), 123–29, 133
nation as female:
femininity/Acadian patri-
otism, 84–85; free trade as
rape (poster), 35–38, **36**, 64, 69;
mother's corpse/Acadian
culture, 78–80, 82; in national
odes, 135–36
nation as food: gluttony/anti-
British imperialism, 82–83,
90n12
nation as horse (*See* Canadian
Horse)
nation as land: Indian/land (*as*
land not *on* land), 294–95, 298;
land/Canada, 122, 123, 132
nation as nature, 119, 131;
pastoral idylls/social ideals
(*Golden Dog*), 95–97, 98–102,
104–6; pastoral idylls/social
ideals (*Jacques et Marie*), 81;
tree/cultural longevity, 79
nation as ship (national odes):
ship/Canada, 122, 123, 125
nation as single subject (national
odes): anthropomorphism,
122–24; asleep/awake as
national formation, 122, 131,
143n1; biography of nation
(Anderson), 124–27; limits of
(Frye and de Man), 128–31, 134;

White, John, "A Woman of Florida," 304

White, Urania, 58

The White Rose in Acadia (Jennings), 88n1

Who Killed Canadian History? (Granatstein), 9–11

Who's Who in New York City and State (1904), 240

Whyte Museum of Canadian Rockies Schäffer archives, 305, 317

Wickman, Matthew, xix

Williams, Catherine R., *The Neutral French*, 88n1

Williams, Raymond
  on "recalling" as political act, 4–5, 6, 31–32
  on relation between formation and project, 8

Wilson, Edward O., 233

Wilson, Elizabeth, fashion and race, 304

Wilson, Red, 9

Wilson, Tom, **331**

Winnipeg demonstration, Great War Veterans Association (1919), **23**

Winnipeg General Strike (1919), 20–21

Wolin, Richard, on allegory, 103, 104

"A Woman of Florida" (White), 304

Woman's Christian Temperance Union, 264, 279n6

women's movement
  conservatism of newspapers, 267–68
  critical interest in, 277–78
  discourse elements, 263–65
  maternal feminism: *Grip* cover of MacDonald, 38, **39**; Lady Aberdeen and, 315; Sara J. Duncan on, 261–63

medical school exclusions, 273–74

metaphors: inquisition and heresy, 265, 269; maternal, 38, **39**, 262; religious, 265; sisterhood, 264; slavery, 260, 262–63; war, 260, 279n3

national myths, exclusions in (Francis), 11

post-WWI conditions and citizenship, 19

"redundant woman" issue, 53

religious affiliations, 264

social class, 264

See also Duncan, Sara Jeannette

Woolf, Virginia, *Three Guineas*, 314

working class
  domestic labour: Aboriginal women and, 48–49; colonial wives as manual labourers, 46–48, 72n9; role of *The Imperial Colonialist*, 319; servants in fur-trade society, 151, 160–64
  habitants: as settlers, 231–32; in *The Golden Dog*, 97–98; horses of English and *habitants*, 225, 228; in Krieghoff paintings, 212, 225–29, **226–27**, 232
  national myths, exclusions in (Francis), 11
  in photography: of family groups, 310, **311**; female as labourer, 322
  post-WWI conditions and citizenship initiatives, 19–22
  progressive movements, 267
  social class and animal cruelty, 228
  See also social class